MW01025964

My Way of Life

Pocket Edition of
St. Thomas

The Summa Simplified
for Everyone

BY

WALTER FARRELL, O.P., S.T.M.

AND

MARTIN J. HEALY, S.T.D.

1952

Msgr. Austin P. Bennett, JCD, P.A.
Director of the
CONFRATERNITY OF THE PRECIOUS BLOOD

5300 FORT HAMILTON PARKWAY, BROOKLYN, N.Y. 11219
0303

NIHIL OBSTAT:

THOMAS W. SMIDDY, **S. T. L.**
Censor Librorum.

IMPRIMATUR:

✝ THOMAS EDMUNDUS MOLLOY, S. T. D.
Archiepiscopus-Episcopus.
Brooklyniensis.

Brooklyni, XXIII Augusti 1952.

Foreword

HERE IS PRESENTED the masterpiece of St. Thomas — the Summa Theologica — in simplified form. This vast summary of Thomistic teaching which deals with every worthwhile truth from a to z, from the attributes of God to the zeal of man has been distilled into this little volume. It is, in truth, a miniature and simple Summa for everyman.

As its name signifies, the Summa Theologica of St. Thomas is the sum total of all theological knowledge, a vast synthesis in which is unfolded all that can be known of God and man. It is divided into three parts which deal with God, man and the God-man, respectively. It comprises 38 tracts, 631 questions, about 3,000 articles, 10,000 objections and their answers.

Obviously all of this vast material is not contained in this small volume. However, an earnest effort has been made by the authors to translate and re-present St. Thomas in concise form for the use of everyman.

THE CONFRATERNITY OF THE PRECIOUS BLOOD in presenting this volume, aims to do for the Summa of St. Thomas what it has already done for the Missal—to place it into the hands of all men. The millions who have found Father Stedman's "My Sunday Missal" so helpful and practical for the Mass of the Altar will find "My Way of Life" equally helpful and practical for the "Mass of Life".

St. Thomas begins the Prologue to his great work with these words: "Because a teacher of Catholic truth ought not only to teach the learned but also to instruct the beginners, in accordance with the words of the Apostle: *As unto little ones in Christ, I gave you milk to drink, not meat (1 Cor. 3/1,2)* we purpose in this book to treat of whatever belongs to the Christian religion in such a way as may tend to the instruction of beginners."

THE VOLUME, HERE PRESENTED, is in full accord with the purpose of St. Thomas. It brings his message from the halls of learning out into the market place and into the home. While primarily meant for everyman, it is profound enough for the most erudite. Hence it can be readily recommended to father and mother, sister and brother, to the high-school and college student, to the convert, the study and Newman Club, to the Confraternity class, to the religious and the priest, in a word, it can be recommended to everyone.

Part I is the work of the noted Thomist, Walter Farrell, O.P., who died shortly after its completion.

Parts II and III were written by Martin J. Healy, Professor of Dogmatic Theology, at the Seminary of the Immaculate Conception, Huntington, N. Y.

(Rt. Rev. Msgr.) Joseph B. Frey

Feast of the Assumption
1952

God and His Creatures

BY
WALTER FARRELL, O. P.
Master of Sacred Theology

Part I

PART I

✠ ✠ ✠ 𝕲𝖔𝖉 𝖆𝖓𝖉

*Refers to questions in the Summa

His Creatures ✠ ✠ ✠

CHAPTER I

The One God

CHAPTER I

The One God

THE ROAD THAT STRETCHES before the feet of a man is a challenge to his heart long before it tests the strength of his legs. Our destiny is to run to the edge of the world and beyond, off into the darkness: sure for all our blindness, secure for all our helplessness, strong for all our weakness, gaily in love for all the pressure on our hearts.

IN THAT DARKNESS beyond the world, we can begin to know the world and ourselves, though we see through the eyes of Another. We begin to understand that a man was not made to pace out his life behind the prison walls of nature, but to walk into the arms of God on a road that nature could never build.

LIFE MUST BE LIVED, even by those who cannot find the courage to face it. In the living of it, every mind must meet the rebuff of mystery. To some men, this will be an exultant challenge: that so much can be known and truth not be exhausted, that so much is still to be sought, that truth is an ocean not to be contained in the pool of a human mind. To others, this is a humiliation not to be borne; for it marks out sharply the limits of our proud minds. In the living of life, every mind must face the unyielding rock of reality, of a truth that does not bend to our whim or fantasy, of the rule that measures the life and mind of a man.

IN THE LIVING OF LIFE, every human heart must see problems awful with finality. There are the obvious problems of death, marriage, the priesthood, religious vows; all unutterably final. But there are, too, the day to day, or rather the moment to moment choices of heaven or hell. Before every human heart that has ever beat out its allotted measures, the dare of goals as high as God Himself was tossed down: to be accepted, or to be fled from in terror.

GOD HAS SAID SO LITTLE, that yet means so much for our living. To have said more would mean less of reverence by God for the splendor of His image in us. Our knowing and loving, He insists, must be our own; the truth ours because we have accepted it; the love ours because we have given it. We are made in His image. Our Maker will be the last to smudge that image in the name of security, or by way of easing the hazards of the nobility of man.

THE GREAT TRUTHS that must flood the mind of man with light are the limitless perfection of God and the perfectibility of man. The enticements that must captivate the heart of man are the divine goodness of God and man's gratuitously given capacity to share that divine life, to begin to possess that divine goodness even as he walks among the things of earth. The truths are not less certain because they are too clear for our eyes. The task before our heart is not to hold a fickle lover but to spend itself.

WITHOUT THESE TRUTHS, and the others that fill out the pattern of a man's days, we are underfed weaklings, starving waifs, paralyzed in our living not only by lack of strength but even more by lack of light. To live a man must move by the steps of his heart; and how can he move until he can see and be drawn by the beauty of Goodness and Truth?

NO MAN CAN GET SUCH WISDOM of himself in time to begin living his life or, indeed, in time to end it. Wisdom must be given to him, for it belongs to God. He can have this wisdom that must be had; but not through the stumbling steps of his own reasoning. He can have it if he will take it from his Maker. He can see in the darkness if he will look through the eyes of God. He can begin life with wisdom lent by God, and have his heart flooded with gratitude for the loan; or he can prefer the false light of the illusion that tells him he is self-sufficient, and die before he begins to live.

A MAN HARDLY DARE face mere natural life alone; alone, he cannot even dream of sharing the divine. Yet, to escape disaster, he must not only so dream, he must make the dream come true.

IF MAN BEGINS LIFE with wisdom lent by God, he ends by possessing that wisdom; if he guides his steps by a light that is not his own along a road too high and hard for his feet, he ends united to that eternal Light, and at home forever in a world that is God's.

THERE ARE MEN AND WOMEN who do not know God. They are made for happiness; every perfectly designed item of their sublime nature strains for that fulfillment which is happiness. Ignorance commits them to frustration; they have eager hearts, pushed to the breaking point by all of nature's demands for happiness, but these hearts have only the wrong places to go. In a very real sense, there is a kind of knowledge of God buried deep in every man, as deep as his demand for happiness. Frustration here is basic, soul-searing, catastrophic. Man makes his way to the illusory havens offered by false gods, but always through a sea of tears shed by his own individual nature.

THIS TRAGIC THING can happen to men of all ages. It has happened. Yet it is not that God is so far from us, since in Him we live, move and have our being. Nor is it that the living God is so deeply hidden from the minds of men. The world is a mirror flashing back different facets of divine beauty, and all that is, by that very existence, shouts aloud God's name: He Who is. Of course there is no adequate picture of God to catch the eyes of men and hold them spellbound. It would be less impossible to expect to hold the world in the embrace of our arms than to encompass the divine perfection in the thimble-capacity allotted to any creature.

YET THE LITTLE that we can see of the infinite perfection of God is an entrancing picture; to escape it, one must glue his eyes to something close, tangible, and blinding. The infatuated see little of anything, and even less of God.

ORDINARILY IT TAKES TIME, effort, and a kind of violence to become so fatuous. To simple men, as to the very wise, the pressing crush of movement that pushes things in the ordered direction that we know as natural, a faithful, daily execution of cosmic chores, has always been as awesomely revealing as the surge of the sea, and as paradoxically mysterious; for both are so inherently blind and incapable of originating such motion.

ONLY AN ADULT who has lost the clear vision of childhood begins to think of his acts, and of himself, as self-sufficient, entirely his own, springing from nowhere, in contradiction to history's short record of the ages of activity. To most men, that a man can lift his hand to thwart an enemy's blow or to encourage a friend has been a wonder that enticed the mind along a path of thinking that brought him to the God on whom all activity depends, Himself so divinely independent.

T HE MYSTERY OF LIFE'S END, and the even greater mystery of life's beginning, the ebb and flow of things beginning and things ending, the steady succession of the sadness of Fall and the glad promise of Spring, prevent the unfettered and uncluttered mind from missing what these were meant to make clear: a life without beginning to explain all beginnings, a life without end to explain death; an infinite Creditor of life to explain all the reckless loan of life to the living.

T HE WORLD, AND THE MEN IN IT, are full of glad surprises; yet the surprises do not come from the things that are part and parcel of either men or things. If we know a man's humanity, we know all of it and there is no room for surprise. But a glimpse of the truth that is in him, a momentary contact with his goodness, a recognition of his nobility—all of these are at once a joy, a surprise, and a rich promise. In each case, what is seen or embraced is so obviously not the whole story. These perfections are as enticing as far horizons, or the limitless stretches of the sea's dark waters. They promise the heart and the mind long journeys and rich rewards, treasures beyond the capacities of any counting room. For these things have no fence about them; traces of them shining forth from the limited things of the world are the allures of the infinite, minute flakes of the precious perfection that belongs in its fullness only to God.

T HE STAMP OF INTELLIGENCE is printed deep in the very being of the universe of unintelligent things; for the theme of that cosmic poem is a theme of law and order shining forth from creatures totally incapable of themselves of disposing things to any end, let alone to cosmic ends. Whether we look at the harmony of the universe and see order written in the capital letters of unvarying procedure and effective subordination, or at the minute organization of microscopic details in the leaf of a tree, the ear of an animal, or the eye of a man, there is that same clear evidence of a gigantic, an infinite intelligence. We have been given a share in that intelligence that we might read the poem that only infinite intelligence could have written; though, of course, the full beauty and meaning of it is reserved to the mind that wrote it.

THE BOOK OF JOB describes God. "He is higher than Heaven, and what wilt thou do? He is deeper than Hell, and how wilt thou know? The measure of Him is longer than the earth and broader than the sea." (11/8-9) There is profound truth in this if we understand the depth of God as His searching knowledge of hidden things; His height as the supreme power of His omnipotence; His length as the endlessness of eternity; and His breadth as provident love embracing all things. For, of course, God is not to be reached by plunging into depths, or scaling heights, or by rushing to the edges of the world. He is not a physical bulk to be approached by steps of the body; He is everywhere, and is to be approached by steps of the soul. It is in this same way that we abandon Him and take up our abode far from Him, though He is in us and about us. It is our heart, not our feet, that rushes to His embrace or flees from His judgments.

WE SPEAK OF GOD'S LIFE, His divinity, His power because our language breaks down before the splendor of the infinite. We do our learning from the things that have been put together by divine genius and power; and so we speak and think of God in those same terms of parts joined to make a whole. For the brilliant beauty of rich simplicity staggers our minds: God is life, unlimited, eternal; He is goodness, without qualification or limit; He is power, boundless and omnipotent. These are not divine possessions; rather, God is each and all of these limitless perfections. What has life and is not life is creature caused by life infinite.

THE IMAGES OF GOD are necessarily imperfect, among others, our very selves; for images are by no means reproductions of the original, infinite model of all creation. They mirror God as far as He can be mirrored; and the divine simplicity can be represented in the created world only by increasing complexity through added perfection. For we, like all other creatures, have something of life, something of goodness, something of truth; and we reach out day by day for still more.

THERE IS no measuring rod of God. Nor is God the measure of creatures in the sense in which we might call a perfect plant the measure of the imperfect plants of the same kind. It is only in this sense that God is the measure of things and men: the closer any thing or any man comes to God, the more there is to that thing or man in its own line of perfection. A man is more a man for drawing closer to God; a man is more godlike as he perfects his humanity.

ST. HILARY STATES the simplicity of God in words simple enough to be worthy of that divine simplicity: "God Who is strength, is not made up of things that are weak; nor is He Who is light, composed of things that are dark." In us, as in all creatures, perfection is reached by greater and greater complexity with more and more perfect order; the enriched powers and smooth precision of cooperation give a created image of the absolute simplicity that is divine richness. Created organization is the best possible reflection of divine unity.

CREATURES ARE INDEED LIKE GOD, though God is not at all like creatures, any more than a man is like a statue, though the statue is like a man. We necessarily stumble badly when we attempt to speak of the perfection of divinity, yet "though our lips can only stammer, we yet chant the high things of God." Every least perfection in the meanest of creatures tells us something of God, for the perfections of all the universe are in God from whom they came. While the revelation of the divine splendor is insistent and constant, it is never more than dim, obscure, inadequate: a finite shadow's revelation of the substance of infinity.

GOD IS GOOD. When that statement calls to our minds the reckless generosity of His gifts, running the gamut of life's beginning to eternity's endlessness, we have actually missed the point of His goodness. The gifts tell us of His love, His mercy, His benign providence; but His goodness does not bring things to us so much as it takes our hearts away from us. The good God is that ravishingly attractive Being Who is resisted only when He is not seen; He is infinite enticement, rapturous beyond a man's most extravagant desires, captivating lovableness to tear the heart out of a man. Confronted by divine goodness, the heart of man bursts into such a flame as to

make a torch of his whole life. Fascinated by the
invitation inherent in such goodness, a man finds no
journey too long, no danger too great, no obstacle
too wearying; here is strength, courage, daring for
the weakest of men, for if this goodness be achieved
nothing is lost, if this be lost everything is bitterly lost.

T HE CHARACTERISTIC NOTE of all goodness is its
desirability; its demand is for love, which is no
more than the recognition of the heart-filling character
of goodness. With us, oddly enough, it is not the substantial goodness with which we begin life that makes
this challenging demand for love, but the goodness
that comes to us with the years in the practice of the
virtues. We are rather a promise of goodness; we
become, through the grace of God, an image of that
divine goodness, and so beloved of men. In God,
there is no slow step from promise to fulfillment; but
instant, eternal, unlimited attractiveness that permits
of no moment of disillusionment or delay. This is the
end of the heart's quest and the beginning of its
fullness.

A S WISDOM INCREASES, and the subtle fragrance
of holiness makes its unobtrusive way into the
least crevices of the hours of a man's day, more and
more hearts go out to him; he is a better man, a
more lovable man, for he is more of a man. There is more
to him, he is fuller, bigger; more of his powers have
been put to work in completing the image of God
within him. On the same count, every step downward
a man takes in vice the more isolated he becomes;
if there are hearts that do not shun him, it will be
because they have not discovered his vice, or because,
loving Another so measurelessly, there is room in
their hearts for even so nearly loveless a one as this

man. There is simply less to the vicious man; he is more empty, shrivelled, dwarfed to such distorted proportions that only God, or one seeing through the eyes of God, can find that small nugget of goodness that justifies love.

PERHAPS THE CLEAREST REVELATION of the intimate connection between goodness and fullness, evil and emptiness, the lovable and the real, is to be had from the obvious futility and desolation of the human heart that is nourished only on dreams. Our mind does not produce reality, it merely recognizes it; and dreams are the products of ourselves, not of the producer of the world of things as they are. To live in a dreamworld is to attempt to have our hearts captivated by nothing outside of ourselves and the pitiful shadows that we can produce in the mental world of our own making. If evil is a destruction of the real, and so of the lovable, the shadow world of dreams is an evasion of the real, and so of the lovable.

THE GOODNESS OF GOD keeps the wheels of the universe whirring; it is this same goodness, or some distorted image of it, that furnishes the driving power of human living. We set our feet on a road because there is goodness at the end of it; we keep our hands at a task because the goodness at the end of it makes all the labor well worth while; our minds probe into every corner of the universe because our hearts are hungry for the goodness to be discovered in the universe and its Maker; we listen to the words of God and conform to their high demands because those words are the square stones of a highway that leads back to the unutterable goodness of the Speaker. Goodness, or the mistaken appearance of it, is the only reason for the ceaseless activity that makes a man's life or engulfs it. We are made for action because our hearts are made for goodness, as the eye is made for color and the ear for sound.

B EAUTY IS FOR THE EYE, not for the heart. It catches the heart, not because of the splendor of its lustrous order but because of perfection, the goodness that is at the root of this brilliant beauty. Beauty is a bitter, galling thing, as shocking as sin in the sanctuary, when it proves a mirage enticing the heart to the embrace of emptiness or evil. Beauty is no mate for wickedness; this ugly companion inevitably destroys even the appearance of beauty.

T HE ALLURE OF THE GOOD is an ennobling invitation; for it is essentially a promise that we can become a part of this loved thing or make it a part of ourselves. It is this same characteristic that accounts for the debasing corruption of a false good. We do indeed become the thing we love. The enticement of personal goodness lies precisely in its promise that we can become so like to this person whose goodness ravishes our heart, that we can move before men in a shared likeness of this beloved person. God is the supreme source from which all goodness takes its rise, the infinite reservoir of all that is desirable, containing and surpassing all that is found lovable in creatures; to love Him is to be caught by the promise of that infinite allure, to become like God and to move in His image before the eyes of men, a likeness of the divinity surpassing all the pictures drawn by the varied beauty and goodness of all the universe.

T HE SAINT, head over heels in love with God, finds the most perfect fellowship with every least and greatest thing in the universe, with every least and greatest man and woman. He understands them, he is at one with them, being himself so closely one with the God Who is their source, the model on which they are formed, the goal to which they are so drawn. He is close to the world and to men because his heart is so close to God. His only hate will center on the disfigurements and mutilations that are wrought on the images of God to hide from the eyes of men the ravishing beauty of divinity.

WE OURSELVES give testimony to the infinite reaches of the being of God both by contrast and by likeness. By contrast with divinity, we are not happy with too much of space. We enclose our hearts with the embracing arms of a few friends, our minds with the absorbing labor of a few interests, our lives with the comforting walls and roof of a home. We are steadily grateful that there is a sky to mark the limits of heights, ground to put an end to depth, and horizons to mark off the boundaries of length and width. We are not God but His creatures, and this protective limitation is in sharp contrast to His boundless being. Yet we are made in His image. We are impatient in heart and mind perpetually, restless, almost discontented; for every truth we know, every good we embrace only serves to convince us that the road stretches out still further. It is especially in the mind and heart of a man that the image of divinity is most apparent; we reach, heart and mind, for the infinity which He is, even while we cower under the cover that we must have as His creatures.

ON THE OTHER HAND, we are not hidden from God by our cowering, nor is our reaching for Him a matter of distance. He is indeed not far from any one of us; rather, He is in us, as He is in every created thing, profoundly, intimately, more present to us than we are to ourselves. Our very being, and the being of everything we have, we are, or we meet is a borrowed thing, as the firelight is a loan from the flames. An instant of separation from God would be instant annihilation, for every moment of our life is nourished from the very life of God, more dependent on that life than an infant in the womb is upon the life of the mother. Our hearts can wander far from God, but God is not far from our hearts for we are more His than our own.

IT WOULD BE MORE ACCURATE to say that God contains us rather than that we have God within us, just as the soul more properly is said to contain the body than to exist in the body. A man can be put in prison, or an animal in a pen; but spiritual things like the soul of a man, the angels, or God are not contained by the strongest or most subtle of fences. We are, in a very true sense, wrapped around with God, penetrated by divinity, held up every instant by divine power that saturates all of reality and exceeds it. God fills the world as summer sunlight floods a room, He is everywhere in the world as the soul is everywhere in the body; where He is not, nothing is.

THOUGH HIS GREAT POWER reaches to the least crevice of our lives, though every futile step of our wandering hearts is clear to His fatherly eyes, though every beat of our pulse proclaims His supporting presence, this is still not close enough for God. As His knowledge and love of us put us in Him rather than Him in us, so through the gift of His grace, He is the Guest of our minds and the Lover enclosed by the arms of our love. He will, in His divine eagerness for the fullness of our happiness, be ours; in us by our act; known, desired and loved, and so given His sole free and hearty welcome in all the physical world that so depends upon Him.

GOD, WHO IS SO HUMBLY OUR LOVE and so majestically our Lord, is unchangeably Lord and Love. He Himself has said: "I am God, and I change not." How indeed could He change? He can gain nothing, who is infinite Perfection; He can lose nothing, who is supreme Lord. His creative power determines, before things are, that they shall be; and that same power marks out the limits of existing things, determining when they that now are shall no longer be. But what power will dictate to the supreme Power on which all else rests? What there is of change is always in us as we bask in the warmth of His love or perversely smash our lives against the wall of His power in rebellion against the Giver of all good gifts.

FOR US TO REMAIN UNCHANGED in this life of ours would be disaster, for the unattained heights always stretch before our laggard feet. We can hardly think of the utterly unchanged since we are necessarily immersed in the flow of time's moments from yesterday, through today and into tomorrow. The unchangeableness of God excludes a beginning or an end, a truth we pack into the awful majesty of the word "forever." We can think of eternity only in terms of interrupted time, of a precious moment caught, transfixed, enduring to the exclusion of past and future; yet eternity is rather a cloak embracing all of time as no more than the pin point center of the uninterrupted circle of God's existence. God is now as He always was and always will be; yet He is ours and we are His: the King of ages, immortal, invisible, the only God.

Though God is so close to all His creatures, and particularly close in the minds and hearts of men, He is yet above and beyond everyone and everything else. The chasm that yawns between the Creator and the creature, the infinite and the finite, is bridged by the mercy of God, not by a watering down of His divine nature. It is not by a weakening or debasing of His nature that He comes close to us, but rather by its utterly simple perfection that He is at once so immanently close and so transcendentally the Absolute One.

"Hear O Israel, the Lord our God is one God." He is not a complex of perfections doled out in shared portions, not a divided God or one capable of analysis into sections, but the infinite, utterly simple and absolutely Perfect One. Not a God of parts, then, nor yet a God capable of multiplication; for the difference that would make two or more gods possible would be a declaration of the defect by which they differed, of perfection had by one and lacked by another. The variety in the world and men is a gracious unveiling of the splendor of God, dimmed lest it blind our poor eyes. We can recognize that variety in humility's inspiring fashion by noting the goodness we lack shining forth from the lives of others; or we can mount the judgment seat so natural to pride and point out all the goodness that we have, lacking in these poor mortals who pass before us for sentence. But there can be no complexity or difference in the source of all variety; which is to say that the divine wellspring of the complexity of the world lacks nothing of the perfection it shares so prodigally.

CHAPTER II

Knowledge and Love
of God

CHAPTER II
Knowledge and Love of God

W E CAN OPEN OUR EYES to the sharp hints of
divine glory in the eager promise of spring, the
austere cleanliness of winter, or the lush richness of
late summer's fulfillment; our days can be a steadily
widening discovery of the nobility of the image of
God in the least of men. The minute details of nature's organization can stagger our minds with their
multitude and complexity and so give us an insight
into the horizons of divine wisdom. Left to ourselves,
we would have to be content with this, yet know
acutely how much more there was to see and to love.
If only the veil could be torn away and our eyes
strengthened to bear the luminous brightness of
divine glory!

I T IS SO PLAIN, from what we know so well of ourselves, that this would be a hopeless dream. What
are our bodily eyes to demand such a vision when
they miss so much of things as obvious as the un-
clouded sparkle in a child's eyes, the freshness of
sky and countryside after a spring rain, or even the
triumph of artistic coloring in a single petal of a rose?
We see so little of the bodily things for which our
eyes were made; we can hope for nothing from them
of the invisible and unlimited splendor of God. Our
minds plunge easily, even eagerly, beneath the surface of physical things to the intangible realities that
enrich and nourish our minds; yet how much we miss
of the courage of little men, of stubborn hope, of
dreams, regrets, and loves too fine for the rough
wrappings of words. These things our minds can see
for they fit into the finite limits of a concept—the

wedding garment essential for every guest of our minds. Not so the infinite perfection of divinity.

GOD IS INFINITELY KNOWABLE, for He is infinite Truth; and we are forever on fire to know the truth that is still unknown, to search further, unappeased by anything less than the whole of truth, infinite Truth. It is not in vain that the fires of this divine discontent have been kindled within us. By the gracious kindness of God, what is impossible to human powers is accessible to men by divine gifts. We can see the very essence of God, the full, unveiled glory of His beauty. Our eyes are given a light to see in a brightness greater than all the suns; and infinite truth comes to our minds, not enclosed in finite concepts, but immediately, nakedly, with no intermediary to limit the full intimacy of the union of mind to truth. That is the vision at the end of the road of a life well lived, the answer to all the desires that hurry a man's feet, the essential, intense activity that endures for all of eternity's moment.

NO MAN NEED ever be ignorant of God. Every single thing in the universe is plainly signed with the name of the divine Artist; and each thing has a distinct truth to tell about its Maker. To those who will admit the limits of our poor human minds, even truths too big for us can still be ours on the word of God Himself. It is thus that faith gives man so many of the truths about God that can be had only from God Himself. But the story told by the universe is so very inadequate, the story of faith so obscure.

IT IS ONLY IN HEAVEN that we shall have the whole story, that we shall see God, all of Him, and in Him the things that He has made. In the degree in which our heart has welcomed God on earth, our mind shall penetrate the fathomless depths of God Himself in heaven, never exhausting the divine riches, for we are not God but seeing God as He sees Himself; for here indeed we are like God and one with Him in an eternal union.

IN THIS LIFE we can talk about God because we can know Him; but we can never say the last word. We can name Him, but not with a perfect, comprehensive name that will say all that is to be said. We speak truth about an artist because we know his works, even though we have never seen the man. We can say a great deal about a man merely in denying him the defects of infancy, the ravages of disease, the corrosion of crime. So, knowing the creatures of God we can know and say much of the truth about Him; we can say still more by denying Him all the defects we see in the creatures of the world; we can go much further by seeing the truth of the divine eminence in all that is good in the created world: the limitless life, unqualified goodness, absolute justice and so on.

IN ALL THIS we are indeed saying something, seeing and saying what is true; in fact, these latter things are more properly true of God than they are of ourselves. For the justice of a man is only a shrunken image of the justice of God, as the life of a man is a flickering shadow of divine life. Yet life and justice are true of both God and man, but proportionately for man is the creature, and God the Creator, God the Architect and man His work.

IT IS TRUE that the word "God" often slips lightly from the lips of men; yet even its most profane use is a true tribute to power and majesty, an invocation of the only judgment capable of sealing a man's eternal doom. Here, too, is tribute to the universal care, the sovereign dominion of Creator over creatures. That reverberating note of hovering and universal care echoes from the word "God" wherever it is let loose in the universe; everywhere and always it has a timbre that stirs a quivering response in the very fibres of our being. This word is a bell ringing out, exultantly or despondently, the intimate life of God in our life and our life in His.

IT IS GOD HIMSELF Who gives us the best name for God. "Moses said to God: Lo, I shall go to the children of Israel, and say to them: the God of your fathers hath sent me to you. If they should say to me: What is His name? what shall I say to them? God said to Moses: I AM WHO AM. He said: Thus shalt thou say to the children of Israel: HE WHO IS hath sent me to you." (*Exodus* 3/13-14) Only in this divinely given name can we express the utter independence of God, the sea of infinite perfection that is divinity, and the eternal now that is beyond all past and all future. So much did the Son of God say with divine conciseness: "Before Abraham was, I AM."

IT IS TRUE that "the things of God no man knoweth, but the Spirit of God," (I *Cor.* 2/11) yet the obscure glimpse of divine things given to us more than justifies St. Paul's heartfelt exclamation: "O the depth of the riches of the wisdom and of the knowledge of God." (*Rom.* 11/33) We have a clue to the vastness of those riches in the wide halls of our own minds; we can play host to all the physical universe because our souls, in their spirituality, escape the enclosing barriers of the material and approach the infinite. This is, of course, no more than a clue, a hint, of the divine riches; for compared to the wisdom and knowledge of God, the Infinite Spirit, the contents of our own minds are the paltry pennies of a beggar's purse.

ONLY GOD can know God as He deserves to be known. Even in heaven itself, where we shall have an unobscured view of divinity, our knowledge will be joyously incomplete, stopping as far short of exhaustion of the ineffable as the finite stops short of the infinite; through all the length of eternity, there will always be more for us to know of God.

THERE IS A SPECIAL COMFORT in appreciating God's knowledge of us and of our world. It is a dreadful thing to be totally unknown. The bleakest reaches of loneliness do not quite touch such fearful isolation; for, however lonely we are, we are among our fellows who at least know what we are, for all their disregard of who we are or where our dreams are calling us. Even when loneliness is routed by the eager companionship of love, we writhe in an agony beyond human relief, of not being known enough and not knowing enough; in this sense we are always alone, alone because we cannot say all that is within us, cannot see all that is in the one we love. The fear of discovery that haunts our secret hours is a terror of inimical or indifferent hearts; it is only to our enemies that we fear to be known. Where love and understanding are guaranteed, it is not pain but blessed relief to have even our most despicable weakness seen and ministered to. That "All things are naked and open to His eyes" (*Heb.* 4/13) is not to our terror but to the banishment of our deepest loneliness; it is to our constant comfort to remember that He reaches "even to the division of the soul and the spirit, of the joints also and the marrow, and is a discerner of the thoughts and intents of the heart; neither is there any creature invisible in His sight." (*Heb.* 4/12-13)

NOR IS THIS THE WISHFUL THINKING of a lonely heart seeking refuge in hopes no more solid than the walls of a dream. Anything less than the illimitable wisdom of God is unthinkable. God knows how far His hand can reach; everything that is escapes annihilation only insofar as the hand of God supports it. He knows the shimmering reflections of divine beauty in the pool of creation, knowing that divine beauty so perfectly. "Not because they are," says Augustine, "does God know all creatures spiritual and temporal, but because He knows them, therefore they are." For ourselves, we wander through the days of our life discovering, with a child's wonder, the things that God has made; but God's knowledge is not the accumulation of discovery. The command of His reason was the fertile word at which all that is leaped from nothingness into being. He is the divine Craftsman not to be surprised by any detail of the work He has so wisely wrought.

ETERNITY IS A CLOAK wrapped about and enclosing yesterday, today and tomorrow in one moment that never ends. Of all this, God's single glance, which is yet eternal, misses nothing: what He has made, what He could have made, the evil that is a tear in the fabric of the good, even what could have been and would have been had we not failed Him. Everything is naked and open to His eyes; down to the last beat of a heart, the first fluttering of desire, the strong steps of hope.

"ALL THE WAYS of a man are open to His eyes." (*Prov.* 16/2) Our feet cannot carry us beyond the vision of God. The most wayward heart is still within reach of His understanding eyes. Triumph and failure, faded dreams, the ebbed courage, the flicked insults of ingratitude, and all the tantrums of childish rebellion do not have to be explained to God. He knows us, knows better than we can ever know; and loves us infinitely from the infinite depth of that understanding knowledge. His image is in us, however deeply buried under the debris of our living, and heaven is never beyond the reach of our fingers.

GOD'S KNOWLEDGE begins to take on its true stature in our eyes when we see His mind as the source of all that can be known, as the fountain from which gushes forth all reality that, known by us, gives us our proud grasp of truth.

THE TRUTH WE POSSESS is a humble thing; no more, in fact, than the mirroring of the real world about us. When we substitute the product of our minds for the products of God's mind, we fashion a world of fancy to replace the world of things as they are; by this, we cut ourselves off from truth, retiring from the real world into one of our own making, isolating ourselves in solitary confinement. When we see the real world in grotesque, distorted fashion, we are in error. To feed the minds of other men that distorted view is a surer guarantee of blindness than plucking out their eyes. We do not create truth; we discover what is real. It is God Who is truth and the source of truth.

THE INFINITE REALITY which is God can be known infinitely, and is so known by the infinite mind of God. It is not so much that God possesses truth; rather He is truth, infinite truth, creative truth. The world of reality is real insofar as it mirrors the divine mind, thus being true to itself; we get our insights into divinity by mirroring in turn the reality which hangs in instant dependence from the mind of God. The source of reality is the ultimate source of the truth of things as they are.

To CUT OFF THE SOURCE OF TRUTH, denying God, is to summon up an unreal reality as monstrously impossible as the uncaused effect that so satisfies the sick minds of our day. There is tragic loss in this casting off of truth's beauty. The tragedy mounts when we realize that this precludes our ever coming into contact with the world outside ourselves; in this condition, we shall never see a single thing as it really is. The supremely tragic note, however, comes from the fact that this blindness is self-inflicted in the very name of the truth whose light is being extinguished. With laborious care, men lift some of the mysterious outer wrappings of reality, and their eyes are caught by the beauty of the vision of complex order and smooth harmony. There is wonder and beauty here indeed, something of the wonder and beauty of God; the fallen angels were caught in just such an enchantment by the vision of their own beauty. To refuse, as the angels did, to look beyond that first glimpse of reality is to make the whole thing unreal and put an end to the pursuit of the full vision of truth.

UNTIL TRUTH GIVES LIGHT to a man's mind, his heart is immobilized more effectively than the feet of a man in the pitch blackness of a strange place. Unless the mind of a man is nourished on truth, his heart is shrunken and starved. If error, not truth, is the diet of the mind, then the heart gorges itself on poison and is doomed to bloated frustration and the writhings of despair. We can reach out only for what we know; if the light of knowledge be false, we can make nothing but missteps. Our hearts can be aflame only with the fuel offered by our minds. Nor can we change ourselves, adapting mind and heart to any light, to any diet; only truth is light for the eyes and goal for the heart. We are real, we live in a world of real things, our hearts are not to be nourished on fantasies or nightmares but on realities.

BEAUTY AND GOODNESS come into a man's life only in the train of truth. Even the enemies of beauty and goodness, making their burglarious entry, must wear the disguise of the beautiful and the good. Perhaps the mind may never see through those disguises; but the heart of a man cannot be deceived perpetually. Ultimately the diet of evil, however good it is made to seem, sickens a man; and ugliness revolts his soul with its loathsomeness. It is to just such sickness and revulsion that leaders and teachers of men condemn the little ones when they deny them the truth. And God is truth.

ONLY OUR VERY BEING is more fundamental to us than truth. We must have truth; only then can we begin to live, only then can we rest in beauty's contemplation, and have our hearts first stirred then filled with good. It was the Word, the Wisdom of God, Who became man and lived amongst us, in order, as He Himself said, that men "might have the truth, and the truth might make them free." He was, He said, "the way, the truth, and the life." He lived for truth, and died rather than mouth the lie that would deny His divinity. Without truth, there is no way for a man's feet to walk, no light for his eyes to see, no goal for his living. He is a slave of the lie that has usurped the throne of truth. Perhaps truth has been denied him with ruthless malice, perhaps the denial came through a teacher's naive, wide-eyed, well meaning stupidity, perhaps it was the individual's own cowardly fear of his own humanity and its demands for courageous living. Whatever the reason, culpable or not, malicious or well meant, the utter, fundamental destruction of the lives of men is exactly the same. We must have truth.

IS GOD ALIVE? This seems a silly question in the light of God's knowledge and truth. It is plain enough to us that a dead man cannot follow an argument nor give a rebuttal, a fact that makes abuse of the dead a safe outlet for a coward's malice. Only the living can understand. Yet again and again men have played the game of living with a dead God, making Him a symbol, an impersonal cosmic thing, a promise of the future, or a product of the hands or the minds of men. It is very much to the point in our time to ask: is God alive? And, if He is, how much of life is there in Him?

THE STRONG PULSE OF THE SEA, the waters of a mountain stream scampering as if for warmth, or the smooth strength of a broad river are all in striking contrast to the waters of a stagnant pond. We speak with reason of "living waters." The water in the river, brook and sea does look alive for it is never still, and it is activity, after all, that is our measure of life. If that activity is from without, we know that we are not watching the progress of a living thing but a likeness of life that can be enchanting or foreboding. The violent rush of storm clouds has all the air of a personal attack, while the carefree patch of white idling its way across a summer sky seems an open invitation to our own dawdling. The persistent tap of rain on a window is not a demand for entry, it just sounds like that; and the harsh anger of a pounding sea has no life in it, though we see it as a living threat. All these are likenesses of life, but they are dead things driven from the outside. Life's activity is always from within.

ON THE OTHER HAND, to see a man driven is to see the likeness of death in the living. Gusts of anger, the dominance of drugs, or the escape of drink drain the life out of a man's actions because they take over command and drive him to things he detests. The inherent horror of a concentration camp is not different from the fundamental repugnance inseparable from all slavery; these things make dead men of the living without killing them, they drive men from without along paths not of their choosing.

LIFE IS ACTIVITY FROM WITHIN. Dionysius, picturing it as a trumpet blast let loose on the world, says "The last echo of life is heard in the plants." Certainly it is true that we easily recognize higher levels of life and precisely on this basis of activity, as we step from the plant to the animal, to the human heights; not only is there more activity as we go up the scale, the activity is more truly from within and for the inner perfection of the living agent. A man has more of life than an animal, not because he can run faster and farther, not because he can see more clearly or hear more acutely; but because he can understand and love, because he can reach out to welcome all the universe into his mind, and can em-

brace or reject any single thing in it. He is not driven.
And his knowledge and his love stay within his very
self to his own perfection, rather than flowing out of
him for the nourishment of others.

GOD IS BEYOND all driving from without: His
knowledge and love are perfectly within Himself, in fact His very self. He is the unmoved Mover
of all else, the Source of all activity and its goal.
Eternally and infinitely intense knowledge and love
is the very essence of divinity; an activity of intellect
and will that is eternally at white heat, not cooling,
not needing refueling, without fatigue or surcease.
It is not that God has life, He is life; not that He
shows activity, but that He is Pure Act; the living
God Who is life itself and "in Whom we live and move
and have our being." In a very real sense, all living
things live by the life of God, sharing something of
that divinely intense living power as a gift lent for a
time to the portrayal of divinity before the eyes of
men. A dead God is a contradiction in terms; to deny
God life is to invoke death on all the universe, to
move in a realm of shadows more ghastly than a
world of the dead who still live.

THE MOST INTENSE LIVING is to know and to love,
for this is most active and the most completely
intrinsic of the living borrowed from God. Even our
ordinary speech betrays our complete acceptance of
this truth, for we see and speak openly of the "second
life" or "second nature" a man can build within himself by his knowledge and his love. So any work in
which a man delights, towards which he has a bent,
on which he spends his time, and to which his life
is ordered is said to be the life of a man; thus we
speak of a man living a life of indulgence, a life of

virtue, an active life or a contemplative life. The Gospels have in fact given just such a definition of life with God: "for this is eternal life, to know the one true God." What we mean by this, of course, is that just as life is the principle of activity in a man, so the habits, good or evil, that he builds within himself are also principles from which flow the actions that give the distinctive color to each man's living.

To know something of ourselves is already to know a great deal about God for we are made in His image. Our life is a drudgery without love; it is vacuous, stupid without knowledge; it approaches the hot flame of intensity when the fires of mind and heart are fed with the fuel of truth and goodness and fanned into a conflagration by the rush to far horizons. The inner life of God is an infinitely intense life: a life of infinite truth comprehended and infinite goodness wholly embraced. With us, our minds lift veil after veil to show us goodness that is still lacking, still to be reached for; so our will, the faculty of our desire and our love, is in ceaseless pursuit of goodness, pausing only in passing for momentary rest and enjoyment of what little of goodness is already within our grasp. On this earth, our life is one of seeking, of constant pursuit; God's life is one of eternal, complete possession. His will has no need to pursue; it need only love.

If we see last in God what is to be seen first, we will most surely distort the divine beauty. So if we see His will as a thing of terror, an insurmountable challenge to our will, an irresponsible cause of evil, or a constant worry to our best efforts to be in harmony with it, we have distorted the will of God and we recoil from a monster of our own making.

That divine will must be seen first in its primary and eternal activity—as a roaring flame warming all the halls of eternity with the fervor of its love. We must see, in other words, something of the sublime attractiveness of the divine will before we can begin to see rightly its might, its mysterious working with our own will, and with the world.

AMONG OURSELVES, we can judge the fineness of genuine worth as against the coarseness of worthlessness in terms of a person's capacity to love. The selfish, the petty, the cowardly are easily and accurately ranked inferior to the generous, the great-souled, the recklessly gallant whose love does not count dollars, hours, sufferings, nor even life itself. In God, we see a love that measures up to the infinite lovableness of divinity, a love worthy of God, the love of a will completely at rest yet ceaselessly active in an eternal embrace of a good beyond all measuring: this is the original of all that we can ever see of superb generosity in human love. Compared to this, even so shining a love as Our Lady's is only a spark. Behind and through every other activity of that divine will is this roaring flame of eternal surrender that is the first and never ceasing action of the will of God.

THE DIVINE GOODNESS, perfectly known, is utterly irresistible, even to God; His love of the divine goodness is inescapable, more necessary than the regularity of sunrise or the eternal security of the saints' vision of God. This God Himself must do: He must love His divine goodness, and infinitely. Any other supposition is absurd: as if God could find something not lovable about infinite perfection, or a rival to entice His heart away from divinity's beauty, or an ignorance that makes Him blind to all that is good. God necessarily loves Himself. His divine will goes out to all else besides Himself, not necessarily but freely; yet even these things God must love for His own sake.

TO SAY THAT GOD WILLS ALL for His own sake is not a statement of infinite selfishness; it is only saying that there is no defect in God, there is no good outside of Him for which He must reach, no lack in His infinite perfection. For Him to will for His own sake is not a miser's greedy grabbing of every last penny despite his hoarded wealth; rather it is the extravagant sharing of one whose riches cannot diminish no matter how widely they are shared. One who has all can only share, he cannot acquire more; that is what the theologians mean when they speak of God as the perfect agent whose only mode of acting is sharing the fullness of His goodness. We, who have so little, must constantly be reaching for more; for us, to act for our own sake is to lay out a program of aggrandizement. Even our most generous, most unselfish acts of self-sacrificing love are never separable from the process of perfecting ourselves; in fact, we do most for ourselves when we think least of ourselves and most of God and our neighbor. We are imperfect agents whose every act must perfect or destroy perfection. To see God's will in the light of our own is to be blind to that first, essential, unending activity of the divine will: the eternal embrace of divine goodness that leaves the will nothing to desire and everything to share.

WITH THAT FIRST ACT OF GOD'S WILL in sharp clarity before our eyes, we can understand Augustine's profound words: "Because God is good, we exist." There is no other cause to be assigned to

God's willing, for there is no rival to the divine goodness to entice God's will into action. It is His will that is the ultimate source of the creative movement that brought us into being; and that movement could be sparked by nothing other than the divine goodness. Because God is good, we exist; because God so loves His infinite goodness, we are called into being that we might share that goodness and that love.

WHAT IS THERE OF TERROR in the fact that a will that makes dim the fire of a Seraph's love is omnipotent, unfailingly effective? Love can, indeed, be terrible, but not with a tyrant's ruthless contempt; rather it is terrible as a rebuke to the unloving, as a condemnation to those who spurn love offered so unconditionally, as a chastisement in its refusal to force itself on those who hate themselves, hating love. It is a blasphemous monstrosity so to distort that flaming love which is God's will into a searing flame of destruction to men, for this is to make God a devil. From the beginning until now, men have hurled themselves into hell; but, as Augustine says, "No wise man is the cause of another man becoming worse. Now God surpasses all men in wisdom (and in love). Much less therefore is God the cause of man becoming worse." We become worse by rejecting the love that brought us into being and that is offered to us for eternity; our hell, on earth and in eternity, is to have our choice confirmed: to lose forever the God we would not welcome.

YET EVEN IN THE FACE of the failure of men, we see an awful confirmation of the unfailing divine love. Love cannot be forced, nor will it use violence; in His image, He made us free and His love refuses to take back any of that original gift, refuses to violate our freedom. If we love Him, we do so freely, for love is a gift or it is nothing. We do not thwart His will when we spurn His love. Slamming the door on His love, we open the door to His justice that yet does not go beyond the declared intentions of our free will: we will have nothing of God; so be it, and the choice stands for eternity. The terror is not in God's will but in the fickleness and perversity of the hearts of men.

THAT SAME INSIGHT into the eternal activity of God's will, its eternal loving, forbids the foolish despair that smothers so many lives in the face of the unchanging character of God's will. Again, we are victims of a monstrosity of our own concoction. Surely there would be good reason for despair if there could be a change, if the divine will could cease its loving and the sharing of its love. The immutable will of God is not a granite wall against which men dash their lives; it is not a blind, heartless fate that renders vain the prayers, the sufferings, the battles, the works of men. These things of men, prayers, merits, sufferings, and all the rest are by no means futile; they are the coins by which heaven is bought, not because they change the will of God but because they fulfil it.

THERE IS NO MAN God does not wish to be saved; but there is no man God will save against that man's will. It would be a poor kind of love that made us in His image and left us nothing to do for ourselves; it is a divine love that sets out a man's work for a man's life and stands by a man's own decisions. He has indeed left us something to do with our mind and our will as well as with our hands and our feet. If we do these things, we are fulfilling the divine will;

if we do not, we are not thwarting God but ourselves, for our eternal happiness hangs on the condition of our activity. This is not a reason for despair; rather it is a divine tribute to the nobility of the nature of man.

IF PRAYER WERE A CRINGING, whining, coaxing of a whimsical God, it would debase a man; where, in fact, it is the shouldering of the burden of his own destiny, a doing of his part in winning heaven, it is the ennobling thing that has so set apart the saints from the cowardly braggarts who deify themselves and the whining cowards who dehumanize themselves. Of course there is difficulty in understanding how we, so utterly dependent on God, are yet free agents working out our own lives with full responsibility; but there is no difficulty in understanding that we cannot retain our freedom if we cut ourselves off from God. That freedom, too, is a reality, not a dream, and everything real depends every instant for its reality on the God of the world of things as they are. To demand a freedom that is totally divorced from dependence on divinity is to ask that men be God; in other words, to destroy both man and God. To ask for a complete comprehension of how God's will produces and preserves our freedom is to ask for the mind of God in the head of a man that the divine infinity be fully understood; which again is to destroy both man and God. We are not God. We are men, made in the image of God, with the fate of our soul entirely in our own hands because of the daring goodness of God's sharing.

WE MUST DO THE WILL OF GOD if we are not to destroy ourselves. Yet, this is not a demand of a grim-faced tyrant obscenely reveling in the crushing power of His will. What it does mean is that we

must answer God's love with our own, to the unending
goal of sharing both His life and His love. What is
the will of God? Our salvation, our happiness, our
eternal union with Him. How can we discover it,
where is it hidden, how can we fathom its infallible
directions? What is the will of God for me in this
particular matter? How can I be *sure*? Will I, in spite
of my best intentions, make a mistake about His
will and wander off the road?

HIS ENCOMPASSING LOVE has left little grounds
for our uneasiness. There are the explicit statements of His will in the divine prohibitions, precepts
and counsels. For judgment in the entangling circumstances of particular occasions, He has given us minds
of our own, imaging and sharing the divine light of
His own mind, and therefore to be followed confidently; and there is the advice of those wiser than
ourselves. Beneath, behind and through it all there
is the stupendous truth that no man loses God by
accident, no man wanders off the road home in spite
of himself, no man is in rebellion against the will of
God except by his own open declaration of war.
Perhaps the months or years will show us that we
have taken a roundabout path; but if our heart is
right, our feet will find the ultimate goal of God:
our salvation.

OFTEN ENOUGH WE MUST RESORT to figurative
language when we speak of God simply because
the arms of our mind will not go around the infinite
truth that is God. To speak of the anger of God, His
hope, desire, or sorrow gets something said of Him
as long as we remember that we are borrowing from
the poets to hint at things we cannot say; for all these
things literally indicate that God is in some way

vulnerable, that there are avenues of inimical invasion
of divinity, or that He needs help to reach what is
still lacking to Him. We are talking in metaphors and
must speak with the utmost caution. But when we
speak of love in God we are talking in literal terms;
this is true of God and cannot be said too strongly,
there is no need for caution, no apology for the
seeming extravagance of love's language.

ST. THOMAS, FOR EXAMPLE, makes so bold as to
say: "A lover is placed outside himself, and made
to pass into the object of his love, inasmuch as he
wills good to the beloved; and works for that good
by his providence even as he works for his own."
To apply this general truth of love to God, he calls
on Dionysius, lest he seem to be going too far: "On
behalf of the truth we must make bold to say even
this, that He Himself, the cause of all things, by His
abounding love and goodness, is placed outside Himself by His providence for all existing things." (1 a,
q. 20, a. 2, ad 1 um) Much bolder things must be said
when it is a question of the divine love that God
places in a man's heart, the love we know as charity;
the point here is the truth that thrusts its sharp point
at the very heart of the universe: God loves.

THE GOODNESS OF THE WORLD and of the men
and women in it is a lover's invitation to our
heart to come forth from its lonely castle; on the
contrary, God's heart is not called forth to love, rather
it is His love that calls from nothingness all the
goodness that He loves in His creatures. We wander
the world alert to the discovery of something worth
loving, helpless to produce that lovableness; so in all
our loving there is a note of surprise, of delight, of
exultation that never loses humility's unobtrusive

grace: all this is so obviously not from us. We cannot make goodness; we can only discover it and gratefully embrace it. God's love is always productive of goodness, creative, effective; His heart does not wander the world searching goodness but scattering it. Wherever the love of God lights, lovableness springs into being and is divinely cherished.

IN A VERY REAL SENSE God loves everything that is, for to every existing thing God has effectively willed some good, otherwise it would not be. And this is love's best definition: to will good to another, and to get it done. "Thou lovest all things that are, and hatest none of the things which Thou hast made." (*Wis.* 11/25) This is not to say that every soaring bird or growing shrub is a friend of God's; that is a privilege reserved for us who can return that love and share the divine life He leads, as becomes a friend. All the rest of creation is loved by God for Himself (to the sharing of His goodness) and for us, His friends, for there are services they can render to us. Perhaps it is this last that so shrivels our pride in our own love: that this Friend should put omnipotence to work in the making of a universe that we, His friends, might find our way home to Him. We get so little done for our friends, and demand so much as the price of continued friendship. Even the greatest sinner, scorning friendship and declaring war, does not cut off God's love for him; God hates the sin that is destroying this friend of His, not the man on whom He lavishes the wonders of a universe.

FOR US WHO ARE HIS FRIENDS, who have minds to understand and hearts to love, the very universe He has made for us opens up the heart of God, for it tells much of the story of His loves. There is no comparison between the love God has for a puff of dust carried along on a passing breeze and His love for a man striding boldly and purposefully towards the heights of God. Every touch of God's love produces something of goodness; so the record of goodness, of the share in divine existence given to every creature, is a note in the scale of divine love. What has more has been loved more by God: the non-living, the plants, the animals, men, the angels. Yet this scale of natural perfection is not the whole story. Because supernatural gifts have been poured into the worlds of angels and men, our fuller knowledge of God's love must wait for heaven; for now men can be better than angels, have more of divine life, and so more of divine love. Of all creation, the humanity of Our Lord clearly ranks highest in the love of God; no other creature has been as close to God as substantial union, no other has had such absolute fullness of shared divine life or grace, such heights of glory. The next in certain preference is surely the Mother of God, above all the saints and all the angels. Beyond that we cannot go. To attempt to determine the degree of God's love for Peter or John or James, for this or that man or woman of our acquaintance, is a presumptuous invasion of the privacy of God. "The Lord is the weigher of spirits", and no other. (*Prov.* 16/2)

AN UNJUST LOVER is as impossible as a vicious saint. How can we lay claim to the name of love if we will not even give this dear one what is his due? Love's fortifications tumble in ruins when injustice breaches any part of them. While it is true that justice may endure for some time without love, not a single stone of love's mansion can be raised without the

solid rock of justice as its foundation. The soft sand
of sentimentality or of passion can shift in a moment
to an unfairness that totally undermines love's whole-
hearted dedication to the happiness of another. It is
not a reflection on God's eager love of men but
rather a defense of it to insist that "God is just
and loves justice."

IF JUSTICE IS LOVE'S MINIMUM DEMAND and its
solid foundation, we should see it in terms of some
of love's allure, a precious thing calling forth our
heart's loyalty and a strong refuge against the threats
levelled against love. Yet justice, particularly the unfailing justice of God, remains for us a source of
terror. The just Judge stands in complete contrast
to the loving Savior, the cross to the throne of judgment; and this in spite of the fact that it is the same
son of Mary Who hangs on the cross and sits on the
judgment throne, no less loving in His majesty than
in His agony. Love and justice are not implacable
enemies but inseparable friends.

IN OUR PANIC, we have traced our terrors to the
wrong roots, and we strike out blindly against the
justice of God; if God were a little less just, our
terrors would vanish. But it is not the justice of God that
gives rise to our terrors; an unjust God would not
set our hearts at peace. We are terrified not because
of the acts of God but because of our own acts; it is
not God's justice but our injustice that reduces us to
mortal fear. The real root of our justified fright is
our sinful acts; the injustices we perpetrate against
God are what brings down on our heads at our demand the awful wrath of the living God.

THE JUSTICE OF GOD is no more terrible than
truth; it has no less of scintillating beauty, no

less of luminous splendor in sharp contrast to the repulsive ugliness of a lie. For in actual fact, the justice of God is the truth of God at work. It is the divine Architect's measuring mind tracing in creative lines the pattern of all that is, as His carpenter Son would later trace out in human gestures the perfect pattern of the just man. This divine mortising of the universe into a whole solid with order is the creative justice of God; its correlative is the distributive justice of the Sovereign Lord of Hosts meting out the treasures of perfection with a heart and hand strong enough to preserve all the delicate nuances of proper proportion, in contrast to an indiscriminating coddling of spoiled children. A sentimental or cowardly denial of justice to God is an insertion of the festering decay of falsehood into the perfection of divinity. This is not done in praise of God but in mockery of Him by way of defense of our own desertion of the beauty of truth and the solid bulwark of justice.

L OVE BUILDS ON JUSTICE or it is not love at all; just as truly, justice rests ultimately on mercy or it has no field in which to work. Mercy and justice are no more rivals in dogged opposition to each other than are justice and love. Mercy does not lessen justice but goes beyond the demands of justice; justice does not cancel out mercy but presupposes it.

B EHIND ALL THE DIVINE JUSTICE, there is the first merciful ministering by God to our nothingness. It was the divine mercy that filled up our emptiness from the plenitude of divinity by creation's summoning of the world from the abyss of nothingness. Men had to *be* before there could be any question of a claim in justice to truth, to beauty, to virtue's helps.

Without mercy, there is no justice for there is no one to whom there can be something due.

IN THE DIVINE BOUNTY TO US, we can see God's goodness sharing itself from sheer beneficence, His justice respecting the rights divine wisdom gave to each nature, His liberality alert to all that is helpful to us, and His mercy quick to minister to the defects, the miseries before which we are so helpless. The multitude of defects which the years make plain in us, and which we achieve as our harvest of the years, fixes our eyes more and more on the divine mercy. It is to the mercy of God, as we know ourselves better, that we look for the full fruits of His goodness, His justice, His liberality. Of ourselves, we slide back easily to the nothingness from which His mercy called us.

THE PROUD DREAMS OF YOUTH, nurtured by young strength and unfettered hopes, are dissipated by the pitiless light of facts as we gradually face our limitations and defects. In the light of these defects, in view of the terrific risks we run in each moment's choice between heaven and hell, with the present held in fragile control and the next hour or the next day outside the scope of our most careful planning, there is a serious temptation to act as thoughtless children: living from moment to moment as though we would never die, pretending that nothing really counts, feigning contentment with what our hands can grasp and hold for the moment. Much of the enticement of this temptation comes from the slight savor of truth there is in it. We can face life without the madness of despair only by seeing ourselves as children; but as thoughtful, appreciative children, not thoughtless infants merely playing a game. The frailty that is ours loses much of its terrifying quality when we see ourselves as children growing to eternal life under the eyes of an almighty, infinitely wise, and divinely loving Father in a world that is wholly His.

MORE AND MORE, as the years go on, we lean on the providence of God, which is to say on the fatherliness of God. Our Father is providing, seeing ahead, arranging all details, taking care of all the things to which children's eyes are blind or which children's minds misinterpret. Nor is this a poetic escape from the realities of human life. The child's limitations in comparison with its human father are much less than our own compared to God. Our eyes see only a few steps down the road, our minds grasp only a few details of the ordered universe, our hearts contact only a fragment of the goodness about us, and our hands are weak and fumbling. God has all the human child mistakenly attributes to its father: He knows everything, He can do all things, His love is unvarying and completely understanding, He is sure refuge in every need.

WE SEE THIS more exactly when we understand that every detail of all the universe, every moment of every life, every hair of every head are all orderly parts arranged from eternity in the mind of God. Nor is this any more than a statement of the intelligence of God. All creation is His work, a work intelligently done, and so planned, seen ahead of time. In our own planning of our limited labors, we attempt this same thing; but our plans falter under the weight of ignorance and weakness. We cannot know everything, so the unforeseen can wreck our most careful arrangements; we cannot do everything, so our plans can be thwarted by rival plans. Neither lack of knowledge nor lack of power is possible in God. His plan of creation is complete from eternity; nor is that plan upset by unforeseen events or rival powers.

MEN MISTAKE THE MYSTERY of the perfection of providence for the impossibilities of a contradiction if they insist on limiting God's mind by the measure of their own. We must take things as they are, use them, minister to them; for our constructive capacity does not go beyond the world of the artificial—houses, barns, clocks and cloaks. We do not make trees or cats or sunrises. Because these things are beyond our planning, we absurdly conclude that they are beyond all planning, that they need no mind behind their orderly existence. These things do not need men, so they do not need God; they are necessary, with no word of explanation of that necessity!

WE FALL INTO THE SAME ABSURDITIES when we attempt to read the plan of God within the limits of our own vision. Why do hurricanes roar about the world; why must grass be killed that cattle be nourished, or cattle die that men might live? Why must men be hurt by the evil actions of other men? A pinpoint of the map of the centuries falls under our eyes and we pass judgment on the whole infinitely wide plan, much as a petulant child will scream in protest at details of cleanliness that make no sense within its infant horizons. If we were God, we would not allow such things; if the child were a parent it would not inflict such a regime on its children. The difference is that the child's horizons eventually reach out as wide as the parents', while the creature can never embrace the horizons of God. We remain children under God with better reasons to trust our heavenly Father than we have to trust ourselves.

PHYSICAL EVIL gives up its reasons under the pressure of even such wisdom as ours. Given enough patience for the slow working of our minds, years enough for us to look down a longer length of the road, the fog of passion and ignorance lifts enough for us to see such things as the destruction of vegetables for the nourishment of animals as a necessity for the ordered maintenance of the world; we may even see the physical suffering of men in the form of punishment preserving justice or in the form of tribulations tempering virtue to a flexible toughness impossible to men whose strength has not been humbled. If we get to be very wise indeed, then we may awake to the fact that it is the good in the world, not the evil, that surpasses all explanation; that we take the truly mysterious entirely for granted and concentrate all our thinking on what is almost self-explanatory. The perpetual wonder is that God is so good and so much of His goodness has been scattered before our eyes.

A CHILD SELDOM SEES more than one side of a question, and many a human father has unjustly suffered pity, scorn, or open rebellion from his children at precisely the moment that his love and reverence for them were passing their greatest tests. It is, it seems, the common lot of fathers because their love must meet the common failing of children. Certainly the heavenly Father of men has not been spared this injustice. The sins of men are judged a slimy blot on the beauty of God's plan if we look only at the undoubted freedom of men; that sins occur in

KNOWLEDGE AND LOVE OF GOD

the world at all is seen as unfair to men, harsh indifference to their destiny, a self-evident refutation of God's goodness, if we look only at the omniscient power of God. A child's blindness to all angles but one lets men see God's eternal knowledge of the conquest or loss of heaven by these individuals as an invitation to fatalism and utter despair, as the destruction of man's control over his life, the end of his freedom. The same childish failure lets other men so fix their eyes on the free mastery of a man over his days as to conclude to complete presumption, even to open denial of God, and so to a much more reasonable fatalism and despair. The heavenly Father is pitied as helpless before the wills of men, scorned for His reverence for the gifts He has given men, rebelled against because men suffer and souls are lost.

THE TRUTH, OF COURSE, is that God and man are not enemies at each other's throats, that their actions are not mutually exclusive; the knowledge of God is not the destruction of man's mastery over his life, and man's freedom is not evidence of a limp in omnipotence. These truths of God and man must be seen together and in their proper order, not as opposed but as harmoniously complete. It is equally true that God is omnipotent and omniscient, and that man is free to win heaven or to choose hell. That our Father will not violate our freedom, even in the very moment of our deepest insult to and betrayal of Him, is not a gesture of contempt for us but of profoundest reverence for the sovereignty He has given us; indeed, at this very moment we must have the benefits of His justice and mercy or we would cease to be. Like a Sovereign completely sure of His power, He has liberally shared with us the power to act from intelligence and free will; in all our positive actions He, the Source of all reality, must be behind and through the reality of our activities. But in our sins, we need no help, for this we are quite sufficient unto ourselves; for here we are not in the order of realities but of negations, here we are producing nothing but the lack of order. For what is lacking we are always sufficient; the real wonder again is not the evil but the good, the mystery lies not in what we refuse to do but in what we get done. It is here that man's least action demands the supporting hand of omnipotence, it is here that the explanations go far beyond the reaches of the finite mind of man.

IF GOD LOVES US SO, if He is so provident a Father, why does He let us commit sin? The answer is that He is God, reverently respectful of His children, and He has made us men. Why, since He knows from eternity which of us will lose our souls, did He make us at all? The question is a coward's complaint against his humanity and the share of divinity given to men. If we are to have a chance at heaven, we must run the risk of hell; no man is in hell who did not have, time after time, the chance of taking heaven in his grasp. Heaven is worth the risk of hell; God is worth the risk of the devil. It is dangerous to be a man lifted up to the heights of God; dangerous, but a danger well justified by the goals that are open to us. The shared power of God that is ours does not destroy His omnipotence, nor does His eternal knowledge destroy our freedom: we are men and He is God, and we can live that divine life with Him forever if we will, or we can start our hell on earth and preserve it for all of an eternity.

CHAPTER III

The Trinity

The Height of Mystery

A Proof of Love

The Indwelling
of the Trinity

The Inner Life of God

Divine Reasons for Sharing
the Mystery of the Trinity

CHAPTER III

The Trinity

WE HAVE REASONS in abundance for trusting our heavenly Father, not the least of which have been evident proofs of His love. Every lover is driven by the double necessity of talking and listening, of revealing and discovering; for it is an authentic mark of love to desire to know and to be known. In our human loving, this double desire is never fully accomplished: our fondest gestures bear an air of frustration for they fall far short of the things we would say by them; love's most penetrating glance never exhausts the possibilities of discovery. How can we make ourselves known to another when we know ourselves so sketchily? How can we know another as love demands since we cannot search the inviolable regions of a man's mind and heart? We say what we can, unveiling sacred things to trustful eyes, and depend on another's belief in our words and gestures; we listen to all that we can hear, accepting it all on our faith in the beloved's words for in no other way can these things be ours.

OUR HEAVENLY FATHER is at home in our hearts, no stranger in the halls of our minds; to Him, we are known, known as completely as even His infinite love could demand. And we are aghast at the generosity of the love that could endure in spite of such knowledge. But, loving us, He would also be known by us, by us who cannot even penetrate to the soul of a man let alone to the depth of divinity. So, as lovers always do, He tells us His secrets, truths that we can have in no other way than by our faith in this divine Lover's words. He can indeed tell us of Himself, for He knows Himself as we can never know ourselves.

ONE OF THE SUPREME CONFIDENCES God has made to His human friends, a divine secret that only God could know, is the story of the impenetrable activity within the Godhead, the story of the family life of God. He has, in His lover's eagerness to be known, told us of the mystery of the Trinity: the mystery of three divine Persons in one divine nature, Father, Son, and Holy Ghost who are yet, by their unity of nature, one God. The intense life of divinity itself is told to our trusting hearts: the Father, who is God eternally knowing, eternally generating; the Son, who is God eternally known, the Word eternally generated; the Holy Ghost, who is God eternally loved, the breath of love proceeding eternally from the perfect Knower and the perfectly Known. These are three Persons, distinct one from another, but completely identical in their divine nature. This is a lover's surrender of secrets. It is not a truth told to stagger our minds and so to impress us, though certainly the truth is much too big for more than our most timid caress. The secret has been revealed to further and deepen our happiness, a contribution of love to the happiness of us who are so loved.

EVEN TO OUR DULL EYES, there is a tremendous kindness, a gentle protection of our love in this divine confidence. In our stumbling human fashion, we might so easily have seen God as utterly alone, as lonely as a bishop in his study, aloof from everything for lack of equals, cold for lack of a goodness worthy of His great heart; and, seeing Him thus, we might have given Him pity instead of admiration, adoration and love. In our human experience activity and change are so intertwined that we might easily think of the unchangeable God as condemned to a life of idleness, completely inactive, stagnant, with nothing to do and all eternity to face; and so have our own hearts go dead within us in a sorrow that would be close to revulsion. Because we have direct experience only with human persons, we might easily make the mistake of conceiving of God as an impersonal being, some kind of a huge blob of goodness, spectral, ghostly, without eyes or heart; and thus have rendered ourselves incapable of so intimately personal a relationship as love.

IN THE TRUST that love so eagerly gives to a lover's words, and so helplessly since there is no other way of knowing what must be known, we know now that there is no loneliness in God, no lack of equals, no lack of lovableness worthy of infinite love. Rather, the joy, the truth, the beauty, the love of that divine life has spilled over in its abundance to make a world and to quench the thirst given to men for the life that is proper to God. He has told us that truth's bright beauty is never veiled and the allure of goodness never dimmed; in other words, that the activity of mind and heart that can shrink the hours to minutes in our clumsy world of time, flames through all eternity with infinite intenseness. In that divine life, on the word of God, Love is so personal as to be a Person, Wisdom and its Generator so far superior to anything we can conceive as to *be* Persons. Father, Son, and Holy Ghost are divine Persons; the revelation of their eternal life is the divine answer to the absurdity of an impersonal God, the divine invitation to a love so penetrating as to be victorious possession and unconditional capitulation.

GOD IS MOST ANXIOUS that we know these divine secrets; He tells them plainly though they be beyond our mind's power to understand. Depending with a lover's trust on His word, the very knowing of the existence of the Trinity will do so much for our love of God, so much for our living, so much for the honor and respect we will give to men who are to share that divine living now and for eternity. Knowing that there are three divine Persons in one divine nature lets us know there is truth indeed in the lover's quest for union, however frail an image we achieve of the union of the divine Three. It tells us there is truth in our estimate of activity, great activity, above all the activity of mind and heart that is entirely within our very selves; while it makes it no less clear that we are very wrong in identifying change, gain and loss, with the activity that is the very core of life. The fact of the Trinity reassures us in our defense of truth in our minds and love in our hearts even at the cost of physical life, we are right in seeing these as the priceless gifts that cannot be surrendered; we are right in seeing falsehood and hate as the living death of a man. Love and truth are close indeed to the very life of divinity; falsehood and hate are most completely opposed to that divine life. By love and truth we are closest to God; by falsehood and hate, farthest from Him.

GOD'S SECRET OF THE TRINITY lets us know clearly that God does not need creatures for His Fatherhood; nor creation for the expression of His Word; nor men or angels for His Love. Within divinity itself there is eternal Fatherhood, the infinite Word, and living Love. Everything that God has done outside the Godhead is the work of all three Persons, a work done by virtue of the divine nature which is common to them all. It is to our comfort, and as an emphasis of the infinite personalities of the Trinity, that we speak of the works of power as works of the Father, works of wisdom as works of the Son, and works of love as works of the Holy Ghost.

THERE IS NEW MEANING in the solemn truth that we are the abode of God, His temples, now that we have been told of the Trinity. The Trinity, Father, Son and Holy Ghost, living the infinitely intense divine life, abide within us as we share that divine life by the gift of sanctifying grace. We know as God knows by the virtue of faith, we love as He loves by the virtue of charity; thus God is in us in a very special way, as the object of knowledge and love, a special way that smacks strongly of the Trinitarian way of Knower, Known, and Loved. Grace is the seed of glory; heaven begins in the meanest house on the vilest street in the most disordered city when grace enters the soul of a man living there; his life touches on the burning intensity of divine life and the eternal fire is lighted in his soul. We begin to be at home in the family of God when the Trinity makes its home within the house of our soul.

CHAPTER IV

Creation

CHAPTER IV

Creation

WHEN WE TURN OUR MINDS to the consideration of creatures we do not by that fact turn away from God; our creature world is not an alien one into which divinity enters timidly by our gracious invitation or is excluded by our inhospitable provincialism. It is, in fact, not nearly so much our world as God's. If we insist on an exclusive concentration on ourselves and other creatures, we miss most of what has captivated our eyes; and what little we see is distorted into a grotesque ugliness that offends the mind and revolts the heart of a simple man.

A SCRUTINY OF THE BEGINNINGS of creatures confronts us with the magnificent spectacle of omnipotence sharing infinite goodness. To look at creatures themselves is to marvel at the perfection of detail and symmetry of organization in the executed plan of the divine architect; infinite wisdom achieving the patterns of divinity, dazzling reflections of divinity glittering before the eyes of men. A glance ahead, down the road along which each creature rushes so intently, shows us the fixed purpose of all nature: to get closer to God, to struggle to that individual perfection which is a better imaging of the infinite perfection, to come to the beginning and the goal of all that is.

IF OUR EYES ARE REALLY OPEN to the world in which we live, then every detail of it shows us God: God sharing His infinite goodness; the divine Architect achieving cosmic plans down to the minutest detail; God the ultimate Perfection calling forth all the world's activity that each thing in the world might, in its own finite measure, reach for and come to rest in that only final goal. All the world is filled with the happy, ceaseless clamor of all its creatures shouting from the very depths of their natures: "God shared His goodness with us; what we have is God's; we are hurrying back to Him."

WE COULD ENJOY the story of creation if we were sure it were not true. The story of God's will effortlessly plucking from nothingness the whirling suns of the universe could be as pleasantly mystifying as a magician's tricks if we were as sure that this too was a divine trick; not really so, quite beyond our immediate understanding of how the trick was worked, but still only a trick with its own radically simple explanation.

FACED WITH THE FACT that the story of creation is true, that God did indeed so call everything from nothingness, we are caught up breathless, almost incapable of protest. The magnitude of the thing so far outstripping all our ordinary ways of getting things done hits us with something of the terror of a man suddenly gone blind, for when we plunge into this truth we cannot see. It is not only that creation stands at the brink of the world; every time we dare to look at that great truth, we stand on the brink of the world of our understanding, caught between the terror of mystery's invitation to step out into the darkness and our mind's stubborn insistence on knowing the truth. There is humiliation here for a proud man; this truth is so much bigger than the widest stretches of his own mind. There is comfort here for the wise man, the comfort of knowing that there are truths too big for the mind of man, of knowing that this paltry mind of ours is not the full measure of all truth.

Wise or proud, terrified or enticed as we may be, the truth stands: "In the beginning, God created heaven and earth."

OUR MINDS DO NOT ACCEPT the boon of mystery easily. They writhe and wriggle, twist and turn, pout and rebel, like an infant fighting off the food that alone will preserve its life and give it growth. No matter how many blankets of centuries we pile on the question of the beginning of things, that question is not smothered. That the world began yesterday or a million years ago has nothing to do with the mystery of how it began. It is no help to plunge into the middle of things and go on from there, pretending that there was no beginning and will be no end, or that beginnings and ends are trivial things compared to the zest of the world right now. It is amusing, but not effective, to hide behind a contradiction as a child hides behind its own hands, explaining gravely to ourselves and the world that "at some time, Random gathered itself together and the world began." But this is obviously a child's game, not meant to deceive even the child; for the phantasy of a world giving birth to itself is no less ludicrous than that of an infant bringing itself forth from its own womb.

CERTAINLY GOD'S WAYS are not our ways. We are only cooks, and our cookery is no better than the food we have to work with; sometimes a great deal worse. Our labors, even the greatest of them, hardly escape the level of puttering. At least we must have something given us to work on, material whose nature we must take as the gift it is: we do not author the solidity of stone, the live beauty of wood, the brilliance of the spectrum's colors. Given these things, with time, labor, some gift of artistry, we can do wonders.

We stand off in admiration of the finished product in an exultant kind of paternity and say: this is mine, I made it. Of course it is much more God's than ours. We are makers, not creators; in all our works there is the presupposed material, the process of change where genius has its innings, and the finished product. In thinking of God's work, we must cross out the first two of these steps. The finished product jumps instantly into existence at the creative command of God.

GOD, YOU SEE, IS FIRST; there is nothing before Him, not even some vague material for His workmanship. He is omnipotent; He has no need of time to bend stubborn material to His purposes, no need for laborious assembling of parts. There is no measure of His strength and ability in terms of time, or in any other terms. He serves no apprenticeship, He does not come to the peak of His powers through the years. The world is not a growth in the womb of God living by His life, nor is it a parasitical growth adhering to the very substance of God, it has not oozed out of some mysterious divine stuff: it has come into being and is sustained in its existence solely by the intellect and the will of the Almighty.

MODERN MAN CAN STAND PROUDLY beside the gigantic machine that belches such wonders and smile at the notion that omnipotence is behind the birth of the universe. The mountain labored and brought forth a mouse! Imagine omnipotence behind the pettiness of an insect, the lowliness of a worm, the fragility of a hummingbird; infinite wisdom behind the senseless badgering of dust by vagrant winds! It would be well for the self-made god to look to the obvious truth that power is manifested not only in what is done but in how it is done. With time and patient labor, ants can pile up grains of sand; a child in a moment of play can heap sands higher than the ants could ever manage. Medical care and natural recuperative powers mend many a broken leg over weeks and months; the divine touch heals it perfectly in an instant and we recognize a miracle, we see that we are in the presence of greater power than the world can muster.

THE LEAST THING brought into existence by creation is clear and vivid witness to omnipotent power at work. Nothing but omnipotence can work with absolute independence of all else. Only in this way can the dependent things of the world have had their beginnings, for only omnipotence, absolute independence can be unqualifiedly First. The world is in fact about us; nothing in it, nor all of it taken together can make any pretense at omnipotence and at such independence while time grinds out its sentence of ultimate extinction and the facts make their stubbornly just claim of things beginning. We have little choice: to deny that the world and ourselves exist at all; or to submit to the fact of creation by which alone things could begin to be. For all of its mystery, for all its incomprehensibility, for all the terror and challenge of its darkness, it is the stark truth. "In the beginning, God created heaven and earth."

THE NEWBORN INFANT works wonders of reform and perfection on its parents, piercing the hard shell of defense that has hidden them from disinterested or hostile strangers. With that shell broken, a beaming kindliness, understanding, cleanliness is let loose on the world; even strangers passing by are warmed by the fires of nobility, of generosity, of self-sacrifice that have been lighted by the infant in the hearts of a man and woman. We miss most of the truth when we dismiss all this in terms of "doting" or "proud parents." These people are not proud but humble, humble from the personal confrontation of the mystery of creation.

MOTHER AND FATHER KNOW, with an overwhelming sense of humble gratitude, that the soul which gives life to their infant, spiritual and immortal, reaching out to the ends of the universe and beyond to garner truth, soaring to the heights of God Himself to fill the cup of love, this soul was none of their making. They know, and stand in silenced awe, that they were not even the instruments of the production of this soul, not playing even so humble a part as that of hammer or saw in the making of a bench. For a spirit, such as this soul, is not made *out* of anything, it has no parts, it is not produced in slow stages; not even God Himself could give an instrument a part to play in the wondrous work of creating a human soul. These parents know that their child is much more God's than their own and in that knowledge come close to the joy in the hearts of Mary and Joseph on the first Christmas night.

THAT RICH VEIN of humility so extravagantly given to parents can be mined by any man who dares to face the stupendous fact of creation. One does not know he is engulfed by the awful power of omnipotence and at the same time coddle the illusion of proud self-sufficiency. A man must turn his eyes from the mystery of creation before he can find allure in pride's ugly daughters—ruthless ambition, hypocrisy, boasting presumption, and quarrelsome contempt for men. And God has made it very hard for a man to blind himself to omnipotence at work all about and within himself.

TRACES OF THE TRINITY are plainly marked in the non-human world which serves the interests of men: a shadow of that independence of the Father in the individual integrity of every substantial thing; the wisdom of the Son in the minutely detailed perfection of every kind of thing; the burning will of the Holy Ghost in the smooth order of one thing to another to make up the harmony of the universe. There is more than a trace, there is a positive image of the Trinity in every man's distinctly human activity of mind and will: man knowing reflects the perfection of God Knowing; his generation of knowledge is the temporal image of the eternal generation of divine Wisdom; and from that knowledge proceeds the love that is at the same time the dynamic source of all his action and the reiterated proclamation of the eternal flow of Substantial Love, the Holy Ghost, from Father and Son.

THE TRACINGS OF DIVINITY in our world are as inadequate and unsatisfying as music so faintly heard as to be almost illusory. Each creature is a tiny cup while divine goodness is a boundless ocean; how much of the awful majesty of God can be protrayed in the miniature of creatures even by a divine Artist? No one thing in the world gives more than a hint of the splendor of divinity; all the universe taken together can show forth only a fragment of the divine beauty. But all this is true only in contrast with the limitless source of the goodness, the majesty, the beauty of it all; it can easily dazzle our eyes and our heart by its sheer magnificence, though it was meant to light burning fires of desire for truth without limit and love without end.

TALKING IN OUR HUMAN FASHION, we would say that the first creatures God would think of creating would be those most like Him, the angels; and then the things most unlike Him, all the world beneath man. For the angels are, like God, pure spirits whose life is a white heat of knowing and loving, independent of all but God, strangers to death; while the world beneath man is a spiritless world, incapable of the intellect's soaring and the heart's surrender, dependent in every moment and in every activity on things around it and beneath it, constantly devastated by death and renewed by birth. The wonder to our minds is that divine ingenuity should ever have hit upon such creatures as ourselves: both spirit and matter, dissatisfied with anything less than infinite truth and yearning for love's holocaust, dependent on all the world beneath us yet scorning the limitations of time and space with mind and heart, saddened by death and inspired by birth, yet both terrified and rejoiced by the certainty of eternal life.

CHAPTER V

The Angels

Bodiless Spirits

Their Number and Variety

Angelic Knowledge and Love

Angelic Sanctity and Sin

CHAPTER V

The Angels

THE CREATURES MOST LIKE GOD, the angels, show forth best the goodness, the majesty, the glory of God; these are His most perfect images, and so the ones to be multiplied with divine extravagance. Heaven and earth are indeed full of His glory. Because the angels are bodiless creatures, pure spirits, it is too often concluded that they are supernatural beings; they are not, God is the only supernatural being. The angels are natural beings, they belong in, and, indeed, dominate our world. They are creatures as natural as oaks, or sunsets, or birds, or men. To call them supernatural because they are not like ourselves is a part of that provincial pride by which a man puts human nature at the peak of the universe, primarily because he himself is a man.

TO PRETEND THEY DO NOT EXIST because we do not see them is like pretending that we never sleep because we have never caught ourselves asleep. There would be much more sense in the angels exiling us from the world of nature on the basis of a majority vote. We have no monopoly on nature, not even on free will and intellectual knowledge in nature; we have big brothers far outstripping our puny powers, yet nonetheless brothers, a part and parcel of the created world that is so truly ours.

SEEING OURSELVES from the plant or animal level, we can with reason marvel at the nobility of men; if the animals were capable of such things, they would see us as godlike creatures. Looking up at the angels from our level, we promptly shrink to our proper proportions: of all the created world, we have the least, the most earthbound, the feeblest of all created intelligence and love. Lest that be too humiliating, we can reflect that somewhat the same is true of the angels: seen from our level, they are creatures so wondrous as to make men doubt their very existence; but seen from the heights of God they are so inadequate an image of His splendor as to be insignificant in comparison with the Infinite.

IT WAS NO TRICK to fill the heavens with a heavenly host on the first Christmas night. The stars that sparkle on the body of night are a mere handful of jewels compared to the numbers of the angels. The prophet Daniel gives only a hint of their number when he says: "Thousands of thousands ministered to Him, and ten thousand times a hundred thousand stood before Him." Dionysius humbly confesses: "There are many blessed armies of the heavenly intelligences, surpassing the weak and limited reckoning of our material numbers." All the men in the world at any time are a handful, a scattered gathering easily lost sight of in the myriads of pure spirits who most perfectly image the Creator of both men and angels.

VARIETY IS DEAR TO US, as it should be for it is dear to God. We appreciate changing seasons, the differences of trees, flowers, animals; and we are particularly grateful that all men and women do not look exactly alike. We like change and differences, not because we are fickle, or just for the sake of change, but because no one moment, no one climate, no one expression of beauty or goodness exhausts the possibilities of reflection of the divine perfection. There are so many pleasing combinations of human creatures, so many pleasing patterns of human virtue, so many pleasing colors, sights, sounds; such inexhaustible aspects of truth, so many alluring insights into goodness. The variety of the world is at one and the same time a declaration of the imperfection of created things, each one giving us only so much, and of the extravagant generosity of God.

AS IN NUMBERS, so in variety, the angelic world is a splendor that dims the variety of the physical world into a plainness approaching homely monotony. There are no angelic families or races; each individual angel stands apart from all others more distinctly different than an elephant from a fly. The pleasant individual differences we notice from man to man and woman to woman are as far from the differences between the angels as a ripple on a pond is from the towering power and smashing violence of a stormy sea. At each encounter in the heavenly courts, the angels see differences greater than those which distinguish a rose from a woman. Multiply this by the countless numbers of the angels; the heavenly choirs are a luminous image of divinity's perfections stupendous in its beauty, staggering in its wide variety. Yet all this is no more than a foggy outline of the beauty of God.

ONCE CREATED, the angels live forever, depending, as we do, on the steady support of the hand of God but on nothing else. All the things that pertain to us because we have bodies have no place in the angelic world: growth, nourishment, sickness, pain, the decline of old age, and ultimately death. They are so much more like God than we are that their whole being reflects something of the divine eternity, immortality, independence. Angels are neither old or young, sick or healthy, men or women, infants or ancients, tall or short, fat or thin; they are the bright flames of life, unflickering, unfading, indestructible, flames that are fed by nothing but God.

THE PRINCELY DIGNITY of Gabriel standing before Our Lady, the easy competence of Raphael protecting the young Tobias, the majesty of Michael with his flaming sword guarding the gates of a lost paradise gives us some little vision of the nobility of the angels. We are in danger of blinding ourselves to that vision if we forget that these were angels stooping to our limitations, bowing to our penchant for thinking in pictures; thoughtful angels who delight us as a mother delights her infant by imitating its gurgling and chuckling. This is not a mother's normal speech; nor is this the angel's normal appearance.

ANGELS WERE NOT MADE TO GIVE LIFE to bodies as were our human souls. The bodies in which they have appeared from time to time among us were the appearances of bodies taken on for our comfort; not real, but apparent that we might the more easily accept the angel, his message, his companionship. None of the things that are proper to living bodies could be accomplished by these apparent bodies of the angels: they could not digest a meal, beget children, become tired, or wake refreshed from sleep. For us to lose our body is the tragic thing called death; the body belongs to our integrity, without it we are not men and women but disembodied souls, we are only half ourselves. It is hard for us not to feel a little sorry for the angels' lack of bodies, forgetting that if the impossible thing happened and an angel had a real body, it would not be benefited but debased by that fact. Its completely spiritual nature in its independence and power has no need of a body. It can get far more done than any strong man, indeed than any material force. It is free from the barriers that the physical inevitably imposes on our knowledge and our love: free from the sluggishness, fatigue and distraction that makes our lifetime harvest of truth so skimpy; free from the frustration inherent in all our loving gestures of union, of all the feeble faith that supports our love, of all the helplessness that is our love's bitterest fruit.

NOT EVEN A CHILD is puzzled about how an angel gets its clothes on over such huge wings; for it is clear to everyone that the wings we give to angels are a symbol and nothing more. The swift flight of a bird contrasted with the trudging step of a man is a fitting symbol of smooth, untrammeled, rapid movement, and so a centuries-old expression of the celerity of angelic passage. In our own times, we might appeal to the soundless swoop of a diving jet plane to help our stumbling minds to follow the flight of an angel; we would come closer to reality by following with a flick of the eye the almost instantaneous thrust of lightning. We have the most accurate measurement of that angelic progress in the time it takes our own minds to jump from city to city, across oceans, over five, ten, or fifty years; for it is thus that an angel moves.

IN OUR THINKING about the angels, we must draw much more on our knowledge of God than on our knowledge of men, for the angels are finite pure spirits modelled on the infinite Pure Spirit. We do not locate God by surrounding Him, He is not contained within the easily discerned outlines of a body, a town, a country; He is where He works, and so is everywhere, for nothing can continue to be unless it is supported by His omnipotence. Nor can we locate an angel by surrounding it; it, too, is a pure spirit. To ask where an angel is means to ask where it is working; only thus is an angel in place. Obviously no place can be too small for an angel, no place too big, no place too distant; for with the angels, it is not a question of squeezing a body into uncomfortable quarters, of spreading its arms wide to cover more territory, or of easing it out of a town quietly. No angel is everywhere, for no angel is God, no angel is omnipotent; but neither is an angel human, to be circumscribed by the length of its arms or the horizons of eyes. It is pure spirit, to be limited in place only by the degree of the power and perfection proper to the nature given it by God.

THERE IS A FASCINATION for us in thinking of the angels, a fascination that springs from the fact that a healthy mind welcomes nourishing truth as enthusiastically as a healthy stomach welcomes a hearty meal; with the difference that there is no such thing as a stuffed mind. The more of truth we learn the hungrier we get, though the happier and more satisfied we are. These angelic big brothers of ours have much for our learning: much of God, whose closest image they are; and much of ourselves, to deflate our pride and stimulate our humility as we learn from them how dim a light marks out our path and how wavering a heart supports our love. But to learn any of the lessons there to be learned, we must remember that angels are not God, neither are they men.

GOD KNOWS HIMSELF PERFECTLY, and knowing Himself knows all else. We never do know ourselves directly, we learn of ourselves, like any outsider, from the things we do; and our conclusions usually contain a good margin of flattering error. The angels, like God, do know themselves directly; like us, they know nothing else from knowing themselves for, like us, they are not the source of creatures but part of the family of creation. Divinity is the Creditor of the angels as of us; from the infinite intellect which God is, they too borrow a limited intelligence and hold it on the terms of God. Though the amount of their loan is so very much greater, it is as true of angels as of us that they have limited intellects, they are not intelligence itself. We walk through our days with the impact of the world beating on our senses like a pelting rain. From this downpour, properly filtered, we quench our mind's thirst though it is dangerous business; for the same flood furnishes us with all the risks of deception from the wandering phantasms that take over so completely in the dreamers or the insane. God and the angels live their eternal lives in perpetually sunny weather, with never a drop of this rain falling into their world. As Gregory has it: "Man senses with the brutes, and understands with the angels."

WE ARE VAGRANT PROSPECTORS searching the world for effortless strikes that will give nuggets of truth, but actually subsisting on the flakes and dust that make up our usual find. We spend our lives in laborious attempts at a piecemeal assembly of the pattern of truth from the shattered fragments that fill the world about us. Men search the earth for their knowledge, for we are close to the earth; for the source of the angels' knowledge we must look not to earth but to God, for angels are close to God. As creatures less than the angels sprang from the mind of God into the physical world, from that same divine source, they sprang into the knowledge of the angels.

THE ANGELS' KNOWLEDGE, THEN, IS ALL that ours is not: accurate, complete, absolutely firsthand, coming to them directly from First Truth itself. All this, not by way of a special gift but by natural right; by the very fact of their purely spiritual nature, their proper way of knowing is by ideas infused into their minds by God. As the years roll by, we may become learned, or even wise; but our knowledge and wisdom are the products of the years and of our labors with many a weed harvested along with the good grain of truth. The angel has all his knowledge in the first instant of his life; whenever, through all his ageless career, an angel uses any one of those infused ideas there is no laborious thinking involved. The thought of an angel, swifter than light, deeper than a sword thrust to the heart, an intuitive plunging to the very depths of truth, leaves no room for doubts, for error, for indecision.

WE, WHO ACHIEVE OUR LITTLE WISDOM so painfully, are decidedly interested parties in any discussion of the mind of the angels. They are our only intellectual relatives in the whole of creation, relatives who have millions to match our intellectual pennies, and there is no possible threat to their great wealth. Moreover, we do not stand afar off in poverty's frustration at the walls of snobbery or the great distances of social strata; these intellectual brothers of ours slip in and out of our days with an ease and intimacy unknown to the most loved members of our immediate family. We should know more about them; and, almost instinctively, we want to know more about them not only because they can do so much for or against us but also because they are all so very close to us and to our living.

SOME OF THEM ARE FRIENDLY with that staunch friendship that endures, even heightens, throughout our weaknesses, our failures, our pettiness, our positive malice; so friendly as to be on guard for us twenty-four hours in the day. It is good to know the powers of such friends, good for our courage, for our hopes, for our loneliness, for our self-respect. Other angels are relentlessly hostile, fired with a hate we did nothing to generate and which we can not dissipate by apology or appeasement. They will stop at nothing less than our total destruction, and even that will not satisfy but rather intensify their hate. In sheer self-defense, we cannot disregard the information possessed by such an enemy.

WE MAY BE ONLY MILDLY INTERESTED in the fact that an angel knows itself immediately and perfectly, that, seeing itself as the divine image, it knows God, and that it has complete and intimate knowledge of other angels; though by this we miss all the implications for our own humility, the substantiation of our dreams, and the inherent frustration of our love's desire to know all. But we must come up sharply alert at the angels' knowledge of this physical world of ours. In that regard, they approach closest of all creation to the instant, omniscient comprehension of God. They know the details of the physical world, not through the often murky filter of sense and imagination but directly, without possibility of incompleteness or distortion. They know the world, all of it, not in the blurred fashion of a dilettante's surface expertness, nor in the vague general way of a mind that is just too tired to keep its hold on details, but sharply, concretely, with firm mastery. They know, in other words, more about all the things we have so laboriously studied through the centuries, and know them better than we ever will however more centuries are at the service of the labors of the minds of men.

ABOUT OURSELVES, THE ANGELS KNOW ALL there is to be known from the post of an observer who needs no relief, misses nothing, forgets nothing. Beyond that, the angels, all of them, easily penetrate into the regions of our imagination and memory, areas about which the human observer can only guess; which means that our daydreams are not purely private affairs, they are shared by the whole of the angelic world, our sentimental journeys into the dear days of long ago are never solitary trips. We are not nearly so much alone as we imagine, whatever the hour or the place. In relation to the friendly angels, this is to our infinite comfort, and often enough to our acute embarrassment; while it brings home clearly our weak defenses against the hostile horde of devils, the help we unwittingly and constantly give to our bitter enemies, and our own desperate need for help from powers on a par with these enemies who so completely outmatch us.

THE ANGELS CAN INTRODUCE PICTURES into our imagination, they can reach into the storehouse of memory and parade the past before our mind's eye; but there the great natural powers of the angelic world grind to a halt before the impregnable sovereignty of our intellect and our will. Not even the highest of the angels knows what a man is going to do next; the most gifted of the angels cannot know what I am thinking at this moment. In this privacy of soul, we are the equals of the angels; this territory is inviolable to all but almighty God Himself. Such is the stature of man's dignity. We are spiritual as well as physical; we are free; our intellect and will are not to be tampered with by any created force. So our thoughts, our deliberate desires, our loves are our own; for them we ourselves must take full credit or full blame. The angels can suggest through imagination and memory, they can coax, entice, threaten, or frighten through these avenues of our sense nature; but we are the ultimate masters in command of our lives.

BOTH ANGELS AND MEN BOW DOWN in humble union in matters of faith. Here every truth is God's secret not to be discovered by anyone less than God, not to be known unless God Himself make the truth known. That divine life can be and is shared, that heaven's welcome waits for those who welcomed God, that hell's misery confirms the sinner's choice, that the Son of Mary is also the Son of God, that the living Christ is present in the Eucharist, Calvary renewed in the Mass, that grace pours into the soul through the sacraments—all these the angels know only as we do: by believing them on the word of God. Angels are a part of nature, as we are; their powers are natural powers. What they have of the supernatural, whether it be life, truth, action, or goal, is theirs only through the boundless generosity of the only supernatural Being, God Himself.

JUST AS IN US, the sweep of knowledge marks out the horizons of love, so in the angels, to match that superb knowledge, second only to God's, there is a driving power of appetite that comes closer than anything else in creation to imaging the power, the intensity, the constancy and finality of the divine will. Knowing a little we can love a little; loving a little, we insist on knowing more of that lovableness; knowing more, we love more and insist again on more knowledge that there might be more love. The heart never actually outruns the head, for we have to see to love and the heart has no eyes. To know something of the magnificient perfection of angelic knowledge is to prepare oneself for the breathless rush of angelic love.

THE ANGELS ARE NOT DRIVEN to their activity by a knowledge outside themselves, directed by another intelligence, as are the plants; they are not caught up necessarily in the immediate appeal of this or that particular good, as are the animals. Rather, like us, they are free agents; their love is their own. They can take or leave any good that creation has to offer. The explanation of this is roughly paralleled in our capacity for vision. Our eyes can see brown, black, purple, blue, violet and all the rest precisely because they are not determined to any one of these things but to color in general, any color, all colors; if they were made only for brown, they would see nothing else. Our wills, and those of the angels, are not fixed to any one good, but to good, any good, all goods, even the infinite good; and so our wills and theirs can reach out to any good, or they can reject any good save goodness itself seen nakedly in the vision of God.

BUT ANGELS ARE CREATURES, they are not God. Like ourselves, they cannot rest content within themselves without excluding happiness and making a home for misery. Like ourselves, they must reach outside themselves for the lovableness that will still the insistent demands of the will. Only God is totally sufficient unto Himself, for only God is infinite goodness, only God has no end to attain but only goodness to share. Only God is home for the love of the angels, as He is for our love; they too must make their way home or remain forever exiles, wanderers in a world as empty and cold as a prison cell, for love's fire is the divine flame or it gives no warmth.

TO THE APPRECIATION OF OUR NOBILITY be it said that the angels are no more free than the least of men. Liberty does not come in spoonfuls, it is not doled out in differing degrees; it is magnificently full or it is non-existent. We are, then, no less responsible than the highest angels for the use we make of that liberty; and it is this awful splendor of responsibility that frightens men into an attempt to deny their humanity. The record of our use of it gives us grounds primarily for humility, since we are so often wavering, weak, timid both in our virtues and our sins. The angels suffer no such imperfections: their virtues are gestures of sweeping grandeur, their sins plumb the depths of the malice of hell. The movement of their wills, in other words, is a worthy complement to the instantaneous perfection of their knowledge.

IT IS AN AWESOME THING to be loved or hated by an angel; one hardly less overpowering than the other. Nothing will arise to change that love or hate, there will be no belated discovery of goodness or evil, no error of judgment to be corrected, no rival to detract from the totality of love's embrace or hatred's spleen. The angel loves or hates instantaneously, with all the intensity of its unimpeded nature, irrevocably, with utter generosity or malice, in a roaring flame of consummation of its desire. This is the way we think of our love in its springtime vigor, the way we dream of love in its perfection; but we know in the depths of our hearts that only God can make it come true in us, and we are astounded that even God can work such a wonder within us. We are so easily afraid of utterly final surrender, so aghast at reckless gallantry, so cautious in giving, so demanding of gifts.

THE ANGELS' LOVE AND HATE suffer no limitation from physical causes, the limits that are perpetually insisted on in us by our bodies. We can be terribly angry, but for just so long: new joys can dim the sorrow that provoked anger, new sorrows swamp the old in their magnitude, old joys come back to dim the memory of injury; or we just get too tired by the violence of anger to seek the revenge it demands. Our love suffers the same distractions, the same rivals, the same opposites, and even the same fatigue. There are no such passions in the angels, for they are pure spirits, unencumbered by anything of the physical; in them there are only those corresponding movements of the will for which we have no other names than the tags we have put on the movements of passion: love, hate, desire, aversion, joy, sorrow and all the rest. Clearly, the fury of a devil far surpasses the anger of the loudest, most violent, most vicious of men; quite aside from its superior intensity and wholeheartedness, there need be no lessening of it, no end to it, indeed it is certain that it will never be less consecrated to destruction than in its first moment. So too the love of an angel reduces the breathless wonders of our love's first moments to the echo of a whisper, to a light dimmer than a candle's light in the heart of the sun.

THERE IS LOVE AND HATE in the world of the angels, love and hate that separates angels into the world of heaven and the world of hell, bringing home to us the humbling lesson that even the greatest of God's creatures can fail, it is only God who cannot. There is among the angels an evil love which was the undoing of the very best, the most perfect of them, a love that was hatred of self by its very refusal to look beyond the staggering beauty that was God's gift to the angels. That hating self-love gave birth to unremitting hatred of God, the Giver of the gifts that so blinded the vision of these evil angels; a hatred of their fellow angels who saw beyond the gift to the splendor of the Giver; and a hatred of men and of all the things that God had made. There is in the world of the angels a glorious love, an utterly unselfish love that ushered angels into the family of God and the life of heaven for all eternity, the love that fulfilled even angelic desires and completed their imaging of the magnificence of the Godhead.

THE WORLD OF THE ANGELS was not always so rent asunder by the brutal violence of sin. From all eternity, and beyond all time, the intense life of the Trinity filled up the infinite measure of the Godhead before ever there was a creature to image that boundless perfection. When, in God's generosity, the time came to share that goodness, God made the world; all of it, not a part here and a part there, but all of it, the angels along with the rest of creatures. As they came from the hand of God in that bright morning of the world, the angels were as clean as a dawn at sea; sin was an unknown stranger in a world that God looked upon and saw that it was good.

INDEED IT WAS GOOD, superbly good, divinely good, and at its very best in its angelic details. The creative word of God brought the angels into being free of all spot or taint, with innocence as deep in their nature as it is obvious on the face of a sleeping child; they were perfect, with absolutely no defect. Concretely, that means that in the first instant of their lives, the angels' minds were fully possessed of all their natural knowledge, their love instantly went forth to wrap itself about all that was good; they were, from the very first moment of their lives, in full possession of natural happiness, with nothing lacking, nothing to fight against, nothing to labor for, no steps to be taken. This was the springtime of the world, and never since has spring matched the exuberant joy of this first blossoming.

WITHIN THE LIMITS OF NATURE, there was nothing more that could be given to the angels; natural resources had been tapped to their utmost, natural capacities for happiness had been exhausted, natural joy could not bear the slightest increase. But God, who made nature, is not imprisoned by His creation, He is not held within natural limits. All that had been given to the angels was still not enough for the generosity of God. Divine wisdom devised a way to give infinitely more than the fullest cup of natural happiness, to give a share in the life, the action, and the goal of God. For the angels, that same first instant of fullest natural happiness was also the first instant of their supernatural life; they were created in sanctifying grace.

ON THIS LEVEL OF DIVINE LIFE, there was indeed much still to be had, there were steps to be taken, a goal to be won. By this gift of shared divine life, the angels faced the terrific risks of virtue and vice, of merit and demerit, of heaven and hell; for heaven is natural only to God Himself. To all the rest of us, angels included, the glory of heaven is the final fruit of the seed of grace, the reward to be merited by our own actions flowing from the life-giving principle of grace. It does not belong to us, it is not thrust upon us, but by the kindness of God it can be had for the taking. The angels had the same terrifying responsibility of a final choice between heaven and hell, between God and creatures; not all of them chose well.

THE NATURAL HAPPINESS of all the angels was a possession impregnably secure; if they had been created in glory, it would have been impossible for them to lose heaven. The goodness and beauty of God, once seen face to face, suffers no rival, it cannot be rejected; and it is only by a creature's deliberate rejection that God can be lost. Some of the angels, we know, did reject God. Like us, all of them had the gift of grace and with it the divine virtues of faith, hope and charity; these were the instruments by which they were to build their eternal mansions in heaven. Without them, they would be utterly helpless to advance towards God, as would we; with them they could know God as He knows Himself, love Him as He loves Himself, and walk confidently home in the strength of His strength. The point is that they faced a moment of trial and assumed full responsibility for the outcome of that trial.

IT NEED ONLY HAVE BEEN A MOMENT. Unlike us, there was no necessity in the angels for the long period of trial that makes heaven so uncertain to our flickering strength. We fall and, by the grace of God, rise again only to find our stumbling hearts tripping us up again; perhaps the greatest splendor of our long fight comes from the unyielding courage that is willing to try again and again despite the testimony of the years to the feebleness of our defenses. The angels suffer none of the obscurity of ignorance, none of the violence of passion, none of the inconstancy of will which so weaken our strongest efforts. In them, as in us, grace is the perfection of nature; their supernatural life is the story of the divine perfection of their natural powers. Their supernatural love then is too an instantaneous, complete, irrevocable embrace. For them one act of charity is decisive for all eternity; there is no dallying by the angels in the face of a choice of heaven. In that one instant, the time of their trial was over; one instant marked the end of their merit; in one blinding flash of love, their place in heaven was fixed forever.

PROBABLY THE PATTERN of supernatural splendor in the angelic world parallels the natural, though this is guessing at the gifts of God; the lowest angel could, receiving greater gifts of grace, easily surpass the Seraphim. But since each of the good angels rushed to the embrace of God unhindered and with all the intensity of its being, it can be reasonably supposed that the divine design matched the splendid variety of the angelic natures with proportionate perfections of the divine life of grace. Here there would be no question of laggards and enthusiasts; according to the degree of grace given, each angel, with the full fury of its nature, rushed wholeheartedly to the welcome of God or, in the same kind of headlong plunge, spurned Him utterly to concentrate wholly on itself and so to destroy itself.

THE CONSEQUENCES OF THIS SINGLE MOMENT of trial of the angels are staggering. There is no such thing as a second chance for an angel, no period of contrition and penance. Their freedom from ignorance and passion, their instantaneous grasp of truth removes all possibility of a change of will for them. They love or hate at once and beyond recall; as fixed by that instant as we are by death. When the moment had passed, the sinless angels were securely at home with God, and forever sinless. God, once seen, shrinks all rivals to their proper insignificance. It is not only true that the angels will not sin, they cannot sin now that heaven has been attained; and in that very impossibility they are most wholly free. To choose what defeats the deepest desires of the will, to turn from goodness to evil, is not liberty but its abuse; a truth that needs no argument for the sinner as he writhes in the chains his sins have forged for him yet goes in shamed disgust to sin again.

THE EVIL ANGELS, in that first instant of their abuse of liberty, rejected God. Caught in a deliberate fascination of their own beauty, they refused to look to that beauty's source, refused to seek for happiness outside their own satisfying self; and so attempted to find in themselves what can be found only in God— the answer to the will's divinely given desire for goodness without limit. These devils can now sin all they like, and know themselves less free with every sin; the abuse of liberty mounts with each sin, the chains grow more galling, the self-imposed slavery more bitter, and the hatred more consumingly intense. Their choice was freely made, abusing liberty; and it is eternally confirmed to make up hell's most despairing torment.

UNKEMPTNESS IS A COMMON NOTE of all sins; they are all born in disorder, rollick through dishevelled days, to a climax of shabby disintegration that can no longer keep up the pretense of self-respect. Dirt and decay are steadily more familiar companions from which only darkness gives a momentary escape in forgetfulness. This unkempt note is particularly evident in the sin of the angels, not only because disorder is in such marked contrast to that superbly ordered world, but fundamentally because the angels face the psychological impossibility of choosing evil. They cannot make the fatal error of seeing good where none exists, and so taking evil to their hearts. To sin at all, the angel has to take an embraceable good, but in a disorderly fashion, with a deliberate uprooting of that loved good from its proper place. It is no exaggeration to say that the bad angels introduced chaos into the divine neatness of the universe, and that darkness and disarray are the atmosphere of hell.

TO EXCLUDE EVIL as a possible choice of angelic sin seems to limit the angelic horizons of sin extremely. Actually the limits are much narrower than this would indicate. None of the wide fields of sin opened up by the seductiveness, fear, or violence of the passions were possible to the angels; as pure spirits, without bodies, the appeal of the senses which is passion's domain is outside the world of the angels. The only avenues of rebellion for them were the purely spiritual ones of pride and envy. When we stop to realize that only a fool is envious of a good infinitely beyond his reach, we see that the angels would sin by pride or they would not sin at all. Surely they had much to be proud of, and there was more reason for pride as the scale of angelic perfection soared to the highest of the Seraphim. The very perfection of the angels, in other words, exposed them to the constant danger of the gifted, the danger of enchantment with the splendor of the gifts to the denial of the Giver.

GRANTED THAT FIRST SIN of pride in the angels, envy is ceaselessly busy in all directions. Pride hurled them down, and in their fall they passed rank after rank of less perfect angels, down past the best of men, beneath the feeblest infant barely clinging to life, even below the most hardened sinner who still has the breath of life in him. All these are still recipients of the gifts of God; all of them have heaven either in their grasp or still within their reach; yet all of them are so much less than what these angels could once have been.

THAT A MERE MAN, the lowest of intellectual creatures and so far beneath the devils in natural gifts, should, by the grace of God, go beyond the limits of nature to eternal life in the home of God is galling to the devil and a constant prod to his envy. That this particular soul should reach such heights triumphing over Satan's diabolic genius is a bitter humiliation and added fuel to the fire of his hatred of God. Both that envy and hatred are fed by the devil's disgust with the sins of men. True, he knows that he is guilty of all the sins he induces men to commit; but that guilt is a far cry from any affection for the things that so easily enslave a man. A man surrendering to the allure or violence of passion, immersing himself in the world of sense, playing the slave to things designed to serve him—all this is revolting to the devil's purely spiritual nature even when he is playing the principal part in bringing about such a degradation of a man. His utter disgust with the depths to which man can sink is still more reason for his envy that such creatures can still aspire to heaven while Satan himself must grovel eternally in hell.

ALL THESE GROUNDS for envy and hatred would hold if only the least of the angels had sinned. According to the probable view of theologians, we must start not with the least but with the greatest of the angels in reading the story of evil. It was Lucifer, the highest of the Seraphim, the most perfect image of God in all creation, who took the road of pride to eternal misery. By his example and exhortation, some of every angelic hierarchy joined him in the self-sufficiency that would exclude God. Not that there was a rousing campaign for evil in the angelic courts. Time is our burden, it is for us to deliberate and proceed by argument. The angelic sin was an affair of a moment, enduring eternally, with a leadership of brilliant intelligence. Our Lord has told us of the "everlasting fire which was prepared for the devil and his angels," indicating a leadership in hell. "The order of divine justice," says St. Thomas, "exacts that whosoever consents to another's evil suggestion, shall be subjected to him in his punishment; according to *II Pet.* 2/19: 'By whom a man is overcome, of the same also he is the slave.'" The greatest creature God created spurned his Creator; those who followed him are his slaves, not catering to his comfort but augmenting his misery.

BY FAR THE GREATER PART of the angels won their way to heaven; for the rejection of God is too violent a perversion of nature to achieve a wholesale victory without such allies as ignorance and passion. It is a different matter with us. We grow up so reluctantly, so easily slip back into the irresponsibilities of immaturity; and all our sins have an air of the immature, the incomplete, the underdone about them. We start all our actions from the senses. Stopping at that starting point, refusing the labor and responsibility of going beyond that to the strong domain of reason, is the general story of most of men's sins. Because it is so much easier to start a thing than to finish it, much of men's lives never get beyond the level of the senses; so sin is easily common to the majority of men, but a shocking exception in the world of the angels.

THERE ARE DEVILS ENOUGH to make the working out of our salvation a task to be approached in fear and trembling. These are enemies from whom we can expect no quarter. Hatred has put the full force of the splendid perfection of angelic nature to work for our destruction, for the sin of the angels took nothing away from their natural perfection. They still have that encompassing knowledge; that power to affect and penetrate our senses, our memory, our imagination; that movement swift as thought; that ageless experience; that unwearying vitality, that shrewd intelligence so far above our own. What they have lost only serves to make them more dangerous enemies, for it is the supernatural that has been stripped from them: the supernatural love with its blossoms of peace, joy, mercy, kindness; the supernatural knowledge of the mysteries of faith with its revelation of the nobility of man in the light of the splendor of God; the supernatural hope that keeps despair, and all its collapse of the defenses of virtue, safely at bay. Only the mercy of God restrains the violence of the devil's hate of us.

THERE IS NOTHING OF JOY in the devil's enduring natural perfection. Take the matter of his great knowledge as an example. There is no happiness in a creature's grasp of what is on its own level or beneath it; that happiness is to be found only in reaching to what is above the creature. With ourselves, this is clear, though the embrace of the opposite error is a modern tragedy on a huge scale. The fact remains that there is no more than a passing exhilaration in our knowledge of the details of the world about us; there is a more lasting satisfaction in what knowledge we can gather of the angels, for they are above us in the scale of perfection. But it is only in our knowledge and love of God that we can rest; at every other level, we must substitute the pursuit for the goal to ease the gnawing discontent of our empty hearts and heads. For the devils, there is no happiness in knowing others of their kind; no happiness in their profound knowledge of men and of the world. None of these is above them, and they have forever excluded God.

JOY IS A STRANGER TO HELL, not because it primly avoids so evil a place but because, paradoxically, the miserable in hell will not tolerate its presence. All the inhabitants of the infernal regions are there by their own free choice; and the essential step in the process of gaining admission there was the deliberate exclusion of the sources of joy. There is a kind of sorrow that, too, is barred from hell by unanimous agreement. It is the sorrow unknown to the innocent and impossible to the damned, the sorrow that pours its bitter waters over our soul to kill every least sprig of joy and make a desert waste out of our hearts; yet if the flood be deep enough, it will deposit new, rich soil for an even more abundant growth. This is the sorrow of remorse, the sorrow for the guilt of the sins we have committed. That guilt turns all the world gray and changes every ordinary source of joy into an escape route for the impossible flight from ourselves. If we are sorry enough, sorry to the length of perfect contrition, the sun shines again and joy beats at our hearts for the smiling welcome which is its right. We can be forgiven and guilt can be destroyed. There is no such prospect on any of the horizons of hell.

THE SORROW THAT RULES the skies of hell is hopeless, despairing, as cold and barren as a leaden sky in November. The sorrow that belongs in hell is a sorrow for punishment, not a sorrow for guilt. The devils are bitterly sorry that happiness is forever lost to them, bitterly resentful of the limitations that punishment places on their angelic natures. There is nothing they can do about remedying that sorrow; indeed, there is a violent rejection of the very notion of doing the only thing that would remedy such sorrow—contrition, repentance of the sins that brought it about. Their bitterness turns penetratingly on themselves, leaving them without even that small, fictitious comfort of putting the blame on someone else.

WE THINK OF THE DEVILS as being in hell, and so we should for that is where they belong because of the guilt that destroyed God's life within them. But there is another count on which the devils, some of them, are to be found not in hell but wandering the earth; that is the divinely ingenious purpose of exercising men in virtue. Even by their sin the devils did not become altogether useless in the working out of the purposes of the universe. It is God's wise and universal plan that inferiors be led to their perfection by their superiors; that responsibility rests on the whole angelic world and is accomplished directly and joyfully by the good angels leading men to God, indirectly and in spite of themselves by the bad angels in their testing, and strengthening by that exercise, of the virtues of men. It is a further humiliation to these sinfully proud spirits, that they should be reduced to little more than exercise boys to the conditioning of the race they so envy and for which they have the utmost disgust.

THE DEVILS IN THE WORLD are by no means on vacation from hell. Wherever they are, that fundamental and unending sorrow of hell which consists in the loss of God is their close companion. Wherever they are, they are keenly aware that the humiliation of a spirit's limitation by so material a thing as fire awaits them; the infernal fence of fire that supernaturally marks the narrow boundaries of their eternal cell is as galling a memory and a forecast on earth as it is an actuality in hell itself.

CHAPTER VI

Man and His World

Human Splendor

The Truth of Humanity

The First Man and Woman

Life in Eden

CHAPTER VI

Man And His World

THE ANGELS BLIND US by their splendor. Everything about them seems so superb as to test our capacity for absorbing truth. It is so easy here to be incredulous because it is all nearly too good to be true. Men blind us by their very ordinariness. We ourselves are men, and surrounded by our kind; human things, under our eyes all the time, are easily dismissed as prosaic. We miss the splendor of men through that same blindness to the obvious that allows us to take grass and trees, sun and rain, even love and life, for granted, while we stand in open-mouthed wonder before a machine that coughs out cigarettes.

OUR HUMAN SPLENDOR is a living splendor. By that fact, we are set apart from stones and dirt, clouds and mountains. By it we join ranks with all the living, from the least plant through the highest angel, to Life unlimited from Whom is all life. A dead plant, a dead animal, a dead man are all things whose inner spark of life has been extinguished, the splendor is gone, and only memory gives some dignity to the burnt out ashes of death.

WE KNOW THIS CAN HAPPEN, for we have seen it; the vital principles by which things live are lost and death takes over the kingdom that once belonged to life. Each living creature has that vital principle, its soul, by which it is alive; a thing not to be weighed and measured, yet not to be doubted in the face of the graphic facts of life. Here we touch on a mystery, a profound mystery for a world that sees only bodies as non-mysterious; these souls are not composite things to be taken apart; they are not bodies but the principles by which bodies come alive.

SOULS ARE NOT PECULIAR TO US, but the common characteristic of all living creatures; the living possess a vital principle by which they live. We begin to enter the realm of distinctively human splendor when we notice that we can know all bodies; a feat as impossible to a soul with anything of the corporeal in it as it would be for a man with a bitter taste in his mouth to detect sweetness or a colored eyeglass to show us the variety of the rainbow. There is an independence here that marks out the beginnings of a startling truth: that our souls are not only not bodies, they are fundamentally independent of the corporeal world which they dominate.

WE BEGIN TO APPRECIATE THIS when we notice that the souls of the animals are so tied up with the corporal that they cannot work without it; they produce no vital actions without a decided, sometimes a disastrous, physical change in the body. Notice the contrast, for example, between too much of light for the eye or too much of sound for the ear as against a truth too great for the mind or a goodness too great for the heart. Too great a perfection of light blinds the eye, too loud a sound deafens the ear; the very things that make possible sight and hearing, if they be too perfect, destroy vision and hearing. On the other hand, the greater the truth, the greater the perfection of the intellect contacting it; the greater the goodness, the more ennobled the heart that reaches out to embrace it. The faculties of our souls are not destroyed by the perfection of their goals but rather challenged and improved. These things, truth and goodness, do not demand a physical, bodily change, they carry no threats of destruction to the seeing mind and the loving heart.

OF COURSE WE DO GET TIRED. Yet it is not our mind, but the ministering body that is the subject of fatigue. Our eyes and ears, our memory and imagination must haul the rough material of our knowing; and they are physical things that can and do need rest and refreshment from the burden of labor. As far as our soul is concerned, such fatigue is as accidental as the termination of a painter's inspiration by fading light or the architect's failure to finish a building because of lack of material. The fact is that we do things beyond the physical: we bypass time to plan for the future and to recall the past, we bind men together by bonds that are purely political, we discover the living beauty of divinity in the dead things of the world and imprison it in poetry, we trace relationships that leave no physical trails, and uncover universal truths in a world of singular things.

IT IS THIS NOTE of independence that is the startling wonder of man's soul. The souls of plants and of animals are not made up of parts, not to be located in roots or leaves, head or tail; for by the soul the whole creature lives, roots as well as leaves, head as well as tail. The principle of that living is the soul. That is wonder enough and mystery enough for our time. The added wonder in man is that not only has his soul no parts, vitalizing as it does the whole man, but neither is there any substantial dependence in it. An animal cannot be killed by taking its soul apart as a fresco is destroyed by scraping it off a wall inch by inch; but just as the fresco can effectively be destroyed by demolishing the wall on which it is painted, so can the soul of the animal be eliminated by destroying the body on which it depends.

N O SUCH THING is possible in man. His soul cannot be taken apart, as no soul can, for it has no parts; but neither can it be destroyed by destroying the body of a man. The death of the body is not the end of the soul, for the soul has its own independence, its own actions transcending the physical and corporal, it has its own life which it gives to the body but which is not surrendered with the death of the body. The soul of man can be separated from the body, (and we call that separation death) but not destroyed.

T HE SOUL OF MAN, in other words, stands alone in the physical universe, for it is spiritual, bodiless, independent, living by its own life. Once brought into existence, that soul is as immortal as the angels; it cannot be destroyed by disintegration nor by any attacks on the body which it vitalizes. The soul of every man who has been born into the world lives forever; there is no end to a man's knowledge, no wall that marks the end of his life, no escape from a responsibility that stretches the length of eternity.

T HE WONDER OF MAN IS that he is a little less than the angels and considerably more than all the rest of the universe: a little less than the angels because he is body as well as spirit, so much more than all the universe because he is so utterly different from the physical world in which no other spirit lives. In our blindness to the obvious, it is easy for us to draw a contrary conclusion. There seems so much resemblance between a sleeping man and a sleeping dog, the struggle of the two from the depths of sleep, the morning stretch and yawn. But it is not the dog who makes coffee, draws up plans for the day, and goes his entirely unpredictable way piercing the imprisoning walls of time and eliminating distance with his mind and heart even as he paces off the roads with his feet.

THE FIRST AWAKENING to the wonders of our soul carries the real danger of a kind of spiritual snobbery. It is easy to be tempted to sniff at the body as a lowly, animal sort of thing vulgarizing and profaning its beautiful spiritual consort. It is in this frame of mind that the body is seen as the prison holding the soul in temporary confinement, or as a mere tool to be tossed aside as its edge is blunted; the implication is that man is his soul, and the body merely a nuisance or at best a clumsy impediment to the soul's glorious powers.

THIS IS, IN FACT, a groundless illusion springing not so much from admiration of the soul as from contempt for man's humanity. It is in obvious collision with the facts. It is a man who sleeps, not a body; it is the same man who eats and who thinks, who has toothaches and ecstasies, who loves and who dies. We are not angels, and it is no compliment to our humanity to pretend that we are. It is a guarantee of despair to demand of men that they move on the level of pure spirits; they will surely fail before this impossible demand however heroic their efforts, fail so completely and so repeatedly as to kill all hope. To see the glory of the soul as obliterating the body is to be blind to the soul itself; for it is the vital principle of the body, not a disembodied spirit. Surely this is to be blind to man's humanity. Man is not his soul; body and soul unite in one substantial unit that we call a man. When these two are separated by death, the soul is no more the man than is the corpse which lies dead before us; it is not John Jones who is then admitted to purgatory, but half of him, his soul. It is only when body and soul are reunited in the resurrection that the man lives again.

IF ANGELISM DOES NOT become a man, neither does bestiality. We are not angels, but then neither are we merely animals; yet that is what the fashionable error of our time declares when it sees man as no more than his body, when it smiles pityingly at the notion of a soul that cannot be bathed or spanked. This error, like its twin, does not spring from an admiration of the particular bodies we pass on the street but from a contempt and a fear of the humanity of man. It too is an invitation to despair, for it asks man to live humanly while it denies him the centers of control that make responsibility possible to him. Its popularity lies in its apparent release from the awful burden of human responsibility; yet it punishes crime and admires virtue in the same breath in which it traces all action to subrational sources quite beyond our control. Again, the collision with facts is obvious: there are saints and sinners, we are by turns nasty and noble, we are rightly ashamed of our pettiness and exalted by meeting love's challenge by unselfishness. There is justice and choice and responsibility in our human world, things utterly foreign to the plant and animal world.

THESE THEN ARE SOME of the wonders of the obvious in ourselves, wonders that we so easily take for granted and to which we become blind. We are alive. We live by a life dramatically different from any other life in the physical universe. The vital principle within us, the soul, easily outraces time, eliminates distance, and pierces the wall of death. We are not angels, though spiritual; we are not animals, though physical. Of all the physical world, we are in control of our actions and our life, responsible for both; made to be masters, first of all of ourselves, and then of the physical world in which we live out our days.

GOD'S MASTERPIECE OF CREATION in the physical universe is ourselves. To appreciate the divine genius and its masterpiece, we must see ourselves in that physical world, yet not confuse ourselves with any part of it. It is true that we have, like the plants, the vegetative powers of nutrition and growth, yet we are not plants; we have, like the animals, powers of movement, sense knowledge, and passions, yet we are not animals. There is a flavor, an accent, a bent in all these things in man; to disregard that distinctive characteristic is a kind of vandalism which aims its destructive blows at the artistry of God.

WE, AND WE ALONE, not only see a sunset but also see and revel in its beauty. We do more than hear sounds; we grasp their meaning or, injecting order into them or discovering that order, open up the whole world of music for our enjoyment. Our taste has commanded and perfected the art of cookery. The fragrance of flowers has been distilled and brought from the ends of the earth for our delicate pleasure. Our touch forever brings a message or carries one, a message of reverence or contempt, of love or hate, of appreciation or disgust. It must be so, for our vision, hearing, taste, smell and touch are human things, far above the level of the animal world to which they bind us; human things, and so working humanly at human things in the human manner dictated by intelligence and will. Like the animals, we too have imagination, memory, an instinctive kind of judgment and coordination of the data of the senses; but in us, all these things are so uplifted by that refining contact with intellect and will as to soar far above the level of their operation in animals. The wonder of man is that in him the plant and animal world is united to the spiritual and made one, a human one, not to be confused with anything else in all of God's creation.

A MAN MUST BE COURAGEOUS to face the truth of his humanity. Cowardice finds the animal world much more comforting and eagerly seeks family resemblances to the animals that it might renounce humanity. It is not so much a matter of taking the animals to our bosom as of unbosoming ourselves of our human nature; we would like to have the relationship with animals an intimate family tie, not because we love animals but because we are afraid to be men. The animal parallels adduced in support of that hairy relationship are superficial and misleading; the resemblance is much too faint and fanciful to justify claims to an animal heritage.

O NE OF THE FAVORITE PARALLELS is that of passions in men and animals. The animals follow the dictates of passion along paths laid out by a physical necessity that assures control, though it is not the animal that is doing the controlling. The happy conclusion is immediately reached that men and women must run wild or do violence to their nature. The fact that animals do not run wild is blithely overlooked. The central fact of control is brushed to one side in order that we might forget the terrifying truth that our own reason must furnish the control in ourselves that physical necessity imposes on the animals. Human passions are not violated or frustrated when a child is forbidden to overeat or when a man stops at one drink instead of going on to drunkenness; human passions are perfected by just such control. They were made to operate under reason, and it is under reason that they reach their greatest perfection. It is not the glutton or the drunkard but the saint who is the passionate man; the first two are the victims of a dehumanized passion, a passion gone wild and thus a kind of freak in nature.

OUR JUDGMENTS OF THE MANLINESS of a man or the womanliness of a woman are not based on vegetable or animal grounds. Our eyes are not made merely to see, our ears merely to hear; they are to furnish the rough material for a vision and an understanding far beyond the world of the senses. Our human touch has a meaning or it is not human, our human taste leads to judgments possible only to man or it is the animal's guzzling. Our passions are brutalized beyond all human resemblance when they are in command of our actions; in that false role, they destroy both the man and the passions themselves. The grounds of our judgment of excellence among men are human grounds: control, capable direction, mastery, responsibility. Or, to put it in one word, the norm of excellence is virtue.

THIS IS THE WONDER of man that so frightens the cowards: every man is in control of himself; his acts are his own, he has full responsibility for every moment of every day, the success or failure of his life rests squarely on his own shoulders. He, and he alone in all the physical universe, is free: free to choose between the paths to his goals, or to abuse that freedom and abandon the human things for which he was made. He has a spiritual appetite commensurate to his spiritual knowledge; his will measures up to his intellect. He can know truth and goodness without limit; so his heart is free in the face of any one particular good since his mind can see its limits, the promises it does not make, the desires it leaves unfulfilled.

WHAT THINGS THAT FREE WILL of man chooses in this life make or break a man. The evil we know may do us no harm if it does not stir desire, at least no harm beyond wasting time and energy that are not sufficient for a knowledge of all good things. But the same is not true of our loving. To know a base thing, we must lift it up to our level, spiritualizing it for entry into our minds; to know what is superior to us, we must cut it down to the proportions of our own mind. Our will is not a host but always a guest; to love a base thing means to go out to it and identify ourselves with it, to love a noble thing means to go to its heights and rest in its embrace. In this life, it is quite true that it is both better and worse to love than to know; for love can be either disastrously degrading or breathlessly ennobling. Our happiness or misery now is a matter of the objects of our loves.

IT IS STILL TRUE that we must know in order to love; the heart does not outrun the head. The priority of our knowledge, the superiority of its rank comes out clearly in our eternal life with God. There we know God, not by cutting Him down to our size, not through the means of a concept or idea, but directly, face to face, through the direct union of the divine essence to our intellects. It is, in other words, by our act of knowing in heaven that we possess God, and the possession of the Infinite is our eternal happiness. The joy and love in the will is an effect of that happiness, not its cause. Here on earth, we have a foretaste of heaven by the divine love in our hearts; there we possess heaven by the eternal vision of God.

THE BATTERED HULK of a ship limping home from stormy seas gives but a poor estimate of the proud strength and sure swiftness of it at its launching. If we are to appreciate to the full the wonder of man, it is not to what man has made of himself but what God made of him originally that we must look. As the first human couple came from the hand of God, they were the product of omnipotent genius working directly and unimpeded at the high point of physical creation. It is not hard to see something of the complete physical perfection of Adam and Eve; they were as physically perfect as it can ever be given to a man and woman to be. Our dreams of human strength, beauty, and grace are more than wishful thinking; they have about them the flavor of haunting memories of an earthly paradise, of a man and woman not as they should be, or could be, but as they were.

THE INTELLECTUAL PERFECTION of man and woman in this first beginning of the race was even more stupendous than the physical fullness. Adam and Eve came into being as adults. They had no time to learn through the slow formative years of childhood; in their first moments they were already long past the pliability and elasticity of childhood. Moreover there was no one from whom they could learn. Rather than a disciple of a master, Adam was to be the teacher of the human race, the source of its intellectual completeness as well as of its physical being. In all fairness, he could not be started off on such a life empty-headed; in justice, he would have to be given the perfection of mind proper to an adult, to a teacher, indeed to the master-teacher of the whole race. His ideas, and the equipment of imagination necessary for their use, would have to be given him immediately by God; and with that absence of stinginess characteristic of divine action. We see Adam, then, as the wisest, most learned of all men of all ages, short of the man Jesus Christ Who also was God; he possessed all natural knowledge, surely in its principles, and all the supernatural knowledge necessary for himself and his children.

THE FATHER OF THE RACE had his physical and intellectual gifts directly from the fullness of God's justice, without personal effort or dependence on any other creature; and, consequently, without the least shadow of defect. Still, he was no more than a man; the human limitations on knowledge were to be found in him as they are in every man. He did not see God face to face, for he was not God; he had no direct knowledge of the angels, for he was not an angel. The object of his knowing, as of our own, was the sensible world, the natures of sensible things, and all the rich harvest of truth that can be garnered from such humble, earthy roots.

ON THE SIDE OF APPETITE, Adam was no less sound. He was a man of good will in the fullest sense of those words. His heart did not run down blind alleys, through devious ways, or in secret sorties to dark places; it was not crooked, twisted, nor blinded by the glaring appeal of lesser things, least of all of artificial things which are the world that a man makes. He was a man of great passion; which is to say that he had strong, healthy sense appetites,

appetites which were not weakened by abuse, not distorted by ignorance of his humanity, not dehumanized or brutalized by the loss of man's mastery over himself.

SINCE ADAM, NO MERE MAN has ever stepped into the arena of his living so powerfully armed and splendidly arrayed by nature. With no more than this much of the story told, we have the picture of the superbly perfect man within the limits of human perfection. Yet to stop here is to miss the sublimity of divine ingenuity in the production of this divine masterpiece. With no more than this, Adam had within him positive guarantees of constant civil war and ultimate disintegration. Such a man, perfect as he was, would ultimately have to die; his body, like every body, would wear down and its capacity for rebuilding be gradually weakened until death overtook it. This man, with no more than all that nature could give him would be subject to violence, disease, and senescence. Such a man would necessarily be a man of battle within his own kingdom. No matter how perfect the work of the divine artisan, a perfect body and a perfect soul mean distinct appetites answering to proper objects of desire—and inevitably clashing in the kind of battle we know as the war of the spirit and the flesh. To maintain human control, i.e., the supremacy of the spiritual appetite or will, demands a constant lesson of subordination to be drilled into the passions; and that means war.

MORTALITY AND CONFLICT are deficiencies inherent in human nature; they are not to be corrected through any tinkering with nature, not even the tinkering of a divine mechanic. They can, however, be supplied for by drawing on the divine treasury for gifts to which human nature has no claim; man can be given preternatural and supernatural gifts to be more than a man, and so to escape the defects of humanity through the omnipotent generosity of divinity.

THE FIRST HUMAN COUPLE were loaded down with just such gifts from the divine Giver. They were protected from the fatigue, discouragement and defeat of conflicting appetites by the gift of order, of perfect subordination of the body to the soul, and the world to the whole man. Against disease and senescence, there was the gift of external immortality, a gift that held death at bay through the renewing nourishment of the tree of life. Against violence and its threats of injury they were secured by the gift of impassibility, a gift that gave them so alert a prudence and far-sighted a wisdom as to make the avoidance of injury mere routine.

ADAM AND EVE LOOKED OUT on their days to a life of profound internal peace and complete security from all external threats. They would be forever strangers to injury and disease, and death was powerless to inflict its violent termination of living and loving. They could live their life vigorously, heartily; in it there would be no dark corners of ignorance or malice; passion would not extinguish the guiding light of reason. The shutters of their minds were thrown wide open to the sunshine of truth, the paths to all goodness lay clear and level for their eager hearts; their days well filled with the stimulation of labor's challenge to the strength and skill of their hands.

ALL THIS WAS STILL not enough for man in the eyes of the Creator. Exhaustive natural perfection and abundant supplementing of humanity's defects were hardly more than foundation stones of the edifice planned by the divine Architect. It was not enough to make man a little more than man. God lifted Adam and Eve above themselves to such heights as to enable them to share in divine life, divine living, divine knowing, and divine loving. Like the angels, Adam and Eve were created in sanctifying grace, created, in other words, sharing the divine life. They were given all the supernatural habits of virtue that make divine living possible to men even on earth: faith to see through the eyes of God, hope to share His strength and fidelity, charity to walk into the heart of God; and all the moral virtues that let the fire of charity sweep through the whole life of a man in a roaring conflagration. Their souls were made perfectly subject to God, and that subjection to their Maker was the foundation of the perfect order running through man's nature, the subordination of body to soul and of the world to man; indeed it was the foundation of all the gifts that had been given to man.

A S THE FINAL DIVINE TOUCH, all these gifts correcting nature's defects and lifting it to divine levels were not limited to the purely personal area; they were given by way of family traits. Every father possessing these gifts from Adam on down would pass them on to his children. As Adam and Eve looked about their earthly Paradise, their eyes searched horizons of happiness that would never again fall under human eyes. All these things were theirs, to be possessed in peace for themselves, their children, and their children's children. There was no dimming of truth's bright beauty, no flickering of love's fire, not an instant interruption to the reign of happiness and joy. One day, at God's good pleasure and without death, they would be transported to eternal living face to face with God in heaven. Such we were as God made us.

FOR ALL THEIR WONDROUS GIFTS, Adam and Eve were still human beings, their world was a human world and was to continue so. In it people would eat and sleep, grow tired and be rested. There would be marriage, the generation of children, and all the homely treasures of routine family living. The inhabitants of that human world would be as strikingly individual as the inhabitants of our present world; no two would be alike. The inequalities inherent in variety would be found among them but without imperfection. They would differ physically, morally, intellectually.

SUCH VARIETY IS A PART OF A HUMAN WORLD; necessarily, some men would hold high offices, some low, some none at all. There would be teachers and students, masters and disciples. There would be political organization, government, and law. All such things are the necessary implements of human social life. However loyally Adam and Eve guarded their precious gifts and so passed them on to their children, and however many generations of such perfect men walked the face of the earth, there could still, at any time, have been sin. At sin's appearance, the preternatural and supernatural gifts would be stripped from the sinner, leaving him a nature shorn of those quasi-family traits of perfection and so incapable of giving his children more than the damaged nature that he himself possessed. It could have happened that the world would have been peopled by a mixed race: the descendants of sinners and the descendants of perfect men; men and women with all the defects inherent in human nature plus the added burden of sin, and men and women as humanly perfect and as divinely elevated as the common parents of the race. In actual fact, the splendor of that first perfection was shattered before ever it was passed on to a child.

CHAPTER VII

God's Work in the World

Divine Government

World Dependence

Divine Independence—
Miracles

God in the Mind and Will
of Man

CHAPTER VII
God's Work In The World

THERE IS NOTHING OF ANARCHY in the world except the apparent chaos produced by wilful men. For the rest, the world goes on with an obedient regularity as assured and as effective as the dull patience of a setting hen. Even the wars of the animals and the rages of the elements are predictable and obedient pursuance of the narrow paths to determined ends which is the stable characteristic of the natural. The world moves on, and everything in it, from sunrise to sunset, from new moon to full moon, from century to century, as if it had intelligence; as an arrow flies to its mark as though it had eyes. The arrow is in fact directed by eyes, but by the eyes and hands of the archer; the world too is directed by an intelligence, by the intelligence of God.

THE DISCOVERY OF SOME of the less obvious details of that assured direction makes up the great triumphs of scientific investigation. The formulation of the discovered details of order, the unveiled evidences of divine intelligence in nature, are scientific laws; the progress in the formulation of such laws and their constant correction spell out in huge letters the supremacy of divine and the plodding limits of human intelligence. It is right that we demand sharp intelligence and long training for the human mind that sets out on the search for the details of divine intelligence in the world of nature; for order is the product of a directing intelligence, and not to be discovered or appreciated except by doggedly intelligent pursuit of truth. The intelligent course of the world is evidence of intelligent direction or government on a divine scale.

THE SAME INSPIRING TRUTH is readily arrived at if the search starts, not from the facts of the world but from the truth of God. He is infinite goodness. Such goodness demands that the world created by it be directed to perfection, that is, governed; it is a contradiction to goodness to picture divinity as abandoning the created world as perversely as a wicked mother abandons a new-born infant. God is infinite intelligence, and His provident plan of the universe includes every detail of this stupendous work; to deny the execution of that plan to God is to deny the infinite wisdom that drew it up or the infinite power that puts it into operation. The plans of men too often fall short of completion because there are things men cannot know in making their plans, and there are rival powers strong enough to make men's efforts futile. There are no defects in the plans of infinite wisdom, no thwarting of infinite power's execution of those plans. The government of the world is the execution of the Providence of God.

IT DOES NOT DO to push God out of the picture and explain that the orderly world is nature's work. True enough, nature is the cause of the order in the world; but not nature in capital letters. The order stems from particular natures: the nature of an oak, of a dachshund, of a worm, of sulphur, or gooseberries. Our confusion results from our inevitable practice of hauling God up for trial in a human court. We can impose direction on things only from the outside, as the archer imposes a violent direction on the arrow. We can do nothing about the inner principles of things, about their very nature, for natures are not our product.

God suffers no such human limitations for natures are precisely His products. His directions are not extrinsic, violent things. The finger of God writes His directions in the very fibres of the things He makes and directs; those divinely written directions we call nature's directions or nature's laws. And so they are. But nature and nature's necessity are not substitutes for God; rather they are a record of His governing intelligence.

To THOSE WHO RESENT GOD as an intruder on a self-sufficient world, chance, that is coincidence or accident, has seemed a much more appealing explanation of nature's order than the omnipotent government of divinity. Chance, however, is not an agent at the root of the history of the world; it is a vague name given to the clash of causes each of which was going its own way in determined obedience. A bird struck by a lightning bolt is a victim of chance, but obviously both the bird and the lightning were acting in obedience to nature's determinations. Chance is a handy explanation of upsets of order, but it is an impossibility unless a previous order is in the process of execution. It does not make order but supposes it, and is necessarily limited to the area of causes which can be impeded by other causes. There are no surprises for God in the long history of nature's activity. Omnipotence and infinite wisdom are not to be caught off balance by coincidence or accident. Chance is not God's rival but His instrument in the interlocking pattern of nature's activity.

The ORDERLY COURSE of the world is not the result of democratic processes in government. There are no aristocratic governing boards laying down the rules. The aristocracy of science does not make the laws but rather discovers the laws already made. There is but one Governor of the world, as there is but one Architect and one Creator; for all three of these, omnipotence and omniscience are necessary, and only God is all powerful and all wise. No one thing in nature is the cause of nature's order, rather everything in nature is a part of that order; nothing in nature is the goal of nature's order, not even that universal order itself. The world does not exist for itself any more than it exists from itself; it does not fulfill itself any more than it gives birth to itself. It is from God; and it is to Him that every bit of its order is directed. Nature bends all its energy to a return to God, becoming more like Him as it sharpens the divine image by reaching to its natural perfection.

THERE ARE NO AREAS of anarchy in nature; no successful secession from the divine government of the world. Men can, of course, rebel against the order of charity whose goal is heaven; by that rebellion they do not escape divine government but plunge into the order of justice which confirms their choice of hell. Punishment is no less evidence of orderly government than the awards given to heroes. All the world exists on a loan from God, a loan that is vital not only for the first production of things but for their moment to moment endurance. Successful separation from the divine order would be instant annihilation; a thing not to be achieved by the borrowers of existence but by a recall of the loan by the creditor. By the goodness of God, annihilation never happens.

HUMAN GOVERNMENT QUICKLY ENDS UP in an absurdity that is often both comic and tragic when it attempts to legislate minute details of dress, of conduct, of conversation. It is on just such a basis that our minds easily balk at the detailed government of the world by God. How can we understand the ordered supervision of each moment of development of all the children in the wombs of pregnant women in all the universe? How can anyone plan and execute the detailed intricacies of organic and inorganic structure, let alone the infinite details of organic and inorganic activity? All this is merely saying that such detailed government is too much for a human governor. The conclusion is not that such detailed government cannot possibly be, but rather that it must be the work of a mind bigger than man's, bigger than any mind within the orbit of nature's order. Such government can only be through an intelligence beyond nature, a supernatural intelligence, the intelligence of God.

THE DIVINE GOVERNMENT of the world is not a democratic government, nor the government by an aristocracy; but neither is it a government by one so weak as to fear any sharing of his power, a dictatorship. There is no place in omnipotence for fear of rivals, no basis for cautious hoarding of power, no reason for denial of direction to subordinates. Rather, the secure sweep of omnipotence gives every reason for bestowing real power on creatures.

IT IS TRUE THAT THE SUN rises on atheists too, that those ignorant of God can think, digest, and generate; for it is not our knowledge of God that makes these things possible to men, but rather God's knowledge of us. We do not destroy God by denying Him, we destroy only ourselves. There are real causes in nature, causes producing real effects by their efforts, whether God is thought of or not; but none of thir is true without God. It is precisely because there is a God Who created and governs nature that things come about through natural causes. God not only governs, He makes subordinate governors whose power is real. The powers of men are a testimony to the secure power of God and to the divine reverence for creatures.

"THE FOOL SAID in his heart: there is no God." Such foolishness has had a long life, and taken a great variety of forms. Sometimes, satisfied that the world is doing very well without God, it simply waves Him out of existence with a wand of words. Some men, not more wise but less intolerant, are willing to let God be if He will keep the place they assign to Him: a foreigner totally outside the world, a guest in the world, or even a part of the world. In any case He had better obey nature's laws or He will not be tolerated. Others, foolishly exposing their foolishness, make it plain that man's helplessness is the measure of all strength. Men cannot escape nature's bonds in any least act; so of course there is no such latitude to be allowed to God. God is all very well, but let us not have any of these tales of wonders or miracles.

ALL THIS IS MORE than a little childish. The fact is that we cannot have the world without God; and there is no question but that we have the world on our hands. Indeed we are an integral part of the world at which we peer and poke, and for which we solemnly lay down conditions of acceptance and rejection, as if it were an immigrant of which we do not quite approve. We have much less chance of doing away with God than with the world; and a very good thing, for in either case we would do away with ourselves.

THERE IS AN INHERENT ABSURDITY in the notion that omnipotence by sharing its goodness through creation lost something of its power and all of its freedom. We have managed to swallow this indigestible morsel on the human level in our own times. It has been seriously argued, on both sides of the Iron Curtain, that the State which is man's created instrument for political life automatically supersedes its creator. The radically revolutionary argue that the state devours a man; the merely liberal, that it absorbs him. In either case, he is small change compared to the state. To accept this same humiliation on a cosmic scale is to replace the fact of creation and divinity's perfection with a Frankenstein myth of total universality. God's creation towers over Him and ultimately destroys Him. The enlarged proportions of the tale do not diminish its childishness. Common sense would put aside this pettishness and look squarely at the obvious question: what can God do in the world?

CAN GOD, FOR EXAMPLE, DISPENSE with active causes in producing changes? The philosophical argument that omnipotence can effect all it has given creatures the power to do is unnecessary in the light of the shining beauty of the first instant of the life of the Son of God upon earth. The Virgin Mary, because the Holy Ghost came upon her and the power of the Most High overshadowed her, virginally conceived her Son, Jesus Christ. Of the beginning of all human life upon earth, it is written: "God formed man of the slime of the earth." God has done this; a thing beyond the power of any angel or any devil. Nothing in nature can work without natural causes.

IT IS WITHIN THE EASY POWER of angel, devil or man to move a body, as easy as a mother's effortless rocking of her infant. This is hardly a thing to be denied to God's omnipotence; yet our minds are apt to stumble over the absence of hands and arms in God's lifting. We are vastly more surprised than we should be at the story of the deacon Philip in the Acts: "when they were come up out of the water, the Spirit of the Lord took away Philip; and the eunuch saw him no more . . . But Philip was found in Azotus; and passing through, he preached the gospel to all the cities . . ." No straining muscles, no labored steps; for it was omnipotence at work.

WHEN IT IS A QUESTION of God's actions in our sovereign powers of intellect and will, we are not in the field of the unusual, the startling, where ordinary causes are supplanted by God Himself. This is the prosaic routine of every moment of man's rational actions. The university professor is no more than a servant; at best, he serves food that must be eaten and digested by his students, he merely presents truth. He cannot make a gift of that truth to the mind of his students, he cannot stamp it on their minds, he cannot give them his vision. To see something of God's action on the mind of every man, we must go behind the teacher's work and beyond its greatest effort. It is from God that every man has the power to know at all; a power that the professor hopefully takes for granted. In all his actual knowing, man is never alone; God must play His part here, the part of the First Cause of everything real. This act of knowing, too, is a reality, not a fiction; it depends in its every instant on the cause of all reality or it ceases to be. We know truth, but not completely by ourselves, not in absolute independence; not divinely but as creatures moved and sustained by the Creator in every instant of real motion. Only God can work thus *within* the mind of a man; it is the privilege of the First Cause and the sole explanation of anything getting done by the mind of man.

COULD THIS BE TESTED FROM EXPERIENCE? Well, hardly; for who but God is to get inside the mind of a man? Yet it is not to be challenged under pain of treason to common sense. Common sense is right in its insistence that one never finds something coming from nothing, activity from passivity, perfection from imperfection. As we pass from the condition of potential knowers to actual knowing, we cannot in common sense cherish the illusion that knowledge has given birth to itself in our minds, that the unknowing intellect has given itself knowledge. We do indeed know truth; that knowledge is rigidly personal, it is ours. Behind our knowing is the God of all reality, causing and sustaining our knowing and our knowledge in the world of the real.

THE SAME MUST BE SAID of the divine activity in our will's free choice if both the choice and the freedom of it are to be real. If a man, his action, and that action's freedom are all real, then all three are intimately dependent in every moment on the Cause of all reality. Escape from the divine motion is a plunge into nothingness. God's activity within our will is not an affront or an impediment to our free choice; rather it is the absolutely indispensable and completely first cause of that freedom. Under that divine motion, we do our own choosing humanly, for we are men; not divinely, for we are not God. Absolute independence would destroy both us and our freedom.

WE HAVE DIFFICULTY with this truth, not only because it is necessarily mysterious since it involves the infinite divine motion, but primarily because we insist on putting God on trial in a human court. For ourselves, we can move things, and men, only from the outside; our movement of others is always a kind of violence even when it is no harsher than allure or enticement. We never get inside any creature to move it by its own principles. Stubborn men have shown us convincingly that we cannot move men's wills; certainly we cannot move them and have them freely. So, of course, it just cannot be done. The proper conclusion from this human helplessness should be that we cannot understand how it can be done, but we can know by common sense alone that it has to be done.

GOD MUST WORK in every agent, in every action, or there is no reality to the agent or the act. The divine motion is not a brutal blow putting an end to all opposition, the rule of the mailed fist. If there is irreverence for an individual nature in the world, we can be sure indeed that the irreverence is not from God; He moves all things according to their natures. So the sun, the moon, the trees and the animals are moved necessarily to their goals, for freedom has no part in their natures. Man is moved freely to his goals, for necessity has no part in his moral nature. It is equally true that this action is mine and is God's, His because He is First Cause of all reality, mine because God stands behind the execution of the powers He has given me. To ask to understand *how* God can move from the inside, freely, from the principles proper to man's nature is to demand a comprehension of the infinite motion of God by the finite mind of man. God's part in our freedom is not a contradiction but an assurance of reality.

GOD'S ACTIVITY WITHIN our very minds and wills is mysteriously wonderful beyond words; but it is not extraordinary. It is, in fact, routine; an every day affair, so prosaic as to be taken for granted or completely overlooked. What rivets our attention is the extraordinary. Can God work miracles in the world; can He do the really extraordinary? Can He work outside the order of nature which He has established? Christ's answer to the disciples of the Baptist leaves no room for doubt: "Go and relate to John what you have heard and seen: the blind see, the lame walk, the lepers are made clean, the deaf hear, the dead rise again, to the poor the gospel is preached." At the moment the Baptist's disciples had come with their questions, Our Lord had lavishly displayed the divine power: "in that same hour, He cured many of their diseases, and hurts, and evil spirits: and to many that were blind He gave sight."

THE NEW TESTAMENT IS REPLETE with details of the limitless power of God. The incarnate Son of God did things nature can never do, as when, in His glorified body, He walked through locked doors to give peace to His disciples. At His word, the dead Lazarus came alive and walked from the tomb, the man born blind could say to the nagging Pharisees "now I see." Nature too gives life, but not to the dead; it gives sight, but not to those born blind. Many other things He did which nature does, but not in this divine way: stormy seas grow calm, but not at the sound of a voice; fevers burn themselves out, but not in an instant at the touch of a hand. God is not fenced in by His creation.

ST. AUGUSTINE DESCRIBED A MIRACLE as "something difficult, which seldom occurs, surpassing the faculty of nature, and going so far beyond our hopes as to compel our astonishment." We marvel at miracles, not so much because of their wonder but because of their infrequency. It is a wondrous thing that seed brings forth the harvest of wheat to feed all mankind; but it happens year after year. On the other hand, it is rare indeed that five thousand are fed with a few loaves and fishes. It is not that we should wonder less at the miraculous, but that we should come awake to the marvel of the ordinary, and wonder most of all at the Lord of the universe and the flashes of His omnipotence that gives us, with the same ease, both the miraculous and the prosaic.

CHAPTER VIII

Creatures' Work in World Government

Angels and Devils

Guardian Angels

Physical World . . .
the Moon and the Stars

Man's Will

Man's Mind

CHAPTER VIII

Creatures' Work in World Government

"THIS IS THE DIVINE UNALTERABLE LAW, that inferior things are led to God by the superior ones." These profound words of Dionysius give the basis of every creature's nobility and humility, stating with uncompromising exactness the place on the stage and the words to be spoken by every creature playing a part in the government of the universe. From these words it is plain that superiority is not a title to service but a commission of serious responsibility; on the other hand, inferiority is not a relegation to labor that superiors might have ease, but a title to the superiors' utmost help. The least are led to God by the greatest; talent is not a mere personal favor but a social responsibility.

THE UNIVERSAL LAW of creature participation in universal government finds its first and rigid application in the world of the angels. Holy Scripture names nine choirs of the heavenly spirits, ranging from the least of the angels to the greatest of the Seraphim. The doctors and theologians of the Church have grouped these nine choirs into three hierarchies on the basis of their offices and superlative gifts. In this vast world, whose numbers defy all our computation, the orderly subordination of lower to higher is without exception, flawless; the help of the higher to the lower is without interruption. The higher angels have truth and love to give, the lower angels have truth and love to receive. Both the truth and the love are without limits, while the hunger for both rather than being appeased grows steadily keener, happily sharpened by the very richness of the diet and the eager devouring of the food.

THE ANGELIC WORLD could be seen as a great school, if it were possible for us to think in those terms without the unpleasant memories of long labors and fragmentary results. The higher angel can and does share his greater knowledge with all his lesser fellows; the truth possessed by the superior angel runs down from the heights like a great river to every plot of the fertile minds of the lesser angels, a refreshing flow of living water, fruitful, enriching, prodigal of its benefits. "In that heavenly country", says Gregory, "though there are some excellent gifts, yet nothing is held individually." In the words of Dionysius: "Each heavenly essence communicates to the inferior the gift derived from the superior."

THE OPEN HANDED SHARING of knowledge in the angelic world is a model of the use of God's gifts urged upon Christians by St. Peter: "As every man hath received grace, ministering the same one to another; as good stewards of the manifold grace of God." There are, in fact, none of the reasons among the angels that contribute to our own stinginess with truth; none of pride's blindness that gives an air of justification to snobbish disdain, none of jealousy's hoarding lest a rival surpass us. There is no fatigue in the teaching, no labor in the learning, no impediments to knowledge, no interruption of the flow of truth. Here it is most perfectly true that the lower is brought to God by the higher.

YET THE ANGELIC COMMUNICATIONS are not all in one direction, with the lower angels having never a word to say. It is true that these lesser angels cannot teach the higher ones. By that, the angelic world is set off sharply from the world of men. Among ourselves, until a man has learned to listen he has no business teaching; until he realizes that every man has something of truth and wisdom to offer he does not begin to learn; it is only when he sees how each of his fellows surpass him that a man begins to be wise, to himself and his fellowmen. It is not so among the angels. The lesser angels have nothing to teach their superiors, but they do have gifts to give to those above them, personal things not to be had except by way of gift. The lower angel cannot teach, but he can and does talk: talks to the highest and the least of his fellows, even to God Himself. He has much indeed to talk of, the width of the angelic world is no hindrance to the effectiveness of his least whisper, the crowded halls of heaven offer no impediment to the privacy of his speech.

THE SUPERIOR ANGEL'S HELP in the matter of love is much more limited than in the matter of truth. Every intellect can be moved by truth, indeed must be moved by truth; but every heart is master of its loves. Only infinite goodness plainly seen can dictate to a created will, be it human or angelic. No one angel can move the will of another. One can give reasons for loving, yes; lovableness and its enticement can be shown most attractively; but that is as far as any creature can go in influencing the love of another. There are no degrees of freedom. The least of men and the highest of the angels are equally free in their embraces. In this matter of love, a creature, man or angel, can be helpful, kindly, persuasive; but we always stand in uncertainty, cap in hand, hoping for a gift that cannot be commanded or purchased.

T HAT PART OF THE ANGELIC WORLD which is the prison of the fallen angels has its fundamental order of higher and lower devils intact; but the highest of the fallen is, by way of punishment, subject to and dominated by the least of the blessed angels. Hell's order is intact, but not its operation. No one in hell is going to God. Superior devils have no reason whatever to share their natural possession of truth with their inferiors. On the contrary, they are bitter, proud, envious, hating everyone and everything; everyone of them is totally against anything that remotely smacks of help or kindness. There is speech in hell, yes; but the words of that speech are a liar's words, not unlocking the gates of the heart but as a usual thing throwing up a wall against all communication. When, in the odd case, the truth is told, it opens a fetid heart to add to the horrors of hell.

A NGELS HAVE BEEN BADLY TREATED by the men of our time. Where they have been given any consideration at all, they have been locked off in a separate compartment somewhere apart from the world of reality in order that men might the more easily forget about them and concentrate on the physical and tangible. But then the soul of man has received hardly less cavalier treatment, and for the same reason. In both cases, men have failed to remember that the angels are an integral part of the natural order; they cannot be excluded from that order without distorting the whole picture of nature. As natural, the angels have a part in the government of the universe that cannot be confined to the angelic world. In fact, by virtue of the universal law that decrees the superior's help to the inferior, the angels should have more to do in the government of the universe than any other creature in the world.

IT MAY WELL BE that pagan philosophers, like Plato and Aristotle, proceeded from a deeper penetration of a profound truth rather than from mere ignorance of scientific laws when they saw the angels as movers or governors of the heavenly bodies. Surely it would be in harmony with the security of omnipotence and the generosity of infinite goodness that the power and wisdom of administration over the physical world be widely distributed among the subordinates to divinity. It is the perfect complement in action to angelic superiority over the physical world. At the same time, it is no detraction from the accuracy of scientific knowledge of sun and stars, of tides and winds; for administration by superiors does not imply destruction of inferiors, nor elimination of the inferior's own degree of self-sufficiency. The error is much more likely to be on the side of the moderns rather than on the side of the ancients; for it is our tendency, not theirs, to give every creature an independence approaching that of divinity.

THE ANGELIC PART in the government of the universe is not a justification in fact for the pleasant absurdities of a child's fairy tale. No angel has the power to change a man into a horse, a villain into a snake, a river into a mountain; like ourselves, the angels can do nothing about the inner natures of things. The idea of administration of natural things does not involve the abolition of natural laws; quite the contrary. In nature, it is only like that generates like; angels do not generate anything. They cannot cause natural things to be, dispensing with natural causes. The wicked witch and the fairy godmother are fantastic creatures with purely imaginary powers; and, in fact, they are never summoned from the world of fantasy by the children for whom they were devised. It is only adults who make fantasy from facts and facts from fantasies.

THE ANGELS' POWER to move bodies seems to border on this world of fantasy but that is because we insist on thinking of angels in human terms. It is certainly true that the angels' power to move things suffers none of the limitations that experience has led us to expect when we see a man pushing at a car or tugging at a rope. Our souls are, like the angels, spiritual; but they are the vital principles of bodies. What a human soul does to the physical world is done by the physical energies of the body which is enlivened by that soul. Piano movers accomplish their tasks not by purely spiritual power, nor yet by purely animal power, but by human power; the intelligent use of physical strength. The angel is not limited to a body, it is not the vital principle of any body; its power to move physical things is greater, more perfect, more unlimited than any power in the universe.

THE SMOOTH SWEEP of such effortless power dazzles us. Perhaps there is a touch of envy in our readiness to disbelieve in its existence. There is evidence enough of this spiritual power in the tantrums of the devil tormenting such men as the Cure of Ars. There is no reason to doubt it beyond the fact that our imagination cannot give us a picture of an angelic piano mover. In our envious stubbornness, we might even settle for a contradiction and agree to see the piano as taking off on its own power rather than admit such prodigious capacities in the creatures we like to relegate to the sweetly helpless delicacy of pious decorations.

STAGGERING AS THAT ANGELIC POWER IS in the physical world, it stops short of the miraculous. If an angel ever has a part in the performance of a miracle, that part is a purely instrumental one played as humbly as the part of a brush in the hand of an artist. Miracles are God's. They are outside nature's order and so are not to be accomplished by anyone who is himself a part of that natural order. Miracles are possible only to the one Being Who is outside of nature, the supernatural Being Who alone is the cause of all natural things. The angels can surprise and astonish us by wonders beyond our powers or outside our knowledge; but these wonders are not outside all natural powers but the products of creatures, the angels, who are themselves a part of nature. The prodigies are real enough, as Augustine pointed out long ago: "when fire came down from heaven and at one blow consumed Job's servants and sheep; when the storm struck down his house and with it his children—these were the works of Satan, not phantoms."

SUCH WORKS ARE WONDROUS TO US, not because they are supernatural but because they so far surpass our own powers. Indeed, as Augustine points out, the prodigies of the devil are really lying wonders: "either because he will deceive men's senses by means of phantoms, so that he will not really do what he will seem to do; or because, if he work real prodigies, they will lead those into falsehood who believe in him." This hoary procedure of Satan has been employed for so many centuries that it has become almost a rigid routine in winning his dupes: startle them into a blind faith in him by showing them novelties beyond human power in order that, in that blindness, they might accept the poisonous evil he has prepared for them. Men invite this very catastrophe when they search for knowledge of the future from stars, ouija boards, cards, tea leaves, palms, bumps on the head or the self-induced darkness of the seance room. It is the element of reality behind good-luck charms, love potions, and voodoo curses; all these are invitations to the devil to exercise a power superior to that of the physical world.

THE SPECIAL DANGER OF THIS SORT of thing becomes apparent when we remember the angels' wide field of effective action on men. Our bodies, and all the physical avenues to our souls, are wide open to the angels. Any effects on our sense that can be produced by any physical agent in the universe can also be produced by an angel, from a black eye or a broken bone to the caress of spring winds or the steady murmur of the distant sea. There is no phantasm which cannot be produced by the angels in our imaginations; no depth of memory that cannot be easily and instantly dredged to give up the most deeply buried relic of our past. On this score of our senses, imagination and memory, we have no defense against the invasion of the pure spirits, good or evil; that we suffer so little from the devils in this way and are helped so much by the good angels is the most constant testimony to the limitless mercy of God.

THE GOOD ANGELS ARE EASILY the supreme teachers of men. All our knowledge takes its rise from the world of the senses, and memory and imagination are tireless laborers ceaselessly hauling the material for our knowing; every angel has the key that gives easy, independent admission to senses, imagination, and memory. No need for the angel to search for a word, to cast about for illustrations, or smear up a blackboard with diagrams. He can indeed offer us truth for our knowing, comforting strength to our minds by his presence, and a gracious clothing of the too great splendor of naked truth in the physical robes to which we are accustomed. For all that, the angel's role in giving us truth is never more than the teacher's very humble work. Not even an angel can put truth into our minds. Our intellects are spiritual faculties enjoying a sovereignty sacred to all but God Himself. Short of knowledge given directly by God Himself, we must do our own learning, reap our own harvest of truth.

THE GREATEST ANGEL is as helpless before the will of the least of men as he is before the will of any other angel, as helpless as one man is to produce love in the heart of another. Our will as well as our intellect is sacred and inviolable; no one penetrates there but God. All others circle about its ramparts seeking some weak point that may be threatened, or call boldly at its gates offering treasures great enough to induce us to throw wide the gates. Angels can offer us inducements to love, they can awaken our sense appetites and enrich our imaginations; they can persuade, coax, cajole, argue. But none of this amounts to moving the will of man. We are not driven by anger, fear, desire; indeed, we are not driven by anything. Man is free in his love, free of every created agent, even of the highest of the Seraphim.

ALL THIS IS NOT IDLE SPECULATION or unfounded dreaming. Angels are sent to men. "And there appeared to him (Zachary) an angel of the Lord, standing on the right side of the altar of incense ... but the angel said to him: Fear not, Zachary, for thy prayer is heard ..." "And in the sixth month, the angel Gabriel was sent from God into a city of Galilee, called Nazareth, to a virgin espoused to a man whose name was Joseph, of the house of David; and the virgin's name was Mary." "But while he thought on these things, behold the angel of the Lord appeared in sleep to Joseph, saying: Arise, and take the child and His mother, and fly into Egypt . . ." "But when Herod was dead, behold an angel of the Lord appeared in sleep to Joseph in Egypt, saying: Arise and take the child and His mother, and go into the land of Israel . . ."

THESE WERE SPECIAL OCCASIONS, but the merely occasional is not characteristic of the angels' work for men. We are guarded by angels. "Behold I will send my angels who will go before thee" is literally true for the least of men in the universe. The guardianship of men is not a lowly work undertaken in a spirit of humility or humiliation by the pure spirits who are so close to God; neither is it a compassionate or patronizing gesture called forth by the pitiable condition of men. This is a part of the general order of the universe, a dictate of the invariable law that leads inferiors to their perfection by superiors. It is an angelic responsibility, consequent on complete, accurate knowledge and irrevocable love, that they should take over the guidance of our stumbling minds and fickle hearts. This is not a small boy's wishful thinking, nor the poet's fragile dream, but an integral part of the divine government of the universe. It is a predictable thing; to be expected; a protection that is in no sense an effect of our will, our morals or our merits.

THIS TREMENDOUS TRUTH must not be left in the field of generalities. St. Jerome probed its sig-

nificance when he said, "Great is the dignity of souls,
for each one to have an angel deputed to guard it
from its birth." St. Thomas explains the truth with
words of simple beauty. "Man while in this state of
life is, as it were, on a road by which he should journey
towards heaven. On this road man is threatened by
many dangers both from within and without . . . And
therefore as guardians are appointed for men who
have to pass by an unsafe road, so an angel guardian
is assigned to each man as long as he is a wayfarer.
When, however, he arrives at the end of life he no
longer has a guardian angel; but in the kingdom he
will have an angel to reign with him, in hell a demon
to punish him."

FROM THE FIRST MOMENT of human life, a particular angel is assigned to lifelong guardianship of
this man. To that work, the angel bends all his
mastery over the physical world, all his command of
human senses, memory and imagination, all the
angelic deposit of truth, all the raging fire of angelic
love. That guardianship never relaxes for a moment,
night or day, year in and year out, until the last spark
of life is extinguished. It is a benefit given to every
single man, not by reason of his belief or his sanctity,
but by reason of his humanity.

NO MAN WHO HAS EVER LIVED was deprived of
this particular angelic guardianship. Guardian
angels were necessary for Adam and Eve in the
Garden of Paradise for, as was proved by the event,
they were under the threat of the demons from without, however perfectly ordered their souls were within. ". . . just as the infidels and even Antichrist are
not deprived of the interior help of natural reason; so
neither are they deprived of that exterior help granted

by God to the whole human race—namely, the guardianship of the angels. And although the help which they receive therefrom does not result in their deserving eternal life by good works, it does nevertheless protect them from certain evils which would hurt both themselves and others. For even the demons are held off by the good angels, lest they hurt as much as they would. In like manner Antichrist will not do as much harm as he would wish."

F ROM THE FIRST MOMENT of life until the last, each one of us is engaged in a battle to the death. "The demons are ever assailing us, according to I Peter: 'Your adversary the devil, as a roaring lion, goeth about seeking whom he may devour.' Much more therefore do the good angels ever guard us." We are children in the face of the keen strength of angels and devils so our first thanks for our angel's guarding are for the effects consistent with childhood's helplessness: the warding off of the demons, and the prevention of bodily and spiritual harm. We are not wrong in this spontaneous burst of gratitude to our rescuer. Yet, because we are responsible adults faced with the final choice of heaven and hell, our angel's guardianship is ordered principally to our enlightenment by instruction, as the devil's attack is ordered principally to darkening of our minds by frauds and lies. Truth is the light by which a man guides his steps home.

I N THE LIGHT of our own angel's magnificent and unceasing help, there is something of the braggart's pitiful absurdity in the pride we take in the truth we learn and the love we give. There is, too, a note of terror in the exclusive responsibility we have for the success or failure of our own living. Nothing in the universe can withstand the angel's powers, except our own choice. The angel who guards us is of the lowest of the heavenly choirs; yet his power is more than enough for all the physical universe, more than enough for the greatest devil, bowed as the devils are in punishment to the least of the good angels. The only effective obstacle to the angel's guarding love is our own intellect and our own will. We ourselves can defeat such guardianship; and we do in every sin.

EVEN IF ANGELS HAD NEVER SINNED, leaving man free to work out his salvation with no external enemies to fight, we would still have had this guardianship. In the face of the fact of angelic betrayal of God, "our wrestling is not against flesh and blood; but against Principalities and Powers, against the rulers of the world of this darkness, against the spirits of wickedness in the high places." We, who command our own appetites only with great effort and generous divine help, are no match for such enemies from hell roaming the world like roaring lions. For all our sovereign intellect and will, our battle with the legions of Satan would be a hopeless slaughter of weaponless pygmies by armed giants were it not for divine mercy's restraint of the devil's powers and the protection we receive from the army of heaven.

FOR ALL HIS MALICIOUS ENERGY in the cause of disorder and ruin, the devil in spite of himself falls neatly into place as a factor in the divine government of the universe. Despite his most vicious gestures of hatred of God and man, when the results are totaled, the devil is shown to be, not the prince of the world, but the servant not only of God but of man. His malice is explanation enough of the consistency of his attacks on us; his pride apes divinity's assignment of guardian angels for the protection of men by a nomination of destroying demons for the ruin of men. Yet his campaign of disorder is turned to the purposes of God. Let him entice man to sin, and in reality he offers man an opportunity for the practice of virtue; irritations are builders not destroyers of patience, honesty is stronger, not weaker, for its battles against the lazy ease of injustice. Let the devil carry out divine decrees of punishment, his own hatred and malice does not lessen the merit of the culprit's humble acceptance and penitent return to the arms of a love strong enough to be severe. The devil's attacks on men are, in the divine government of the world, for the perfection of the very ones the devil works hardest to destroy.

WE COULD VERY WELL DO without the devil. Virtue gets exercise enough from the world and the flesh. And there is temptation enough, though never sufficient for the malice of Satan. This truth is plain when we understand that temptation really means a trial or a test. Thus tests are imposed on man by God for the refining and strengthening of virtue. A man may try his physical strength or his intellectual acumen for a better knowledge of himself; or he may try the virtue of a woman from curiosity, vanity, lust or malice. The devil tries men always and only for their ruin and destruction. The radical and climactic perversion of human nature is to be found in the man who tempts others for the ends of the devil: invading the integral goodness of innocence and, from sheer wickedness, disfiguring its pure beauty. Here is the perfect agent of hell who reaps hell's rewards: deeper misery for himself and ruin for those defiled by his touch.

WE HAVE GREAT REASONS for thanks to the restraining mercy of God and the powerful guardianship of the angels when we remember how well the devil can know us. He is the perfect newsman, missing no details of a man's life, completely up-to-date on each man's history, with a comprehensive grasp of the images that people a man's imagination and of the vast storehouse of a man's memory. There are limits to his knowledge, but only those limits that mark out the territory known surely only by God and the individual man: the affairs of a man's heart, the acts of his intellect, the motives that give life or death to his actions. The devil's frighteningly intimate knowledge of us does not, in other words, overwhelm our mastery; our sins are still our own, not the devil's.

MANY OF OUR SINS come as a pleasant surprise to the devil. Many of them are ushered into our lives by ourselves without the devil's being so much as an occasion of them. It is, in fact, only our sins that are wholly and exclusively our own. The angels take part in all our good works; behind and through them, as behind and through us, there is always the omnipotence of God giving the ultimate explanation of the mystery of goodness in our actions. We cannot approach God without His help, but we can very well fall into sin with no help at all.

ST. CHRYSOSTOM, POINTING OUT the solid basis of our serenity in the face of the devil's consuming hatred, says: "the devil does not tempt man for just as long as he likes, but for as long as God allows; for although He allows him to tempt for a short time, He orders him off on account of our weakness." The mercy of God and the strong help of the angels turn satanic temptations into moments of great significance for men: the blows struck for virtue against temptation build up the sinews of a man's soul, deepening the wellsprings of virtuous action, laying down valid claims for an increase in grace and a title to eternal glory, and welding that companionship of guarding angel and wayfaring man into a unity too strong to be broken by the assaults of evil.

THERE IS YET ANOTHER EFFECT, pointed out by St. Ambrose, and not to be lightly passed over: "The devil is afraid of persisting, because he shrinks from frequent defeat." The bitter taste of defeat is too galling for pride's stomach, and pride is synonymous with the diabolic; yet, there is a kind of stupidity from pride's blindness that sometimes drives the devil to persistent and violent attacks on the holiest of men and women, dashing Satan again and again head on into the invulnerable wall of sanctity like an enraged animal battering itself to death in blind fury. Here too the mercy and justice of God are clearly to be seen: mercy, unleashing more of the devil's power where it cannot conquer; justice humbling satanic pride by repeated and crushing defeats.

MATERIAL THINGS, TOO, have a part to play in the ordering of the universe. This truth has so struck the modern mind as to blind it to all the other agencies of divine government, and lead it to the conclusion that man is at the mercy of the physical universe. To pass from the purely spiritual activity of the angels to the purely material activity of physical creatures is not to escape from divine government. Acids cut through man's flesh, fire warms his house, spring rains bring life to frozen earth, and summer sun brings the fields to rich maturity. The more minutely we examine the chemical, plant and animal world, the more expertly we observe winds and clouds, heat and cold, the more our mind is overwhelmed with the detailed organization and minute activity that keeps the world on an even keel. A mind robbed of insights into the human, angelic, and divine worlds, is reduced to numbness by the magnificence of the divine government of the physical world.

MEN DID NOT WAIT for our time to marvel at this cosmic organization; ancient peoples were not blind to the intrinsic sufficiency of nature; it was not our scientists who first saw that like generates like. It was fifteen centuries ago that St. Augustine wrote: "Of all the things which are generated in a corporeal and visible fashion, certain seeds lie hidden in the corporeal things of this world." St. Thomas, explaining Augustine's words, takes the blur out of the magic word that our time has used to explain all things. ". . . in the whole corporeal nature, living bodies are the most perfect: wherefore the word *nature,* as the Philosopher (Aristotle) says, was first applied to signify the generation of living things which is called *nativity:* and because living things are generated from a principle united to them, as fruit from a tree, and the offspring from the mother to whom it is united, consequently the word *nature* has been applied to every principle of movement existing in that which is moved. Now it is manifest that the active and passive principles of the generation of living things are the seeds from which living things are generated. Therefore Augustine fittingly gave the name of *seminal virtues* to all those active and passive virtues which are the principles of natural generation and movement."

"THESE ACTIVE AND PASSIVE VIRTUES may be considered in several orders. For in the first place, as Augustine says, they are principally and originally in the Word of God as *typal ideas*. Secondly, they are in the elements of the world, where they were produced altogether at the beginning, as in *universal causes*. Thirdly, they are in those things which, in the succession of time, are produced by universal causes, for instance in this plant, and in that animal, as in *particular causes*. Fourthly, they are in the seeds produced from animals and plants. And these again are compared to further particular effects, as the primordial universal causes to the first effects produced."

IT IS NOT RECENTLY that men have discovered that the tides are the response of the oceans to the pull of the moon, or that the sun's light and heat play a crucial part in the development of all forms of physical life. Our improved observation has corrected the old notion that the sun spontaneously generated the lower forms of life; yet we still make the ancient error of subjecting man to the sun, the moon, and the stars. Surely man's body, like every other physical thing, is affected by these heavenly bodies; but they do not produce a man's actions nor do they forecast his future. A man is more than a body; the truth he acquires and the love he gives away are not things he suffers from without but things he does.

ASTROLOGY HAS NOT DIED, though there is nothing of vigorous health in it; it has escaped death through the genius of the devil and the gullible cowardice of men. With a false gesture of mercy, it explains away the evil of men's actions by pointing an accusing finger at the stars while it weeps over the helplessness of the stars' victims. Men are absolved from all responsibility because certain stars looked down on their birth. At the same time, astrology coddles the truth that contradicts this lie, assuming full credit, freedom, and responsibility in each man for his good acts. The cake is not only both eaten and had, it never grows stale! The fact is there is no inescapable fate before which a man must bow in helpless futility. There is no blind force driving a man to his foredoomed destiny. There is no nemesis dogging the footsteps of man and defeating his best efforts at mastery of his life. There is a divine Providence, a divine government, that guides a man, but not to his ruin and destruction; there is a power greater than man that moves him but precisely to his responsible mastery of his own life.

FOR ALL THE WONDERS OF IT, the material world plays the least part in world government, and plays that small role without choice. Material things act as if they had intelligence because they proceed in orderly, law-abiding fashion; but the intelligence apparent in their actions is from outside the things themselves. They direct no one, no thing, not even themselves. They are directed. They play no more than a bit-part in the drama of the universe, which is the drama of the salvation of men. They can neither teach nor learn, love or be loved. They are servants to be trained, ministers, hewers of wood and drawers of water; they are to be used, in sharp contrast to men and angels who must not be used under penalty of destruction from both nature and nature's God. This material world is the inferior thing that exists for its superiors, with never a note about it of rest, of finality, of goals achieved. In the physical world, we see man as its master or we miss the world itself.

OUR MASTERY, HOWEVER, IS NOT that of a sovereign Lord. We are but stewards to whom the universe has been committed for the working out of the supreme value of our world: the eternal life of individual men. We can shout at the seas but they will not be calm. We can say the creative words over and over again, but nothing happens. Nature does not move at our nod. We have no creative power over God's creatures. We can bring no single thing into being by a fiat of our will, nor can we so cause its destruction. We cannot change natures any more than we can produce them. The inner principles by which particular natures are what they are escape our stewardship; we must take the world as God made it, and go on from there.

THERE HAVE BEEN FABLES to the contrary in every age, for men have always fretted at their human limitations though the full human glory is often too much for their courage, and the splendor of divinely lived human life has comparatively few enthusiasts. Men would like to be much more than they are, but without the labor of virtue. This desire has given birth to stories of mysterious powers, easily had, particularly powers of destruction: the searing malice of witches, the dark domination of voodoo experts, the blight of the evil eye, and so on.

THE ELEMENTS OF TRUTH in these things are not at all mysterious. The devil is not one to refuse an invitation to share in the destruction of men; in every age he has been a willing agent of men and women whose thirst for power was mad enough to enlist even his help. Then, too wickedness can so corrode a man or woman as to achieve an almost tangible malignity. This concentrated evil, glaring out of a man's eyes as from the windows of his debased soul, seems to soil the very air; its impact, particularly on the innocent, has all the force of a crushing blow. There is a sickening revulsion at contact with such evil; but this is no secret power of evil but rather the sound reaction of healthy innocence.

THE ONLY BODY WE CAN MOVE at will is our own, the one enlivened by our immortal soul and joined to that soul in a substantial unity. Whatever activity we exercise on things about us will have to be through our bodies and by the use of the natures about us as we find them, not as we would like them to be. The spiritist's array of unauthored trumpet blasts, knocks, cavorting tables, and garbled messages cannot be laid to the souls of the dead. Once separated from its body, the human soul is powerless to move any physical thing. The spiritist's tricks may indeed be nothing more than trickery; they are definitely within the limits of the devil's powers; but only a miracle, a direct intervention of God could make it possible for separated souls to do these things. It is quite certain that God is not a partner to these tricks whose atmosphere is dark confusion and whose goal is deceit; so sure, indeed, that no spiritist ever dreams of inviting God to a seance.

WE ARE NOT MORE HELPLESS than the greatest of the angels in our lack of dominion over the intrinsic principles of things as they are. The angels, too, suffer a creature's limitations: they, too, have no power to change, generate, or destroy the natures in the world. But we are much more helpless than the angels as far as movement of things in the physical universe is concerned. They are bodiless spirits; their power thus is not limited to one body but sweeps over the whole vastness of physical things. Our soul is a spirit, but a spirit limited, determined to one body. It has direct powers over this one body alone, the one to which it gives life; if we move anything in the world it will be because we use our muscles to push or to pull, or use our intelligence to put other physical forces to work to do the moving for us.

THE WONDERS OUR TIMES HAVE ACHIEVED in putting the physical world at the service of men are a reason for pride, but not for an unreasoning pride that refuses to compare man's lordship with that of the angels or of God. As long as we fight off the natural desire to raise our eyes above the world beneath us, we can tell ourselves there is nothing above us. But we hardly convince ourselves. We work no miracles. We accomplish no creative results. We get nothing done in an instant and without labor. The truth is we are lowly ministers in a cosmic government; we have great powers that are to be used with great labor, and the results are achieved only by the efforts of the abrasive years.

YET WE ARE INDEED MASTERS of the physical universe. Everything else in it is driven; we alone choose our paths. It is only for us to *use* nature's powers, to direct them to our purposes rather than to be driven by them. We oppose these powers one to another, harmonize them, limit them or free them from their own limits, combine and separate them, all to results which have waited on our genius for their appearance in the world. We have a great part in the divine government of the universe; but only a human part under God.

WE NEED ONLY GLANCE above ourselves to avoid pride's puerile illusions and so recover the firm ground of humility's truth. We have absolutely no power over that part of nature which is the purely spiritual world of the angels. Angels are in no way subject to our orders. They are immune alike to our physical blows or caresses. They are beyond our direct knowledge. They enter the world of our love only because the walls of nature have been breached to give us a knowledge beyond our own powers.

THE FIELD OF OUR TEACHING stops short at the edge of the world of the angels. Even the greatest of us know nothing that is not already grasped in a superior fashion by the least of the angels. "There hath not risen among them that are born of woman a greater than John the Baptist; yet he that is lesser in the kingdom of heaven is greater than he." "Therefore angels are never enlightened by men concerning divine things. But men can by means of speech make known to angels the thoughts of their hearts; because it belongs to God alone to know the heart's secrets." These gifts alone we have to share with the angels: the secrets of our hearts.

IT IS IN THE WORLD of our fellows, among our equals, that we find our greatest contributions to the government of the universe; not in the angelic world so far above us, nor in the physical world that exists merely as our instrument. In these great human works, our high nobility is written clearly in refutation of all those who would underestimate a man; no less sharply witnessed is our humble state, against all those who would make gods of men. This, after all, is the whole truth of the matter: that a man towers above all else in the physical universe and is infinitely less than the God Who made him; and it is in the whole of the truth that the solid glory of man has its firm foundations.

IT IS GIVEN TO MEN to generate their kind. This is an almost insignificant thing to those who submerge men in the animal herds of the universe. But it is a work of high nobility when we see man truly, when we realize that the individual human being is the supreme work in the physical universe. Nature intends the enduring, is careful with the species and utterly careless of the individual; on this score alone, the value of a man is clear, for every human being outlasts all physical species since his immortal soul is destined for eternal living. For the humility of parents, the fact is plain that their child is more God's than theirs. They cannot create anything, let alone a spirit that will never die; yet in every human conception, an immortal soul comes into being. Procreation is a work done under God and directly with Him; the parents in each case prepare the material for union with a soul that comes directly, in each case, from God Himself. Parents have a right to be proud, but their pride must focus on the beneficence of God in giving them so humble a share in so great a work. They people the earth with citizens of heaven; and, in deepest humility, they dedicate themselves to the children that have come to them from God.

A MAN'S LIFE JOSTLES THOSE of countless other men and women in the course of his living, and with concrete results for good or for evil. No man comes to the end of his days devoid of influence on the lives of others; in this sense, no man lives alone, no life is a purely private affair. The number of those we have pushed towards heaven or turned towards

hell is known only to God; a secret whose very existence is for our caution and our comfort for it leaves
us with never an excuse either for presumption or
discouragement. So very much, indeed perhaps most,
of this influence on the lives of others is not by our
direction or government, it is not through our efforts
as delegated participants in the ordering of the
universe. Rather, the results in others are indirect
effects from our lives; echoes of our living ring down
the valleys of the lives of others like the voices of
distant bells, quietly, impartially, implacably reaching out to the most secluded, almost forgotten
hamlets of men.

OUR LIVES SWEEP THROUGH THE LIVES of other
men and women like wind over the waters of
the sea, whipping up waves that lash their ways to
distant shores. Our kindness, a sympathetic word
from our lips are seen and heard, imitated, and in
turn are fresh breezes dissipating the selfishness in
other lives. Our sins are seen, heard of, suffered;
then spread like a corrupting plague. All this is no
small part in the fate of the human world; but it is
not by our design. This is not the work of a governor
or his delegate, this is that good or bad example that
the scholars call a formal cause. For all its indirect-
ness, it is by no means ineffective. By it saints have
renewed whole cities, and the vicious have corrupted
whole communities; of the two, the victims of vice
have won more numerous imitators for the roads they
travel are so much easier in their beginnings.

THERE IS AN ENTICEMENT, quite aside from mere
example, that beckons from one life with a depth
and extent of appeal beyond the realization of the man
who so draws others to goodness. The perfume of a

saint's life, the wholesome happiness of innocence, the strong serenity carved in the face of the man who has dared to be good, the quiet happiness of an unselfish woman who, seeking nothing, yet possesses all things—all these are a parade of goodness, of lovableness, of happiness before hearts hungry for just such things. Their allure awakens at least a nostalgia in the most hardened of men, and often enough lights a roaring fire in the greenest wood. There can be no question but that such enticement plays a great part in the lives of men and women; but again this is not by our design, it is not by our direction or government of these people, but rather by the appeal, the allure, the seduction of goodness. Goals so universally desirable are openly displayed in their concrete reality and men move to them not by the force of commands but by the much more subtle force of attraction.

OUR DIRECT PART in the divine government of the world of men is not by the formal causality of example, nor by the final causality of good's attraction, but by efficient causality, by what we can do to men. It is by his communication of truth, by teaching his fellows, that man plays his chief part in divine government. Not all teaching is confined to classrooms, but even staying within those limits it is easy to see the tremendous power given to men who teach: one generation of ignorant or wicked teachers who feed the minds of men on falsehood instead of truth can corrupt a whole nation; nor is the power of good teachers any less. The reason for the sweeping effect of both on the lives of men lies in the fact that each man steers his life by his own reason, that is, by what of truth he has been able to grasp. Each man can find something of truth for himself, moving by way of discovery from the little he knows to what has been until then unknown. Or, profiting by the wisdom gathered by others, he can learn by instruction. However he attains to it, a man must have truth to live.

THE SUPREME IMPORTANCE of the teacher's work for the direction of men can be readily appreciated both from the side of the student seeking truth and from the side of the truth he seeks. Left to himself, devoid of instructors, a man finds truth slowly, far too slowly to keep pace with the race of the years of his life; he learns with a heart-breaking labor that can easily prove too much for his courage; whatever his genius, the truth he uncovers will be spattered with errors, and each error paves the way for tragedy in the attempt to live it. On the other hand, from the beginnings of his life each man has a desperate dependence on the light of truth. He must have that light from the first moment he begins to walk towards his goals, that is, from the first moment of his human living. Without it, in a condition of ignorance or in the distorted gloaming of truth's perversion, a man faces all the helplessness of the blind, all the terrors of impenetrable darkness, all the misery of the misguided and betrayed.

THE TEACHER HAS MUCH MORE to do than merely jog the memory of his students. We do not start life with an equipment of sluggish knowledge, or with a handy gadget called a race memory; we start off with a blank sheet on which we write the truth that we gain either by discovery or instruction. The students sit at the feet of the teacher, not in the hope of getting a slice of his knowledge, nor in watching the parade of the professor's own wisdom. The student must see for himself, must know for himself, must possess the truth personally or he is still blind, he has not learned, he has not been taught. Again, in this greatest role of government or direction of men, the nobility and humility of our work are inextricably intertwined. We give what men must have or fail in their living; yet we give it in a lowly, ministerial fashion, as extrinsically as a doctor gives health.

IN OUR TEACHING OF MEN, we hardly do more than the housemaid's humble chore of raising the blinds to let sunlight stream into the house. The teacher's work is to remove the impediments to a man's own seeing, to remove the things that would block the light. He cannot reach into another man's mind to insert knowledge; neither can he furnish the light to that mind by which it will see the truth. He merely sets nature free to work, as a doctor's medicine allows nature to throw off a disease; his is the humble work of helping nature, imitating its procedures, but never supplanting it. He takes another by the hand and leads him from known truths into the unknown, gradually, showing the steps to be taken by his contrasts, his examples, his similes, hoping the learning mind will follow the steps and come to truth. He cannot offer the comfort of a superior intellect, as an angel can, for in fact his intellect is not superior; it is of exactly the same kind as that of his student. He brings the material for knowing to the mind of his student, lays that material out in order, removes the impediments to knowing; and then hopes for the splendid result of knowledge.

IT IS NOT SURPRISING that the Incarnate Word of God should have spent so much of His three short years of public life among men teaching and preaching, and confirming His doctrine by a profusion of miracles. For this is man's great privilege, his supreme sharing in the government of the universe: that by his efforts, other men may have truth. Truth is crucial to men's living; so crucial, that the Lord could say of Himself: "For this was I born, and for this came I into the world; that I should give testimony to the truth." To His disciples He promised: "You shall know the truth, and the truth shall make you free." Man perishes in the darkness for he was made for truth's kingdom of light.

Man:
The Image of God

BY
MARTIN J. HEALY, S. T. D.

Professor of Dogmatic Theology

Seminary of the Immaculate Conception

Huntington, N. Y.

Part II

✠✠✠✠✠✠✠✠✠✠✠✠✠✠✠✠✠✠✠✠✠

PART IIa

✠ ✠ ✠ Happiness

* Refers to questions in the Summa

✠✠✠✠✠✠✠✠✠✠✠✠✠✠✠✠✠✠✠✠✠

CHAPTER I

The Nature of Happiness

Happiness:
   the Goal of Mankind

False Goals

The True Goal:
   the Vision of God

Happiness and Intellect

Happiness and Will

Happiness and the Body

Happiness and Friendship

The Possibility of Happiness

Happiness and Freedom

CHAPTER I
The Nature of Happiness

WITH THE LOVING LIBERALITY of a Lord whose wealth is never lessened, no matter how much He gives away to others, God has made man an image of Himself, a being with mind and free will, with the power of self-mastery; and then, with an excess, as it were, of divine generosity, He has given man a share in the government of the corporeal world. "Let us make man to our image and likeness; and let him have dominion over the fishes of the sea, and the fowls of the air, and the beasts, and the whole earth, and every creeping creature that moveth upon the earth. And God created man to his own image; to the image of God he created him." (*Genesis, I,* 26-27)

IN THE LONG HISTORY of man upon the face of the earth we read the tale of his efforts to fill the earth and to subdue it. In the rise and fall of empires and kingdoms, in the mounting and falling waves of civilizations and cultures, and even in the slight ripples caused in the vast sea of life by the individual actions of individual men, we see man seeking to master himself and the world God has given him. And whether man does his work in the world well or poorly, we know that the world gives glory to God; for God is the absolute Master of His world.

BUT WHEN WE LOOK at the bewildering complexity of man's work and the manifold motives that drive him to work, we cannot help asking what inner compulsion moves man to his labors. Does the poor man work just for a crust of bread or a roof over his head? Is the rich man seeking only to build up large reserves of wealth? Is the roué interested only in pleasure? Is power the only goal of the ambitious? If mankind is really one, if all men really possess a similar nature, what is the key to all their actions?

BENEATH THE MULTITUDINOUS and even conflicting desires of men we can see the one desire which gives unity and meaning, force and decision to all human desires. All men seek what they seek for one reason: they think it will satisfy them, they believe that the accomplishment of their desires will make them happy. Happiness is the goal of all human activity, precisely as it is human, that is, free and deliberate. The child with his nose pressed longingly against the pet shop window is seeking, not just a dog, but happiness. The miner in the bowels of the earth is seeking, not just coal, but happiness.

BECAUSE HE CAN THINK, man can always look beyond the action of the present moment to the goal which he seeks in all his work. The goal of his acts is a lamp lighting the way for his will. Because the goal beckons him on, man goes the way of his life, from act to act, from free choice to free choice. And the common goal, the ultimate end of all human acts is happiness, the perfect good which satisfies all human desires.

THE SEARCH FOR HAPPINESS is the common ground on which all human desires, all human ambitions meet. The child riding the tight circle of a merry-go-round, the jet pilot flying swifter than sound the vast circuit of the earth, the beachcomber avidly sifting his little treasures from the sands of the seashore, and the great banker seriously charting the course of financial empire, all are searching for happiness.

THE TRAGEDY OF MAN is not that he cannot find happiness, but that he looks for it in the wrong places. Because the desires of man are boundless, no particular good, whether outside himself, or in himself can perfectly satisfy him. The wealth of the earth, whether natural or artificial, can never completely satisfy him. For the natural goods of the earth, such as food, can only be used in a certain measure, though the desire for more still remains. And an abundance of money, the artificial wealth of the world, brings, not rest, but a restless striving for even more. Nor can honor, fame or human glory bring man the complete happiness he desires. For these goods are outside a man; they are the world's acknowledgment of the good which is inside a man. Nor again can power, even absolute power, satisfy all man's longing; for power does not bring that rest and repose which is characteristic of happiness. Rather, power is not an end, but a beginning; for power must be put to work, and so demands further actions, for further ends, for new goals. Besides, power can be used for good or evil; whereas happiness is concerned only with man's good.

NOT EVEN THE PARTICULAR GOODS of a man's body or soul can bring him that complete satisfaction which is happiness. The goods of the body, health, strength, beauty and pleasure, are delicate things; they wax and they wane, and at death they cease to be. The body itself exists for the soul; it is the soul's instrument for man's work in this corporeal world.

SURELY, THEN, WE MUST SAY that man's happiness is to be found in the good of his soul. And in a way this is true. But just as the hunter must be more

wary as he approaches nearer to his quarry, so we
must be most careful as we come nearer to the end of
our quest, the definition of real happiness. Obviously
happiness is not the soul itself; if it were all men
would be happy from the beginning. But this is contrary to all our experience. Nor is it some particular
perfection of the soul, such as science, or prudence
or virtue. For these, once again, are particular goods,
which always leave something further to be desired.
No, the only object which can completely satisfy all
human desire is the absolutely universal good, which
is outside man, even outside the whole created world.
Nothing can satisfy man's will completely, except the
universal good, which gives complete rest to his
appetite; and this is to be found, not in any creature,
but in God alone. Man's happiness, then, is to be
found in the possession of God. Briefly, God is the
ultimate object, the ultimate end of all man's desires;
and the possession of God by the soul is happiness.

BUT CAN MAN, whose powers are all limited, attain
God, the Infinite Good? It is clear that man cannot attain God by any of the acts of his body. Since
God is a pure spirit, man cannot consume God as he
consumes food in nutrition. Nor can he see God with
the eyes of his body, or hear Him with his ears, or
touch Him with his hands. If man's desire is to reach
to that Absolute Spirit which is God, he must do so,
if at all, with his own spiritual powers of intellect and
will. Only the vision of God, then, can fully satisfy
all man's desires.

ONLY THE INTELLECTUAL VISION of God, Who is
all Truth can put an end to the quest of man's
intellect for an understanding of the Cause of all
truth. Only the intellectual vision of God, Who is all

Good, can bring rest and never-ending enjoyment to the quest of man's will for the universal good which leaves nothing to be desired.

IS THIS VISION OF GOD really possible to man? Can man contemplate the Essence of God as it is in itself? The puny, limited intelligence of man is not in itself equal to the task. The small cup of man's mind cannot contain the ocean of being and goodness and truth which is the Essence of God. By himself, then, man does not dare to assert that he can see God. But God Himself has told us that He will make it possible for us to see Him. "Beloved, now we are the children of God, and it has not yet appeared what we shall be. We know that, when he appears, we shall be like to him, for we shall see him just as he is." (*I Epistle of St. John*, III, 2)

THROUGH THE GIFT OF GOD, promised by God Himself, Who can neither deceive nor be deceived, we can hope for what seems impossible, the vision of God Himself.

TO SEE GOD as He is in Himself, this is the essence of perfect happiness. But this is an act of the mind, of the intellect. And men, even after death, when the soul is separated from the body, are not just intellects. It is natural for us to ask what happens to our wills, which seek God in love; to our bodies, which are our soul's instruments in the search for God; to our friendships with other men, who helped us to reach God.

AS FOR OUR WILLS, the answer is obvious. Through the intellectual vision of God we are in possession of the Sovereign Good, and our wills necessarily take delight in the presence of God.

AS FOR OUR BODIES, it remains true that the essence of perfect happiness is the soul's vision of God. The soul is entirely at rest in the vision of God. But because it is natural for the soul to desire to enjoy God in such a way that the body may share in this enjoyment, God has promised us the resurrection of the body at the time of the Last Judgment. Then our souls will be reunited to our bodies, and in such a way that the fulness of happiness in our souls will perfect our bodies spiritually.

IT IS CLEAR, TOO, that when this blessed condition of soul and body has been achieved, we shall no longer need the material things of this world, such as food and riches, which are necessary for the imperfect happiness of this present life. The external goods of this present mortal life are needed to support the animal life of our bodies. But our risen bodies will be spiritualized, immortalized by the power of our beatified souls.

AS FOR THE FELLOWSHIP of friends, once again, it is not necessary for perfect happiness. God alone is that Sovereign Good which sets all desire at rest. But the fellowship of friends will add charm to happiness. And if there are friends also enjoying the vision of God, our own love of God will lead us to love them in God. The love of friends, therefore, will accompany perfect happiness. How is this perfect happiness to be attained? Since the vision of God, the essence of perfect happiness, is beyond the natural power of any creature, it follows that it can be attained only through the gift of God. This is supernatural, surely, and a mystery which we must accept humbly, trusting in God's word.

Bᴜᴛ ɪᴛ ɪꜱ ɴᴏᴛ ᴏᴘᴘᴏꜱᴇᴅ to the proper independence of the human personality. Strictly speaking, an all powerful God could have created us not simply with a tendency to find our happiness in the vision of Himself, but with the actual enjoyment of such a vision. Then we should enjoy perfect happiness without ever having asked for it, without ever having had the freedom to accept it or to reject it. But God has respected the dignity of each human being too much to have acted in that way ... God has created each of us with free will so that we may turn to Him of ourselves, asking Him for the gift of perfect happiness. God has given us our freedom so that we may seek and find Him by our own free acts. Although perfect happiness is a gift from God, nevertheless, those who achieve it, do so through the proper use of their own free will. Part of the charm of man's ultimate happiness is the fact that he has chosen it for himself.

EXᴘᴇʀɪᴇɴᴄᴇ ꜱʜᴏᴡꜱ ᴜꜱ, ᴛᴏᴏ, that this perfect happiness cannot be found in this world. No man sees God face to face in this present life. Besides perfect happiness leaves nothing to be desired. But true happiness must be everlasting; else man could always desire it to be so. Since this present life always ends in death, no present happiness is everlasting, and, therefore, cannot be perfect happiness.

Pᴇʀꜰᴇᴄᴛ ʜᴀᴘᴘɪɴᴇꜱꜱ can be achieved only in the next life, only in eternity. As the life in the apple seed cannot produce the tree, nor the blossoms, nor the fruit unless the seed die in the earth, so also, man's free will, even with God's grace, cannot bring forth the fruit of perfect happiness, until the man dies and grows into eternity.

How FOOLISH are those men who cry petulantly for perfect happiness in this life! They are like the overtired child who weeps and stamps his feet and shakes his fist at his father because he is not allowed to stay up as late as his parents. As the child grows, and grows stronger, his childish weakness will be replaced by the strength of maturity. So it is, too, with the life of men in God. In this present world, we are as children, who must be satisfied with the work and the enjoyment proper to children. If we live according to the power and the rules of conduct which God, our Heavenly Father, gives us, we shall one day grow up to the Everlasting Day of eternal happiness.

CHAPTER II

Human Acts: Steps to Happiness

CHAPTER II

Human Acts: Steps to Happiness

MAN'S FINAL GOAL is the vision of God. Human life is a journey from earth to Heaven, a journey from this world of time and space to the timeless world of the vision of God. To arrive safely at this destination man must have a means of traveling there and know the proper road or course to follow. If we imagine man's journey to God as a walking trip, then we can say that man walks to God by his human acts. Every creature reaches its own perfection by its own activity. Men reach God by their own actions. The proper road is the path of goodness and virtue. For how can a man reach God, the Perfect Good, except by seeking the good? The wrong road is evil and sin. The road-map which enables man to distinguish the right from the wrong road is law. The divine invitation which prompts man to the journey is God's grace.

TO ACCOMPLISH THE JOURNEY successfully we must understand all these things. In the present chapter we shall consider human acts, man's steps to happiness in God. In later chapters we shall be concerned with the proper path to God, the road-map which outlines this path, and with God's invitation to the journey.

MAN WALKS TO GOD by his human acts. Since, as we have seen, no creature below man can reach the vision of God, it is obvious that man can reach this vision only by acts that are truly human, acts that are superior to the actions, e.g., of rivers or roses or rabbits. What is it that distinguishes man's truly human activities from the activity of the creatures below him?

MAN IS DIFFERENT from everything else in the world of nature because he is free. He has control of his actions. If a stone is unbalanced on a mountain side it must roll down. If a tomato plant is planted in good ground and given sufficient nourishment, light, and moisture it must grow. If a hungry dog is given food he must eat. But if the agents of a foreign country offer a hungry prisoner food on condition that he betray the military secrets of his own country, he can accept or refuse. This is because man is the only agent in nature who can know a goal as a goal and recognize the relation of suitability between a means to a goal and the goal itself. Because man can know that his final goal is the good in general or happiness in general, no temporary, partial good can force him to act. Because a man can know that treason will not bring him perfect happiness, he can refuse the bread which is the price of treason. Man not only moves himself to his own acts, as the dog may be said to do, but he can move himself to his acts with the knowledge that they will lead him to his goal or turn him away from his goal. In his truly human acts man enjoys freedom.

THE SECRET OF EACH MAN'S FINAL DESTINY lies in the proper use of his freedom, in the proper direction of his control over his own acts. If men won the vision of God by one act, the story of man's journey to God could be told simply and quickly. But, as experience shows us, men normally must make innumerable free choices in the course of a lifetime. And the proper direction of freedom is either hampered by opposing forces or given direction by the conditions in which the free act is made. If freedom is to be used properly these forces or conditions must be recognized and their bearing on the direction of man's acts evaluated.

FREEDOM IS A SPIRITUAL PREROGATIVE. It frees man from the restraint of matter. It is like the flight of a bird whose wings free it from the earth and give it the limitless horizons of the upper air. A prisoner freed from jail, or a sick man finally released from the relentless routine of a hospital feel light and light-hearted and free. But this spiritualizing effect of freedom is neither easily won nor easily preserved. The bird must work at flying or he will fall back to the earth and be broken. The released criminal must keep the law or he will find himself back in prison. The convalescent must guard his health or he will be back in the hospital. Freedom of will must be won and preserved against the forces in the world that oppose man's freedom.

FREEDOM HAS ENEMIES both within and outside of a man. Outside a man there is force or violence used against a man's will. Within a man there are fear, concupiscence and ignorance which can weaken or destroy man's freedom.

THE MOST OBVIOUS ENEMY of man's freedom, though in reality it is the weakest, is violence—force applied to man from outside himself. A gorilla, with its great physical strength, might lay hold on a man and drag him into the jungle. Force prevents the man from running away. But force cannot prevent his will from wishing to run away. Force can prevent a man from accomplishing his desires by his external actions. But force alone cannot destroy the freedom of his will.

THE REALLY DANGEROUS ENEMIES of man's freedom come from within himself. They are fear, concupiscence and ignorance.

THE CAPTURED SOLDIER who is threatened with physical torture may, through fear of suffering, betray the military secrets of his own army. Fear has made him do something he would not wish to do in ordinary circumstances. But his act is still voluntary. He is willfully seeking his own safety. Only a fear so great that it destroyed his power to know what he was doing would completely destroy his freedom.

THROUGH CONCUPISCENCE, or desire, a poor man in desperate circumstances, may steal five thousand dollars. The urgency of his desire has influenced his will. But his act of theft is voluntary. He wants the money. Desire can destroy freedom only when its strength and vehemence destroy a man's power to know what he is doing.

THE WORST ENEMY of freedom is ignorance. Freedom is based on man's ability to know his goal and the means that lead to the goal. Ignorance prevents a man from seeking either the proper goal or the right means to the goal. Sometimes, it is true, the ignorance may be involuntary and inescapable. The driver of an automobile crosses an intersection after observing all the proper precautions. But suddenly a child runs into his path against the traffic light. The ignorance of the driver in running down the child is involuntary and so blameless. But sometimes the ignorance is voluntary. A man can refuse to learn or neglect to learn the income tax regulation of his country because he wishes to act against or outside the law. In this case ignorance does not destroy his freedom but leads him to abuse his freedom.

IN THE SEARCH for perfect happiness man must conquer these enemies of his freedom. Only knowledge of the true significance of his acts will give man the mastery of his acts. Only the proper mastery of his acts will lead man to his ultimate goal.

The true meaning of a man's acts is determined not only by the inner freedom of his decisions but also by the concrete conditions in which he acts. It may be correct for an engineer to blast rock from a hillside in order to build a road. But it is wrong if a party of picnickers is sitting on the rock at the time. It may be right to practice shooting a rifle in order to be a marksman. But it is wrong to do the practicing in a crowded street. The actual condition in which a human act is done can influence the direction of the act to man's ultimate goal. The chief circumstances which affect the significance of a human act for happiness are found in the answers to the questions "Who, what, where, by what aids, why, how, and when?" So, for example: it is a good thing to celebrate Mass, but only for a priest, since he alone has the power; for anyone else to attempt to do so would be sacrilege. It is a bad thing to steal. It may be a good thing to take a bath, but not in the middle of Times Square. It is a good thing to give alms to the poor, but not when it is someone else's money. It may be a good thing to go to church, but not when your intention is to steal the money from the poor boxes. It may be a good thing to pat a little boy on the back, but not if you hit him so hard you break his backbone. It may be a good thing to play the organ in church, but not when the priest is preaching the sermon.

S O FAR WE HAVE SEEN that man achieves perfect happiness by his free, deliberate, controlled actions. The use man makes of his free will determines his final destiny. The direction in which his free will takes him can be influenced by fear, concupiscence, and ignorance within him and by the actual circumstances in which his acts are done.

B UT TO UNDERSTAND man's freedom better we must consider the details of any human act. Any free human act, any deliberate, controlled act of a man involves the activity of both his reason and his will. It is necessary to see the interaction of reason and will in a human act in order to understand human freedom.

L ET US TAKE an individual human act and examine it closely. A husband gives his wife fifty dollars for her birthday with the command to buy something for herself. The wife realizes that the money is to be spent on something that will make her happy. She wants to be happy. She intends to be happy through the spending of the money. But should she buy the wrist watch she has wanted for a long time or a new Easter outfit? Either one would bring her happiness for the time being. She decides to buy the watch. So she goes to the jeweler's, pays for the watch and puts it on her wrist. For the rest of the day she looks at the watch frequently, enjoying the possession of it.

I N THIS LONG SERIES of actions the reason and the will of the wife have each in their turn contributed to the accomplishment of her desire. When she first received the money her reason recognized that something good was within her power. Her will responded by wishing this good. This is simple volition, the turning of the will to good. Then her reason judged that this good that could be bought with money should be bought. Her will replied by intending to take some means to achieve this possible good. Her reason took counsel with itself about the means of achieving the desired good. It proposed that the desired happiness might be found in either a wrist watch or a new Easter outfit. Her will consented to the good in both of these means. Her intellect then made a preferential judgment in favor of the watch. Her will freely chose to purchase the watch. Her reason intimated to the will that she would have to go to the jeweler's to get the watch. Her will commanded her to walk to the store, ask for the watch, pay the purchase price and put the watch on her wrist. When the watch was hers, her will rejoiced in the possession of this good thing, and in the happiness it brought her.

IN THE LONG SERIES of actions on the part of human reason and will there are four things that are especially important in this chapter on the direction of human actions to the pursuit of happiness. First, the will always follows the intellect. Second, the will always seeks what is good. Third, freedom is found chiefly in the act of choice. Fourth, command is the guiding force of the human act.

THE WILL ALWAYS FOLLOWS THE INTELLECT. By itself the will is blind. It is an appetite for what is good, a tendency to what is good. But until a man recognizes what is good by his intellect or reason, the will cannot reach out to the good. It might be said that even the intellect needs to be moved by the will to its activity. Therefore, we have an impossible situation: the will cannot move without reason and reason cannot move without an impulse from the will. The answer to the difficulty is found in nature and in God the Author of nature. The first movement of the intellect or reason in man is due to nature itself. Man is plunged body and soul into the activity of the world. He cannot escape the impact of the world and of his own body on his consciousness. The pangs of hunger in the body of an infant force themselves into his consciousness, such as it may be, and he cries aloud for food. Thus, at the dawn of reason in the child he apprehends that there are things, such as food, clothing, parental love, etc., which are good for him and his will which is made for good tends to these goods. From then on in his life we find the constantly repeated interaction of the reason and will—reason recognizing the good in things and the will reaching out to these goods.

THE WILL ALWAYS SEEKS GOOD. It is a power made for the good, a constant tendency to the good. When we reflect that in fact men often seek what is harmful to them it might seem a begging of the question to say that the will always seeks the good. The solution lies in the nature of the will. The will is a rational appetite. As an appetite it is an inclination to something. When we will anything we are inclined to it, we seek it. But every inclination is toward something suitable to the being with the inclination. The good is what is suitable to a thing. But the will is not only an inclination. It is a rational appetite. It seeks what is suitable insofar as reason recognizes something as suitable to man, as good for man. The will seeks therefore not simply the good, but the good as apprehended, as recognized as good by human reason. Hence, though the will seeks only the good, it is possible for man to seek something harmful to him because it appears to him to be good. So theft is really harmful to a man because it detours him off the road to perfect happiness, but it appears good to the thief in one way at least for it brings him the money he desires.

IN ITS TENDENCY TOWARD GOOD the will moves naturally and spontaneously. Good in general is the object of the will. In this respect man's will is not free. Man's will can only move toward a good or at least something apprehended as good in some way. It is God, the Supreme Good and the Author of all the good in the universe Who moves man's will naturally to the good. Freedom then is not found in the will's spontaneous tendency to what is good.

RATHER FREEDOM IS FOUND in the choices man makes in selecting the means of achieving the good. In the example given above the wife naturally and spontaneously sought the good which the money meant to her. But in the choice she made to purchase a watch as a means of achieving good, of attaining some imperfect happiness, she was free. If her husband, instead of giving her money, could have given her the vision of God, she would have accepted it spontaneously but necessarily. In that case her will could not have refused the perfect satisfaction of all its desires. But her husband could not make such a gift. Only God can make this gift. In this present life only particular good things—not the good in general nor the Supreme Good which is God—can be attained by men. But since no one of the good things or even the collection of all the good things in this life can perfectly satisfy the will, man's will is free to seek or not to seek any particular good. The freedom of man's actions is found in his choice of means to attain the good.

WHAT IS IT that gives the will the impulse to set about the business of achieving the ends of desire? What moved the wife to go to the jeweler and purchase the watch? It is command, the message the human reason gives to the will that such and such is to be done in order to satisfy the tendency of the will to the good it desires. Command is the general, the guiding force of human activity. If a man did not command himself to act he would never achieve his ends. We all know the ineffectiveness of the man who can never bring himself to do what he wants to do. Without the command of reason telling the will to take the steps necessary to accomplish its desires man would never achieve his happiness through his actions. Through the command of reason the will sets in motion the action of all the powers of man needed to accomplish the desired end or goal. Because the wife desires in her will to find imperfect happiness through the possession of a watch her reason commands the will to set in motion the movements of her body in walking to the store, the actions of her reason in talking intelligently to the jeweler in making the purchase, the actions of her eyes and hands in paying the money for the watch, etc. Although command is then an act of man's reason, it presupposes an act of the will, the free choice of the will to seek good in a certain way.

THE PROBLEM OF SUCCESSFUL LIVING, that is, of so living as to attain ultimately perfect happiness, is a problem of free choice and command. Man will reach perfect happiness by properly directing his human acts to that goal. But an effective direction is impossible without the proper free choices and command. To reach perfect happiness man must make the right choices and he must accomplish the object of these choices. A man can only accomplish his long journey to the vision of God by walking in that direction. He is walking in that direction when he freely chooses to do the things that lead in that direction and commands the execution of the acts that lead to the vision of God.

CHAPTER III

Happiness and Morality

Meaning of Morality

False Foundations of Morality

Reason: the Measure of Morality

How Reason Measures Morality

Morality and the Human Will

Morality and External Action

Reward and Punishment

CHAPTER III

Happiness and Morality

IN THE LAST CHAPTER we examined human acts, the steps man takes in the pursuit of happiness. In this chapter we shall consider the question of the morality of human acts. For morality, by showing the rightness or wrongness of human acts, shows us the foundation of the road to happiness and the road to despair.

EVERYONE UNDERSTANDS, at least in a general way, what we mean by the morality of a human act. The morality of an act is its rightness or its wrongness, its good or its evil, its suitability to praise or blame, to merit or punishment.

BUT EVERYONE DOES NOT AGREE on the foundation of morality. What makes a man's actions good or bad? deserving of praise or reproach? Some would say that morality is merely custom or convenience. It is based on a set of rules for conduct which men have adopted merely because they have found it convenient or easy to live in a certain way. At the whim or the arbitrary will of society the rules, they say, may be changed. What was right yesterday may be wrong today, if custom or convenience approve the change. In this view divorce and remarriage are wrong when men do not approve of them and right when they do approve of them.

OTHERS HAVE SAID the foundation of morality is to be found in authority: in the authority of the State, or of the civil law, or in the Church, or in ecclesiastical law, or in the authority of a father as head of the family, or even in the authority of the individual to rule himself. In this view men act morally when they obey the voice of some human authority. But the authority itself has no other sanction but custom or convenience.

STILL OTHERS HAVE, in theory at least, destroyed all morality by making man the slave of biological, psychological, or sociological forces. Men do what they do, not through a reasoned control of their actions, but because they are driven to their actions by the physical and chemical forces at work in their bodies, or by the psychical forces at work in their subconscious minds, or by the heavy pressure of the socio-economic forces at work in society.

BUT NONE OF THESE EXPLANATIONS is adequate. Man, as we have seen, is free. He is not the helpless slave of biology, or psychology, or sociology. He is in control of his own actions in the pursuit of happiness. Therefore, the authority of no group or individual can be the total explanation of the morality of his actions. A man obeys the authority of the State, or of the civil law, or of the Church, or of his father, or of himself, not just because it is an authority with the power to force him to do its will, but because he recognizes that obedience to legitimate authority is a good thing—it can lead him to happiness. Again, man is a particular kind of being, and the kind of being that he is makes some things good for him and other things bad for him. This is true of all things. It is good for the fish to dwell in the depths of the ocean. The fish was made for this; he is equipped for this. But it is not good for man to try to live all his life submerged in water. He is not made for this; he is not equipped for this. Hence the basis of morality cannot be mere custom or convenience. It must be something that is concerned with the suitableness or the unsuitableness of things or actions for man as man. Rightness or wrongness, good or evil are determined not by custom but by the answers to the question, "What should this thing be?" Granite should be hard, solid and heavy. If it is then it is good granite. A dog should be a live animal, with a body, having eyes to see with, ears to hear with, etc. If it is it is a good dog. But if it has no eyes or no ears then it is defective, and we call this defect an evil in the dog. The dog is not all that he should be. What a creature is, determines what is suitable or unsuitable for it. When it possesses what is in accord with its nature, then it is said to be good. When it lacks something which it ought to have, then it is said to be defective or evil. A bird ought to have wings because a bird is meant to fly. Without wings it is defective. But an elephant with wings is only a whimsical fantasy because the elephant is not meant to fly. So likewise a human action will be good or evil, perfect or defective according as it is or is not all that it should be.

BUT, AS WE SAW in our last chapter, man's controlled free actions are meant to lead him to perfect happiness. A man's free actions will be good or evil then insofar as they are suitable or unsuitable in relation to his ultimate destiny, the attainment of perfect happiness.

NOW IT IS HUMAN REASON which recognizes what is suitable or unsuitable for man in the pursuit of happiness. It is reason which recognizes the last end or goal of all human acts, namely, the good in general or happiness in general. It is reason also which makes the judgment that some actions will lead to this end while others will not. The judgment of human reason on the appropriateness of a human action to bring good to man is the immediate rule for human actions. The judgment of reason is the immediate foundation of morality in human actions.

THERE IS NOTHING ARBITRARY about this rule for human actions. Things or actions are not good or evil simply because the mind of man thinks them to be such. The judgment of reason is based on reality itself. The appropriateness of any particular good for any particular creature is based on the nature of the creature itself. Sunlight is good for corn because corn is meant to grow through the influence of light and heat. Wings are good for a bird because it is meant to fly. Some actions are good for man because they lead him to the perfect happiness for which he is intended in the order of God's creation. Others are not good for him because they do not lead him to the end for which he is intended by his nature. The judgment of reason then in questions of morality, in questions of the suitableness or the unsuitableness of human actions to man's last end is not created by the human mind. The mind of man only discovers this characteristic of appropriateness or inappropriateness in reality itself.

BUT CREATED REALITY is only an imitation, a reflection of the infinite perfection which is God Himself. Ultimately then things are good or evil, human actions are good or evil insofar as they accord with God's conception of what they ought to be. Behind the law of human reason there lies the solid foundation of the Eternal Law in the mind of God. But even here in the mind of the omnipotent God there is nothing of the arbitrary. Whatever God makes in the creature, whether it be by way of creation of the creature itself or of the production of the perfection or of the activity of the creature, everything that God makes in this world is an imitation of what He is Himself. But since He Himself is absolutely unchangeable, the essences of the things He makes in the world will also be unchangeable. Not even God then can make a *good* dog without the perfection that a dog should have, e.g., eyes, ears, etc. So too with human actions. The Eternal Law in God's mind is based on the natures of things as they reflect His own perfection. The Eternal Law for human actions is based on the nature of man and the nature of human actions insofar as they reflect the perfection of God realized in man. The judgment of human reason on the morality of human actions is only a reflection or a participation of the human mind in the eternal, unchangeable mind of God.

BUT HOW, IN FACT, does human reason evaluate the goodness or evil in a human act? By measuring the suitability of the act from the point of view of the object of the act, the end or human purpose of the act, and the circumstances of the act.

THE OBJECT OF THE HUMAN ACT is the natural purpose accomplished by the act. The purpose accomplished by eating, as far as the act of eating is concerned, is the maintenance of the health of the body. The object or purpose of theft is stealing, taking unjust possession of someone else's property. As the examples show the object or purpose of the human act in itself is the basic determining factor of the morality of the human act. Human reason can see that some acts are good because their natural purpose is good, what they accomplish is good, and that other acts are evil because their natural purpose is evil, what they accomplish is evil. To give alms to the poor is always a good object. To steal is always a bad object for a human act.

BUT THE OBJECT, the natural purpose, of a human act is not the only source of its morality. The person doing the act can direct its natural purpose to some further goal. Thus the man who spends hours training in a gymnasium may intend not only to be healthy and agile but also to use his acquired strength and agility to commit a series of second-story burglaries. Though physical agility in exercise is a good in itself, here the man's intention to use it for an evil purpose makes his acts in acquiring it evil. An evil intention can make evil an act whose natural purpose is good. The contrary, however, is not true. A good intention cannot make an evil act good. A man cannot steal five thousand dollars to help the poor. Though his intention is good his act is evil in itself.

THIRDLY, THE CIRCUMSTANCES of a human act can help determine its moral character. An evening at home seems good to a tired man. It seems better if there is peace and friendship and love there. An evening at home will seem bad to a tired man if there is no love between him and his wife and his children. It will seem worse if his wife is actually nagging him and shouting at him and the children. Similarly the actual circumstances in which a man is acting can make the goodness or the evil of his act better or worse. To love is a good thing, but to love your enemy is better, for it takes greater effort. To steal from a rich man is bad, but to steal from a poor man is worse.

SOMETIMES THE CIRCUMSTANCES of an act may play a larger role in the morality of an act. Sometimes a circumstance may be so important in the mind of the man acting that it really becomes the object or part of the object of his action. Murder is evil, but it is only one sin, the sin of murder. But when a man who hates God and religion kills a priest precisely because he is a priest then it is not only murder but sacrilege, an act of irreverence and hatred for God Himself.

IN THE PURSUIT of the good which constitutes happiness man determines the morality of his actions by the judgment of his reason on the object or natural purpose of his act, the end or human purpose of his act, and the circumstances of his act. If reason judges that all these elements of the act are good, that is, suitable to man as a creature seeking happiness, then his act is morally good. But if his reason judges that the act is unsuitable, evil from any of these points of view, then the act is sinful and will not lead man to happiness.

THIS, OF COURSE, is not the whole story of goodness or evil in human actions. When human reason has given its verdict on the goodness or evil of a proposed human act there is still the act of the will choosing or rejecting the act and beyond the internal act of the will there may be the external action itself. Both the will and the external action are related to the morality of man's actions. The will as the commanding power is the active source of good or evil. The external actions of man are the means he uses to accomplish good or evil in the world.

THE WILL OF MAN is good or evil according to the purposes which it seeks to accomplish. The proper object of the will itself is always the end or goal which man seeks through his acts. When we are speaking of external acts we distinguish between the object or natural purpose of the act and the human purpose or end of the act. A man goes to church to steal the money in the poor boxes. The object or natural purpose of the external act of going to church is to enable the man to be present in the church. This object may be good or evil. But the end or human purpose of the act, stealing money from the poor, is evil. Wherever we are considering an external act we can distinguish these two ends or purposes in the act. But when we are concerned with the internal acts of the will the object of the act of will and the end of the will are identical. For the will, simply as will, is always concerned with ends, with goals. Hence the goodness or the evil of the will is measured by the goodness or the evil of the ends which it chooses.

THIS DOES NOT MEAN that the end justifies the means. It does not mean that a good intention justifies an evil act. A man cannot rightly steal because he intends to use the money for a good purpose, e.g., to help the poor. The intention or purpose of the will gives form to any human action. But this inner form of the action must be measured against the form which the judgment of human reason proposes for the act. So in the case of a man who goes to church to pray, the act of the will intending to pray is good because reason judges that prayer is an action or a goal which will lead to the attainment of man's last end, happiness. On the other hand in the case of a man who goes to church to steal money from the poor boxes the act of the will intending to steal is evil because reason judges that stealing will turn the man away from the achievement of his ultimate goal, happiness.

In the last analysis, behind this judgment of human reason measuring the good or the evil of the ends sought by the human will there lies the Eternal Law in the mind of God. Human reason is a reflection of the Divine Knowledge. It may happen in a particular case that a man following human reason seeks a goal which is not in conformity with God's Will. A man works to achieve great wealth. But God does not wish him to be wealthy because God knows that great wealth will corrupt the man and lead him away from his ultimate happiness. But the difference of will between man and God in such a case is not a formal difference, i.e., the man is not consciously willing a goal against what he knows to be the Divine Will in the matter. Formally both God and the man are willing good for the man. As long as man follows the judgments of right reason he is seeking the good and his ends will be God's ends formally even though materially they may differ.

The external actions which the will commands also have a relation to good or evil. When the external action is evil in itself the end or intention of the will cannot make the action good. Stealing is an evil even though the thief intends to use the money for a good purpose. But when the external action is good in itself or at least indifferent then the end intended by the will can make the action good or evil as the end of the will is good or evil. We praise the man who gives money to the poor to help them in their need. But we think poorly of the man who gives money to the poor only for reasons of vanity, to gain applause for himself.

This idea of praise or blame introduces us to the last question to be considered about the morality of human acts. It is customary for men to judge other men by their acts. We say that the man who pays his debts is a good man. We call the thief a bad man, a sinner. We think it right that a man be rewarded for his good acts and punished for his evil acts.

IT IS FASHIONABLE in some circles to ridicule the idea of sin and so to discount the ideas of praise or blame, merit or demerit. But facts are facts and the human mind must face them. To deride the notions of sin or praise or blame is reckless sentimentalism. It is a refusal to face facts. It is like the sentimentalism of a mother who persists in considering her son a model of goodness when she is faced with overwhelming evidence that he is a thief and a murderer.

THE JUDGMENTS of reason or of God on the morality of human acts are based on the nature of reality itself. They are as inescapable as reality itself. An act is good and worthy of praise when it can be properly directed to man's last end, perfect happiness. It is sin and worthy of reproach and punishment when it cannot be ordered to man's last end.

THE MORALITY OF HUMAN ACTIONS is pregnant therefore with important consequences for man. When a man so lives that his actions are directed to true happiness according to right reason he will ultimately attain true happiness. When his actions are not so directed or are incapable of being so directed he will lose his ultimate happiness.

MORALITY IS FOUND in every truly human act. Every deliberate, controlled act of a man will take him toward happiness or away from it. The dignity and the power of each man's freedom and control over his own human actions is clear. When a man's controlled command of his own actions is directed by right reason to his last end, then that man is capable of reaching out beyond the space-time limits of the whole universe to the ageless, limitless horizons of the vision of God. When his deliberate, controlled actions are directed against the dictates of right reason to some other goal than perfect happiness then that man is descending into the smallest region of the confining and restraining limits of his own meager self. Good is an expanding force, capable of opening up the soul of man to the limitless vistas of the Divine Being. Evil and sin are constraining and limiting forces, capable of imprisoning man in the narrow confines of his smallest self.

M AN'S TASK IS TO CONTROL his action in the direction of good so that he may grow from time to eternity, from the smallness of himself to the greatness of God. The means of this control, right reason and good will, are within the power of every man. They are not the privileges of rich or poor, of the powerful or of the weak of this present world. By using the reason and the will properly every man can direct his steps unerringly forward to the vision of God in which his true happiness is to be found.

CHAPTER IV

Happiness
and the Passions

CHAPTER IV

Happiness and the Passions

THE POWER OF MAN to reach perfect happiness is based on his control of his own actions. This control is exercised through the use of human reason and free will. If man were a pure spirit like an angel we could proceed at once to a consideration of the habits of reason and will which make man's progress to happiness easier or more difficult. But man is not simply a pure spirit. Man is a natural unit composed of body and soul. The soul of man is destined by nature to union with man's body. It is the whole man, both body and soul, that seeks perfect happiness.

AS A SOUL, man is made to live in the spiritual world of universal truth and universal good. But as a body man is made to live in the material world of nature. In his soul, man is superior to the material world of sticks and stones, of flowers and irrational animals. But in his body man is part and parcel of this world of matter. As part and parcel of the world of nature man must somehow seek his ultimate perfection through a spiritual mastery of the material world in which he naturally lives and acts.

TO PARAPHRASE AN OLD ADAGE, the perfection of man demands a sound mind in a sound body. But the soundness of the body depends in part upon its adaptation to life in the material world. Now just as God has given to irrational animals an inclination to seek what is good for them in the world and to avoid what is harmful to them, so also has He given man a similar natural inclination. This inclination to seek good and avoid evil in the material world is called the sensitive appetite or the sense appetite. In both animals and men this appetite is manifested in those movements towards good or away from evil which are called passions. In irrational animals these passions move naturally and necessarily and hence have no moral character. But in man, the rational animal, the movements of the passions are subject to the control of his reason and his will. They can have, therefore, a moral character in so far as they move man to actions suitable or unsuitable to man. For this reason passions are important in the pursuit of happiness.

B UT WHAT IS PASSION? Everyone knows something about passion. A young girl may say she has a passion for candy. A young woman may say she is passionately in love. A man who strikes his wife in anger is said to have acted in a passion of rage. In these and similar examples we seem to be referring to the intensity of some craving or emotional drive. But intensity is only a quality of passion. What is the essence of passion? Perhaps an example will enable us to discover the essence of passion.

A FRIEND INVITES A MAN to a steak dinner. Since steak is his favorite food he loves the idea at once. His mouth waters at the thought of the steak. He desires to eat it. He accepts the invitation and goes to the dinner. As he eats he enjoys the steak. The taste and the feel of the steak in his mouth give him pleasure. When he has eaten his fill he stops. His sense of fullness kills his desire for more steak. But there is still some steak left and his generous host urges him to take more. Because he feels full he dislikes the idea of eating more. When his host still urges him on he begins to hate either the steak or his host because he perceives that they are now dangerous for him. They may lead him to overeat and become ill. When he sees that his host means to have his way he begins to fear that he really will become ill. Trusting to the good sense of his host he compliments him on the quality of the steak and the cooking, but politely declines to take more. His hopes are in vain, however, and his daring to no avail. His host still insists. What shall he do now? He may become angry at his host's insistence which he now regards as a present evil. A sharp and curt refusal in an angry tone of voice may win him release from the present evil. If so, he sighs in relief and enjoys the removal of a threat to his well-being. Or, if he is weak, he may despair of avoiding the evil, eat the steak and suffer the pain of indigestion.

IN THIS RATHER ORDINARY incident at a dinner table we can find all the ordinary passions of man at work. More importantly we can discover what passion is and how the passions are related to one another.

IN THE FIRST PLACE we can see that three things are involved in every passion: knowledge, a movement of the sense appetite and some change in the body. Before the man loves or desires the steak he must know of its existence and the possibility of attaining it. When he knows it he feels inclined toward it as something good for him, or later, when he has eaten all he desires, he is inclined to avoid it as something harmful to him. The steak as either a delectable object or a dangerous object attracts or repels him. In the man this attraction or repulsion is a movement of his sense appetite. Lastly these inclinations toward or away from the steak are associated with a bodily change. When he first hears about it he feels good and his salivary glands begin to work almost as if the steak were in his mouth. When he is eating it the feel and taste of it give him a sensation of pleasure. When he is afraid that more will make him sick his stomach seems about to turn. If he becomes angry at the insistence of his host the blood rushes to his head, his face becomes red and his voice becomes loud and sharp. When he gives in despairingly he feels a sinking sensation in his stomach. When indigestion develops he is in actual pain. In the case of every passion involved there is some change in the condition or action of the body.

ALTHOUGH KNOWLEDGE, movement of the sense appetite and some bodily change are found in every passion, it is the second, the movement of the sense appetite, which is essentially passion. Every passion is a movement of the sense appetite in relation to some apprehended good or evil. The sense appetite of man is his natural inclination to seek the sensible good of his body or to avoid what is evil or harmful to his body. The passions are the movements of this sense appetite toward good or away from evil.

THE PASSIONS OF ANIMALS OR MEN are set in motion by the apprehension of good or evil. From this point of view men or animals are passive under the action of good or evil objects distinct from themselves. It is this passivity which accounts for the name of passion. It is the steak as perceived by the man which moves him to love and desire or to hate and anger. This element of passivity in the passions, however, should not lead us to underestimate the importance of the passions in human life. Although man is in a certain sense passive in the movements of the passions, nevertheless the passions are the great motive force behind most human acts. It is the passion for the natural goods of the body such as food, clothing, and shelter which drive men to work in the world. It is the passionate desire for pleasure which impels man to attain the things which he judges will give him pleasure. Passion is a power driving man to accomplishment in the world. Without passion man lacks initiative, is inactive like a blunt discarded tool incapable of doing its proper work in the world.

I**N THE EXAMPLE OF THE MAN** invited to a steak dinner we can see the principal passions which drive men to achievement. When the steak was proposed to him he loved it, desired it, and, when he could eat it, enjoyed it. When the proposal of more than he needed appeared evil to him, he hated the steak, disliked it, feared it, hoped to avoid it, dared to refuse it, and ultimately, either grew angry at his host, or submitted in despair and became sad. In other words the man went through the whole scale of the passions: love and hate, desire and aversion, pleasure and sadness, hope and fear, daring and despair, and anger. It is true that in this example the passions are concerned with something comparatively small and trivial—a good steak. But it is these same passions that move men to the accomplishment of great good or great evil.

A FURTHER STUDY of this same example will reveal the relations between the various passions and the fundamental direction of their power. Food is good—even necessary—for man's body. Hence the invited guest loves it, desires it, and enjoys it. But overeating is harmful or evil to the body. Therefore the guest hates the surplus of steak, dislikes it, fears it, hopes to avoid it, becomes angry at it, or despairs of avoiding it and becomes ill about it. But in all cases it is clear that the passions are concerned with the good of the man. He is either seeking good for himself directly or he is seeking good indirectly by trying to avoid evil. This is the first important characteristic of the passions in human life. The passions are all ordered, whether directly or indirectly, to the good of man. If they lead a man to evil, whether physical or moral, it will be due to some defect in man's perception of what is good or evil for him or to some defect in his will which leads him to choose what is physically or morally evil.

THOUGH ALL THE PASSIONS are concerned with man's good they do not all seek it in the same way. Nor is the difference between them limited to the fact that some of them are exercised in the pursuit of good while others are exercised in the avoidance of evil. The story of the dinner guest shows us also that the difficulty which sometimes hinders the attainment of the object of the sense appetite distinguishes some passions from others. Love and hate, desire or dislike, pleasure and pain are concerned with good and evil considered without any perception of difficulty. But hope and despair, fear and daring, and anger are passions that come into play when there is difficulty either in obtaining the good or in avoiding the impending evil. So the dinner guest simply loved and desired the steak when it was made easily possible for him by the invitation to dinner. When he had it in his possession at the meal he simply enjoyed it. But when it became apparent to him that it would be difficult to avoid the evil of overeating, then he hoped to avoid it through some appropriate excuse. With this hope he dared to refuse. When his refusal was not accepted then he began to fear the impending evil of illness. When it was clear that he could no longer avoid it he either became angry as a means of avoiding it or he despaired and submitted. If he avoided the danger he was again at rest in his well-being and so took pleasure in his escape. If he submitted in despair he was simply sad at the presence of evil. The passions which deal with good or evil simply—love and hate, desire and dislike, pleasure and sadness—are called concupiscible passions. We might call these the simple passions since their action is not complicated by the knowledge or apprehension of any difficulty in the way of the attainment of their objects. The passions which deal with a good difficult to obtain or an evil difficult to avoid are called the irascible passions. We might call them the emergency passions since they are only called upon in the emergency associated with difficulty.

I T IS CLEAR ALSO that all the passions are grouped in contraries, with the exception of anger. So love is contrary to hate, desire to dislike, pleasure to sadness, hope to fear, and daring to despair.

L ASTLY IT IS IMPORTANT to note that love is the source of all the other passions. It is love of the good which moves a man to desire and pleasure. It is love of the good which leads a man to hate or dislike an impending evil or to be sad at an evil when it is present to him. It is love of the good which gives impetus to hope or daring, or a cutting edge to despair and sadness. It is love of the good which gives power to anger. The all important role of love in the movements of all the passions shows once again that all are fundamentally manifestations of the basic tendency of nature to good rather than to evil.

T HE RELATIONSHIP OF THE PASSIONS to morality can be seen easily. In the animal the passions move the animal to its actions spontaneously and necessarily. But in man the movements of the passions can be controlled by reason and free will. Though a man loves a steak he can still refuse an invitation to eat one. Though a man may hate to overeat, he can still freely choose to do so. When human reason perceives that a passion has for its object something which can lead to truly human perfection, then man sees that the object can be morally good and that the pursuit of it will be a morally good action. Human reason knows that a healthy body is good for man. It knows that food is necessary for a healthy body. It sees that a good steak will help to keep the body healthy. It can therefore approve the acceptance of the invitation to dinner and the eating of the steak as morally good acts. But it can also see that overeating or gluttony is bad for man and so it can perceive it as morally evil. The will in its turn can choose to follow the judgment of reason or to act against it. If it follows the judgment of reason then the passions have led man to moral good as well as physical good. If it acts against the judgment of reason then the passions have led man to moral evil, whether physical good is achieved or not.

THE PASSIONS ARE POWERS given to man to attain what is good for him in this world. But they must be under the control of reason and will. And this control must be in the direction of moral good, else the passions will lead man astray. But the proper control of the passions demands some knowledge of the particular passions, especially love—which is the source of all the others—and of the similar emotions in the spiritual soul of man. We shall begin with the simple or concupiscible passions and conclude with the emergency or irascible passions.

THE FIRST of the concupiscible passions is love.
It is only fair to say here that we are using the
word love in a much more profound sense than is
usual in ordinary conversation. By love we mean here
whatever is the source of movement toward the goal
that is loved. In this sense we can find love even in
inanimate things. For love is concerned with appetite
or the inclination of everything to seek its own good.
Rivers by nature flow downward to the sea. This is
good for them because it is the inclination of their
natures. Poets then can rightly say that rivers love
to flow into the sea. This kind of love is called
natural love and it means the natural adaptation of
an inanimate thing for the goal of its nature. In inanimate things, or, more generally, in things without any
knowledge at all, it is God who knows what is good
for them and moves them to their proper goals. In
animals the process is different. The animal has sense
knowledge. He can perceive what is good or evil for
him. But because he is incapable of reason and free
will the animal's appetite moves necessarily to what
he perceives as good or to the avoidance of what he
perceives as evil. In man there is both sense knowledge and intellectual or rational knowledge. Man can
perceive what is good or evil for him in the order of
the senses and in the order of the spiritual world of
reason and free will. Man is capable therefore of both
sensitive love and intellectual love. Sensitive love is
the movement of his sense appetite toward a good
perceived by his senses of sight or touch and so on.
Intellectual love is the movement of his will towards
a good perceived by human reason. In both cases
man can exercise free will, for even his sense appetite
is to some extent under the control of reason. Both
sensitive and intellectual love are the adaptation

respectively of his sensitive or intellectual appetite to some good. They are a feeling of complacency in a perceived good. In man all love is this: a complacency in the realization of the harmony between some good and the appetite—sensitive love if the harmony is only between the sense appetite and a good of the senses, rational love if the harmony is between the will—or rational appetite—and the good of reason.

IN HUMAN ACTIONS we can see two kinds of love— selfish and unselfish. When a man loves cigarettes because of the pleasure they will give him, his love is selfish in the sense that he wishes this good which he derives from smoking for himself. This is called technically the love of concupiscence. When a man so loves another man that he wishes him well, i.e., wishes him health, success or virtue or the like, then his love is unselfish. He wishes good to the other man not for his own sake, but for the other man's sake. This is called technically the love of friendship.

IT MUST NOT BE THOUGHT that the love of con- cupiscence, or what we have called selfish love— is necessarily evil. In fact the man who has no love for himself will probably have no love for anyone else. It is natural for man to love himself. It is even necessary. For it is self-love that will lead a man to seek the perfect happiness for which he was made. The point we wish to make here is that there are two ways in which a man can love something—for his own sake or for the sake of the other thing itself.

IT IS TRUE though that the love of friendship is a higher kind of love than the love of concupiscence. For selfish love makes a man grow in humanity only to the extent that the goods he acquires through the influence of this love make him richer in himself.

But the unselfish love of friendship makes a man grow in humanity in the sense that he grows into the lives of other men, sharing their joys and sorrows, their defeats and triumphs. In this latter love man grows out of the limitations of his own small self into the larger world of intimacy with other free spirits, human, angelic and divine.

THE GREAT AND SOMETIMES STRANGE multiplicity of human loves has often led men to say that love is blind. But while some particular loves may seem unexplainable to most men, it is not so much love itself as the objects of love or the actions which flow from love which are mysterious. For the causes of love itself are well known. They are knowledge, goodness and likeness or similarity.

KNOWLEDGE IS INDISPENSABLE for love. The appetite, whether sensitive or rational, is moved only by an object which attracts it or repels it. But this attraction or repulsion cannot take place unless the attractive or repulsive object is known and recognized as such. This explains the true meaning in the statement that love is blind. Either the passion of love is not moved at all because no lovable object is proposed to it by the senses or it is moved to an unsuitable object because only the good in the object and not the evil is proposed to the appetite. Without knowledge there is no love.

BUT THE KNOWLEDGE of the object of love need not be perfect. A man can love a steak perfectly even before the actual eating of it acquaints him with all its perfection. The point is that some knowledge of an object as good and therefore lovable in some way is necessary for love to exist at all in the appetite.

GOODNESS IN THE OBJECT—when perceived—is the fundamental cause of love. Love is a movement either of the sense appetite or the rational appetite. Like all appetites it is then an inclination to good. This is why we said above that love is complacency in good. A man loves a friend either because he perceives that the friend is good in himself or good for him. Goodness is the universal magnet drawing all love to itself. Likeness is also a cause of love. Musicians love other musicians. Teachers love teachers. This is because love always tends to union of the loved object with the lover. But when men have similar virtues or tastes then they seem to be united to one another.

IT MIGHT BE OBJECTED that opposites attract one another. A little man marries a tall woman or a spendthrift marries a thrifty woman. But even here it is likeness rather than unlikeness which causes the love. The small man likes to think himself tall and so he marries a woman with the quality he admires and would like to have.

WHEREVER WE SEE LOVE in action it is apparent that love aims at a union of the lover and the thing he loves. It is love which drives the young man to spend as much time as possible with his fiancée. It is love which makes a wife yearn for the presence of a husband who is away on a business trip.

THIS UNION CAUSED BY LOVE is found at its best in the intimate life that lovers lead in one another. A man in love with a woman has the thought of her with him always. She lives in his mind and imagination. She lives in his will for when she is with him he is pleased and when she is away he desires her presence. The lover seeks also to live in his beloved.

He desires to know everything about her. This explains why courting couples find so much to talk about. They are trying to get into one another's personalities by learning all they can about one another. The lover seeks even to live in the heart and will of his beloved. So a woman is never satisfied with one declaration of love. She wants a man to say he loves her over and over again. When this unifying effect of love is found in both parties then human love between human beings exists at its highest.

LOVE IS ALSO ECSTATIC. To be in ecstasy means to go out of one's self. But it is characteristic of love that it makes a man think less of himself and more of the object of his love. It will even move a man to make personal sacrifices for the sake of the one he loves. In this way love is also the cause of zeal and jealousy. A lover is zealous and energetic in trying to do good things for the person he loves. Or he is jealous of anyone or anything which seems to threaten his exclusive possession of the one he loves.

BUT LOVE CAN also injure or wound man. It is a movement of the appetite, whether sense appetite or rational, to good. But sometimes a particular good thing is not suitable to a man. Food is good for man. Too much food at one meal is bad. When a man's love for good food drives him to gluttony then his love has injured him. Love must be under the control of the judgment of right reason or it can harm a man more than it benefits him.

DESPITE THE DANGER of reckless love, love is basically an inclination to good. As such it is the source of all human actions. Whatever a man seeks, he seeks because he loves it. Love is the inspiration of all human effort. It is the motive power behind all human accomplishment.

THE CONTRARY of love is hatred. Love is the initial movement of the appetite toward the good. Hatred is the movement of the appetite away from evil. When a hostess sets a cup of coffee before a man at the end of a meal he considers it good and loves it. Were she to set before him a glass of iodine he would recognize it as harmful and he would hate it. Good is the object of love. Evil is the object of hatred.

BUT EVEN though evil is the object of hatred, still love is the cause of hate. A man hates evil only because the evil object threatens to deprive him of some good. A man hates the glass of iodine because the drinking of it would deprive him of his life which he loves. All hatred is based on some previous love.

HATRED SOMETIMES makes a strong impression on a man's life and gives such a distinctive coloring to his actions that men often regard hatred as a stronger force than love. But a little reflection will show that love is always the stronger. For as we said above every hate supposes some previous love. A strong hate means a strong love. A man has a strong hate for poison only because he has a strong love for life.

SINCE HATRED is based on love it follows that hatred is also a great power for good in man's life. Hatred enables man to avoid the evils that would destroy him. But like all the passions it must be under the control of right reason and will if it is to benefit man.

DESIRE, OR CONCUPISCENCE, is a power flowing from love in the pursuit of good. When a man loves a cup of coffee, he desires to enjoy the pleasure it will give him. Desire occupies a place midway between the love of something good and the actual enjoyment of that good thing. Desire is love in actual pursuit of the pleasure or joy that good will bring.

DESIRE is distinct from love. Love is simply a complacency in the good. Desire is a tendency toward a good which is not yet present to the appetite, not yet enjoyed. When a man has what he loves, he no longer desires it; he only enjoys it.

DESIRE IS THE ENERGIZING FORCE behind human actions. It is the desire for good that sets men in action pursuing the goods they do not yet possess. But when we examine the multitude of things that men pursue in the course of a lifetime, we can see that some of their desires are natural and others are acquired. Men have natural desires for whatever is required by nature itself for their well-being. So all men desire food and shelter. But men also possess reason and through reason they can see good in many things which nature does not absolutely require for man's well-being. In this way men seek, for example, the pleasure to be derived from smoking tobacco. Reason has discovered some good in tobacco for man. Since the power of reason to discover truth and goodness is universal, reaching out to everything in existence, desires acquired through reason can be limitless. So the man who thinks wealth is good, can desire not just a limited wealth, but as much wealth as is possible. Natural desires, on the other hand, are satisfied with what nature requires. A man naturally desires only enough food at any one meal. He does not desire naturally a mountain of food at each meal.

THE CONTRARY OF DESIRE is dislike or aversion. This is the weakest of all the passions. Simple dislike is never very productive. For that reason dislike is sometimes not very admirable. No one admires the person who never does anything simply because he dislikes everything. Hate shows a capacity for great love. Dislike seems to indicate an inability to love anything strongly.

DESIRE MOVES MEN TO ACTION. Because men desire things they work to attain them. Desire is always aimed at the enjoyment of the things we love. The end of desire is always pleasure or joy. Pleasure is the movement of the appetite in the presence of good. We call it a movement because the appetite possessing the desired good, is in action. Actually we could say also that the appetite is at rest. It is resting in the possession of the good it formerly desired. So a man rests or is at ease in the possession of a good when he relaxes in the refreshing coolness of the ocean after a hot day at the office in the city.

THE REPOSE OF THE APPETITE in good can be either pleasure or joy. When the sense appetite reposes in the possession of something that appears good to the senses, then the repose is called pleasure. A man takes pleasure in smoking a good cigar. When the rational appetite, the will, reposes in the possession of a good approved by reason as leading to perfect happiness, then the repose of the will is called joy. A man is joyful at the discovery of truth. Pleasure is always accompanied by some change in the body. But joy is simply a movement in the will of man, although sometimes a great spiritual joy can, as it were, seep over into the body and give pleasure.

STRICTLY SPEAKING the spiritual pleasures reached by the will and the intellect are better in themselves than the sensible pleasures of the body. A man takes delight in driving an automobile. But he takes more delight in understanding what an automobile is.

BUT THE PLEASURES of the body seem stronger to men than intellectual pleasures. This is due to the fact that the pleasures of sense are better known to men and produce a feeling of well-being in the body which intellectual pleasures may not give. Again, the pleasures of the body frequently offset the pains of the body and so men seek them as an antidote to pain.

SINCE LOVE SEEKS UNION with the thing that is loved, pleasure is found in any union with the loved object. The greatest pleasure or joy is found in real union. But it is possible to take pleasure in a past remembered union or in a future anticipated union. The husband separated from his family takes delight in remembering the times he was with them or in anticipating the time when he will be reunited to them.

THIS UNION effected by love can make even the actions of others a pleasure for us. Our friends may do good things for us, or make us conscious of our own goodness by admiring us or paying us compliments.

ON THE OTHER HAND when we do good to those we love, we enjoy it because we look on our friends as ourselves. Or we expect them to return the favor by doing good to us. Or when we are generous we are pleased because our generosity makes us aware that we have so much good ourselves that we can afford to share it with others.

LIKENESS OR SIMILARITY is also a cause of pleasure. We are happy when we are in the company of friends who have the same interests, tastes and virtues.

THE SENSES OF SIGHT and touch are the greatest sources of sensible pleasure. Sight gives us pleasure because it enables us to know the many good and delightful things in the world. Touch gives pleasure because it is by touching and holding things that we put them to our own uses. As long as we are concerned only with the pleasures of the body, touch is more important than sight. But when we seek the pleasures of the mind, then sight is better than touch for it leads more immediately to knowledge.

THE OBJECTS OF PLEASURE are as many and varied as the things which bring delight or joy to the soul. But the general causes of pleasure are few in number.

SINCE PLEASURE requires the attainment of a suitable good and the knowledge of this attainment, activity is a cause of pleasure. Men must act to attain their desires. Every pleasure is the result of some action. Change or movement is also a cause of pleasure. Man is by nature changeable and what is pleasant to him at one time, later is not.

EVEN WONDER OR CURIOSITY can give pleasure. For when we desire to know something and have a chance of gaining the desired knowledge, then we are pleased in anticipation. A woman can be pleased in the thought that a friend will bring her all the latest news or gossip.

IN ALL CASES it is clear that love is the cause of pleasure or joy. Consequently the greater the love for something, the greater is the pleasure or joy in its attainment.

WHEN LOVE HAS LED A MAN through desire and hope to pleasure or joy, the first result of delight is a feeling or a consciousness of growth. We are, as it were, enlarged or enriched by the enjoyment of the good we desired but did not possess before. In this we can see the expansive force of love. Love makes men grow. If their loves are right, they grow rightly and strongly, like a tall evergreen. If their loves are wrong, they grow, but in a distorted way, like a tree that has been blighted by poor soil, dry climate, fire and lightning.

BUT PLEASURE OR JOY also results in exciting a desire for more pleasure. Since sense pleasures are not always perfectly possessed, it is possible to seek more. A man enjoys a steak. But if there is not enough, he will desire more. As for intellectual joy, since human reason is made for all truth and the human will for all good, man seeks joy without limit. Only the vision of God, the Supreme Truth and the Supreme Good, can fully satisfy man's appetite for joy.

PLEASURE CAN PREVENT the proper working of the human mind. The feeling of pleasure can be so intense that it distracts the mind and hinders its proper functioning. Sometimes pleasure can bring about such violent changes in the body that it completely prevents the mind from functioning. Excessive drinking of alcohol can take away reason altogether.

L ASTLY, pleasure can make human action more perfect. We do well the things in which we take pleasure.

S INCE PLEASURE OR JOY is the goal that man aims at in his loves and desires, the morality of our pleasures is of great consequence in our lives. Their morality is to be judged by the standard of right reason. If they lead to man's final goal, the vision of God, they are in accord with right reason and therefore good. If they turn man away from his final goal, then they are not in accord with right reason and so are evil. The highest pleasure possible to man is the enjoyment of God in the beatific vision of God. All other pleasures are subordinate to this final pleasure or joy. The good things of this world are only a foretaste of the joy of Heaven. It is the task of reason to determine whether or not earthly pleasures lead to the joy of the vision of God. If reason judges that they do not, then man pursues them at the peril of losing his greatest joy. If reason judges that an earthly pleasure or joy can lead a man to God, then man can act to secure that pleasure with a confident hope that it will lead him ultimately to the greatest joy of all.

T HE CONTRARIES of pleasure and joy are pain and sorrow. Pain is the movement of the sense appetite in relation to evil. Sorrow is the movement of the will in relation to evil. As always in the case of the passions, pain and sorrow come only through the knowledge or apprehension of the presence of evil.

P AIN AND SORROW have a depressing effect on man. They prevent him from enjoying the good things he possesses. The man who is plunged in grief at the death of his wife cannot find pleasure in his children or friends or possessions. If his grief is profound it may even prevent him from working.

THE BEST REMEDY for pain is pleasure or joy. When a man can take pleasure in something, then he is at least beginning to rouse himself from the depression caused by pain. Tears, as everyone knows, are a natural relief from depression. The sympathy of friends or a new interest can also drive out sorrow.

MEN USUALLY REGARD pain and sorrow as evil. In part they are right. In so far as they are concerned with the presence of an evil, pain and sorrow are evil. But sometimes they are the means of safeguarding or attaining real good. A pain in the abdomen is an evil thing in itself. But it may warn a man that he has acute appendicitis and so lead him to take the steps necessary to save his life. Remorse for a sinful act is not pleasant. But it may lead a man to repentance and spiritual good health.

THIS CONCLUDES our consideration of the simple passions. As we have seen, they are concerned with good and evil simply as objects to be sought or avoided. But in life most good things cannot be attained easily. Nor can all evils be easily avoided. God has given us the emergency passions to cope with the difficulties we meet in the pursuit of good and the avoidance of evil.

THE VALUE OF THE EMERGENCY PASSIONS should not be underestimated. We all think poorly of the man who can never attain the good he loves or avoid the evil he hates, because he lacks the energy to overcome the obstacles in his path. It is the emergency passions which enable men to meet difficulty successfully.

THE FIRST of the emergency passions is hope. Hope is a tendency to a future good which can be attained, but with difficulty. A man who has been shipwrecked will cling to a piece of driftwood for hours because he hopes to be rescued.

DESPAIR IS THE CONTRARY of hope. A man runs away from a future good because he regards it as unattainable. The timid man never asks his employer for the raise in salary which he deserves because he feels sure that his employer would never grant it.

HOPE IS BASED ON EXPERIENCE and, strangely enough, on the lack of it. The young are full of hope because the experience of failure has not yet shown them their own limitations. A young girl with no singing voice at all will still hope to be some day a prima donna at the Metropolitan Opera. But hope is at its best when based on successful experiences. The lawyer hopes to win a difficult case because he has often won such cases in the past. Hope is a help to action because it arouses effort and leads through success to pleasure or joy. Despair on the other hand tends to paralyze action and kill effort.

AFTER HOPE AND DESPAIR come daring and fear. Daring springs from hope. When a man hopes to attain good, he dares to face difficulty and danger in the pursuit of good. The fireman dares to rescue the child trapped in a burning building. When daring is based on reason and experience it is more constant than when it is reckless. The daring of a mature man whose hope of victory is based on successful experience is a stronger and more lasting force than the daring of inexperienced youth.

OPPOSED TO DARING is fear. Fear is the movement of flight in the appetite in the face of an impending evil that seems irresistible. Fear arises when danger is right at hand. Men seldom fear dangers that are far in the future. When death seems far away men seldom fear death or God's anger. But when danger is just around the corner, then fear seeks to escape it.

FEAR WEARS MANY FACES in human life. In a man who fears work it is laziness. In the man who fears future disgrace it is shamefacedness. In the man who fears present disgrace it is shame. In the man who faces an evil whose extent and magnitude seem immeasurable, fear appears as amazement. In the man faced with a sudden and unlooked for danger we find stupor—a paralysis of his whole being. When a man fears a future misfortune which he cannot foresee, his fear is called anxiety.

THE BASIC CAUSE of fear is love of good. A man fears something because it will deprive him of some good. The second cause of fear is a man's feeling or conviction that he is unable to cope with the danger.

THE FIRST EFFECT of fear is a paralysis of man's power to act. A woman confronted by an angry rattlesnake is frozen with fear. She is powerless to attack or run away. This is the great evil of fear—that it prevents man from acting for his own good.

SOMETIMES, when danger is still far off, fear will move a man to seek the advice of others. When the advice is sought from prudent and courageous men, this effect of fear is good. But fearful men are not good advisers for other fearful men. The timid will usually counsel either timidity or reckless daring.

THE LAST of the emergency passions is anger. Anger is a mixed passion. It is concerned with both good and evil. When a man strikes an enemy who has been spreading lies about him, his anger has two objectives. He seeks revenge, which he regards as something good—a recompense or satisfaction for the damage done to him. And he hates the man who has lied about him as something harmful to him.

SINCE ANGER seeks vengeance for some damage that has been done, it implies a comparison between the damage done and the vengeance sought. Anger deals then with questions of justice. We are angry when we think that some injustice has been done to us, and, in anger, we seek revenge on the evildoer.

IN LIFE MANY THINGS can cause anger. But they all involve some real injury or fancied injury to ourselves. We regard the injury as a symbol of contempt on the part of the one who has injured us.

ANGER often produces pleasure. We are pleased when we have secured a recompense for the harm done to us. It also impels men to action. The angry man is energetic in the pursuit of justice. But anger can destroy the reasonableness and prudence of our actions. Frequently angry men exact a greater vengeance than the injury done to them merits.

ALL THE PASSIONS OF MAN, from love to anger, are powers given to man to enable him to seek what is good and to avoid what is evil. Under the control of reason and will their action can be morally good or bad. The man of many desires can forget God in the pursuit of pleasure. This is what the drunkard or the libertine does. The fearful man can desert

God in his desire to avoid all difficulty or pain. The passions must be brought under the control of right reason and will. Their powers must be directed to what is morally good. The passions are like the power in an automobile. As long as the driver is in command of the automobile, the driving power of the car will take him safely where he wishes to go. But if he loses control of the car, both the driver and the car come to grief. When properly directed by right reason the passions move man to accomplishment. They help man to dominate the world for his own happiness and God's glory. When a man loses control and allows himself to be ruled by his passions they lead him to destruction—to the ruin of his human personality.

IF WE THINK OF THE ROLE of the passions in the present world in which we are living, it appears that we have emphasized the simple passion of pleasure and neglected the emergency passions, especially hope and daring. People are too interested in pleasure. Our great technical inventions and natural resources have made life too easy for us and our moral fiber is in danger of disintegration. Laziness prevents us from making sufficient effort to achieve our real happiness. But great goals are achieved only through great effort. The vision of God is not brought to us on a serving platter. The kingdom of Heaven is won by violence—that is, by effort.

LOVE OF GOOD, of the real good, must be the motive of all human activity. Through love man grows, and society grows with him. Love, under the control of right reason, is the force that will make the world fit for man and man fit for God.

CHAPTER V

Happiness and Habit

CHAPTER V
Happiness and Habit

MEN WALK TO GOD by their free, morally good human acts. They walk away from Him by their morally evil human acts. But the choice between moral good and moral evil is not always an easy one. Did you ever observe carefully a child's effort to be generous? How reluctantly he shares his toys or candy with someone else. How slow he is to give anything away. His internal struggle with selfishness shows itself in the slowness of his actions as he transfers a treasured possession to someone else. His hands move slowly and hesitantly. His eyes roam anxiously from his toy to the other child, to his mother and back again. As often as not he snatches the toy back or begins to cry. If every free decision in human life required as much effort, life would be an intolerable burden.

FORTUNATELY FOR MEN the difficulty of making free decisions is eased by that quality of human nature we call habit. The generous man finds it easy to be generous because he has acquired the habit of being generous. The dishonest man finds it easy to decide to steal because he has acquired the habit of being dishonest. Habits make it easy or difficult for men to be good. They also make it easy or difficult for men to be evil.

HABIT IS A QUALITY in a man that disposes him well or poorly in relation to his human nature or to his human actions. To be disposed to something means to be put in order to or for something. But only something that is composed of different parts or elements can be put in order. A single bowling pin cannot be put in order. But ten bowling pins can be put in order or properly arranged for a game of bowling. The separate parts of an automobile must be put in order or properly disposed in relation to one another before we have an automobile capable of transporting people from place to place.

MAN IS ALSO COMPOSED OF PARTS. He has a body and a soul. His body is composed of different organs or members. His soul, since it is a simple spiritual thing, has no parts in the proper sense of the word; but it has different powers—the intellect, the will, and the passions of his sense appetite. These parts or elements of human nature must be put in proper order before we can say that a man is well-disposed or poorly disposed in his human nature or in relation to human actions.

NOW WE DO NOT CALL every order or arrangement of parts a habit. The arrangement of the parts of an automobile is not a habit in the automobile. It is the form that man imposes on the parts of the automobile. The union of soul and body in man is not a habit. It is natural to him. It constitutes his nature.

WE RESERVE THE NAME HABIT for something that is added to the nature of man. It is in this sense that we sometimes call habit a "second" nature. But not all natures are capable of habits. For habit we require first a nature that is capable of some perfection which it does not yet have. Since God is infinitely perfect, He cannot have or acquire habits. Secondly we require that a nature be capable of being determined to different things or perfections. The eye is determined by nature only to the perception of light or color. Hence it cannot acquire habits. Thirdly we require that the nature be capable of being determined to something in different ways. An animal will seem to act differently in its pursuit of good and avoidance of evil. Actually it always follows blindly the prompting of animal instinct. But man can freely choose whether to follow good or evil and what way to follow them. The dog who hears footsteps in the hall must rush to see who it is. The man can continue to read his newspaper. He can choose to learn what is new in the paper rather than what is new in the hall.

IT IS BECAUSE man's tendencies have a character of universality that man is capable of habit and needs habit for efficient action. The goals of human action in this world are many and they can be attained in different ways. Man's mind seeks all truth. Since man does not possess all truth at once as God does, man can choose which truths he will seek. Man's will seeks all good. Since man does not possess all good at once as God does, man can choose which goods he will seek. But the attainment of any truth or good requires the easy direction of man's powers. Without what we call habits man would be frequently paralyzed or frustrated in his actions. In the face of the great multitude and variety of good things in the world how could man choose efficiently which ones to pursue and acquire? His sense appetite tends indiscriminately to all the pleasures of the body. His intellect tends to all truth; his will to all good, whether real good or only apparent good. The powers of man must be determined or slanted in one direction to one object, if man is to act efficiently. It is habit which gives this determination or slant to human powers.

HABIT IS A QUALITY in man that lies midway between his powers to act and his acts. Man's

will is capable of choosing to tell the truth. But before
man can choose efficiently to tell the truth in any and
all circumstances, he must acquire the habit of
truthfulness. Truthfulness is the determination or
slanting of his will toward telling the truth. A farmer
has water in his artesian well and he has fields. But
before the water can be brought efficiently to the
fields to irrigate them the farmer must either dig
canals between the well and the fields or he must
lay pipes from the well to the fields. If he tries to
carry the water a bucket at a time he will never succeed in irrigating the fields in time for planting,
cultivating and harvesting. Similarly man is capable
of acquiring many goods and avoiding many evils.
But if each act of will or reason requires as much
effort as the farmer who must carry water by the
bucket, then man will never efficiently accomplish
his ends. Habit is the secret of man's efficiency in
the moral order. Habit is the canal or pipe which
carries the energy of human power to human action.

HABITS ARE CONCERNED with human action.
They can be related to human action directly or
indirectly. It is man who acts. It is his human nature
that acts. But his human nature acts through its
faculties or powers. Some habits then can be found
in the essential parts of his nature—his body and
soul. These habits will affect his nature immediately
and his action only indirectly. Other habits can be
found in his faculties or powers—his reason and will—
and these habits will be directly related to his actions.

HEALTH OF BODY or beauty of body are habits
that affect man's nature directly and his actions
indirectly. Health makes a man's body well-disposed
in itself and a fit instrument of the soul and the

powers of the soul in search of happiness. A healthy man can work better than a sick one.

SINCE IT IS the human soul which gives form and order to the human body, there is no habit of nature that directly affects the human soul. Rather the human soul gives form and finality to human nature itself. The soul does not have to be put in order or properly arranged to make a man human. Rather it is the human soul which informs and vitalizes the body and with it constitutes human nature.

BUT SOMETHING LIKE A HABIT can affect or modify the soul in the supernatural order. The soul is not naturally disposed to exist or operate in the supernatural order. If God calls man to the vision of Himself, the soul of man must be disposed to the divine life in which that vision consists. God infuses this disposition into the soul when He infuses sanctifying grace. We might say—without insisting too much on the resemblance—that what health does for man's body in the natural order, grace does for man's soul in the supernatural order. Health of body enables man to live and act efficiently in the natural order. Grace of soul enables man to live at home in the supernatural world of God's own life.

HABITS SUCH AS HEALTH of body in the natural order or grace in the supernatural order are called entitative habits. This is because they are found in the very elements of human nature itself. They affect nature directly and action only indirectly. But most habits are concerned directly with action. They are dispositions modifying not man's nature itself but man's powers to act. They are qualities which direct or canalize the powers of reason or will or sense appetite to a definite kind of action. These habits are called operative or active habits because they lead directly to action.

OPERATIVE HABITS are found most properly in the powers of the human soul—intellect and will. This is because man's intellect and will are tendencies toward universal truth and universal good. Because they tend to universal objects their activity must be set in channels or grooves if they are to act efficiently. The powers of the body, such as digestion and growth through the assimilation of food, operate naturally and necessarily. They are always slanted or directed in the same way. They cannot therefore be subject to habit. The sensitive powers or passions also operate for the most part naturally. They are however subject to the control of reason and will. To the extent of this control they also can be subject to habit. But in human intellect and will there is almost an infinite possibility of action, since they are inclined to all truth and all goodness. This quasi-infinite power of reason and will needs to be canalized to specific ways of acting if the individual man is to realize efficiently the potentialities of his own human nature.

SINCE HABIT IS THE KEY to efficient action, the source of habits is important. Fortunately the causes of habit are few and easily accessible to all men. They are nature itself, human activity and God.

NATURE ITSELF is the cause of some habits. Nature alone can be the cause of health or beauty. Nature can also help in the functioning or acquisition of other habits. Good eyesight or hearing can help a man to acquire knowledge easily. Or again all men possess by nature an understanding of the first principles of thought. Every man, once he has grasped what a whole is and what a part is, knows naturally that the whole is greater than the part. Through the senses provided by nature a man can grasp what a whole is or what a part is. Sometimes too nature provides the beginning of a habit in man's appetitive powers. The peculiar disposition or temperament of a man's body may give him an inclination to purity or anger or meekness.

THE PRINCIPAL NATURAL CAUSE of habits is human activity. It is by repeated actions of the same kind that man acquires his operative habits. It is by repeatedly telling the truth in any and all circumstances that a man acquires the habit of truthfulness. If a farmer wishes to irrigate his fields from a river nearby, he can do so by digging canals from the river to the fields. It is the steady digging, shovelful after shovelful, that makes the permanent canal through which the water will flow. So it is with human acts and habit. If a man wishes to direct the power of his will easily and permanently to acts of truthfulness, he must dig a canal which will channel that power to truthfulness. He digs this canal by acts of truthfulness. Each act is another spade of dirt out of the canal, enabling the will to flow more easily and more strongly in the direction of truthfulness. When many repeated acts of truthfulness have dug the canal deep and strong, then the power of the will flows easily in the right direction, and it will be difficult to make it flow any other way. A truthful man finds it easy to tell the truth, but hard to tell a lie.

HUMAN ACTS are the chief cause of natural operative habits in man. But God, the Author of human nature, can infuse habits in a man. Because God is the infinitely powerful Author of human nature He can infuse even a natural habit in man, such, for example, as the intellectual habit of a particular language. In this way He might give a missionary a miraculous knowledge of some language he had never naturally learned. But this will be an extraordinary occurrence. More frequently God infuses supernatural habits into men. God calls men to lead a divine life in this world and the next. But the natural powers of man are not in themselves capable of leading a divine life. They must be elevated by God to this capability. This God does when, for example, He gives a man the supernatural habits of Faith, Hope, and Charity. But this point will be discussed later on.

SINCE MOST HABITS ARE acquired by human activity, it follows that they can be increased or lessened. They can grow or diminish. The more frequently a man acts honestly, the stronger becomes his habit of honesty. This will be true only when an honest act equals or surpasses in degree the intensity of the habit already established. The man who pays a debt with great reluctance does not increase his habit of honesty. We can suspect that his reluctance is a sign that he is already on the way to losing his habit of honesty.

JUST AS A MAN can increase the strength of a habit by acting in accordance with it, so, conversely, he can lessen its strength and eventually lose it either by acting contrary to it or by ceasing to use it. A temperate man can begin to destroy his habit of temperance by drinking alcohol to excess. The more frequently he drinks to excess, the weaker becomes his habit of temperance in drinking until he has lost it entirely and acquired the contrary habit of intemperance. He is like a farmer who shovels dirt back into his irrigation ditches. If he pours enough back, he destroys the canal altogether.

THERE ARE MANY HABITS which men acquire in one way or another in the course of a lifetime. Habits are distinguished from one another chiefly by their objectives. As the objectives differ, so the habits differ. Telling the truth is different from helping the poor. The habit of truthfulness is different from the habit of mercy.

HABITS CAN ALSO DIFFER in morality. If they incline a man to a morally good action, they are good habits—which men call virtues. If a habit inclines a man to actions which are morally evil, it is a bad habit—what is called a vice. Gluttony in eating or drinking is a vice. Paying one's debts is a virtue.

SINCE MAN ATTAINS OR LOSES his true happiness by his human actions, and since habits are the channels down which man's powers move efficiently to human actions, a man's habits and their morality are of great importance to him. A man with the wrong kind of habit, with those bad habits which we call vices, is moving very efficiently away from God. In colloquial language he is riding a fast express to Hell. A man with the right kind of habit, with those habits we call virtues, is moving very efficiently toward God. In colloquial language, he is flying a plane to Heaven.

CHAPTER VI

Happiness
and Virtue

CHAPTER VI
Happiness and Virtue

HABIT IS THE KEY to efficient human action. But efficiency is not enough. Efficiency alone can lead either to happiness or to misery. A man can wreck his life just as efficiently as he can make it a success. Efficiency must be constructive rather than destructive. Destructive habits are called vices. Constructive habits are called virtues. Vices wound a man's humanity and tend to reduce him to the level of the beast. Virtues perfect his humanity and increase his likeness to God.

VIRTUE IS A GOOD HABIT by which man lives rightly, and which he can never put to a bad use. Man is made to achieve true happiness by the pursuit of moral good. Since man's intellect and will—the human powers which man uses in the pursuit of good —are tendencies to universal truth and universal good, they must be determined to particular acts of goodness by good habits. Virtues are the good habits which perfect man's powers in the pursuit of truth and goodness.

VIRTUE IS NOT, THEREFORE, a hindrance to good living. On the contrary, it is a necessity for good living. A man without virtue is like a genius who is kept forever in the first grade of school. His power of genius is wasted forever on the trivial task of learning again and again how to spell "cat." But a man of virtue is a man set free. His limitless appetite for truth and goodness finds unlimited opportunity for action and conquest in God's world and ultimately in God Himself. Virtue is that perfection of human power which enables man to act successfully in conquering the world for himself and himself for God.

VIRTUE IS A HABIT by which men work well. Virtues can be related to action in two ways—imperfectly and perfectly. Some virtues give man the ability to work well, but they do not of themselves give him the right use of that ability. A carpenter may know well how to make a desk—he possesses the intellectual virtue of art—but this knowledge alone does not produce a good desk. The carpenter may make a poor desk because of laziness or bad will. His art then makes him a good carpenter, but it does not necessarily make him a good man. His art is only an imperfect or relative virtue for while it makes him a good carpenter potentially, it does not make him a good man. On the other hand there are virtues which give a man not only the ability to work well but also the right use of that ability. The virtue of justice not only enables a man to pay his debts on time but it gives him the right use of that ability. It produces the act of paying the debt. Such virtues are perfect virtues, and so they are called simply virtue.

SINCE VIRTUES ARE CONCERNED with truly human acts, they are to be found only in the soul of man, and only in those powers of the soul which distinguish man from the world below him. Virtues are to be found then in the human intellect, the human will and the human sense appetite. But, because of the differing relationships which these powers have to good acts, virtues are found in them in different ways.

SINCE IT IS THE HUMAN WILL which moves both itself and the other powers of man to the pursuit of moral good or perfection, perfect virtue is to be found only in the will and in the other human powers only in so far as they are under the direction of the will. The intellectual virtues of science, wisdom and understanding are concerned only with the contemplation of truth. By themselves they do not produce morally good acts. They are therefore only relative or imperfect virtues. A man may be a good scientist, but morally a very bad man. The intellectual virtue of art is also an imperfect virtue. It enables a man to know how to make things well, a statue, for example, or a symphony. But it does not necessarily make him a morally good man. A man may be a good musician, but morally a very bad man. The intellectual virtue of prudence, on the other hand, is a perfect virtue because it is concerned with right action, with morally good action.

THE SIMPLE AND EMERGENCY PASSIONS of man when considered only as movements of man's sense appetite are not subjects of virtue. But the concupiscible and irascible faculties of man's sense appetite can be directed in their action by human reason. Under this direction of reason the movements of the passions become sources of truly human actions. The man who eats properly under the direction of reason—because reason tells him food is necessary for life—is performing not just an animal action, but a truly human action. The powers of the sense appetite are subject to virtue in so far as they are subject to reason. The virtues of the passions are their habitual conformity with reason.

THE WILL, WE HAVE SAID, is the proper subject of virtue. This is because it is the will which moves man to good acts. But a distinction must be made here. The will is itself an inclination to the good which is proper to it in accordance with reason. From this point of view the will does not need virtues to make it perfect in its action. Man's will does not need habits or virtues when man is seeking only what is good for himself. But man has relationships with other men and with God. In relation to them he must act altruistically, unselfishly. In this regard the will needs virtues to perfect it, such virtues as justice and charity.

ALL HUMAN VIRTUES will be either intellectual or moral. Human virtue is a habit which perfects man in view of his doing good deeds. But there are only two sources of truly human actions: the human intellect and the human will. Every human virtue must be a perfection of one of these two sources of human action. If it perfects man's intellect, it will be an intellectual virtue. If it perfects his will, it will be a moral virtue. From this it follows that human virtue makes man perfect as man. Virtue is the perfection of the powers of reason and will which raise man above the level of the beast and make him the image of God. God's life consists of His Divine Knowledge and His Divine Love. The perfection of human life consists also of knowledge and love. Man needs therefore the intellectual and moral virtues which enable him to know and love well.

THE INTELLECTUAL VIRTUES perfect man's intellect in the pursuit of truth, which is the good of the intellect. Truth may be known either speculatively or practically. The speculative intellect simply contemplates truth. The mathematician simply contemplates the truth that one plus one equals two. The practical intellect considers truth as the measure of action. The violinist considers the rules of fingering and bowing the violin as the rule or measure for playing the violin well. The prudent man considers the rules for contracts as the measure of making and fulfilling contracts well. Both the speculative and the practical intellect need virtue for perfect action.

A TRUTH MAY BE KNOWN speculatively in two ways. It may be known in itself, or it may be known in and through some other truth. That a whole is greater than any of its parts is a truth that is known immediately in itself. Truths of this kind are known naturally to the intellect. They are the principles—or starting-points—of all other knowledge. The habitual knowledge which man has of these principles of all thought is called the habit or virtue of understanding.

A TRUTH WHICH IS KNOWN in and through some other truth can also be known in two ways. It may be seen as true in the light of its proximate principles. An habitual knowledge of truth in this way is called science or knowledge. Science always deals with a particular subject. So we have the sciences of mathematics, of physics, of biology and so on. In all the sciences we either deduce truths from some other truth or we interpret facts in the light of the principles furnished by the intellectual virtue of understanding.

B UT THE HUMAN INTELLECT is never satisfied with the proximate explanation of truth. It is natural for the mind to seek the ultimate explanation of everything. The habitual knowledge of the ultimate or last explanation of all things is called wisdom. Wisdom is that intellectual virtue which enables the mind of man to see everything in order in its proper place. Wisdom gives man the ultimate explanation of all things. Through wisdom man sees the relation of one truth to another, of one science to another, and of all truths and sciences to the ultimate truth which is God.

A S A RATIONAL BEING man is made for truth. It is natural for him to want to know and understand all things. The virtues of the speculative intellect—understanding, science, and wisdom—are necessary for the perfection of man as man. Understanding is the native endowment of every man. Science and wisdom must be acquired. In our modern world science, especially positive science, is valued very highly. We have been led to think that the advancements of the positive sciences such as chemistry and physics and mathematics will produce heaven on earth for man. The sciences are certainly intellectual virtues that make man perfect. But without wisdom—the highest of all the sciences—they cannot make man as perfect as he should and can be. Wisdom alone gives man the ultimate explanation of things. Wisdom alone answers the ultimate questions: Where did the world come from? Where did man come from? Where is man going? The astronomer may be able to explain how the earth revolves in its orbit around the sun. But without wisdom he cannot explain the origin or the existence of either the sun or the earth. The virtue of wisdom should be the goal of all human effort in the acquisition of knowledge.

THE PRACTICAL INTELLECT of man can also be the subject of virtue. The practical intellect is concerned with the truth about things to be made or things to be done. The virtue which perfects the intellect in the knowledge of how to make things is called art. It is art which enables a musician to know what a symphony is, how it is constructed, how it should be written, how it should be played by an orchestra. Since man is naturally a maker of things, the virtue of art plays an important role in man's life on earth. We all admire—in fact sometimes we envy —the man who can make his own garden, or make and repair his own furniture or furnace. Whenever man is engaged in the making of something, there he needs art. Art is the knowledge of the right way to make things.

WHEN THE PRACTICAL INTELLECT of man is concerned with the right way to act or to do things as a human being, then we need the virtue of prudence. An art is always concerned with something specific. We can have an art of farming, of home-building, of music, of portrait painting, and so on. But prudence is concerned with all human actions precisely as they are human. Prudence deals with the right way to do or perform man's truly human acts, that is, his free acts. Because prudence deals with the right way to act humanly, it is an intellectual virtue. As a virtue its objective is good. As a virtue directing human acts its virtue is moral good. But human actions derive their goodness or evil—at least in part—from the goodness or evil of the goal to which they are directed. Hence prudence is dependent on the goodness of the will, for it is the human will which chooses the goal of human activity. If a man's will chooses to rob a bank, his practical intellect may counsel him on the best way to rob the bank successfully. But it is not the virtue of prudence which makes him a successful thief. Prudence is a good habit, directing man's forces to moral good. If a man wills a good goal, for example, to provide an education for young men who cannot afford it themselves, then prudence will help him to do this well. It is prudence which will tell him the good or the best way to attain the goal of his will.

SINCE MAN ACHIEVES true happiness by his good human acts, and since prudence is the virtue which directs human acts well according to the standards of human reason, it is the presence or the absence of prudence in a man's mind which makes the difference between successful living and dismal failure, between happiness and misery.

UNDERSTANDING, SCIENCE, WISDOM, AND ART are in themselves perfections only of man's intellect. They are not of themselves moral perfections. They do not of themselves make man as man morally good or morally evil. They are therefore in themselves relative or imperfect virtues. But prudence, since it directs man's free acts, is concerned with the pursuit of moral good and the avoidance of moral evil. It perfects man as man and so it is a perfect virtue.

THESE INTELLECTUAL VIRTUES are distinct from what we call the moral virtues. The moral virtues are habits modifying the appetite of man for good. If knowledge necessarily produced moral good in all man's actions, there would be no need for moral virtues distinct from the intellectual virtues. But experience shows that knowledge and virtue are not absolutely identical. A thief may know that it is wrong to steal, but he will still do so. It is true that human reason is the first principle or source of all human acts. But reason is not a totalitarian dictator of all human actions. The appetite of man obeys reason, but with a certain power of opposition. The passions of the sense appetite, for example, often oppose the dictates of reason, and sometimes even override reason. Reason may tell a man that gluttony is evil. But his desire for tasty food or for alcoholic liquors may rebel against reason and lead him to the sin of gluttony. For a man to act well, then, in the moral order he needs not only intellectual virtues to perfect his reason, but moral virtues to dispose his appetite in conformity with reason.

THE INTELLECTUAL and the moral virtues are distinct. But they have some relationships. Moral virtue is impossible without the intellectual virtues of prudence and understanding. Prudence enables a man to choose well the proper means to achieve his goals. The moral virtue of justice in the will enables a man to choose to pay his debts. But it is prudence in the intellect which decides on the proper way to pay the debt. A man without prudence might decide to pay Peter by stealing money from Paul. A prudent man would choose a good means of paying Peter. He would pay Peter from his salary or bank account. Prudence in turn needs the assistance of understanding, the habitual knowledge of first principles of the intellectual or moral order.

ON THE OTHER HAND, though understanding, science, wisdom, and art can be found in a man who has no moral virtue, prudence cannot exist without moral virtue. For prudence deals with particular acts. And particular acts are done by men for ends or goals. They will be good or evil as the goal is good or evil. The goal of a particular act is then the principle or source of that act. Man performs the act because he intends to achieve the goal he has chosen. Prudence then, as a virtue, demands rightness of intention here and now in this particular act. Now rightness of intention in relation to goals is the work of the moral virtues which perfect man's appetite. If the appetite is properly tending to moral good, then prudence can work in the direction of means to the good. In fact it is the right intention in the appetite which gives the intellect a real capacity for judging rightly how to achieve a good goal. A man whose will is just has, as it were, a real capacity for judging well how to act justly in particular questions of justice. On the contrary, a man whose will is unjust finds it hard to judge questions of justice properly. The passion of an unjust man for the bodily pleasures which money will bring will prevent his reason from judging properly when he should pay his debts and when he may defer payment. Prudence then absolutely demands righteousness in the will and sense appetite.

MAN AS MAN IS MADE for truth and goodness, for knowledge and love. The virtues, both intellectual and moral, are the canals which direct the powers of his intellect and will to the attainment of the true and the good. A truly human life is impossible without the virtues. The world is built on truth and filled with goodness. It offers man unlimited opportunities for knowledge and love. From the heights of God to the inconceivable littleness of the electron in the atom, all the universe lies open to the reason and will, the knowledge and love of man. The virtues are the perfections which enable the intellect of man to embrace all truth and the will of man to love all good.

CHAPTER VII

Unity in Human Action

Virtue: the Principle of Unity

Cardinal Virtues

Theological Virtues

CHAPTER VII
Unity in Human Action

IN UNION THERE IS STRENGTH. The world abounds with proofs of the truth of this old axiom. A nation is strong and successful because its government and citizens work together to achieve the common goals of all. An industry or a labor union is strong because all its members work together to realize their common objective. Machines, such as the automobile, are effective when all their parts are properly adjusted and united to one another so that they function together to produce the object for which the machine is made. This is true of man and the pursuit of happiness. Man pursues happiness by the proper use of his powers of reason, will and the sense appetite. But these various human powers must be properly adjusted to one another if man is to function as an efficient unit in the pursuit of his goal. Each of these powers has its own good to achieve. But they cannot work for man's true happiness when they are divided against one another. If they are to function smoothly and successfully in the achievement of man's real good, they must be properly subordinated to one another and to God.

THE PROPER ADJUSTMENT of man's human powers to one another is the work of the virtues. To reach true happiness man must know what true happiness is and how it is to be achieved. This is the work of the human intellect or reason. Reason is adjusted to this task by the intellectual virtues. If man were called by God to a purely natural destiny and if each man were alone in the world, man's will would need no special virtue to enable it to function properly in the pursuit of good, for it is in itself an inclination to seek the good of reason. But man is called by God to a good which surpasses his natural powers—the vision of God—and so his will needs the virtue of charity, for example, to seek and embrace God with a supernatural love. And man lives in this world with other men. His will needs the virtue of justice to incline it to give to other men what is their due. The passions of the sense appetite are in themselves only strong tendencies to seek good or avoid evil. They must be under the control of reason and will if they are to aid man in the pursuit of his true happiness. Further, as experience shows us, left to themselves they tend to revolt against reason and will. They need virtues to adjust them properly to reason and will. Temperance is the virtue which moderates and, if there be need, restrains the simple or concupiscible passions in their pursuit of good. Fortitude is the virtue which moderates and directs the emergency or irascible passions in their pursuit of good.

TO FUNCTION PERFECTLY in the pursuit of good a man needs the equipment of all the virtues. Philosophers and theologians distinguish many virtues in the perfect man. They will be considered later in this book. For the present it is sufficient to speak of the cardinal virtues which make man a perfect agent in the pursuit of natural happiness and the theological virtues which make man a perfect agent in the pursuit of the supernatural happiness of the vision of God.

THE CARDINAL VIRTUES are prudence, justice, temperance and fortitude. These four virtues are called cardinal virtues because they are the principal natural virtues which coordinate human activity and direct it to the good of man as man. They are the roots from which all the other human virtues grow. This is so because these four virtues perfect all man's natural powers in their functions in the pursuit of good. From the point of view of reason man needs to command here and now in any particular situation what is to be done or avoided in the pursuit of the good sought by the will. This is the function of the virtue of prudence. From the point of view of man's appetite for good, some of man's actions are concerned only with the individual himself and others have a social character—they are concerned with what is due to others. Justice is the virtue which perfects the will in man's social actions. Justice inclines a man to give to everyone what is due to him, whether that other be God or another man. As for those actions which perfect only the individual himself, these flow from the sense appetite of man. But the sense appetite consists of both the concupiscible and the irascible faculty. The virtue of temperance is needed to curb man's concupiscible appetite for sensible good. The virtue of fortitude is needed to strengthen his irascible appetite in the pursuit of the difficult good. Any other individual virtues which man may have or need for natural human actions will be related to one of these fundamental natural virtues.

WITH THESE CARDINAL VIRTUES a man is equipped perfectly for the pursuit of natural good. These virtues make man a unit, an efficient unit in the pursuit of good. With them in his possession man is not at odds with himself. His powers are not struggling with one another for mastery. Reason perceives man's true good and the will and the sensitive appetite follow reason to the perfection of man. Without any one of these virtues man is no longer a unit. He is no longer efficient. The conflict between his natural powers will destroy him. The revolt of will or sense appetite against right reason destroys man in the sense that it prevents man from achieving his true happiness and makes him seek false happiness in riches or pleasure or some other unsatisfactory goal. With the cardinal virtues man is at peace with himself, with the world, and with God. Without the cardinal virtues man is like a machine whose cog-wheels or gears are not meshed properly. As they work, their lack of proper adjustment makes them tend to fly apart or injure one another. So it is with man. When the reason, will and sense appetite are not properly adjusted to one another their action tends to injure one another and to disrupt the unity of man. When they are properly adjusted through the cardinal virtues, then man works as a smoothly adjusted machine, applying all his power at the right time to the task in hand.

IF MAN WERE CALLED by God to a purely natural happiness the cardinal virtues would be sufficient for man. But God calls man to the vision of Himself. This goal is beyond the reach of any purely natural powers. If man is to reach it through the action of reason and will, these powers must be made capable of a supernatural activity which will lead man to this goal. It is the role of the theological virtues of faith, hope, and charity to fit man's reason and will for the task of seeking successfully the vision of God. These virtues are called theological virtues because their object is God—they direct us to God— because they are infused in us by God alone, and because they are made known to us by God alone through divine revelation.

IN THE NATURAL ORDER man needs the knowledge of first principles to direct his activity. In the super-natural order man needs the knowledge of supernatural principles to perfect his intellect for the pursuit of God. Through the virtue of faith God gives man this knowledge. In the natural order man's will tends naturally to its object, the good. In the supernatural order man's will tends to the vision of God through the virtue of hope. In the natural order man's will grasps in love the good which it has obtained. In the supernatural order man's will grasps the God of the supernatural in the virtue of charity. The world of God as He is in Himself is not a world naturally open or accessible to man. But the infused virtues of faith, hope, and charity open up this world of God to man. It is as if a poor man were admitted to the palace of his king. He can roam the corridors almost at will, inspect almost all the rooms. And if he stays long enough and learns to behave as one should in the palace of the king, one day he will be admitted into the very presence of the king himself. Faith, hope, and charity set man free in God's palace. By living a life of faith, in hope and charity he is preparing himself to be admitted into God's presence. If he dies with these virtues he will be admitted into God's presence. He will have achieved the purpose of his existence—the attainment of the vision of God.

ALL THE VIRTUES, both natural and supernatural, are intended to make man what he ought to be. The natural virtues will make man perfect simply as man. The supernatural virtues will make man perfect as the child of God and the heir of heaven. The cardinal virtues subject all man's powers to the command of right reason. The theological virtues subject man's reason and will to God. Together they put all man's powers in proper order for the attainment of the vision of God. Properly conceived then, the virtues are not restraining forces destroying man's freedom. The man who shows you the right way to do something has not destroyed your freedom. He has really set you free to use your powers most effectively. Similarly the virtues set man's truly human powers of reason and will free to work most effectively for happiness. Nor do the virtues destroy or unduly limit the passions of the sense appetite. By bringing the passions under the control of reason they enable man to employ all his force in the pursuit of real happiness.

THE VIRTUOUS MAN is not frustrated by his virtues. He is not prevented from entering wholeheartedly into the vast arena of human life to impress his personality upon the world. Rather the virtues enable him to act intelligently and strongly in the world. He knows what he wants, where he is going, how to get there. And he has the strength of will and passion to pursue his course even in the face of obstacles. In a word the virtuous man is the perfect man.

CHAPTER VIII

Striving for Happiness

CHAPTER VIII
Striving for Happiness

THE PERFECTION which the natural and the infused supernatural virtues confers on human reason, will and sense appetite enables man to reach happiness through his human acts. If men were born with all these virtues perfectly formed in them and if these virtues could never be lost, the attainment of happiness would be easy. But men are not born with the full perfection of all the virtues and the different virtues can be lost in different ways. We must now consider how men come into possession of the virtues, how the virtues work for happiness, and how they are to be preserved until they accomplish the attainment of happiness.

NATURE, MAN, AND GOD all cooperate in giving man the virtues he needs for successful human living. Nature gives all men the seeds or the beginning of the natural virtues. For nature gives human reason the knowledge of the first principles of knowledge and action. Every man knows naturally the first truths, which are the foundation of all science and wisdom. Every man knows naturally, for instance, that the whole is greater than any of its parts. Every man knows naturally that good is to be done and evil avoided. This last truth is the source of all the practical knowledge by which reason directs human action to the goal of happiness. Again nature makes the will a natural appetite for good in accordance with reason. Finally, we can see that nature gives individual men a certain slant or tendency toward certain virtues by the disposition or temperament which she gives men's bodies. Some men seem to have by nature an inclination to the virtue of fortitude, for example, or temperance. It is nature then which gives men their first push in the direction of the natural virtues.

TO ACQUIRE THE NATURAL VIRTUES man must follow this push from nature. The natural virtues are habits. They can be acquired therefore in the same way as any natural habit. If a man wishes to acquire the natural virtue of temperance, he must do so by acting temperately. The natural moral virtues follow the norm or rule of right reason. To act temperately a man must follow the rules laid down by reason for the proper use, for example, of food and drink for himself and of the use of sex for the preservation of the human race. Repeated acts of temperance in accordance with the dictates of reason or prudence will form the habit or virtue of temperance in a man. The other virtues will be acquired in the same way.

THE SUPERNATURAL VIRTUES, whether theological or moral, cannot be acquired through nature or natural human action. They must be infused into man's soul by God. The infused theological virtues of faith, hope and charity, have God Himself—as He is in Himself—for their immediate object. Since this Object—God as He is in Himself—is beyond the natural powers of man, the virtues which unite man to this Object are also beyond man's powers to acquire. God Himself must give virtues to man. The infused moral virtues of prudence, justice, temperance, and fortitude do not have God as He is in Himself as their immediate Object. But they are concerned with the right use of man's actions and passions in relation to the Object of the theological virtues, God in Himself. Consequently they cannot be acquired naturally by man, but must be infused by God. How God infuses these virtues will be discussed later. For the present it is sufficient to note that they must be infused by God if man is to act efficiently in the pursuit of the vision of God.

HOW DO THE VIRTUES WORK in the pursuit of happiness? Since all human action is intelligent action, it follows that every human act is directed to some goal. The perfection of any human act and the perfection of the virtue which produces the act will be measured by the goal itself or the suitability of the act to attain the goal. The virtues then will work according to the rule or measure that is proper to them.

THE NATURAL MORAL VIRTUES work according to the mean of human reason. When we speak of the mean of reason we are speaking of the middle path that reason indicated between two other paths that lead to excess. Temperance in eating means to eat just enough to maintain good health. It follows a middle path between gluttony which would destroy health by an excess of food and starvation—or extreme fasting—which would destroy health by an excessive lack of food.

THE MEAN OF REASON or of virtue has nothing to do with the weakness of character which men despise in the timid compromiser. Following the mean of virtue does not paralyze human activity. It sets it free to follow the path of man's real good. The drunkard may taunt the temperate man by saying he can drink him under the table. But the weakness is in the drunkard who cannot control his intemperate appetite. The strength is in the temperate man who can control his appetite. The drunkard debases his human nature by delivering his reason and will to the slavery of alcohol. The temperate man may take a drink. But he will never allow alcohol to enslave his reason and frustrate his free will.

THE NATURAL MORAL VIRTUES, then, follow the rule of reason in the pursuit of natural good. Sometimes this rule of reason is a rule which reason itself places in human actions. Sometimes this rule or mean is dictated by the object of the action.

IN QUESTIONS OF JUSTICE the rule of reason must be conformed to the object of justice, which is to give to everyone his due. If John owes Peter ten dollars, he must pay him ten dollars, no more and no less. To pay him less is to fail in justice. To pay him more is to be more than just. The excess amount is not due to justice but to some other virtue, such as liberality, or perhaps even to a vice such as vanity.

BUT THE MEAN of the other moral virtues is the mean which reason itself decides. It is reason which decides what is temperate for a man or what fortitude requires. This shows that the mean of moral virtue may vary from man to man. A man with a strong body and a tolerance for alcohol may take three drinks and still be temperate. But another man with no tolerance for alcohol may get drunk on two drinks and be intemperate. Similarly it may be fortitude for a trained fireman to enter a burning building to rescue a man. But it will be rashness for an untrained by-stander to try the same thing. It is prudence which determines the mean of the other virtues. It is prudence which determines what the individual can and should do, when he should do it and how he should do it.

THE NATURAL INTELLECTUAL VIRTUES also work according to rule. The object of the intellect is truth. The object of the speculative intellect is truth taken absolutely. The object of the practical intellect is truth in conformity with a right inclination to the good.

FROM THE STANDPOINT of speculative truth, the intellect is measured by things. The intellect must know or express things as they are in themselves. The intellect is perfected by the virtue of science when it knows just what the moon is made of. But it is imperfect when it persists in believing that the moon is made of green cheese.

THE VIRTUES of the practical intellect are art and prudence. Art is concerned with the making of things. Its rule is the rule of reason in so far as reason is conformed to things. When an artisan designs a violin he must make the design according to the nature of a violin. He cannot so design it that when it is made it is not a violin but a saxophone. Prudence is concerned with human actions. It is concerned therefore with the appetite of man, with his will and sense appetite. Prudence then follows the mean of reason. It must measure the actions of justice, temperance, and fortitude according to the circumstances of the individual man.

THE RULE OR MEASURE of the supernatural infused virtues is different from that of the natural virtues. In the case of the infused moral virtues the mean of virtue is not the rule of human reason but the rule of the Divine law or the Divine Mind. Like the natural virtue of temperance the infused virtue of temperance rules the actions of the simple passions of man. But the mean of the two virtues may be different. Natural temperance may lead a man to eat enough to keep his body in good health. Natural temperance is concerned only with the natural good of human nature. But supernatural temperance is concerned with the passions in so far as they are related to the supernatural destiny of man—the vision of God. Supernatural temperance therefore may lead a man to fast from food in order to bring his body into subjection to his soul so that his soul may go more freely and easily to God. The infused moral virtues follow the mean not of human reason but of the Divine Mind.

FROM THE POINT OF VIEW of their object the theological virtues—faith, hope, and charity—have no mean at all except God Himself. But since God is infinite Truth and the Supreme and Almighty Good, a man can never believe too strongly in God, nor hope too confidently in God's goodness, nor love God too much.

BUT BECAUSE MAN IS IMPERFECT it is possible to find a mean for the theological virtues in man himself. Because God is good and all-powerful, man can never hope too much in God. But because man himself is imperfect, he can hope for too much or too little from God. The man steeped in sin may hope to attain the vision of God while remaining a sinner. This is presumption—hoping for more than he deserves from God. Or the man who can still turn from sin to God may not do so because he fears that God, Who is all merciful, will not forgive him. This is despair—hoping for too little from God.

ALL THE VIRTUES work according to some measure, whether that measure be in things, in man or in God. Moreover all the virtues are related in some way to one another. This is not surprising when we consider that the ultimate object of all the virtues is to lead man to the vision of God. The virtues, as virtues, make man a perfect agent. But man acts for happiness. We should expect therefore that the virtues which enable man to attain happiness should have some intrinsic connection with one another.

PRUDENCE IS THE BOND of union of the moral virtues, whether natural or infused. For the virtues of justice, temperance, and fortitude moderate the actions of the will or the passions of the sense appetite in accordance with the rule of human reason—in the natural virtues—or of the Divine Mind—in the infused moral virtues. If a man who cannot swim were to dive into the ocean to save a drowning woman, we would not say he had fortitude. His brave action was not prudent. It had no chance of success.

IT IS ALSO TRUE that prudence cannot exist without the moral virtues. This is because prudence is concerned with the choice of the right means to attain the goal of human action. But prudence presupposes a right inclination in the appetite to a good goal. If this inclination is not made perfect by the moral virtues, then prudence will not exist in the intellect. The man who has no real inclination to act justly through the virtue of justice will not judge prudently when he should pay his debts. This is the situation of those people who are continually in debt and who never pay any of their debts until their debtors force them to do so. Or again, the intemperate man can never judge prudently when he has drunk enough alcohol. This is the situation of those poor unfortunates who always think they can take one more drink without getting drunk.

SINCE THE NATURAL MORAL VIRTUES seek only man's natural good they can exist without the infused virtue of charity. But since the infused moral virtues moderate man's appetite in relation to his supernatural destiny, they cannot exist without charity. Supernatural justice, temperance, and fortitude are impossible without supernatural prudence. But supernatural prudence is concerned with the supernatural means to man's supernatural destiny, the vision of God. Hence it cannot function properly unless man's will is properly ordered to God in the supernatural order. This proper supernatural disposition of the will is the work of the infused virtue of charity. Charity is necessary therefore for the proper functioning of the supernatural moral virtues.

SIMILARLY THE INFUSED MORAL VIRTUES are required if charity is to achieve its end. Charity, love of God, is the source of all human actions that lead to the vision of God. But it cannot have its proper effect unless all man's actions are made proportionate to this goal. It is the infused moral virtues which direct man's actions to the goal of charity.

THE THEOLOGICAL VIRTUES of faith and hope can exist without charity. But then they are not perfect virtues. Perfect virtue enables a man to act perfectly in the pursuit of happiness. But an act of faith which does not proceed under the impulse of charity is not a perfect act of faith. Believing in God without loving Him does not effectively lead a man to God. Similarly hope cannot be perfect without charity or the love of God. The sinner who hopes for Heaven through some future repentance is doing a good thing, but he is not doing it well. To hope perfectly in God's goodness a man must love God and be in union with God's will.

OF COURSE CHARITY ITSELF is impossible without faith and hope. Could anyone love a man if he did not believe it was possible to be or become his friend? Or if he despaired of ever gaining his friendship? So it is with man in relation to God as He is in Himself. Man must believe it is possible to attain a perfect friendship with God in Heaven and he must hope to attain this friendship through God's power before he can love God as his supernatural destiny.

TO SAY THAT VIRTUES are related to one another and that some cannot exist without others is not to say that all the virtues are equal in perfection. Virtues will vary in perfection according to the perfection or goodness of their objects and according to the degree of virtue in a man.

THE GREATER THE OBJECT of a virtue the greater the virtue. The theological virtues whose immediate object is God surpass all the other virtues in excellence. Charity surpasses faith and hope because it is more closely related to God. For in faith we cling to God without seeing him and in hope we trust we will obtain the vision of God which we do not yet have. But in charity we are already united in love with God.

AS FOR THE INTELLECTUAL and the moral virtues, from one point of view the intellectual virtues are superior and from another point of view the moral virtues are superior. Since the object of the intellect is universal truth, whereas the object of man's appetite in this life is always some particular good, the object of the intellectual virtues is in this way superior to the object of the moral virtues. But if we consider virtue in relation to human action, then moral virtue is more excellent because it perfects man's appetite which moves all man's powers to action. Good intellectual habits make a man good intellectually. But good moral habits make man good as man.

AMONG THE MORAL VIRTUES justice is the best. This is so because justice is a perfection of the will, man's rational appetite, rather than of man's sense appetite. It is so also because justice sets a man in proper order to other persons besides himself. Fortitude is more excellent than temperance because it subjects his sense appetite to reason in important matters of life and death.

AMONG THE INTELLECTUAL virtues wisdom is pre-eminent. Wisdom has as its object God as the ultimate cause of all things. Hence it surpasses in dignity the other intellectual virtues.

VIRTUES MAY ALSO DIFFER in excellence according to the degree in which a particular man possesses them. Some men are more temperate than others. Even within the same man the virtue of justice, for example, may be stronger than the virtue of temperance. This difference of virtue between men or within one man may be due either to nature, man, or God. Sometimes nature gives one man a strong push toward temperance and another a strong natural tendency to fortitude. Man himself can consciously develop one or more virtues to the extent that his justice is stronger than his fortitude or stronger than another man's justice. Since God is the cause of the infused virtues, they may differ in degree from one man to another according to the gift of God.

THE FACT THAT ONE MAN'S VIRTUES may differ in strength should not be taken as a denial of the points that the virtues are related to one another and that some cannot exist without the others. These points still remain true. But it is a matter of proportion. A regular outfielder on a baseball team should be a good hitter and a good fielder. But he may be a better hitter than he is a fielder. Another good outfielder may be better at fielding than he is at hitting. The point is that he can be better at one aspect of his job than at another and still be good at the job simply. So one man may be more temperate than constant in fortitude and still be a good man.

BUT THE POSSIBILITY and the actual fact of a difference of degree in virtue among men is a proof that virtue makes man's world interesting instead of boring. Some people think that if all men became virtuous all men would be the same and act in the same way. Humorists sometimes think that in a world of virtuous men nobody would ever be able to go through a door because everybody would be waiting virtuously for everybody else to go through first. The infinite variety of ways in which the virtues can be realized in individual men shows that such views are based on ignorance. If all men were perfectly virtuous, they would all be good. But they would be good in different ways. And this difference would provide us with a more pleasing variety in life than vice does. Vice always leads to boredom and despair because only the good is satisfying. Virtue makes life interesting because it is concerned with good which is always pleasing.

CHARITY and the infused moral virtues are lost through any mortal sin. To preserve them man must avoid mortal sin. Faith and hope are lost only by sins opposed to them and are to be preserved by avoiding such sins. The natural virtues are lost either by neglect or by a series of actions contrary to them. They are preserved and strengthened by acting in accordance with them.

THE PRESERVATION of the virtues naturally brings to mind the question of the duration of the virtues. The virtues enable man to pursue successfully the goal of perfect happiness. But when man has attained happiness in the vision of God, will the virtues still remain? Or if a man has failed and has by his failure condemned himself to Hell, will his virtues remain in him?

I T IS OBVIOUS that the saints in Heaven—since their souls have been separated from their bodies—have no disorderly desires for food or the pleasures of sex. Equally they no longer have any difficulties to overcome or dangers to avoid. They have no need therefore for the material element of the virtues of temperance and fortitude. But the order or conformity to reason—whether man's reason or God's law—which these virtues gave to man will still remain. Temperance will remain, as St. Augustine says, without the rebellion of the desires and will take delight in God who knows no imperfection. Fortitude will remain without any fear of evil and will cling to God steadfastly. Justice will remain even materially in so far as it will make man give to God constantly what is due to God. The intellectual virtues will remain in the sense that the mind will retain all the ideas that it learned in the course of a lifetime. But until the soul is reunited with the body at the general resurrection the soul will not be able to use its understanding to the extent that the act of understanding depends on the functioning of the body's senses and imagination.

F AITH, HOPE, AND CHARITY cannot remain in Hell because the condemned sinner cannot believe or hope that he will be united to God in love. He has rejected God forever. Faith and hope cannot remain in Heaven. In Heaven a man does not believe blindly in God. He sees God face to face. In Heaven a man does not hope to possess God. He already possesses Him. But charity is love of God and man will go on loving God for all eternity in Heaven.

S INCE CHARITY ALONE remains completely and most perfectly in Heaven, charity is the greatest of all the virtues. The permanent character of charity reveals to us also the secret of the unity which the virtues give man. The problem of human life is to make human actions conform to the goal of human life. But the true goal of man is the vision of God. The natural virtues perfect man as man. By themselves they will not enable man to attain the vision of God. The infused supernatural virtues will elevate the perfect natural man and enable him to reach the vision of God. The infused moral virtues enable man to use the world in an orderly fashion to bring him to God. The theological virtues order man's intellect and will directly to God. Charity, or the love of God, directs all man's actions to union with God.

CHARITY, OR LOVE, is the answer to the problem of human life and human action. Without charity there is no prudence. Without prudence there are no moral virtues. And without moral virtues the many things which man does and must do in this life cannot be directed to the attainment of happiness.

ONLY THE FULL PANOPLY of the virtues will enable man to act efficiently as a unit in the pursuit of happiness. Without the virtues man is like a faulty machine whose operation is shaking and tearing it apart. With the virtues man is like a well-constructed machine. He is using well all his powers, both natural and infused, in the successful search for happiness.

CHAPTER IX

God and Human Happiness

Familiarity with God's World

The Gifts of the Holy Spirit

The Fruits of the Holy Spirit

The Beatitudes

CHAPTER IX
God and Human Happiness

GOD HAS GIVEN MAN the supernatural infused virtues to enable man to produce those divine-human acts which lead to the vision of God. But His generosity to man has not stopped here. The world of the supernatural is familiar to God. It is His own world. But it is not familiar to man. If man is to make his way safely and easily in the world of the supernatural he must be led by God. Human reason is a sufficient guide to man in the natural world of man. But in the world of God human reason, even when it is perfected by faith, is not an accurate guide. Human reason can enable man to live familiarly with other men and with his inferiors, the animals, the plants, and the earth itself. But God is infinite perfection. Human reason alone cannot give man that familiarity with God which will enable him to act easily and safely in the world of the supernatural. To overcome this difficulty, to make man's progress in God's world easy, God has given man the gifts, fruits, and beatitudes of the Holy Spirit.

IF MAN IS TO BE LED by God in the world of the supernatural, he must be disposed to accept that divine guidance or inspiration. A teacher cannot lead a pupil to the discovery of truth unless the pupil is docile, that is, unless the pupil is disposed to accept or follow the guidance of the teacher. When man is given the infused supernatural virtues he is ready to walk in God's world. But the unfamiliarity of man in that world demands God's guidance. Through the gifts of the Holy Ghost man is disposed to obey that guidance. The gifts of the Holy Ghost are habits that God infuses in man to dispose man to obey readily the inspirations of promptings of the Holy Ghost.

THE PURPOSE OF THE GIFTS, like that of the virtues, is to perfect man's actions. They will be found then in man's power for action, reason and appetite. The gifts of understanding, knowledge, wisdom, and counsel are found in the intellect. The gifts of piety, fortitude and fear are found in the appetite.

THE FOUR GIFTS which perfect the intellect do so by completing the virtue of faith. They enable us to know the supernatural world both speculatively and practically. Understanding gives us a swift, easy, intuitive grasp of the meaning of the truths God has revealed to us. Knowledge enables us to judge quickly the created things of the world in their relation to God. Wisdom helps us to judge divine things. And counsel helps us to bring all this knowledge to bear upon the decisions we must make in our particular actions. Piety perfects the virtue of justice in the will by moving us to do good to all men out of reverence for God. Fortitude perfects our appetite by strengthening it divinely against the fear of danger. And fear perfects our appetite against the inordinate lust for pleasures.

THE GIFTS ARE GIVEN TO US by the Holy Spirit, Who dwells in us through charity. They are rooted therefore in charity and will remain with us as long as charity remains. Since charity remains even in Heaven, the gifts will remain with man essentially even in Heaven. That is, though some of the matter with which they deal, for example, fear of danger or lust for pleasure, will no longer plague man in Heaven, yet the gifts will remain in so far as they make man amenable to the action of God in his soul. For in Heaven God will be more perfectly in man's soul than He is while man is still here on earth.

THE GIFTS OF THE HOLY SPIRIT are given to us to produce divine-human acts in us. God produces these acts in us but not without us. When we are moved to action by the Holy Spirit, it is still we who move. The actions are ours. They flow forth from our reason and appetite. The student surgeon who performs an operation under the direction of a master surgeon owes the success of the operation to the master surgeon. Still it is the student who has actually performed the operation. So it is with the acts which we produce under the influence of the gifts of the Holy Spirit.

JUST AS AN APPLE TREE works to produce fruit, so man works to produce good acts. Through the gifts God works with man to produce the fruits of good acts. The good acts which flow from the gifts of the Holy Spirit are called the fruits of the Holy Spirit. If we consider the great variety of good acts which man may produce under the influence of the Holy Spirit, we could say that the fruits of the Holy Spirit are innumerable. St. Paul enumerates twelve fruits of the Holy Spirit: "But the fruit of the Spirit is charity, joy, peace, patience, benignity, goodness, longanimity, mildness, faith, modesty, continency, chastity" (*Gal.* V, 19).

ST. THOMAS TELLS US that St. Paul's list of the fruits of the Holy Spirit is an adequate list because it shows us how the Holy Spirit sets our minds in perfect order in relation to ourselves, to our equals, and to our inferiors. The mind of man is properly disposed in itself when it has the proper attitude toward good and evil. "Charity" or love gives the mind its proper disposition to good for it puts man in possession of the Holy Spirit. "Joy" is the necessary result of the union of man with God in charity. But if a man rejoices in the possession of God in charity, then he is at "peace" in the undisturbed enjoyment of the presence of God. As for the proper disposition of the mind toward evil, "patience" prevents a man's mind from being disturbed when evil threatens, and "longanimity" or "long-suffering" prevents the mind from being disturbed when good things are delayed in coming.

IN RELATION to his neighbors or equals, man can have the will to do good to them, and this is "goodness", or he will actually do good for them and this is "benignity." Or if his neighbor inflicts evil on him, he can bear it with equanimity, and this is "mildness" or "meekness"; or he can refrain from doing harm to his neighbor, and this is "faith" or "fidelity." In relation to his inferiors man can have "modesty", which moderates his external actions, and "continency" and "chastity", which moderate his internal actions.

THE BEATITUDES are the most heroic or perfect fruits of the Holy Spirit in man. Like the fruits they are acts which proceed from the infused virtues as perfected by the gifts of the Holy Spirit. But they are the most perfect divinely human acts which man can perform. Consequently Christ Himself has attached a reward to them both in this life and in the next. Christ gives us eight beatitudes in the Sermon on the Mount:

"Blessed are the poor in spirit: for theirs is the kingdom of heaven.

Blessed are the meek: for they shall possess the land.

Blessed are they that mourn: for they shall be comforted.

Blessed are they that hunger and thirst after justice: for they shall have their fill.

Blessed are the merciful: for they shall obtain mercy.

Blessed are the clean of heart: for they shall see God.

Blessed are the peacemakers: for they shall be called
    the children of God.
Blessed are they that suffer persecution for justice'
    sake: for theirs is the kingdom of heaven."
                               (*Matt.* V, 3-10)

ST. THOMAS POINTS OUT to us how wonderfully
these beatitudes given us by Christ describe true
happiness in this life and in the next. Men have sought
happiness in sensuality, in action and in the contemplation of truth. In the beatitudes Christ first pointed
out those beatitudes or actions which preserve man
from the error of seeking only sensual happiness.
A life of sensual happiness consists either in the use of
external goods, such as riches and honor, or in following the impulses of passion. The first beatitude makes
us "poor in spirit" and so preserves us from the dangers of riches or worldly honor and vanity. The second
and third beatitudes safeguard us against the disturb-
ing impulses of the passions. Meekness protects a
man against unruly and disorderly impulses of the
emergency passions such as anger. Those who "mourn"
are moved by the Holy Spirit to give up entirely the
good things to which the concupiscible passions incline them for the sake of a higher good.

TRUE HAPPINESS IS FOUND both in activity and in
contemplation. The beatitudes show us how both
can make us happy. Activity, or an active life, plunges
a man into many relationships with his neighbor.
These relationships must be regulated by justice or by
liberality. The fourth beatitude makes a man happy
by giving him the works of justice for which he thirsts
under the influence of the gift of the Holy Spirit. With
regard to liberality, we are perfected to the extent
that we have mercy on the poor and the afflicted.

GOD AND HUMAN HAPPINESS

As for the beatitudes of the contemplative life, "cleanness of heart" and "peace", they are really the effect of the active life. When a man has perfected himself by humility of spirit, by meekness, by justice, and so on, he has purged himself of ignorance and passion and found cleanness of heart. When he has perfected himself by mercy and justice, then he is at peace with his neighbors. In this way the sixth and the seventh beatitudes are a foretaste of Heaven.

The last beatitude is, as it were, a summary of all the other seven. Because a man is confirmed in meekness, mercy, and so on, no persecution will induce him to renounce them. Hence he has laid hold strongly on the kingdom of heaven.

All the beatitudes are a promise from Christ that those who perform the works of the beatitudes will achieve the blessed vision of God in the next life. But they are also a foretaste of Heaven in this life. For a man is happy to the extent that he has a reasonable hope to attain true happiness. And the man who produces the works of the beatitudes through the virtues and gifts of the Holy Spirit has a well-founded hope that God will reward the perfection of his human acts with the final divine gift of the vision of God.

CHAPTER X

Sin and Unhappiness

Nature of Sin

The Enemy of Virtue

The Distinction of Sins

Mortal and Venial Sin

Sin and Disorder

Gravity of Sin

Sin in the Will

Sin: a Disease of Soul

CHAPTER X

Sin and Unhappiness

AS VIRTUE LEADS to happiness, so vice causes unhappiness. Virtue coordinates human energies under the control of reason or of reason enlightened by divine faith. Vice dissipates human energies in the random impulses of the sense appetite. Virtue gives a man peace within himself, with God and with his fellow-men. Vice sets a man at war with himself, with God, and with his fellow-men.

AS VIRTUE IS A GOOD HABIT, so vice is a bad habit. As good acts form a virtue or good habit, so bad acts form a vice or bad habit. As virtue disposes human powers to good acts in accord with reason, so vice disposes human powers to bad acts against reason.

SIN THEN IS BOTH the cause and the effect of vice. Sin or evil actions lead to the formation of vices or bad habits. Vice in its turn leads to further sin. Therefore the primary cause of unhappiness in human life is sin.

ST. AUGUSTINE DEFINES SIN as a thought, word, or deed contrary to the eternal law. There are two elements in every sin. First there is the act itself, which may be a thought, a word, or an external action. Secondly the thought, word, or deed, is contrary to the eternal law of God. It is this second element which makes the act formally sinful. St. Augustine speaks of the "eternal law" rather than the law of right reason. He does this because the law of human reason is based on the eternal law of God and because the eternal law of God directs men in matters of faith which are beyond the reach of human reason.

SIN IS THE ENEMY OF VIRTUE. Sin and virtue cannot be at peace within a man's soul. They will be at war with one another until one or the other is expelled from the soul. But the power of sin to expel virtue varies with the gravity of the sin and the cause of the virtue involved. Charity, or the love of God above all things, is the root of all the other infused virtues. Mortal sin means that a man prefers some creature to God. It is therefore incompatible with charity and with all the virtues rooted in charity. It is true that the theological virtues of faith and hope will not be expelled with charity unless the mortal sin is a sin against either hope or faith. But in this case, although faith and hope remain, their actions are not meritorious since they are not rooted in the love of God, which is charity. The acquired natural virtues are formed by repeated good acts. Consequently one mortal sin is not strong enough to expel an acquired virtue. An acquired virtue can be expelled only by repeated sinful acts which set up a contrary vice. Lastly, venial sin can expel neither the infused nor the acquired virtues. But venial sin is like the psychological warfare which weakens man's will to resist an invader. It can weaken a man's resistance to the major onslaught of mortal sin and so lead to the loss of virtue.

S INS ARE DISTINGUISHED from one another chiefly by their goals or objects. To take someone's property unjustly is different from taking his life unjustly. The first is a sin of theft, the second a sin of murder. To distinguish one kind of sin from another is to distinguish the different objects of sin.

E VERY SIN WILL BE AN OFFENSE against either the sinner himself, or his fellow-man, or God. The man who deliberately gets drunk sins against his own human nature. The man who steals sins against his neighbor. The man who wantonly sets fire to a church sins against God. We might put this in another way by saying that all human acts must be ruled by human reason or by the eternal law of God. Right reason governs human acts in relation to the individual himself and in relation to his neighbor. The eternal law of God includes the law of reason but goes beyond it to regulate man's relations with God in both the natural and the supernatural order. Every sinful act will be an act against either right reason or the eternal law. It will therefore be a sin against the individual himself, or his neighbor, or God.

WE ARE ACCUSTOMED also to other ways of distinguishing sins. We speak of sins of the spirit as contrasted with sins of the flesh, or of sins of thought, word, or deed, or of mortal and venial sins.

THE MOST IMPORTANT of these distinctions is that between mortal and venial sin. While this distinction does not enable us to distinguish precisely the different kinds of sin, it is important because it enables us to gauge the effect which sin has upon a man's relation to God, the ultimate goal of all human life and activity. Since man exists and acts in order to find happiness in God, God is the ultimate goal of all human acts. When a man's soul is so disordered by sin that he turns away from God, that sin is mortal. If the sinner does not repent of that sin, he will not see God. God does not force anyone to enter the kingdom of heaven unwillingly. On the other hand, a man may sin without actually turning away from God—without rejecting God as his ultimate goal. In such a case his sin is a venial sin. Venial sin is like a sickness in the soul. Mortal sin is like death in the soul.

AS VIRTUE MEANS ORDER in human life, so sin means disorder. In the perfectly virtuous man his body is subject to his soul, his sense appetite to his reason and will, and his reason and will to God. But in the sinful man his body is at war with his soul, his sense appetite is in rebellion against his reason and will, and his will at war with his neighbor and with God. Whereas the virtues are united with one another in directing human acts to the attainment of happiness, the vices of the sinful man are at war even with one another, seeking the destruction of man and his chance for true happiness.

WHILE ALL SINS ARE EVIL, they are not all equally evil. The evil in a sin will vary first of all with the object of the sin. Every sinful act will be an attack on some good, and the greater the good attacked, the greater the evil of the sin. It is a greater evil to take a man's life unjustly than it is to steal his automobile. And a direct sin against God, such as blasphemy will be more evil than a sin against man or his external goods.

THE GRAVITY OF SIN will vary also according to the excellence of the virtue which it attacks. A sin against justice, which is a virtue in the will is more serious than a sin against temperance which is a virtue of the concupiscible sense appetite. Similarly a sin against divine faith is more serious than a sin against justice, for faith is a nobler virtue than justice.

GENERALLY SPEAKING SINS OF THE SPIRIT are more serious than sins of the flesh. We say "generally speaking" because it is easy to see that a mortal sin of adultery is a graver sin than a venial sin of intellectual pride. But, all things else being equal, sins of the spirit are more serious than sins of the flesh. This is so for three reasons. First, it is proper for man's spirit to turn to God and natural for his flesh to turn to the goods of the body. Consequently a sin of the spirit is more simply a turning away from God, whereas a sin of the flesh is chiefly a turning toward the good of the body. Secondly, a man ought to love his neighbors and God more than he loves his own body. Hence a spiritual sin against his neighbor or God is more serious than a sin against his own body. Thirdly, the impulses of the flesh drive a man more strongly to sin than do the desires of the spirit. And the stronger the impulse to sin the less grievous will the sin be.

OTHER FACTORS can also increase the gravity of a sin. Deliberate malice in the will makes a sin more evil. Anything that lessens freedom therefore will also make the sin less grievous. The cold-blooded traitor sins more than the soldier who betrays his comrades under torture.

THE DAMAGE DONE by a sinful act will also affect the seriousness of a sin. To say falsely that a man has money in the bank will be less evil than to say falsely that he is a thief. The first lie may make people think he is stingy. But the second will cause him to lose his job.

THE GRAVITY OF A SIN will be measured too by the dignity or excellence of either the person offended or the person sinning. It is worse to sin directly against God than it is to sin against a human being. Likewise it is more serious for a king or president to steal from the public treasury than it is for a private citizen to steal from his neighbor.

A SINFUL ACT is a human act. As a human act it is a voluntary act. Sin comes then chiefly from the will of man. But it can be found also in human reason and the sense appetite in so far as these human powers are inclined to be moved by the will to actions in the pursuit of good or evil.

SIN THEREFORE is a disease of man as man. This is the frightening thing about sin. It is like a cancerous growth in the human personality precisely where it is most human. It eats away gradually a man's control over his own human actions in the pursuit of happiness. A cancerous growth in the body may begin in a less important part of the body. But it will grow until it prevents the working of a vital organ such as the lungs, or brain, or digestive system and so lead to the death of the body. Sin is a cancerous growth in the soul of a man. If allowed to grow it will ultimately prevent man from attaining happiness. And the failure to attain happiness is the death of man as man.

CHAPTER XI

The Causes of Sin

CHAPTER XI
The Causes of Sin

EVERY SINFUL ACT is a voluntary act. It is an act of will. But it is an act of will that is out of order. It is an act of will against the rule of right reason or the eternal law of God. When a pickpocket steals a man's wallet, the sin is not in his hand which seizes the wallet but in his will which chooses to take unjustly the property of another man. The will is directly the cause of the decision to steal. But this choice or decision to steal is contrary to the law or rule of reason. The will is therefore indirectly the cause of the lack of proper order in the act. But it is precisely this lack of order in the act which makes it sinful. Therefore the will is the cause of the sinfulness of the act. Every sinful act then is an act of the will.

BUT MAN'S WILL can be influenced by his reason and by his sense appetite, by God and by the devil, by man and by sin itself. To understand sin clearly we must measure the influence of all these factors on the human will in the commission of sin. It is well known that men attribute their sinful acts to a variety of causes. Some say they sin through weakness. Some claim that the devil makes them sin. Others excuse their sins by appealing to ignorance. To avoid unhappiness intelligently it is necessary to see clearly the true influence of the various causes of sin.

SINCE A SINFUL ACT is an act of the human will, the basic cause of sin is within man himself. It is his will. But the will is influenced by reason and by man's sense appetite. We shall consider first then these internal causes of sin, that is, the reason, the sense appetite and the will of man.

MAN'S REASON CAN BE THE CAUSE of sin through ignorance. The murderer who says he would not have killed if he had known what he was doing testifies to the fact that ignorance can lead to sin. But the exact relationship of ignorance to sin or to moral guilt must be properly evaluated.

SINCE EVERY SIN is a voluntary act, involuntary ignorance excuses a man from sin altogether. If a Catholic totally forgets that it is Friday and eats meat, he is breaking the law of abstinence. But his act is not a sin. If he had known or remembered that it was Friday, he would not have eaten the meat. When a man's ignorance is not his own fault, then the sinful act which he commits through that ignorance is not a sin at all.

BUT THE CASE CHANGES when the ignorance is voluntary or due to the man's own fault. A Catholic eating in a restaurant wants to order meat. But he thinks it might be Friday. He could learn the truth by asking the waiter or by consulting the calendar over the cashier's desk. But he is in too much of a hurry. So he neglects to ask what day it is. When he eats meat that day, his ignorance is partially the cause of his sin, but it does not excuse him entirely. He could have known the truth easily and he was obliged to discover it.

LASTLY IGNORANCE OF ONE of the circumstances of a sinful act may excuse a man from one sin, but not from another. A burglar is surprised in the act of theft by a policeman. He draws his gun in the dark and kills the policeman. Later he discovers he has killed his brother. Had he known the policeman was his brother he would not have fired the gun at all. His ignorance excuses him from the sin of fratricide. But it does not excuse him from the sin of murder, because he knew he was shooting at a man, even though he did not know that the man was his brother.

THE SENSE APPETITE OF MAN can also be a cause of sin. The strength of the passions can distract a man's reason and so lead him to judge that something can be done which is really sinful. A man and a woman may know generally that sexual intercourse outside marriage is sinful. But they will excuse it in their own case on the plea that they have a passionate love for one another. The strength of their passion does not excuse them. But it has hindered their reason from making a proper judgment on their act. It is for this reason that sins of passion are called sins of weakness. For the strength of the passion weakens the judgment of reason and ultimately weakens the strength of the will in the pursuit of what is truly good.

OBVIOUSLY SINS OF PASSION are due to an excessive love for self. A man commits sins of passion because he has an excessive desire to acquire good things for himself. His excessive desire for the good things of this world shows that he loves himself more than he loves God. He is bartering or exchanging God, Who is the perfect, eternal Good, for the temporary, imperfect goods of this world.

PASSION CAN DIMINISH the malice of sin to the extent that it diminishes the voluntariness of the act. But once again we must make a distinction similar to the distinction made in the case of ignorance. The man who commits a sin of lust after he had deliberately inflamed his passions by reading obscene literature or looking at obscene pictures is fully responsible for his sin. But the man who is provoked to anger by a sudden and unmerited physical attack upon himself, is not fully and wilfully responsible for the blows which he strikes in return. And if his anger rises suddenly and strongly, it may even run away with his will and prevent his act from being voluntary at all. In this last case his act will not be a sin at all.

IGNORANCE ON THE PART of reason and the passions of the sense appetite are causes of sin to the extent to which they influence the action of the human will. We might call them contributory causes of sin. The will itself is the basic or essential cause of all sin.

THIS IS SEEN most clearly in what we call sins of pure malice. A sin is purely malicious when a man's will chooses evil knowingly. A "confidence" man knows that defrauding a widow of her life savings of ten thousand dollars is a seriously sinful act. He knows that such an act cannot lead to true happiness in God. But he prefers the money to God. He prefers a lesser temporary good to the eternal friendship of God. He chooses evil knowingly, that is, he prefers a temporary good to the exclusion of the eternal Good which is God.

SINS OF MALICE ARE WORSE than sins of ignorance or passion. This is so because the will is the basic principle of human acts. The man who sins through ignorance or passion is like a man who is temporarily ill. When his illness passes—when he learns better, or when his passion subsides—he can recover easily. But when a man is chronically ill of a serious disease then his recovery is uncertain and sometimes most improbable. So too the man who sins through sheer malice has a disease of the will itself. Neither knowledge alone nor the cessation of passion removes the disease of a bad will. A man with a bad will has a more or less permanent inclination to evil. And because the will is the basic principle or source of free human acts, sins of malice are more evil in themselves. That is why men forgive sins of ignorance or of passion more readily than they forgive sins of malice. We can forgive a man when we say that he did not know what he was doing. But we resent a man's actions when we say that he does them on purpose.

BESIDES THE CAUSES OF SIN which are inside man himself, there are other indirect causes of sin which are outside man. Men say that God, or the devil, or that other men lead them into sin. We must now examine the truth of such claims.

SINCE GOD IS SUPREMELY GOOD, and not at all evil, it follows that God is never the direct cause of sin. As the cause of all being and all action God is the cause of the being in the act of sin. But the lack of order in the sinful act comes only from the defective or sinful will of the sinner.

SOMETIMES GOD PUNISHES a sinner in this life by withdrawing the divine grace which would enlighten the mind of the sinner so that he would see the error of his ways and soften the heart of the sinner so that he would mend his ways. But it is important to note here that God does this only as a punishment of sin. Often, too, such punishment shows the sinner how much he needs God's help and so it leads the sinner to repentance. But in any case God Himself is still not the cause of sin. The sinner still sins by his own bad will.

THE DEVIL IS CERTAINLY a cause of sin in man. He goes about, as Sacred Scripture says, like a roaring lion, seeking whom he may devour. He hates men and would do them all the harm he can.

BUT, ONCE AGAIN, the power of the devil to make men sin should not be exaggerated. Every sin is a free act. And the devil cannot attack man's freedom directly. The devil leads men to sin only by proposing temptations to men. He can act on men's imaginations or their sense appetites. But he cannot get inside the reason or will of man to force him to sin. It is man's privilege to retain his freedom before God, the devil and other men.

MEN CAN LEAD OTHER MEN to sin through suggestion. But this is also only an indirect cause of sin. No one can escape the responsibility of his own sins by saying that other men tempted him. Every man's sins, from this point of view, are his own because he is free to sin or not to sin.

BUT THERE IS A WAY in which one man's sin caused sinfulness in the whole human race. The sin of Adam, the first man of our race, has made all men sinful. It is a dogma of the Catholic Faith, a doctrine revealed by God Himself that Adam's sin in Paradise is passed on to all his descendants by way of human generation. This is indeed a great mystery. But we have God's word that it is true. The important thing is to try to understand correctly what is meant by this truth.

THE SIN WHICH ADAM PASSES ON to all his descendants is called Original Sin. It is called Original because it has as its cause the first or original human sin, that is, the sin of Adam's disobedience to God. It is also Original because it infects all men in so far as they take their origin from Adam, the first man of our race, by way of human generation.

BUT IF SIN is always voluntary, how can Original Sin be sin at all in the descendants of Adam? We are not personally responsible either for Adam's first sin or for the state of sinfulness in which we are born because of his sin. How then can original sin get into our souls?

THE ANSWER to this perplexing question lies in the fact that in God's plan Adam was the head of the whole human race both physically and spiritually. In the plan of God all men were contained physically in Adam. All men are the physical descendants or children of Adam. We all come from the seed of Adam. This applies also to the spiritual order. God regarded Adam as the spiritual head of the human race. He gave to Adam certain spiritual gifts which were to descend to all his posterity as a gift to human nature. We shall discuss the nature of these gifts later. For the present it is sufficient to note that they were gifts to the whole of human nature as it was contained in Adam. If Adam remained faithful to God, they were to be passed on with human nature to all men. If Adam failed God by sin, then these gifts would be lost to all human nature carnally descended from Adam.

BUT ADAM FAILED. He sinned against God. Consequently he lost these gifts for himself and for all his descendants. As a result each human being who is born by way of carnal generation from Adam comes into the world without the original spiritual gifts that God gave the race in Adam. It is the absence of these gifts which we call Original Sin. This sin is voluntary in each human individual not by his own will but by the will of Adam, the physical and spiritual head of the human race. I have sinned, not by my own personal will, but by the will of Adam acting as the head and, so to speak, the spokesman of the whole human race. I lack the original gifts that God generously gave to all human nature because Adam lost them through his own voluntary act of sin. This lack is sin in me in so far as I was contained in Adam who was the head of the human race.

THE GIFTS WHICH ADAM LOST for himself and for all men are summed up in the name Original Justice. Original Justice is a condition of human nature in which all man's powers exist and act in perfect harmony with one another and in subjection to God. Man, as we know him, is a complex or complicated creature. The facts of human nutrition, growth, disease, and death show that there is in man a life similar to the life of plants. The facts of sensation—in sight, hearing and so on—and motion from place to place show that man has a life similar to that of the animals. The facts of human speech and thought and love show that man has the privilege of intellectual life and love and freedom. But, as the facts also show, the proper balancing of these aspects of human life through the functioning of the human powers of the sense appetite and reason and free will is not easy. The sense appetite inclines strongly to its proper object—the pursuit of sensible good and the avoidance of physical evil. Sometimes this inclination is so strong that it blinds the reason and induces the will to act against man's real good. Sometimes the intellectual desire for knowledge leads a man to neglect his sense appetite unreasonably to the injury of his physical health. When God created man He knew that the delicate balance between man's powers that is necessary for successful human living would be too difficult for nature alone to accomplish easily. So he gave to Adam for the whole race the gift of Original Justice.

THROUGH THE GIFT OF ORIGINAL JUSTICE Adam's will and reason were properly subjected to God in grace. Through the subjection of the will to God man's sense appetite and even, to some extent, his vegetative life, were subjected to reason and will. Original Justice thus established in Adam a perfect harmony between man's various powers. His sense appetite was always under the control of reason and will and his reason and will were subject to God. Consequently Adam was a perfect man, fully equipped to pursue the Vision of God efficiently and easily. Had he remained faithful to God this same harmony between man's powers would have been passed on to all his descendants as a gift of grace to human nature. But he failed and so he lost this gift of Original Justice for himself and for all his descendants.

THIS LACK OF ORIGINAL JUSTICE is the only sin we inherit from Adam. His other personal sins do not affect the human race. Further, this sin affects all of us equally. Just as death is equal in all who are dead, for they all lack life, so Original Sin is equal in all since all lack Original Justice. In all men there is the same lack of harmony between man's powers in themselves and in relation to God.

ESSENTIALLY ORIGINAL SIN consists in this lack of harmony between man's powers in themselves and in relation to God. But once the harmony in man's powers established by the gift of Original Justice is disrupted the sense appetite begins its tremendous drive toward sensible good, even against the rule of reason and to the exclusion of man's spiritual good. This lack of order in man's sense appetite is what we commonly call concupiscence.

ORIGINAL SIN then is like a disease in human nature. Human nature is ill-disposed. It is out of order. The sense appetite of man is struggling with his reason and will. And his will has lost its original subjection to God in grace.

IT FOLLOWS from this that Original Sin affects man's soul, not his body. Original Sin is disorder in the soul of man. And since sin is concerned principally with the will, it affects first of all the will, then the reason and finally the sense appetite.

IT IS THE DISORDER of Original Sin in the soul which makes it easy for the individual man to fall into personal sin. We might be tempted to think that this element in God's plan for men was unfair. But we must remember that the Original Justice which God gave Adam to establish proper order in man was a free gift. God did not have to give it to men. And since sin is concerned the loss of this gift does not mean that men must struggle harder to be good than they would if God had not offered this gift to Adam at all. The power of the sense appetite to cloud reason or weaken the will is quite natural in man. Original Justice made this power completely subject to reason and will. But this was a special divine gift.

ONCE WE GRANT that man comes into this world with Original Sin, that is, with disorder in his human powers, and once we recognize that men commit personal, actual sins, then we must also recognize that personal sin leads to other sins. It is this that we have in mind when we speak of the seven capital sins. By a capital sin we mean a sin that is the source or reason for committing other sins. A capital sin is a vice, or an evil inclination whose goal moves man to evil actions or sins in the pursuit of that goal. Thus excessive pride may move a man to steal in order to keep up appearances, or to lie about others in order to emphasize his own excellence. Or envy will lead a man to lie, to cheat, to steal in order to destroy some one else's property or excellence or reputation.

THERE ARE SEVEN CAPITAL SINS or vices: pride, covetousness, gluttony, lust, envy, anger and sloth. They are all disordered inclinations to seek good or to avoid evil.

PRIDE IS AN INORDINATE DESIRE for one's own excellence. But since perfection or excellence depends on a man's possession of good, pride leads man to sin in the pursuit of his own good. The proud man will lie or cheat to better his own reputation.

COVETOUSNESS IS AN INORDINATE desire for wealth or for possessions in this world. Man seeks possessions because he thinks they will enable him to do what he wants. The covetous man will violate all the laws of reason and justice to gain money or property. And when he has them he will either sin to retain them or will use them to commit other sins.

THE GLUTTON SEEKS inordinately the goods of his own body. So he overeats or drinks to excess. The lustful man pursues excessively the good of sex which is intended for the good of the race. He will do whatever is necessary to gain his sinful pleasure.

THE MAN who is eaten by envy sorrows at the good fortune of others because he regards it as a hindrance to his own good. The angry man will seek by any means to injure others because he considers their good a threat to himself. Lastly, the slothful man will neglect his own spiritual welfare because he is afraid of the labor involved in seeking true happiness. His laziness will lead him to omit to do what he ought to do to be truly happy.

OUR SURVEY OF THE CAUSES of sin in human life shows clearly that the chief cause of sin is the human will. Every man is free to choose good or evil. Reason may be ignorant, the sense appetite may be strong. But in the last analysis it is the will which chooses evil. It is the will which sins. The devil may tempt man. But man is free, he need not fall. Original sin, the sin transmitted to us by Adam, may make us weak in the face of temptation. But it does not destroy free will. Our personal sins are our own sins. In relation to Adam we are to some extent like the children of a millionaire who lost all his money. We cannot begin life with as much power as our father once had. But we have, through our free will and the grace of Christ, the power to build up our own fortune in good works. If we sin instead, it will be our own fault.

SINCE SIN IS CHIEFLY DUE to our own bad will, unhappiness is our own making. If we use our free wills and the grace of Christ to build up the virtues within our souls, we can avoid unhappiness. The wise man is the man who cultivates virtue. The happy man is the virtuous man.

CHAPTER XII

The Effects of Sin

The Wounds of Nature

The Stain in the Soul

Sin and Punishment

Eternal Punishment

CHAPTER XII
The Effects of Sin

MAN EXISTS TO BE HAPPY. Sin causes unhappiness. Sin therefore must in some way injure human nature. In this chapter we shall consider the effects of sin on human nature. We can summarize the effects of sin by saying that sin corrupts human nature, stains the human soul and makes man liable to punishment.

FIRST OF ALL sin corrupts or wounds human nature. This is true both of Original Sin and of personal, actual sin. As we said in the last chapter, original sin means the loss of the special divine gift of original justice. Through original justice the sense appetite of man was subject to reason and will, and the will was subject to God. When this gift is taken away, as it is by original sin, then these human powers are said to be wounded.

THROUGH ORIGINAL SIN man's reason becomes subject to ignorance, his will subject to malice, his concupiscible sense appetite loses its subjection to reason and so is wounded by concupiscence, and his irascible sense appetite loses its strength in the face of difficulty and so is said to suffer the wound of weakness.

BUT THESE SAME FOUR WOUNDS are caused also by men's personal sins. Experience shows that a sinful man has lost his ability to judge what he should and should not do. It also shows that his will has become weak in the pursuit of good, that good actions have become difficult for him and his concupiscence more impetuous. All sin therefore wounds a man's nature in the sense that it makes it more difficult for him to pursue his true happiness. As the virtuous man is a man whose powers are efficiently ordered in the pursuit of good, so the sinful man is a man whose powers are dissipated in the pursuit of evil.

SIN WOUNDS HUMAN NATURE but it does not destroy it. Man remains a reasoning being, even after sin. Hence he retains his freedom. This means that it is possible for man to recover from the disease of sin.

THE POSSIBILITY OF RECOVERY is made difficult however by the fact that sins lessen man's natural inclination to virtue. Since every sin is contrary to virtue, every sin must necessarily diminish a man's inclination to be good. This is why repentance of sin is so necessary. The more a man sins without repentance, the weaker is his inclination to virtue. The multiplication of sins builds a barrier between a man and the possibility of his relinquishing his sinfulness and returning to God.

PHYSICAL DEATH is also a penalty of sin. If Adam had not sinned, he would have been preserved immortal by God. This gift of immortality would have been passed on to his children. But by his sin he lost immortality for himself and for us. Every human being must suffer the death of his body.

BUT WE MUST REMEMBER that immortality of the body is not natural to man. By nature we are subject to death. We would have been immortal only through a special gift of God's generosity. In fact, at the end of the world, God will make us rise again to immortality.

ACTUALLY THE MOST HARMFUL EFFECT of sin is the stain which obscures the beauty of the soul of man. The soul is the nobler part of man. In it God has impressed the light of reason which is a reflection of the light of the eternal law or reason of God. When man is justified by God's grace the soul shines also

with the light or glory of divine grace. But mortal sin
is contrary to the light of reason and to divine grace. It
expels grace from the soul and dims the light of reason.
It is this lack of the light which should exist in the soul
which stains the soul. The soul should be resplendent
with the light of reason and of grace. But sin subtracts
the glory of grace and diminishes the power of reason
to illumine man's soul. When we say that sin stains
the soul we mean that just as an ink stain detracts
from the glorious whiteness of a clean shirt, so also sin
detracts from the glory that should light up man's soul.

THIS STAIN IN THE SOUL will remain as long as man
does not turn away from his sin and return to God.
Sin is a turning away from God to some lesser temporary good. The stain of sin will remain in the soul
until the sinner turns from the lesser good to God. The
act of sin is over and done with as soon as the action is
completed. The lesser good which the sinner sought
may pass away. The thief may spend all the money he
stole. But his soul remains stained until his will turns
back to God.

THE SAD PART OF THIS STAIN in the soul is that it
darkens the light of reason and makes it difficult
for man to see clearly the good he should seek. And,
worst of all, if the stain of mortal sin remains until
death, then the soul of the sinner remains divorced
from God, its only true happiness, for all eternity.

THE SOUL IN THE STATE OF SIN is out of order. Its
sinful act was out of order and the consequent
state of sin in the soul is against the order willed by
God. Hence sin demands punishment.

SIN IS PUNISHED by the authority to whose order it
is opposed. But all sin is either against the order
of human reason in the individual, or against the order

of human reason in the rulers of society, or against the order of the divine law. Sins therefore are punished by one or all of these authorities. In the individual, sin is punished by remorse. When a man's reason sees the disorder in sin, it induces in the man the pain of remorse. In this way every sin brings its own punishment. When man has sinned against the laws of society, then the civil authority imposes its own penalties. In this way men are sometimes punished by fines or prison sentences and so on. Since every sin is against the divine law God also punishes sin.

GOD PUNISHES SIN in this present life and even after death. But the punishment inflicted by God is always proportionate to the guilt involved in the sin. Since sin involves a turning away from God and a turning to some lesser good, divine punishment is measured according to these two elements in sin. The sinner who turns away from God does not want God for his ultimate happiness. God will not force Himself upon such a man. Consequently if a man dies in such a state he will suffer the pain of loss, that is, he will never see God. But the sinner has turned away from God by turning to some lesser good thing in this world. For this he will be punished by the pain of sense.

FROM THE POINT OF VIEW of punishment the distinction between mortal and venial sin is important. Venial sin does not destroy the basic order of man's will to God as his ultimate goal. The venial sinner is not choosing some worldly good to the exclusion of God. Hence he does not merit an eternal punishment. But mortal sin does turn a man's will away from God. In a mortal sin the sinner does choose some worldly good to the exclusion of God. Therefore it merits an eternal punishment. Venial sins will slow down a man's progress to God. But mortal sins put man on the road away from God, on the road to Hell.

SINCE VENIAL SIN HAS, in fact, the dangerous habit of leading to mortal sin, both types of sin are the enemies of human happiness. The wise man, if he has fallen into sin, will try to repair the damage he has done to himself. Now the stain of sin—which remains in the soul after actual sin—is removed when the sinner turns his will back to God. Sin is a disorder in the soul. It is healed by restoring order to the soul. This is accomplished by God's grace. But the penalty of sin still remains to some extent. Sin has broken the order of God's world and the damage must be paid for. The sinner can do this by inflicting some punishment on himself or by accepting the punishments which God may send him in this life or in Purgatory.

THIS DEBT OF PUNISHMENT for sin shows the illusory character of the happiness sought by sin. Every sin must be paid for in one way or another. Every sin begets its own punishment. The punishment may be eternal or only temporary. But all punishment is painful and therefore opposed to true happiness.

SIN IS THE GREAT FOE of human happiness. No disease of the body, no matter how painful or loathsome, can be compared with sin, the disease of the soul. Physical illness can destroy for a time the life of the body. But sin can destroy forever the life of the soul in God. In this life it enslaves a man to the conflicting desires of a soul whose powers are at war with one another. In the next life it condemns a man to eternal agony. As fire destroys a house, so sin destroys happiness. A sane man will neither enter nor stay in a burning house. A wise man will neither enter nor stay in the house of sin.

CHAPTER XIII

Law:
The Road-Map
to Happiness

CHAPTER XIII

Law: The Road-Map to Happiness

LAW IS A ROAD-MAP to happiness. It maps out the direction human acts must take if they are to reach their proper goal. But maps are the products of minds. They are a work of intelligence, a work of reason. Before a map can exist there must be a mind capable of recognizing destinations and the road or roads that lead to them. So it is with the map of human life. There must be a mind capable of recognizing the true goals of human life and the roads that lead to those goals. Law then is always a command or a direction of reason ordering a human act to its proper goal.

THE GOAL OF ALL HUMAN ACTS is happiness. In this life the happiness of the individual man consists in the pursuit of truth and goodness. In the next life individual happiness consists principally in the vision of God, Who is all Truth and all Goodness. But man as we know him does not work for happiness simply as an individual. Man is a social being. He seeks his happiness in and through society. Man works with and through his fellow-men to achieve the goals of human life. It is the function of society—or the union of men working together to achieve happiness—to provide the conditions of life in which men can work successfully to attain true happiness. Society is concerned with the common good of all the members of society. Society—whether it be the family, the nation, or the state—provides the means of life to all, the employment, the food and shelter, the education, the laws and government which make social life and endeavor possible. We might say briefly that society provides the peace and the harmony which enable men to work together to attain the common good of all men. Since the happiness of the individual is possible, in practice, only through the pursuit of the common good of the whole community, law will be concerned always with the common good of all the members of the community.

IT FOLLOWS THEREFORE that the making of laws is a right of the members of the community. They may entrust this right to a king or to an elected legislature. But in that case the rulers or government are only exercising the right which society or the community has given them.

AGAIN, A LAW IS A DIRECTION for human activity. As such it is useless unless it is obeyed. But men must know it, if they are to obey it. Lawmakers must make the laws known to those who are to obey the law To make a law known to those who must keep it is to promulgate the law. Promulgation is not a part of the essence of a law, but is a necessary condition for the effectiveness of a law.

WE CAN DEFINE A LAW then as a rule or direction of reason for the common good made by the one who has charge of the community, and promulgated to the subjects of the law.

THERE ARE DIFFERENT KINDS of law directing human activity to the goal of happiness. There is the Eternal Law in the Mind of God, the Natural Law of reason, Divine Positive Law, and Human Positive Law.

AS WE HAVE ALREADY SEEN, the whole world is ruled by the Providence of God. It is God Who has made every creature and shaped it to the purpose for which He created it. It is the Divine Mind which directs all the activities and movements of all creatures to the purpose for which God made the world. But this direction of all things is eternal in the mind of God. In

God then there is an Eternal Law directing the affairs of the whole world.

E VERYTHING THAT TAKES PLACE in the world is subject to this Eternal Law. The movements of electrons and protons in the atom, the majestic courses of stars in space, the growth of plants, the behavior of animals, the actions of men, all these come under the Eternal Law in the Mind of God. It is clear that only God Himself, Who is infinitely knowing, comprehends this Eternal Law perfectly. The saints in Heaven, who are already in possession of the vision of God, can see this Eternal Law directly, although not perfectly. But here on earth we can only observe the effects of this Law. We cannot see it directly.

B UT SINCE it is the Divine Mind which has determined the goals of all creatures and the roads to these goals, it follows that all other laws will be based on the Eternal Law in the Mind of God.

T HE NATURAL LAW OF REASON is man's participation in the Eternal Law of God. It is the Eternal Law of God which imprints in creatures their inclinations to their proper goals. But man is a rational creature. His reason can recognize his own proper goal and the road that leads to it. Through his reason then man shares in the Mind of God. Man's share in the Eternal Law of God is called the Natural Law of reason.

T HE NATURAL LAW IS BASED on man's recognition of the fact that the natural inclination of every creature is an inclination to good. Recognizing this, human reason sees the first precept of law, that good is to be done and evil to be avoided. All other precepts of the natural law are based on this first precept of the Natural Law. All other laws are intended to achieve the goal of this first law—the attainment of good and the avoidance of evil.

THE TEN COMMANDMENTS, as they are called, are secondary or derived principles of the Natural Law. They are basic principles regulating human behaviour in relation to God and to men.

BECAUSE HUMAN NATURE is the same in all men, the basic principles of the natural law are the same for all men. But law deals with the details of human action. Hence the general principles of the natural law must be applied to particular actions. In the majority of cases they may be applied exactly. But in particular cases the concrete conditions of human action may change the application of the law. Ordinarily, property should be given or restored to its rightful owner. But it would be foolish to restore a gun to a man who intended to kill you with it.

THE NATURAL LAW IS FOUND in all men. All men recognize the force of the first precept of Natural Law—do good and avoid evil. Some of the secondary precepts of the Natural Law may not be recognized by all men. Ignorance or passion may prevent men from applying the law in particular actions. But the basic precepts of the Natural Law are recognized by all.

THE LIFE OF MEN IN SOCIETY is a complicated process. The almost infinite number of human actions, the bewildering conflict of human desires and ambitions, the various tasks necessary to attain the common good of all, in a word, the complexity of social life demands a law to regulate the actions of men and direct them to the common good of society as a whole. The laws which men make to direct the conduct of the members of human society constitute human positive law.

HUMAN POSITIVE LAW is derived from the Natural Law. The precept "Thou shalt not steal" is a general principle for human behaviour. But the concrete conditions in which property is acquired, retained, or transferred are so complex that men must make more particular determinations of law to regulate, for example, the making of contracts, the payment of debts, the arrangements of bankruptcy proceedings and so forth. Human positive law is a particular determination of the Natural Law to regulate the concrete conditions of human acts in society.

IT IS THEREFORE A MEANS to achieve the goal of Natural Law, which is the attainment of true happiness. It must foster religion, which unites man to God. It must establish peace and discipline in society. It must provide for the common welfare of society.

SINCE HUMAN POSITIVE LAW has for its own proper goal the common welfare of the members of society, human laws should be made for the benefit of all, and not just for the benefit of private individuals. As a consequence, whereas Natural Law forbids all vices and sins, human positive law will forbid only those vices which disturb the common good of society. Similarly human law will command only those virtues which work for the common good of all.

WHEN HUMAN LAWS ARE JUST, they bind men in conscience. A human law is just if it fulfils the following conditions: it is directed to the common good, it does not exceed the power of the lawmaker, and the burdens that it imposes on the citizens are distributed with proportionate equality.

SINCE THE PURPOSE OF ALL LAW is the direction of human actions to their proper goals, it is clear that law may be subject to change. It is impórtant though to know what laws are subject to change. The basic precepts of the Natural Law are based on man's recognition of the essential purpose of human life, namely, the pursuit of good or happiness. These basic principles of law can never be changed. They are as unchangeable as human nature itself. The Eternal Law in the Mind of God is eternal and unchangeable. But positive law, whether human or divine, can be subject to change. Such changes may take place when the old law no longer provides for the common good of all or when an old law might prove to be injurious to society. The laws, for example, regulating automobile traffic should be changed according to traffic conditions, the capabilities of automobiles and their drivers, and so forth. In short, the Eternal Law of God and the primary principles of the Natural Law can never be changed because they are based on the unchangeable natures of man and God. But the positive laws that are concerned with the changing conditions of human life can be changed to meet the actual conditions of life.

SINCE ALL OF MAN'S NATURAL ACTIONS are directed either by Natural Law or human positive law, it might seem that these laws would provide man with sufficient guidance in all human activity. But God has called man to a goal which is beyond the power of purely natural activity. Man is called to enjoy the vision of God. It was necessary for God to reveal to man the law which would direct human activity to this supernatural goal. This revealed law is the divine positive law.

GOD REVEALED THIS LAW to man gradually. He gave it to men in two stages. Through Moses God gave what is called the "Old Law" to the Jews.

Lastly, through Christ, He gave to all men the "New Law" or the "Law of the Gospel."

GOD GAVE THE OLD LAW to the Jews to prepare the world for the coming of Christ, the Redeemer of mankind. The Old Law then was a preparatory law. It was not intended to be permanent in all its prescriptions. It was meant to be fulfilled by the New Law which Christ would bring to men.

THE OLD LAW CONTAINED moral, ceremonial and judicial precepts. The moral precepts of the Old Law were chiefly the Ten Commandments of God. These ten commandments are really the secondary precepts of the Natural Law. But God gave them to men by way of revelation to make sure that men would not forget them or remain in ignorance of them. As precepts of the Natural Law as well as of divine positive law they are binding on all men in all times.

THE CEREMONIAL PRECEPTS of the Old Law were intended to regulate the actions of men in the worship of God. Because man is not just a spirit, but also a bodily or corporeal being, and because man is a social being, he must worship God in and by external actions. His external actions must express suitably his internal acts of divine worship. The ceremonial precepts provided for suitable acts of divine worship.

THE JUDICIAL PRECEPTS of the Old Law were particular determinations of the general precepts of the justice to be observed by men in their dealings with one another. The judicial precepts thus included directions to be observed in the relations between the rulers and the citizens of the Jewish nation, in the relations between the members of the Jewish nation, in the relations between Jews and those who were not

Jews, and lastly, in the relations between the members of the same household.

THE OLD LAW THEN, like all law, directed the actions of men in relation to God, themselves and their fellow-men. But, most importantly, the Old Law was, in God's plan, a preparation for the coming of Christ, the Son of God and the Redeemer of the world. Its moral precepts were to last forever, because they were dictates of the Natural Law. But its ceremonial and judicial precepts were only a preparation for the New Law to be given men by Christ, God incarnate among men.

THE NEW LAW GIVEN THE WORLD by Christ is God's final law for all men. It is the road-map to the vision of God. It is then the perfect law, for it will bring men to their true goal, happiness. The efficiency of the New Law in leading men to the vision of God is derived from the grace of the Holy Spirit which is given men through faith in Christ. It is this supernatural gift of grace which puts man on the road to the blessed vision of God. What this grace is and how it is to be attained will be considered later. Now it is sufficient to note that the grace of the Holy Spirit enables man to reach God through human activity. It is true that the New Law of Christ contains precepts just as all law does. It reaffirms the moral precepts of the Old Law and of the Natural Law. It imposes the precepts relating to divine worship through the seven sacraments. But all these precepts derive their efficiency in leading men to God from the grace of the Holy Spirit. Hence this New Law is also called the Law of Grace. For it is grace which makes men's actions equal to the attainment of the vision of God. With the New Law man can rise above the world of nature to the throne of the God who created nature.

THE BENEFIT OF ALL LAW in human life should be easy to see. In the bewildering complexity of human life man needs intelligent direction in his human activities. Law gives him this direction. The natural law and human positive law enable man to direct his activity to the attainment of the natural good of the individual and of society. The New Law of Christ enables men to direct their actions to the attainment of the vision of God.

LAW IS NOT, THEN, a ball and chain dragging at the eager footsteps of human liberty. It is a light enabling men to step forward surely and easily on the right road to happiness. Without law man is a weary, uncertain traveler, halting at each cross-road of life, then stumbling on in twilight or darkness over roads not familiar to his feet nor clearly seen by his vision. Without law man is a slave to the whims, fancies or fears that afflict those who travel in darkness over unknown roads. But with law man is a sure traveler, moving forward in the daylight of human reason and the Divine Mind over a road that is clearly marked to a destination to which he really wants to go. Law gives freedom to human action—the only freedom that really matters, the freedom to seek happiness and to be happy.

CHAPTER XIV

Grace:
The Gift
of Happiness

CHAPTER XIV

Grace: The Gift of Happiness

HUMAN ACTS ARE THE STEPS which lead man to the vision of God. If this is true, it might seem strange, even contradictory, to say that ultimately happiness is a gift from God. Yet we must say that happiness is a gift given to men by God. We must say that man chooses happiness freely by his human acts and yet we must also say that happiness is a gift of God.

THE CLUE TO THIS MYSTERY lies in the nature of man's true happiness. You will remember that we said in the very beginning that man's true happiness consists in the vision of God. But the vision of God is a goal beyond the natural power of any creature. No natural act of man, or series of natural human actions, can enable man to see God. To see God as He is in Himself, to love God as He loves Himself—these are actions that are proper to God alone. The all-perfect God dwells in light inaccessible and no human mind is naturally capable of seeing God. As the stone cannot fly by its own power, as a horse cannot read this book by its own power, so man cannot see God by his own natural power.

IF MAN IS TO SEE GOD, he must be raised to a level of existence and action that is superhuman, that is divine. This is precisely what God has done for man. Through the gift of grace God gives to man the power to see God. Through grace God makes it possible for human acts to lead to the vision of Himself.

MAN NEEDS THE GRACE OF GOD if he is to find true happiness. Man achieves happiness through the proper use of reason and will. But these powers of man must be fortified by grace before their action can lead man to the desired goal. It is true that the natural use of human reason can put man in possession of the truths of the natural order. Human reason can discover the existence of God, the immortality of man's soul, the precepts of the Natural Law, and so on. But human reason alone cannot discover the truths of the supernatural order, such truths as the existence of the Trinity in God, the Incarnation, the Redemption of men by Christ, man's actual call to the vision of God, the grace which makes the vision possible, and so on. To learn these truths the mind of man needs the light of faith which is called the light of grace.

IN ADDITION MAN'S WILL needs God's grace if it is to find God in the vision of God. The human will is capable of performing naturally good acts. But the vision of God can only be attained through supernatural acts. Hence the will needs to be aided by God's supernatural grace to do and wish supernatural good. If man were now existing in a state of perfect human nature, he would still need grace to act supernaturally. Actually, as we have already seen, human nature is now wounded or corrupted by Original Sin. The human will must be healed by grace in order to perform supernatural acts.

AGAIN, IF MAN WERE IN THE STATE of perfect nature in which Adam existed before his fall into sin, he could keep all the commandments of God and the Natural Law. But man is now corrupted in his nature because of Original Sin. Consequently it is impossible for man to keep all the commandments for a whole lifetime without the healing effect of God's grace. Moreover, to keep the commandments perfectly in the way that leads to the vision of God, man needs the elevating power of grace. For no purely human act is capable of gaining the vision of God. Grace is necessary to elevate the character of human acts and make them proportionate to the goal of the vision of God. It is only through the power of grace that man can merit the vision of God.

IF MAN IS TO ACT supernaturally always, and ultimately to enjoy the vision of God supernaturally, he needs an habitual gift of grace. Besides this the human will must be prepared for the gift of habitual grace. Through habitual grace man's will is turned to God. But it must be prepared for this turning to God. The sinner, for example, must turn from his sin to God. He must repent. But to do this he must be moved to repentance by God. God moves his will inwardly and so prepares it for the reception of habitual grace.

MAN NEEDS GRACE even to avoid sin. For the sense appetite of man is not entirely subject to reason and will, and reason itself is not entirely subject to God. Even though man is capable of good, the lack of due order in his reason and sense appetite will lead him into sin unless he is aided by the grace of God. It follows too that man requires the help of God's grace to persevere in the state of grace. For he needs the divine assistance to guard him against the attacks of passion.

THE NECESSITY OF GOD'S GRACE will not seem so surprising if we remember that God's assistance is needed by man even for natural human life and action. The human will needs divine aid even for its natural action. No creature, as we have seen, can move itself to its proper action without assistance from God. The need for this divine aid exists also in the order of supernatural life and action. In this order the goal of action is beyond the capacity of any natural action. Man's nature must be elevated by God to an order of existence and action which is equal to the goal of the vision of God. It is habitual grace which thus elevates man permanently to the order of supernatural action. But just as human reason and will need to be moved by God to their natural acts of understanding and love, so in the order of habitual grace, the sanctified reason and will of man must also be moved by God to their supernatural acts of understanding and love. It is actual grace—a gift of God—by which God moves man to supernatural acts. And just as the will functions freely in the natural order even under the divine motion moving it to act, so too the will functions freely under the divine motion of grace in the supernatural order. In this way happiness, which is the goal of grace, results from the combination of God's gift and man's free choice. Man achieves happiness through his own acts, but his acts are equal to the task through the gift of God's grace.

WHAT IS GRACE IN ITSELF? As we said above, man needs God's assistance in two ways. In the natural order God gives man a rational nature which is the source of the acts of reason and will. Besides this permanent rational nature God also moves human reason and will to their acts of understanding and love. In the supernatural order God provides similarly for man. He gives man habitual grace, which is like a permanent supernature with permanent powers of supernatural knowledge and love. But these powers must be moved by God to supernatural actions. This latter divine motion is actual grace, a temporary divine motion in the soul of man.

HABITUAL GRACE MUST BE A QUALITY infused in the soul of man by God. It enables man to act in the order of supernatural knowledge and love. Since these are spiritual actions, grace, the source of these actions must be in the soul rather than in the body of man. Moreover, since grace transforms man's soul by making it capable of sharing in the life of God, it is a quality infused in the soul. It is a quality because it gives the soul a special form or manner of existing and acting. It gives the soul a participation in the very life of God.

SINCE IT IS A SHARING in the divine life or nature, it is infused in the soul rather than into the powers of the soul. Nature always precedes grace. It is because man has a human nature that he has the powers of reason and will. So also it is because man has habitual grace that he is also endowed with the powers of supernatural knowledge and love.

SINCE GRACE IS A PARTICIPATION in the divine nature, it is obvious that only God can give grace to man. No one but God is the divine nature. Hence no one but God can communicate to man a share in this nature. God may use the human nature of Christ, or the sacraments to impart grace to men. They are however only the instruments by which God, the principal Agent, gives to men a share in His own life.

IT IS TRUE that men prepare themselves for the reception of habitual grace by turning freely to God. In this way men can be said to be disposing causes of grace. They put their own souls in proper order for the reception of grace. But even this turning of man's will to God is due to God's grace. Therefore, from beginning to end, grace is a gift of God.

IN SO FAR AS HABITUAL GRACE joins man to God supernaturally, it is equal in all men. For wherever grace exists, there man is united to God. But this union can admit of degrees inasmuch as one man may be more perfectly enlightened by grace than another. The man who prepares himself for grace by a more perfect repentance for sin or by a more perfect love of God, will receive more habitual grace. Even in this case, though, the more perfect preparation for grace will be due to God's action in the soul of man. Consequently the different degrees of grace in men's souls are ultimately traceable to God.

SO PERFECT A GIFT AS GRACE is clearly the effect of God's love for men. Since men cannot know naturally the supernatural effects of God's love, they cannot be certain that God has given them habitual grace. While God has revealed His willingness to grant His grace to all men, He has not revealed whether or not He has given it to this or that particular man. Consequently no man can believe with certitude that he possesses God's grace, unless God should make a special revelation of that fact to the man in question. But if men do what they can to attain and to retain God's grace, that is, if they receive the sacraments which God has instituted to give grace to men and if they strive to keep the commandments, then they can make a reasonable conjecture that God has given them grace.

IF WE RECALL THE FACT that men come into this world stained and corrupted by original sin, and if we recall the fact that men commit personal mortal sins, then the effect of grace in the souls of men is nothing short of marvelous. If grace unites men to God by giving them a share in God's own life, then grace and serious sin are opposed to one another. A man cannot be united to God in grace and separated from Him by sin. Where grace is, serious sin cannot exist. When grace enters a soul, then sin must depart from that soul.

HABITUAL GRACE THEN EXPELS SIN from the soul of man. Since sin means that man's will is not turned to God, the infusion of grace means that man's will is turned back to God. But man cannot turn back to God without turning away from—or detesting—his sin. The infusion of grace means then that man turns away from his sin. But when man turns away from sin and back to God, his sin is forgiven or remitted by God. The infusion of grace thus remits man's sin and makes man once again the friend of God, the child of God and the heir of heaven.

GRACE MAKES MAN A FRIEND OF GOD because it is the effect of God's love or friendship for man and because it enables man to love God through supernatural charity. Furthermore, because it gives man a share in the divine life, it establishes a community of interests between man and God.

GRACE MAKES MAN AN ADOPTED CHILD OF GOD because it gives man a share in the divine life and happiness. As parents give natural life to their children in the world of nature, so God gives men supernatural life through grace in the world of the divine nature.

GRACE MAKES MAN AN HEIR OF HEAVEN, because grace enables man to attain to the vision of God. Grace is the seed from which the glory of the vision of God will flower. Just as the accident of natural birth gives a child the right to inherit the property or wealth of his parents, so also the accident of grace, which makes man the child of God, gives man a right to share in the wealth of happiness which is God's.

THESE WONDERFUL EFFECTS OF GRACE show us the splendor of God's gift to us. In one sense the creation of the world is a greater work of God than the infusion of grace in the souls of men. For creation means that God makes something from nothing. But from the point of view of the excellence of the thing that is made, grace is superior to creation. For the work of creation brings into being a changeable creature. But grace results ultimately in the eternal vision of God. The gift of the vision of God—which is called the gift of glory—which is given to the saints in Heaven, is a greater thing in itself than the gift of grace to sinful men. But glory is due, in God's plan, to those who die in grace. On the other hand, grace, which leads men to glory, is far beyond the unworthiness of sinful man. Grace is a great mystery of God's love for men.

GRACE LEADS TO GLORY. It leads ultimately to the vision of God. In God's plan grace enables man to merit the vision of God. The vision is given as a reward for grace.

MERIT OR REWARD IS THE PRICE given in return for a work that is done voluntarily. Strictly speaking, the price paid for a voluntary work or service is a matter of justice. Strict justice regulates the relations between persons who are equal to one another. But we also speak of justice in a relative sense of the term, as regulating the relations between father and child, or between a man and his servants. It is clear that God and man are not equals. There can be no question of absolute justice between God and man. But God can make the meriting of the vision of Himself a matter of justice in the relative sense.

THIS IS PRECISELY what God has done in the order of grace. There is no work of man, however great or noble, which would give man a right in justice to the vision of God. But God has made grace the meritorious principle or source of eternal life. In God's plan human acts performed with and through habitual grace will merit the vision of God for men. As Christ tells us, grace is a "fountain of water, springing up to eternal life." (*John, IV,* 14.) Grace is the power of God in us moving us to the vision of God.

HUMAN ACTS PERFORMED IN GRACE are meritorious for two reasons. First, they have the character of merit because God Himself directs them to a supernatural good, the vision of Himself. And secondly, they are meritorious because they are voluntary or free on man's part. Because they are free they proceed from man's will in so far as it loves God supernaturally in charity. Merit then depends on charity. The acts of all the other virtues are meritorious in so far as they are directed by charity to the love of God.

BUT EVEN THOUGH MEN can freely merit eternal life, the vision of God is a free gift from God to man. This is so because the first infusion of habitual grace—which is the source of all merit—is due to God's generosity. No ordinary man can merit this grace for himself in justice. Only Christ, the God-man, had the power to merit grace in justice for other men. In God's plan Christ is the new Adam, that is, He is the spiritual Head of the human race. He can merit from God the grace needed for man's happiness. Other men cannot do this. But, if they are in the state of grace, they are the friends of God. Since they are God's friends, it is true to say that if they perform good works for the salvation of other men, it is fitting that God will grant their desires.

IT IS IMPORTANT TO NOTICE that merit is possible only to those who are in the state of grace. Only those in the state of grace are God's friends and children. Only they have any right to inherit the vision of God. Hence the man who has not yet received habitual grace, or the man who has lost it through mortal sin cannot merit it for himself. Only the divine generosity can give it or restore it to man. The wise man is careful not to lose the grace of God once he has received it.

FAR FROM RISKING THE LOSS of grace through sin, the wise man seeks to increase his grace and charity through good works. Through grace God moves man to eternal life in the vision of God. But this movement or preparation for the vision of God is progressive. As man makes use of the grace already given him, his good use of grace brings further supernatural illumination of his mind and strength to his love of God. By his good works man thus merits an increase of grace and charity in his soul.

SINCE MAN'S FREE WILL remains flexible in this life toward good and evil, it is always possible for man to lose grace through sin. If man dies while in the state of grace, he merits the vision of God as his reward. But man himself cannot provide infallibly for the happy conjunction of death and the state of grace in his soul. Only God, the Master of life and death, can give to man the privilege of dying while in the state of grace. This shows that grace is a precious gift which man must guard carefully. He must persevere in the performance of good works, in the avoidance of sin, in prayers for the great gift of final perseverance in grace until death. If he perseveres in the life of grace, he will receive the reward of grace, the vision of God.

EVERYTHING THAT WE KNOW about grace seems mysterious to us. This is not surprising. The mystery of grace is one of the mysteries which God has revealed to us. We may not understand it completely, but we have God's word for its truth.

BESIDES, THE MYSTERY OF GRACE is part of the greater mystery of God's love for us. Love is always mysterious. The love of men for one another is not completely understood by men. Is it any wonder then that the love of God for men is past all understanding? Men love one another because they find good in one another. But God does not love men because He discovers good in them. Rather God's love for us makes us good. Love is caused in men by the good they find in others. But God's love for men is the cause of all the good which is in men.

SINCE GRACE IS THE EFFECT of God's love in men, and since it is a share in God's own divine nature, we cannot find any exact parallel to grace in the world of nature. But it might be of some help, by way of conclusion to this chapter, to try to compare the mystery of grace to something within the bounds of human experience.

CHRIST HAS LIKENED the Kingdom of heaven to an earthly kingdom. Let us imagine a king who had no heir to his kingdom. For some reason unknown to us he chooses a poor, uneducated orphan boy to be his heir. He adopts the boy as his son. Evidently the boy is not fit for the life or the functions of a king. But the king trains him. Patiently he imparts to the boy the knowledge and the virtue he needs to inherit the kingdom. When he dies, the boy inherits the kingdom. Because of the training the king gave him he rules the kingdom wisely and well.

NOW THIS STORY of the king's love for an orphan is partly like and partly unlike the story of God's love for us as it is made known to us in the mystery of grace. The king knew he would have to die and surrender his throne to some one else. God is eternal. He can never die. But He has determined to share the wealth of His Kingdom with men. Like the king He adopts men as His children in grace. Like the orphan we have no right to be adopted by God. But in the mystery of God's love for us, He has decided to make us His adopted children. Through God's grace we are no longer paupers, children of wrath, but sons of God and heirs to His Kingdom. We can call upon God as our Father.

MOREOVER, THE KING IN OUR STORY could make the orphan his son and heir only by legal adoption. But when God adopts us through grace He does more for us than legal adoption can do. Legal adoption cannot make the orphan the flesh and blood son of the king. But when we are adopted by God through grace, grace gives us a real share in the very life of God. In a real sense then, we become God's real children, sharing His own life.

THEN, JUST AS THE KING imparted to his adopted son his own knowledge and virtue, so God gives us a share in His own knowledge and love. As knowledge and virtue trained the boy to inherit the kingdom, so the knowledge and virtue that come to us through the life of grace prepare us to inherit the vision of God. But whereas the king had to die before his adopted son could inherit the kingdom, it is we who must die before we can share in God's happiness in Heaven. Through death—as long as we die in the state of grace—we come to our divine inheritance in Heaven. In Heaven we become the members of God's royal court. We share with Him the infinite treasure of His own infinite perfection and happiness.

TRULY THE STORY OF GRACE is a story of Divine Love. Its magnificence holds us breathless. Through grace we are no longer slaves to sin or imprisoned in this world. We are the sons of God. And if we are His sons, then we are His heirs also. Ultimate happiness is within our grasp. The Love of God for us offers to us the gift of ecstatic happiness. We have but to reach out for it and grasp it in love. The Love of God calls to us for our love. The reward is God Himself. Who would refuse?

✠✠✠✠✠✠✠✠✠✠✠✠✠✠✠✠✠✠✠✠✠

PART IIв

✠ ✠ ✠ The Divine

*Refers to questions in the Summa

✠✠✠✠✠✠✠✠✠✠✠✠✠✠✠✠✠✠✠✠✠

Life in Man ✛ ✛ ✛

CHAPTER I

Happiness of Mind

God: The Goal of Faith

Faith: an Enlargement of
    Man's Mind

The Truths of Faith

The Act of Faith

The Necessity of Faith

The Freedom of Faith

Profession of Faith

The Virtue of Faith

Effects of Faith

Understanding

Knowledge

Faith: The Beginning of Happiness

Unbelief and Unhappiness

CHAPTER I

Happiness of Mind

DIVINE GRACE GIVES MAN a share in the life of God. It is the divine life in man. Life and action go together. The life of grace then must be active in man. It is active through the virtues—the theological and moral virtues.

MOREOVER, IN THIS WORLD grace is only the beginning of the divine life in man. Like all life it is intended to grow to maturity and bear the fruit of eternal happiness. Grace is "a fountain of water, springing up into life everlasting." (*John, IV.,* 14). The maturity of grace is realized in the next world, where the saints enjoy the vision of God. But in this world grace must grow into maturity as the child grows into manhood. And this growth takes place through the exercise of the theological and moral virtues.

THE STORY OF THE BEGINNING and the growth of happiness in man in this world is the story of the life of the virtues in man. It is a wonderful story because it is a story of success—of man's successful pursuit of God. It is an instructive story—instructive because, in showing man how he can reach God, it also shows him how he can lose God. St. Thomas tells us the story in this part of his great summary of theology.

SINCE IT IS THE STORY of man's pursuit of God, and since the theological virtues of faith, hope and charity have God for their object, we shall consider these virtues first. The moral virtues of prudence, justice, fortitude and temperance deal with the things that lead men to God. Hence we shall consider the moral virtues last.

THE VIRTUES ARE PRINCIPLES OR SOURCES OF ACTION. Now all truly human action is rational, intelligent action. Hence the first of the theological virtues to be considered is the virtue of faith. Faith is an intellectual virtue. It perfects man's mind. It gives man a knowledge of God as He is in Himself and in His action in the world for man's good. It proposes to man's will the great goal of the will—God Himself. It is, as it were, the intellectual principle of all the supernatural actions by which man reaches out to the vision of God.

THE OBJECT OF FAITH IS GOD HIMSELF. Through faith man comes to know God as God knows Himself. Human reason can discover for itself that God exists. It can even discover some of God's attributes or perfections. It can learn that God is good, that He is true, that He is omnipotent, and so on. But human reason can never discover what God is in Himself. It can never penetrate by itself into the mysteries of God's inner life. If man is to know the deep mysteries of the life of God, then God must reveal them to man and man must accept these truths in faith. But God has revealed these mysteries of His own ineffable life to men. And through faith men grasp God in His mysteries.

GOD IS THE OBJECT OF FAITH IN TWO WAYS. In faith God is both the object that the mind of man knows and He is the light by which man knows God. When the human eye sees the greenness of a yew tree in daylight, the greenness is what it sees and the sunshine is the light by which it sees it. When a man assents in faith to the divine revelation that God is Three Persons in one nature, the Trinity is what He believes and God's word is the light by which he believes it.

FAITH IS CONCERNED WITH TRUTH not naturally accessible to the mind of man. However it is a fact that God has also revealed some truths that human reason could discover, such as the existence of God, the immortality of the human soul, and the like. God has done this because He knows that many men, through lack of talent or opportunity, or even through laziness, might never come to the knowledge of these important truths. Whenever men cannot discover these truths for themselves, it is possible for them to learn these truths through faith in God's word. But primarily faith is concerned with the mysteries of God in Himself and in His actions in the world which men could never discover for themselves.

FAITH IS THEN AN ENLARGEMENT of the horizons of the human mind. It lifts the mind of man above the world of nature and sets it free in the limitless world of the Divine Being. It introduces man to that great mystery of the Divine Life, the Trinity. It makes man aware of God's stupendous entrance into human life through the Incarnation of the Son of God in Jesus Christ. It informs man of the divine generosity in making the vision of God possible for men. It gives man a knowledge of the supernatural means by which he can attain the vision of God. Faith does not impose limitations on the mind of man. It removes them. Through faith the mind of man is no longer subject to the imperfections of the senses or of human reason. Through faith man is given a share in the infinite perfection of God's own knowledge. If man's ultimate goal is the vision of God, then faith, which gives man some knowledge, even though an obscure knowledge, of God as He is in Himself, is a beginning of happiness in human life. It puts man on the road to ultimate happiness.

GOD, THE OBJECT OF FAITH, is in Himself absolutely simple. But the simple things are often the hardest to understand or explain. A lever is a simple thing. But how many words, sentences, or even paragraphs may be necessary to explain its power to lift great weights. So it is with God. Because He is absolutely simple, the human mind, which understands things bit by bit, cannot grasp the Divine Being simply. It must, as it were, go round God slowly, viewing Him now from this angle and now from another angle. It will express each of these different views of the one simple object—God—in a separate judgment or proposition. In revealing Himself to man God has taken account of this weakness of the human mind. He has revealed Himself to man bit by bit, sentence after sentence.

THESE TRUTHS OR JUDGMENTS ABOUT GOD, which God has revealed, make up the content of faith. They are many and they were revealed to man over a long period of time, from Adam to Christ and His Apostles. Because God is absolutely one and absolutely simple, some of these truths are contained implicitly in others. From the point of view of the human mind which accepts these truths in faith, we may reduce all the revealed truths about God to the mysteries of the Trinity—God as He is in Himself—and the Incarnation—God as He enters the world supernaturally to accomplish the salvation of men.

SINCE THESE TRUTHS are many and mysterious, and since faith is necessary for those who seek the vision of God, it is both convenient and necessary to summarize these truths in a creed or symbol of the faith. The authority to draw up a summary of the faith belongs to the Church of Christ under the leadership of the Pope. Hence Christ said to Peter, whom He made the first Pope of the Church, "I have prayed for thee, Peter, that thy faith fail not, and thou, being once converted, confirm thy brethren." (*Luke* XXII., 32) Through the creed or summary of the content of faith, the truths of the faith are made accessible to all men.

THE INDIVIDUAL MAN LAYS HOLD of the truths of faith by the act of faith or belief. To believe is to think with assent. Belief is a special type of intellectual act. To understand it properly we must compare it with other acts of the human intellect. When a man understands a self-evident truth—such as the truth that a whole is greater than a part—or when he has scientifically demonstrated a conclusion from its evident principles—such as the demonstration that the three angles of a triangle are equal to two right angles—he no longer needs to think about the evidence for the truths of these judgments. He simply gives a firm assent to these truths. But sometimes a man doubts the truth of a proposition. He lacks sufficient evidence either to affirm or to deny the proposition. Sometimes he has some slight evidence for the truth of a proposition and so he is said to suspect its truth. Or he has enough evidence to think the proposition is true, but he fears that it may not be true. In this case he is said to have an opinion about it. Now faith or belief is like science and understanding in that it assents firmly to the proposition that is believed. Yet the believer has no clear insight into the truth of the statement which he believes.

BECAUSE A MAN DOES NOT COMPLETELY UNDERSTAND the things he believes, there is always some obscurity in the act of faith. This is not surprising. The principal truths of the faith are mysteries of

God beyond human understanding in this life. Even those natural truths which God has revealed are in fact beyond the present understanding of those who have not yet discovered them naturally. But man needs the truths of the faith if he is to achieve the vision of God. In order to attain the vision of God man must first of all believe God, as a disciple believes the master who is teaching him.

GOD HIMSELF HAS SAID that belief is necessary if man is to attain the vision of God. As St. Paul says, "But without faith it is impossible to please God. For he that cometh to God must believe that he is: and is a rewarder to them that seek him." (*Heb.*XI,6)

BELIEF IN GOD'S WORD is a necessary preliminary to the vision of God. As St. Paul says this belief must be at least an explicit or conscious belief in the existence of God and in the fact that God rewards those who seek Him. St. Thomas adds that the object of faith also includes the means to happiness. But the Incarnation is the means to man's happiness. Therefore an explicit belief in the Incarnation is necessary also. Since the Incarnation cannot be believed in explicitly without believing in the Trinity—for how can a man believe the Second Person of the Trinity became man unless he believes in the mystery of the Trinity—it follows that belief in the Trinity is also required for the attainment of the vision of God. By accepting these truths in faith man begins to learn to know God as He really is.

SINCE FAITH MEANS THE ACCEPTANCE of truths which man cannot fully understand, faith is a test of man's good will. Reason is not compelled to accept what God reveals about Himself. In faith reason must be moved by man's will to accept truth, not on evidence clearly seen, but on God's word. Hence the act of belief can be meritorious. When man's will, under the influence of grace and the love of God, moves man's reason to accept God's revelation in faith, the act of belief is meritorious in God's sight.

NATURALLY A MAN'S INNER ACCEPTANCE of God's truth in faith will sometimes find outward expression in his speech or actions. The believer will express his faith publicly. This does not mean that those who believe in God must shout their faith from the housetops on any and all occasions. But there will be times when the believer in God must openly acknowledge his belief. Charity—the love of God and our neighbor—demands that we respect both God's honor and our neighbor's good. Whenever a man's silence about his inner faith would injure God's honor in the world or scandalize men, then the believer must profess his faith openly.

THIS OBLIGATION TO PROFESS one's faith publicly presupposes of course that faith is not just one act, nor even just a series of acts. It implies that behind the act of faith there is a permanent disposition to believe truth on God's word. Faith then is a habitual disposition of mind, and, when perfect, it is a virtue.

ST. THOMAS DEFINES FAITH as a habit of mind whereby eternal life is begun in us, making the intellect assent to truths that are not apparent. This definition, he points out, is equivalent to St. Paul's statement that "Faith is the substance of things to be hoped for, the evidence of things that appear not." (*Heb.* XI, 1) Faith, as a habit of mind inclining man to assent to truths which are not apparent to the mind, is the "evidence of things that appear not." And since it is a habit whereby eternal life is begun

in us, it is "the substance of things to be hoped for."
Through faith man hopes to attain the vision of God,
the object of faith.

SINCE FAITH PUTS A MAN in possession of truth,
of the First Truth which is God, faith is a habit
which perfects man's reason or intellect. It is essentially an intellectual habit. But, as we have seen, in
faith the intellect is moved to assent by the will. But
the principle that moves the will itself to act is the
goal, that is, the good. Now the will is moved or
tends to God as its supernatural goal through the
virtue of charity. As a consequence the act of faith is
truly alive in the supernatural order only when it
functions under the impulse of a will moved by
charity or the love of God.

IT FOLLOWS THEN that the habit of faith is a virtue
only when it is moved to act by the impulse of
charity in the will. It is the function of a virtue to
make human acts good or perfect. But when faith
acts without charity the human intellect is made
perfect, because it tends to its goal, which is truth,
but the human will is not made perfect because it is
not tending properly to its own goal, which is God as
He is in Himself. Therefore faith without charity
does not make man perfect simply as man. Hence
such faith cannot be perfect virtue. But when faith
is moved by charity, then the act of faith is perfect
both in the intellect and in the will, and faith is a
virtue. The act of faith is meritorious in God's eyes
and it enables man to advance in the knowledge of
God and to merit ultimately the reward of eternal
life. When faith acts under the impulse of charity,
then man gives to God a loving obedience of the
intellect and will. On God's part it is grace which

makes man a son of God. But on man's part it is man's free acceptance of God through faith and charity which sets man in motion in the world as the son of God. And it is man as the son of God, that is, man believing God in love, who will inherit the vision of God.

FAITH IS AN ACCEPTANCE of truth on God's word. But God is Truth itself and He cannot lie to men. The man who believes God must believe everything that God says. Human reason can make mistakes. It is possible therefore to accept some things that men say, and to reject others. But God cannot be mistaken. A man must believe everything that God says to him or believe nothing on God's word. A man cannot pick and choose among the truths which he knows God has revealed. Either he has complete faith in God or he has no faith at all. If he rejects any truth which he knows God has revealed, then he rejects all the truths that God has revealed. If he claims to accept any of them it is not because he really accepts them on God's word. He accepts them on the authority of his own mind or because they please him.

WHEN A MAN ACCEPTS TRUTH on God's word, he is certain of the truth. His certainty is founded on the authority of the Divine Mind which is all knowing and all truthful. From this point of view the certitude of faith is more certain than the certitude man gains through the natural intellectual virtues of wisdom, science and understanding. For the Divine Knowledge on which faith is based is more perfect than human reason on which the certitude of the intellectual virtues is based.

FAITH THEN IS AN ABSOLUTE CERTITUDE about truths which are beyond the natural reach of the human mind. It must therefore be a gift of God. In the first place, since the truths of faith are beyond the reach of the human mind, they must be revealed by God before man can believe them. And in the second place since these truths raise man above the limitation of the human mind, he needs a supernatural principle moving him inwardly to accept these truths without doubt. This supernatural principle is God moving man by grace through the infused habit of faith.

MAN'S FREE ACCEPTANCE of the truths of faith sets man on the road to God. More than this, faith, so to speak, establishes the conditions or mood necessary for the successful completion of the journey. If a man were to set out for Washington to ask a favor of the President of the United States, two attitudes of mind would be necessary for success in his mission. First of all he would need to respect the President. If he had no respect for the President, at least for the powers possessed by the President, his behaviour would antagonize the President and make the mission a failure. Secondly he would need to have his mind clear so that he could present his case clearly and forcefully. If his mind is distracted so that he cannot judge properly either the reasons for his own request or the motives which might move the President to grant it, then he will be unable to present his case successfully. Now when man seeks God, his mind must respect God and be clear in its estimate of the goal he seeks and the means to attain it. Faith gives man both of these qualities of mind in man's search for God. Through faith man recognizes the insignificance of man in the face of the magnificence of God. So it instils in man not only a respect for

God, but even a wholesome fear of God. In the sinner whose faith is not moved by charity, this fear is servile fear, the fear of being punished by God for sins against God. This servile fear is good because it can move man to repentance for sin and so turn man back to God. In the good man, whose faith is moved by charity, this fear is filial fear, the fear of losing the supreme good which is God. Filial fear—the fear a son has for a father whom he loves—moves man to avoid anything which would cause him to lose God's love. This loving fear or awe of God is good for man because it makes him humble. He realizes the perilousness of his journey and the need of God's help. He relies not so much on his own strength for the journey as on God's goodness and power to lead him safely to eternal life.

SECONDLY FAITH GIVES MAN the clarity of mind necessary for the successful prosecution of his journey to God. Men, as we know them, are inclined to debase their nobler powers and aspirations by seeking happiness in things below them, in food, drink, clothing, illicit sexual gratifications, and so on. These things clutter up the mind of man. They beget in man's mind a confusion of conflicting desires and ambitions. But faith lifts a man's mind up to God and proposes to him the true goal of his existence—the vision of God. In this way faith begins the purification of man's mind from the errors and conflicting desires which would cause him to lose God. It puts him on the right road to happiness.

BY FAITH MAN ACCEPTS TRUTH FROM GOD, in fact he accepts God, Who is Truth. If this were the only intellectual gift that God gave man, it would still be a magnificent testimonial to God's generosity.

It is good for a child to learn from its parents that it should not drink from the iodine bottle in the medicine cabinet. But the child's mind is more perfect when it learns for itself that iodine is a poison and that poisons destroy human life. So too it is good for man to accept the truths which God reveals to him. But it is better when man gains some understanding of the meaning of these truths.

AND ONCE AGAIN, THE DIVINE GENEROSITY has not been lacking. God has given man through grace two gifts of the Holy Spirit which enable the believer to think out, as it were, the meaning of God's revelation of Himself. The first of these gifts is the gift of understanding. Through this gift God moves the mind of man to penetrate into the inner meaning of revealed truth. Through this gift man begins to understand the truths he accepts by faith.

THE SECOND GIFT OF THE HOLY SPIRIT which perfects faith is the gift of knowledge. Through this gift God moves the believer to judge rightly and with certainty about the true relationship between creatures and God. It enables man to see creatures in their proper perspective. The value of this gift in successful living is almost incalculable. Man is inclined to turn from God to creatures because he is attracted by the beauty and the goodness of creatures and the happiness they seem to promise. But in turning to creatures instead of turning to God man loses his only real happiness. Through the gift of knowledge God moves man to see creatures in their real place in the universe, to see them as pale reflections of the beauty and the goodness which is God, to see that they are to be used when they lead to God and avoided when they take man away from God.

THIS SKETCH OF THE NATURE and function of faith and the intellectual gifts of the Holy Spirit which perfect the action of faith shows the importance of faith in human life. Through faith man accepts God as his goal. Through the gift of understanding man begins to understand God and God's action in the world of men. Through the gift of knowledge man begins to see the world properly in its true relationship to himself and to God. With faith, understanding and knowledge man is intellectually equipped to seek his happiness in the vision of God. In fact, happiness is already partly his. For in the faith which is moved by the love of God, God is already present in the mind of man. Faith is the beginning of happiness in the mind of man.

IF FAITH IS THE BEGINNING of happiness, then infidelity, or the lack of faith, is the beginning of unhappiness. If a man does not believe God and God's message, then he does not know the true goal of human life. If he does not know the goal of life, he cannot attain the goal. But unbelief or infidelity means that a man does not know that God is his goal. It can lead then only to unhappiness.

THERE ARE DIFFERENT KINDS OF INFIDELITY. First of all it is conceivable that a man might never come to know that God has spoken to man by way of divine revelation. In this case he simply does not accept God's message in faith because he is ignorant of the message. This kind of unbelief is called negative infidelity. Secondly there is positive infidelity. This occurs when a man knowingly rejects the faith. This can occur in a number of ways. First of all there is the pagan or heathen who rejects the faith when it is preached to him. Secondly there are those, who have accepted the revelation which God made through the patriarchs, Moses and the prophets, but have rejected the revelation made in and through Jesus Christ. Lastly there are those men who once accepted the totality of God's revelation but have since rejected one or another of the revealed truths—which is the sin of heresy—or have given up the faith entirely—which is the sin of apostasy.

SINCE FAITH IS NECESSARY for the attainment of the vision of God, all infidelity, objectively speaking, causes men to lose God. We say "objectively speaking," because men lose God through sin, and it is not possible for men to judge accurately when infidelity is sinful in a particular person. It is possible that a man may reject the faith without sin because he personally does not know that a particular truth or all the truths of faith have been revealed by God. In the case of negative infidelity, St. Thomas is inclined to believe that such infidelity is impossible in fact. He thinks that, if necessary, God would make a special revelation of the necessary truths of faith to any man who had not previously heard of them. In that case such a man would have the free choice of accepting or rejecting the faith, and so he would have the free choice of accepting or rejecting God as his happiness. In the case of positive infidelity it seems clear that original unbelievers or heretics knowingly reject the faith which is preached to them or which they once accepted. Hence their lack of faith is sinful and if they persevere in infidelity they will lose God. In the case of their children or descendants it seems possible that they may be misled by their parents or leaders or be so poorly instructed that they do not recognize God's word in the world. If this is their real situation then their infidelity is not formally sinful.

AS EVERYONE KNOWS lack of faith in Christ's teaching is widespread in the world. This constitutes a double danger for men. It is dangerous for the unbelievers themselves because they run the risk of losing God. It is dangerous even for those who have the faith because unbelievers fight against the faith. Believers, especially if they are not too well educated or instructed in the truths of the faith, run the risk of losing their faith in the face of the bad example, false arguments or persecutions with which unbelievers attack the faith.

THE CHURCH OF CHRIST, which He founded to propagate and safeguard the faith in the world, must face these two dangers. She strives to overcome the danger to unbelievers by sending missionaries to preach the Gospel to them. She strives to overcome the danger to believers in a number of ways. She counters the bad example of unbelievers with the good example of believing, practising Christians. She answers the false arguments of infidels with the true arguments proposed by trained theologians and apologists. She resists persecution by asserting the right of believers to be undisturbed in their faith and by consoling and strengthening her children through good example, preaching, the Sacraments and the Mass. She advises her children to avoid contact with infidels when such contact might cause them to lose their faith.

BUT IN ALL HER STRUGGLE with infidelity in the world the Church never loses sight of the fact that the act of faith is a free act. She never seeks to compel infidels to accept the faith against their will. She will not even compel the children of infidels to be baptized into the faith against the will of their

parents. Obviously if her own children lose their
faith she can and will impose penalties upon them.
She may expel them from membership in the Church
and so cut them off from all the spiritual benefits to
be obtained within the Church. Since they have
voluntarily rejected God and His Church by their
unbelief this action of the Church is fair and just.

THOUGH UNBELIEF IS ONE of the greatest of sins
because it separates a man from his God, until
a man dies it is always possible, through the grace
of God, for a man to gain or regain the faith. The
Church is as merciful as God. If an unbeliever wishes
to enter the Church through faith, the Church, like
a loving mother will receive him into her arms.

BLASPHEMY IS ALSO A SIN AGAINST FAITH. In
blasphemy a man denies the goodness or perfections of God or reviles God. Since man is obliged
to love and reverence God, blasphemy which shows
that he despises or hates God is by its nature a mortal
sin. It is significant that the devils and the lost human
souls in Hell detest the divine justice and so are
guilty of blasphemy. This shows that blasphemy is
closely related to real unhappiness.

MANY MEN SIN AGAINST FAITH in an even more
subtle way through the sins against the Holy
Spirit, namely, the sins of despair, presumption, impenitence, obstinacy, resisting the known truth and
envy of someone else's spiritual good. The sins
against the Holy Spirit are not sins of weakness or
ignorance. They are sins of certain malice. By despair
a man rejects God's goodness and mercy. By presumption he rejects God's justice. By impenitence
he refuses to turn from sin to God. By obstinacy a
man hardens his will in sin. A man sins in resisting

the known truth because he does so in order to sin more freely. Lastly a man sins by envying someone else's spiritual good because he hates the increase of God's grace in the world. In all these sins there is great danger for man because these sins mean that man is deliberately refusing to consider those truths and motives which would keep him from sin and enable him to turn to God. It is for this reason that the sins against the Holy Spirit are said to be unforgivable. It is not that God is unwilling to forgive any sin. It is rather that in these sins a man shows that he does not wish forgiveness.

THE LAST OF THE SINS AGAINST FAITH are sins against the gifts of knowledge and understanding which perfect faith. They are the sins of blindness of mind and dullness of heart. Blindness of mind rises from lust. For lust withdraws a man's mind from the thought of God and immerses it in the maddening welter of sensual pleasure. This prevents man from knowing or understanding God as he ought. Dullness of heart arises from gluttony which deadens the power of the mind to penetrate to the meaning of truth. Both are great dangers to faith because they withdraw the mind of man from God and plunge his mind and his heart into the base, temporary pleasures of this world.

THE MAN OF WISDOM AND GOOD WILL is a happy man because he accepts God in the loving obedience of faith. His mind is fixed on the far horizons of God where happiness awaits him. Through the gifts of understanding and knowledge nothing can swerve him from his path to God. "Without faith it is impossible to please God." (*Heb.* XI, 6.) With and through faith man is happy because he has already begun to possess God.

CHAPTER II

Happiness of Heart

CHAPTER II

Happiness of Heart

FAITH IS THE BEGINNING of happiness in the mind. It is even more than this. Because faith proposes to man the possibility of attaining the vision of God, it gives man the beginning of happiness in his heart. A man is happy in his heart when he possesses the object of his love or when he conceives that what he desires can be obtained either through his own efforts or through the assistance of someone else. Now faith tells man that it is possible to attain the vision of God through God's assistance. Faith then lays the foundation of hope in the heart of man.

HOPE IS A THEOLOGICAL VIRTUE. It has God for its object. In hope man relies on God's goodness and power to bring man to the possession of God Himself. The divine goodness is thus both the efficient cause and the ultimate objective of hope. It is obvious that faith precedes hope. For unless a man knows that God is prepared to lead him to eternal life he can have no real hope of attaining it. It is faith which tells man that God is ready to assist man to attain true happiness. In this way it is faith which opens the door for hope in the human heart.

CHARITY, OR THE LOVE OF GOD, is more perfect than hope. For charity loves God for the sake of God. It loves God for Himself. In hope man loves God for the sake of the good which he expects to receive from God. But in a certain sense hope precedes charity. For the man who hopes to be rewarded by God is led to love God and obey His commandments.

FAITH MAKES US CLING TO GOD as the source of knowledge. Hope makes us cling to God as the source of our happiness, the goodness and power from which we hope to receive happiness. Charity makes us cling to God for His own sake.

THE OBJECT OF HOPE is eternal life—the vision of God. Since its object is a good, hope is a virtue in the will of man. It is therefore distinct from the passion of hope in the sense appetite of man. The passion of hope moves man to the pursuit of the goods of the flesh. But the virtue of hope moves man to the pursuit of God Himself. It can be found then only in the will.

SINCE HOPE MOVES MAN to seek God, neither the saints in Heaven nor the damned in Hell can have hope. The saints have no hope because they already possess God. A man does not hope to attain what he already possesses. The damned in Hell have no hope because they have already lost God and know that they can never possess Him. Hope is possible only when it is possible to attain the object of love.

BUT HOPE CAN BE FOUND in men in this present life. Moreover when hope is based on faith and inspired by charity, then a man can hope certainly to attain happiness. It is not so much hope itself which is certain, as it is that the faith on which hope is based is certain. The believer knows with certitude that God is ready to lead him to happiness and he knows that God can lead him to happiness.

OF COURSE, AS LONG AS A MAN is still in this present life, his will is changeable and he can desert God through sin. As far as man is concerned then hope can always fail. But the divine goodness on which hope rests can never fail. God is always ready to do what He can for those who truly seek

Him. This certainty of hope does not mean that man can sit back and let God do all the work for man's salvation. Men are not saved, as some heretics have said, simply because they believe in God's goodness. The hope that saves is the hope that works through love of God. It is the hope that leads a man to love God and keep His commandments.

SINCE HOPE CAN FAIL through man's sin, the divine generosity has given man the gift of fear to make hope perfect. We are not speaking now of any purely human fear which a man might have either of God or of anything in the world. We are speaking of that fear which is a gift of the Holy Spirit. It is a gift through which God moves man to fear Him so that the virtue of hope may neither be lost or frustrated.

FEAR OF GOD CAN BE OF TWO KINDS. If a man turns to God because he fears to be punished by God, this is servile fear, the fear which a slave has for his master. But if a man turns to God because of a fear of offending God by sin, then it is filial fear, the fear which a son has of offending the father he loves.

SERVILE FEAR IS FOUND in the man who has faith and hope, but has lost grace and charity through sin. It is good for man, because it can lead him to repentance and the love of God. Filial fear is found in the man in the state of grace and charity. Because he has charity he fears to offend God whom he loves.

IT IS FILIAL FEAR which is the gift of the Holy Spirit. It is filial fear which really perfects hope by leading man to make certain of his salvation by avoiding sin.

FEAR OF THE LORD is the "beginning of wisdom." (*Psalm* CX, 10.) Actually it is faith which gives man the essence of wisdom, for it is faith which tells man the truth about God, the cause of all things, and enables him to rule his actions according to the Divine Law. But both servile fear and filial fear are the first effects of wisdom. For servile fear enables man to rule his actions according to the divine law by holding before him the threat of divine punishment. And filial fear is the beginning, or the first step in practice, of wisdom since it leads a man to fear God and submit himself to the Divine Law.

MEN OFTEN SAY that love casts out fear. When we apply this saying to the love and fear of God it is partly true and partly false. It is true that the love of God takes away the servility or cravenness of servile fear. For the more a man loves God, the less he fears punishment. For the more he loves God the less he thinks of himself, even from the point of view of punishment. And the more he loves God, the more confident he is that he will escape punishment and attain happiness.

BUT FILIAL FEAR, the gift of the Holy Spirit, increases as a man's love of God increases. For the more a man loves someone, the more he fears to offend him or be separated from him. So too, the more a man loves God, the more he will fear to offend Him or be separated from Him.

THE PERFECTION OF HOPE AND FEAR is found in the first Beatitude: "Blessed are the poor in spirit: for theirs is the kingdom of heaven." (*Matt.*, V, 3.) When a man submits to God in filial fear, he ceases to seek greatness either in himself or in anything else but God. As a consequence he no longer sins through vanity or pride in himself or through attachment to the treasures of this world. He is then "poor in spirit." He seeks his happiness only in God. And his reward is the reward of hope, "the kingdom of heaven."

THE ENEMIES OF HOPE are the vices of despair and presumption. To despair is to lose trust in God's goodness and mercy. Presumption is the sin of assuming that God will give happiness to a man when he is not entitled to it. The sinner commits this sin when he hopes to attain the vision of God without repenting for his sins.

OF THE THREE GREAT SINS against the three theological virtues of faith, hope and charity, unbelief and hatred of God are more grievous than despair. For unbelief means that a man does not believe God's own truth. And hatred of God means that a man opposes his own will to God's own goodness. But despair means that a man ceases to hope for a share in God's goodness.

BUT DESPAIR IS MORE DANGEROUS for men than unbelief or hatred for God. For despair means that a man gives up hope. A man without hope has nothing to live for, nothing to seek, nothing to gain. He can neither respect himself, nor others, nor love God. When a man is in this condition he will rush headlong into sin. Every sin will cause him to despair all the more. Since he no longer trusts in the divine goodness, he has no means of raising himself from sin. The man in despair is rushing madly into Hell. Only the great grace and mercy of God can recall him from his dangerous journey to unhappiness.

DESPAIR IS CAUSED CHIEFLY by either lust or sloth. Lust binds a man strongly to the pleasures of the flesh. Hence he has no taste or desire for spiritual good. Or he considers it too difficult to attain. Nothing is left him but despair. Sloth or spiritual laziness casts a pall over man's mind. It makes the pursuit of good seem too difficult and so it leads man to despair.

PRESUMPTION IS NOT IN ITSELF so serious a sin as despair. For presumption does not deny God's goodness. It relies too much on God's goodness to the exclusion of God's justice. For a man is guilty of the sin of presumption when he hopes to obtain happiness even though he has no intention of giving up his sinful way of life.

PRESUMPTION IS CAUSED BY PRIDE. The presumptuous man hopes to obtain glory without merits, pardon without repentance. He does this because he thinks so much of himself that he imagines God will not punish him for his sins or exclude him from the happiness of heaven. The presumptuous man is like the proud husband who mistreats and injures his wife continually, but still expects her to love him because of his fancied perfections.

LIKE DESPAIR presumption drives real hope out of the heart of man. The presumptuous man lives in false hope. The great danger of presumption is that it leads a man to despise the graces of the Holy Spirit which might lead him to repentance. Blinded by his false estimate of his own excellence he spurns God's efforts to lead him away from sin to happiness.

THE GREAT SIN OF THE WORLD of to-day is the sin of despair. Militant atheism in the world has robbed men of faith and destroyed their hope. When men have no hope then violence rules the world. Where there is no hope there are only war and hate. That is why the world is still plunged in the maelstrom of war. That is why the lists of war casualties mount every day, why the number of the starving, the diseased, the homeless and dispossessed has reached appalling proportions. Where there is no real hope in God, there is no love of God. Where there is no love of God, there is no real love of men. A world without hope is a frustrated world. Without hope man has no chance to open the eyes of his soul through the horizons of faith to the infinity of the vision of God. Without hope man is a slave to his passions, to what is lowest in him. Without hope man can never achieve his true destiny.

THE ONLY REMEDY FOR THE WORLD is a return to the love of God through faith and hope. Faith will open man's eyes to the true splendor of God and man. It will give him a vision to live for, a significant journey to make. Hope will give man courage, courage built upon the assurance of the possibility of attaining true happiness. As despair brings the frustration of unhappiness to man, so hope brings happiness to the heart of man. To a man in despair life must seem like a sigh of sadness between two silences. But to the man who hopes life is a sigh of love coming out from a God Who is Love and returning happily and surely to that same God Who is Love.

CHAPTER III

Friendship with God

CHAPTER III
Friendship with God

DID YOU EVER RECEIVE a package wrapped in gaily colored paper and tied with bright ribbons and marked "Do not open until Christmas"? Do you remember the thrill of happiness you felt as you recognized the name of the sender inscribed in the upper left corner of the package? the name of someone you loved, of someone who loved you? Can you recall your heart's delight as it floated along on clouds of mystery, wondering what was in the package? Or, if you thought you knew, how your heart rejoiced in this proof of someone's love for you! With what eager but certain anticipation you treasured the gift until Christmas day when you could strip away the mysterious wrappings and really see the wonderful thing that love had brought you!

THE VIRTUE OF CHARITY is like a Christmas gift of this kind. It is a proof of God's love for you. It is the foundation of your love for God. It brings you God Himself. But, as long as you are still in this present life, it brings you God wrapped up in the paper and ribbons of faith and marked "Not to be opened until eternity."

CHARITY BRINGS GOD TO MAN because it is man's friendship with God. Like all friendship it is a love of benevolence, that is, it is an unselfish love. Charity loves God for Himself. It does not seek any selfish gain or advantage. It rests in God as the supreme Good. Again, like all friendship, charity is based on a community of interests or of living. Through charity God gives to man a share in the Divine Life, and, therefore, a share in the divine happiness. God's happiness is His love of His own infinite goodness and perfection. Charity is man's share in God's love of Himself. It is man's share in God's own happiness. As God is happy in the love of Himself, so man is happy when he shares in that love through charity.

SINCE GOD IS BOTH INFINITE AND SIMPLE, His love for Himself is identical with Himself. It is therefore infinite—a boundless ocean of love, a limitless uncreated fire of love embracing forever the supreme goodness which is God. Charity—man's share in this infinite love—is a created gift. It is a created, limited participation in divine love. Because man is a creature, because his will is a created will, he cannot love God with that same infinite love with which God loves Himself. But through charity he can love God as God loves Himself, that is, he can possess God as the source of infinite happiness, he can possess God as He is in Himself, as the supreme Good.

CHARITY IS A VIRTUE whose rule or measure is God Himself as the supreme Good. It unites man to God Himself as the supreme Good. It is a virtue distinct from all other virtues because its object is God Himself considered as the object of eternal happiness. It is more excellent than all other virtues because it is not self-seeking. It rests in God simply because He is God, the supreme Good. It is more excellent than the moral virtues because they are concerned only with the means that lead man to his goal, whereas charity attains the goal itself, God as He is in Himself. It is more excellent than the theological virtues of faith and hope because faith and hope attain God in so far as we derive from Him the knowledge of truth or the assurance of happiness, whereas charity attains God to rest in Him without any thought or desire for personal gain or advantage.

MOREOVER, SINCE CHARITY ATTAINS GOD precisely as the goal of man, no other virtue can be truly perfect unless its acts are directed by charity to the ultimate goal of all human activity, God as He is in Himself. Human acts of prudence or justice or even of faith or hope do not lead man to his ultimate goal unless they are directed to that goal by charity which unites man to God, the goal of all human acts.

BECAUSE THE OBJECT OF CHARITY is God considered as the goal or end of human life, charity is a virtue of the will. It is the will which seeks goals, above all the ultimate goal of all human activity. Charity then, which unites man to the ultimate goal, must be a virtue of the rational appetite, or will of man.

CHARITY IS MAN'S FRIENDSHIP WITH GOD based on man's share in the Divine Life, in the happiness of God Himself. But man cannot naturally share in God's own life. Man's participation in the Divine Life is a free supernatural gift which God gives to man. Charity then cannot be acquired by any purely human effort. It is a gift of God infused in man's soul by God's goodness and generosity. Charity, like the other theological virtues, is a supernatural virtue infused in the will by God Himself. Who can give man a share in the Divine Love except God Himself?

LIKE ALL GIFTS IT IS MEASURED by the generosity of the giver. God gives charity to men according to His own will. Since charity is a free gift from God to man, no man can say that his own natural virtues or perfections demand a greater share in God's love than the virtues of other men. As St. Paul says, "To every one of us is given grace according to the measure of the giving of Christ." (*Eph.* IV, 7.) The degree of charity—the love of friendship for God—depends not on man or his natural virtue but on God's generosity.

Bᴜᴛ ᴀs ʟᴏɴɢ ᴀs ᴍᴀɴ is in this present world his friendship with God can increase. As long as a man has not yet reached that ultimate union with God which is found in the vision of God, he can always approach nearer to God. In this life charity is a way to God. Hence a man's friendship with God can increase.

Iᴛ ᴡɪʟʟ ɪɴᴄʀᴇᴀsᴇ in the only way in which it is possible for the love of friendship to increase. A man grows in the love of friendship when his love for his friend grows stronger and leads him to do things more frequently for his friend. Consider the growth of friendship between a man and the woman he marries. At the beginning of their courtship he is willing to spend some of his time and his money on her. As his love grows he spends more time and money on her. As it grows still further he begins to admit her to the private world of his thoughts and ambitions, his hopes and disappointments. Then he begins to think of her troubles and sorrows, her triumphs and joys. Later he marries her and shares his life with her. Ultimately he is ready even to give his own life for her. In a similar way man can grow in the friendship of God. As his love of God grows he is willing to give more of himself for and to God. He begins to think more of God than of himself. He is more likely to do things for God than for himself. The intensity of his love for God grows within him until he is ready to give even his life for God. We might state it simply by saying that the intensity of his love for God grows stronger and stronger and becomes more and more likely to burst forth into acts of love of God.

EVERY NEW ACT OF LOVE OF GOD will at least dispose a man to an increase in his love for God. Love actually increases only when it becomes more fervent. A man may be friendly with a woman to the extent of taking her out to dinner and a dance. And the more often he does so, the more likely he is to come to love her more ardently. But his love for her does not actually increase until he loves her enough to introduce her to his family, or to ask her to marry him, or to marry her and share his whole life with her. So it is with man's love for God. Every act of love will dispose man to love God more. But only a more fervent act of love of God will actually increase his love of God.

IN THIS LIFE THE LOVE OF MAN for God is always capable of growth. Charity is a share of God's own love, which is infinite. It is therefore always capable of further growth. Its growth depends on the goodness and power of God which are infinite. And as charity grows in a man through the divine power, so does man's ability to receive a further increase in his love of God.

SINCE GOD IS INFINITELY LOVABLE in Himself, no man can ever love God as much as God ought to be loved. God alone can love Himself infinitely. But man's love for God can be perfect when man loves God as much as he can. This can happen in three ways. A man may love God with the entire devotion of his heart or will. He thinks always of God. He is always actually loving God. This is the perfection of love for God which is found in the saints in Heaven. In this present life man cannot love God with such entire devotion. The need for working or eating or sleeping and so on prevent a man from giving his whole attention to God. But even in this present life a man can try to give to God all the love and attention that are not needed for the necessities of daily living. This perfection of love is possible for man but not common among men. Lastly a man can give his whole heart habitually to God, that is, he will neither think or desire anything contrary to the love of God. He may not be thinking of God as much as he could, but he never does anything that would destroy his love for God.

WE MIGHT SAY THAT THE GROWTH of man's love for God in this life will start with the avoidance of sin, go on to the pursuit of good and end with the desire for union with God in heaven. The reckless youth who has been living a dissolute life falls in love with a good woman. First of all his love leads him to turn from his former irresponsible way of living. To gain the approval of his loved one he avoids his former dissolute companions. He struggles against his own intemperance. Then he begins to seek a good way of life. He settles down, goes to work, starts to save money. Finally he seeks union with his beloved in marriage. The story of man's love for God will follow the same path. When a man begins to love God, first he seeks to avoid sin and the insidious power of concupiscence which would separate him from God. Then he begins to cultivate virtue, to work for happiness. Finally he desires to live with God always.

LOVE IS ALSO CAPABLE OF DECLINE. Purely human love can grow less and less until it perishes altogether. When a man begins to think less and less of his wife, to be less thoughful of her welfare, to do fewer things to make her happy, then his love for her is failing. When he does something evil to her then his love ceases. Charity—man's love for God—can also fail, though not in precisely the same way. Charity will not fail simply because a man thinks less often of God. It will not even fail through venial sin. Venial sin is concerned only with the means that lead to the goal. It does not destroy man's basic tendency to God in charity. But mortal sin destroys charity completely. Charity is the love of God above all things. But in mortal sin man prefers some created thing to God. Hence mortal sin drives charity out of the soul of man. In a certain sense venial sin can lead to the loss of charity. Since all sin is not in accord with the will of God, the venial sinner is gradually disposing his will to give up God. Because he has not followed the will of God in all things, when some crisis arises in his life, he may give up God for some temporary created good.

I F WE WERE TO REGARD CHARITY as if it were only a purely human love, we might be tempted to think that charity is a love that makes man poor instead of rich. Or we might think that God is a jealous lover who resents the thought or affection that his friends give to anyone or anything else. In one way God is a jealous lover. He wants men to love Him above everything else, even above themselves. But this divine jealousy is not at all like the painful jealousy of the neurotic human being who makes his beloved unhappy by his unlimited demands for attention and service. Human jealousy, when carried to extremes, is a force that impoverishes the object of its affections. The jealous man will rob his wife of her parents, relatives and friends, her children, her work and her hobbies. He wants her to love nothing but himself. He wants her to have nothing but himself. But the divine jealousy is a love that enriches man. God asks for man's love through charity not in order to take any good thing away from man but in order to give all

good things to man. For through charity man attains
God, and in God he finds all good both in this life and
in the next. Charity is a share in divine love. But it is
the love of God which is the source of all good in this
life and in the next. It is love, the divine love, which
has created the world and all the good things in it. It is
God's love which has made man himself and the world
in which man is to seek for and to find happiness.
When a man loves God more than everything else, he
finds everything else in God, everything else that can
really make him happy.

SINCE CHARITY IS A SHARE in the divine love, it
follows that it moves man to love all that God
loves. But God loves everything that is good. Hence
man will love in charity everything that is good. He
will love his fellow-men, because God has created
them for Himself. He will love himself, because God
loves him. He will love the whole world because it
gives glory to God. Animals, plants, stones, rivers and
mountains—he will love them all because God has
created them out of love. Man will love his own body,
even though it can lead him into sin, because God
made it good, He made it to lead man to God. Man
will hate the weakness of the flesh which takes him
away from God, but he will love the body in so far as it
enables him to find and to serve God Who is his happiness. Charity will embrace even sinners, not because
they are sinners, but because they are men who are
capable of loving God. Because God loves all things in
the measure in which they are lovable, then charity,
friendship with God, will love all things according to
the same meausre.

FIRST OF ALL CHARITY LEADS MAN to love God
Himself, because God is the fountain of all

happiness. Through charity man loves God more than he loves himself. In God man finds the source of all happiness for himself and for his neighbors. Because he loves God most of all, then he loves everything else in the order in which God loves them. So he loves himself more than he loves his neighbor because he must love his own share in the divine goodness more than he loves anyone else's possible share in God's love. But he will love his neighbor more than he loves his own body or any temporary material pleasure of this world. For he will rejoice more in the thought that God is in his neighbor's soul than he will rejoice in some convenience, even life, in his own body. He will love some men more than others because he will recognize that God has willed that they play a more significant part in his life. So he will love his relatives and friends more than he loves strangers, because he knows that his salvation and theirs is to be worked out together in the plan of God. Ties of blood or citizenship or effort are all part of God's loving plan for men. Hence charity will lead a man to love his family, his country, his fellow-workers. It will also lead man to love his children more than he loves his own parents. For in God's plan his children are more closely united to him. They are a part of himself. He is a part of his parents, but they are not part of him. In charity a man follows the order which God Himself has put in things. So too he will love his wife more than his father or mother. For though he owes his parents love and reverence because they are the source of his own existence, nevertheless in marriage his wife is one with himself, and under God he must love himself more than anything else. For this same reason he will love more those for whom he does good than those who do good for him. He will love his benefactors because they are the source of good for himself. But he will love those for whom he does good even more because he loves in them the effect of his own goodness.

THIS SAME ORDER OF LOVE will remain in heaven. But there may be some modification of this order in relation to other men. Certainly in heaven man will love God above all things. But in relation to other men the order may change. In heaven man's will conforms itself perfectly to God's will. Since God loves more those who are better, then in heaven a man will love more those who are better than himself. Since their greater goodness is due to God's own love and bounty, this means only that man is loving God as He is found in other men. Still, from the point of view of the intensity of the love, man will love himself more intensely, because charity directs his mind to God and this is a part of his love for himself.

CHARITY IS A VIRTUE. This means that it is a power to act. Now the act of charity is love. To be charitable is to love. The love of charity is more than good will. To love is to achieve a union of affection. When two people are in love they have a unity of affection. They love one another, they love what each loves. The love of charity in act attains God immediately and other things as God loves them. When a man loves God, he loves God first and then the things that God loves. He loves God completely. He loves all that God is and all that God loves. In addition he loves God as much as he can. In the love of God when it is perfect, there are no reservations. Man loves God to the fullest extent of his capacity.

SINCE LOVE IS THE MOTIVE FORCE of all human actions and the source of all human effort, we naturally expect that charity or the love of God will have a profound influence on the achievement of happiness. Our expectation is not in vain. Charity brings happiness to both the individual human being and to the human race. Charity produces both interior effects in the individual and exterior effects in society. Or we might say, that since charity follows the order which God wills in the created world, then charity should bring good to the world. The interior effects of charity are joy, peace and mercy in the individual. The exterior effects are beneficence, almsgiving and fraternal correction.

THE FIRST EFFECT OF CHARITY or love is joy. The man who loves a friend rejoices when his friend is present with him or when his friend is happy even though absent. In both these ways charity—the love of God—produces joy in man. For the man who loves God knows both that God is supremely good and happy in Himself, and that through love God is present to him. "He that abideth in charity, abideth in God, and God in him." (I *John*, IV, 16.) Through charity God, Who is the supreme good and the source of all happiness, dwells in the soul of man. If happiness consists in the possession of God, then through charity man possesses essential happiness even in this life.

IT MIGHT BE OBJECTED that even the good seem to experience some sadness in this life. But this is not really incompatible with the joy that charity brings to man. It is true that God is always perfect, always happy. From this point of view the man who loves God can never be unhappy. He can never grieve because God is imperfect or unhappy. A man may be sorrowful because his son is a thief or because his son has been treated shamefully by his wife. But God is always supremely good and happy. Hence those who love God can never be unhappy because of some defect in God's own happiness. But it is possible to be unhappy because one does not possess God as perfectly as one can. So the man who truly loves God may be sorrowful at the thought of his past sins which separated him from God, or at the thought of some possible future sin which might take him away from God. Or he might be sad because he has not yet reached that perfect union with God which is accomplished only in heaven through the vision of God.

THUS, THOUGH CHARITY BRINGS JOY into the life of man—joy in the goodness of God and in the possession of God—still man's joy will not be complete until he reaches that perfect possession of God which is man's reward in heaven. Only in heaven will charity produce its full effect of joy. Only in heaven will man see God face to face and forever. Only in heaven can man be sure that he will never lose that ecstatic happiness for which God made him.

THE SECOND EFFECT OF CHARITY IS PEACE. How the modern world yearns for true peace. But how little the modern world understands what true peace really is. Men think that peace is the result of concord among men. They think that peace is found when men cease to fight with one another for a scrap of paper or a plot of ground or a lode of uranium ore. They forget that there is no true peace among men until there is peace in the individual man. True peace is found only when the conflicting appetites or desires of the individual are harmonized or directed uniformly to the pursuit of the true good of man. As we said above, the individual is not at peace with himself, until his passions are brought under the rule of reason, and until reason itself is directed by the will to the love of God. And until individuals are at peace with themselves, there can be no true peace in society. Now it is the function of charity to direct the activity of all man's powers to the love of God. Charity, therefore, when a man follows its promptings, produces peace in the individual and concord or harmony in society. For through charity the individual unites himself to God and to other men. The peace the world seeks is to be found through Christian charity and in no other way. Only the power of God, through the divinely infused gift of charity, can bring peace to mankind.

THE LAST INTERIOR EFFECT OF CHARITY in the soul of the individual is mercy. Mercy is grief for the distress of someone else, a grief which impels man to help those in distress. If a man loves his neighbor in charity, he is distressed at the misfortunes of his neighbor. The man who loves his wife is in agony when his wife is seriously ill. To feel sympathy with someone else when he is in trouble is an effect of charity. But this feeling of sympathy leads to acts of kindness or of mercy to those in distress. Hence it is not only an effect of charity like joy or peace, it is also a virtue in itself. It directs a man's actions in relation to those of his fellow-men who are in need.

MERCY IS A GREAT VIRTUE because it is fitting that those who possess much should come to the aid of those who are in need. For this reason mercy is a virtue attributed even to God Himself.

Even among men mercy is the greatest of all the virtues which rule the relations between men. It is more perfect than justice or fortitude or temperance.

THE REASON FOR THIS is not difficult to see. God has made the whole world because He is good. The world gives glory to God because He is good. Goodness is the essence of all things. But mercy is a more perfect manifestation of goodness to others than any other tendency in man. Hence of all the virtues that regulate the relations between men, mercy is the most perfect.

CHARITY IS LOVE OF GOD and of our neighbor in God. It is natural then to expect that charity will not only make the individual happy but will also tend to produce happiness in society. Charity does this through beneficence, almsgiving and fraternal correction.

BENEFICENCE IS AN ACT of the virtue of charity. To be beneficent is to do good to someone. When a man loves someone, he wishes him well. This well-wishing leads him to do good things for his friend. In this way beneficence is the result of love.

SINCE BENEFICENCE IS AN EFFECT of charity, it follows that it will be measured by the order of charity itself. A man will do good first to those who are closest to him and then to those who are not so closely related to himself. This is the meaning of the old axiom, "Charity begins at home." Of course, good deeds done for others should be measured also according to the circumstances of those who are to receive the benefit. Naturally a man ought to aid a starving stranger rather than give a luxurious gift to a relative who is already wealthy.

ALMSGIVING IS ALSO an external effect of charity. When we love others, we feel distress if they are in need of anything. We regard them as ourselves. Hence we seek to aid them. The deed that we do to aid them in their need, when it is done out of compassion and for God's sake, is called an alms. Since the object of almsgiving is to relieve someone's need, almsgiving is an act of the virtue of mercy. In this way it is ultimately an effect of charity.

THE NEEDS OF MEN are either material or spiritual. Since man is composed of body and soul, he may be in need either corporeally or spiritually. The virtue of mercy then will incline us to aid our neighbor either materially or spiritually. It is from this point of view that the works of mercy—almsgiving—are divided into the corporal and spiritual works.

THE CORPORAL WORKS OF MERCY ARE: to feed the hungry, to give drink to the thirsty, to clothe the naked, to harbour the harbourless, to visit the sick, to ransom the captive, to bury the dead. Briefly, charity—through mercy—inclines us to care for all the bodily needs of men.

THE SPIRITUAL WORKS OF MERCY ARE: to instruct the ignorant, to counsel the doubtful, to comfort the sorrowful, to reprove the sinner, to forgive injuries, to bear with those who are in trouble and annoy us, and to pray for all. Charity—through mercy —inclines us to care for all the spiritual needs of men.

THE SPIRITUAL WORKS OF MERCY are in themselves better than the corporal works of mercy. This is so because the soul of man is more noble than his body. But in particular cases the corporal works of mercy may be better and more necessary than the spiritual works of mercy. A starving man needs food more than he needs instruction.

CHARITY FOR OUR NEIGHBOR is a matter of precept. Christ Himself has said that the second greatest commandment is to love our neighbor as we love ourselves. Almsgiving then is also a matter of precept. We must love not only in word but also in deed. The precept of almsgiving must be kept whenever the giver has a surplus of goods—that is, when he has more than he needs for himself and those under his care—and whenever the recipient is in real need. It is obvious that the man who has just enough to eat is not obliged to give it to others. It is also obvious that the recipient of the alms should be in need, else there is no reason for giving him alms. When these two conditions are not fulfilled, then almsgiving is not a matter of precept, but only of counsel.

FRATERNAL CORRECTION is also an external effect of charity. When a man sins, his sin is harmful to himself, and sometimes it is also harmful to society. To impose a correction or penalty for a sin which has harmed society is an act of justice. But to correct a sinner in order to lead him to mend his ways is fraternal correction, an act of charity. Sin is an evil in the sinner himself. To reprove him for his sin, even to impose some penalty—if you are his superior—is an act of charity because it seeks the amendment of the sinner. It seeks to do good to the sinner by inducing him to forsake his sin and regain the friendship of God.

THE FRATERNAL CORRECTION OF THE SINNER which flows from charity should not be confused with the annoying officiousness of the professional busybody. The busybody takes delight in reproaching everybody. He feels obliged to report all wrong-doing —even when it is only a matter of rumor or conjecture—to higher authorities. He makes himself the policeman of the conscience of the world. He seeks not the amendment but the punishment of the sinner.

FRATERNAL CORRECTION is an act of charity, an act of love. This means that it will be used always with prudence. It will be used only when, where, and how it ought to be done. Fraternal correction will be used only when it is necessary to lead the sinner to repentance. It will be used with discretion. If a private word of warning is sufficient, that is all that is required. A public denunciation of the sinner is allowable only when his sins are harmful to the community or to other men and when no other means will reform him. And in all cases charity demands that the correction be administered with and through love. This means that we may correct our superiors only with respect and reverence, and our equals and inferiors with kindliness and mercy. Above all, correction is never allowable unless the facts are clear and certain.

WHEN WE CONSIDER THE EFFECTS of charity, it is easy to see that charity could transform the world. Charity itself is an evidence of the entrance of God into the world of men. It is God's love which introduces charity into the souls of men. Charity is a share in the divine love. It unites men immediately to the supreme Love which is God. Through the possession of God the soul of man is filled with joy. Because all man's powers are given direction and unity through the God-centeredness of charity, peace enters the soul of man and spreads concord among men. Charity begets in men's hearts the mercy which safeguards the poor, the weak and the needy. Charity opens the hearts of men to the whole world and enables them to put the mark of love on the world through beneficence, almsgiving and fraternal admonition. If all men lived by charity the world would be the paradise on earth of which men have dreamed since time began.

B UT THE WORLD IS NOT a paradise on earth. This can only mean that charity is not the well-spring of all human action. The lack of joy in the world today, the ominous absence of peace, the cruelty and barbarity instead of mercy, the predominance of sensuality over spirituality, of envy over good-will, of scandal instead of beneficence—all these are due to a lack of charity. Men lie, steal, cheat, foment discord, strife and war because they have forsaken the love of God and men. And the end of it all is hatred, the worst sin against God and men.

T HE WORST SIN AGAINST CHARITY is hatred. To hate God and men means to turn away from them as evil. But God is supremely good. There is no evil in Him. As for men, their human nature, since it is God's creation, is good. In addition, if they have through grace received a share in God's own life, they are also divinely good. Now it is most natural to man to love what is good. Hence hatred of God or men is the most monstrous perversion of man's will. Through hatred man denies what is most natural to him.

S INCE GOD IS INFINITELY GOOD and in no way evil in Himself, it might seem impossible for man to hate God. But love and hate follow knowledge.

Unfortunately man does not see God clearly in this life. Hence it is possible for a sinful man to consider God only as an avenging Judge forbidding sin and inflicting punishment. As long then as the sinner refuses to give up his sin, God will appear to him as something evil to himself. In this way it is possible for man to hate what is supremely lovable in itself.

HATRED OF MEN is due to envy. Envy is sorrow about someone else's good. Since man naturally loves the good wherever it is to be found, hatred of men is the end of a journey not a beginning. In the beginning men naturally love one another. It is only after sin has deformed and destroyed man's natural good will, it is only after a man has seen his own lack of good that he comes to resent the good in others.

HATRED THEN IS NOT so much a capital sin—a source of other sins—as it is the end result of a life of sin. Perseverance in sin leads a man to hate God Who punishes sin and good men in whom there is no sin. Hatred comes to a man after he has lost charity through sinful opposition to the effects of charity.

THE FIRST EFFECT OF CHARITY is joy in the goodness of God. But this joy can only live through the union of man's will with God in charity. And charity demands that man keep all the commandments. Charity demands a fellowship in good between God and man. When the effort to live in this fellowship in good begins to appear too difficult to man he begins to be sorrowful about the infinite goodness of God. This sorrow weighs down the spirit of man and leads him to neglect good. This sorrow is the sin of sloth, sorrow about the goodness of God. Sloth is a capital sin. It leads men into other sins. To avoid

the sorrow or weariness of spirit which is sloth men
will turn from God to the sinful pleasures of the world.

WHEN A MAN FALLS VICTIM to sloth and is
sorrowful because of the goodness of God it
is only natural that he will begin to be grieved also
at the manifestation of the goodness of God in other
men. He will resent good men simply because they
are good. This resentment is envy, hatred of someone else's good. Since the love of our neighbor flows
from our love of God, it is natural that when we
cease to love God's goodness, we will also begin to
hate the goodness of men. Envy, like sloth, is a
capital sin. It will lead men to commit other sins to
destroy the goodness of their neighbors.

WHEN A MAN'S HEART IS FILLED with sloth and
envy the interior peace of his soul which was
the effect of charity is destroyed. The loss of this
interior peace leads to the destruction of the peace
of society. When a man's heart is no longer centered
in God, then his life loses all proper direction. The
order of charity no longer guides his life. When the
love of God is gone he has nothing left but the love
of himself. When a man loves himself without loving
God then he can brook no opposition to his own
judgment or arbitrary will. He can tolerate goodness
in no one else. He will even, by the sin of scandal,
by his own words and example, lead other men into
sin. He must disagree with all men. He must dispute
with them, separate himself from them, quarrel with
them, go to war with them, set the whole of the
community at war with itself.

WHEREVER THE GOODNESS OF GOD is most
manifest, there will the heart of the man who
no longer loves God be most energetic in sowing the

seeds of discord, contentiousness, strife and war. That is why religion and the true Church of God are so viciously attacked in the world today. Those who do not love God are driven by sloth and envy to attack God's tabernacle on earth. When envy and sloth have led men through discord, contention, schism, quarreling, war and sedition to the hatred of God and man, then the sad journey of sinful man is complete. Hatred is the end of the flight from love. But the end of this journey is not a resting-place. Man was made for love. He cannot rest in hate. Love brings fulfilment and rest in the goodness of God in Himself and in His world. But hatred can only bring an agonizing frustration. Hatred despises what man most naturally loves—the good. But hatred cannot destroy what it hates—the good. The goodness of God is eternal. The manifestation of His goodness in the world goes on forever despite the evil of men. The man who hates then lives in a perpetual defeat. His hatred can find no rest because the goodness which harasses him is eternal.

WHERE THEN SHALL MEN FIND peace and joy and rest except in the love of God and men. Only a whole-hearted love of God and of men in God will bring peace to the individual and to society. Love can build a world. Hate can only destroy. Hatred sets men at odds with themselves and with God. They cannot judge correctly the value of men or nature. It is only in God that everything in the world receives its true place and its proper value. Only charity perceives everything as it is in God. Only charity therefore can enable a man to judge both the world and himself properly. And only this true judgment enables a man to find that tranquillity of order which is peace.

CHARITY PERCEIVES EVERYTHING AS IT IS IN GOD. We might more correctly say that charity is the cause of the gift of wisdom. We are speaking not of natural human wisdom which judges everything in the light of the highest cause of things as that cause is known through reason but of that divine gift of the Holy Ghost which enables man to judge divine things and human actions as they are in God. Through this gift of wisdom man is enabled to judge of things, whether divine or human, as God sees them. This is possible to man because in the friendship of charity man shares in the divine life. Two people who lead a life in common can judge the meaning and significance of that life and of their actions in that life in a way that is possible to no one else. To a stranger the harshness of a husband's voice as he speaks to his wife will seem to be an evidence of dislike or hatred. But to the wife who has lived a common life with the husband, the harshness of his voice indicates only his concern for her welfare in the crisis which they are both facing. It is an evidence of love. In charity man possesses God Himself and shares in the divine life of knowledge and love. Through charity and the gift of divine wisdom in the human intellect man can estimate properly the attributes of God in themselves, the effects of God's actions in the world and the relation of human actions to the love of God. Through the gift of wisdom man shares in the divine wisdom. He sees all things as God sees them and therefore sees them most truly. He sees them as they really are. With the truth of this vision man can set his life in order, in the order of charity. With wisdom man moves through the world truly awake and alert, realizing the true significance of everything. Without wisdom man is foolish. The meaning of the world and of life escapes him. His mind is dulled by sin. He turns from God—Who alone is the inner meaning of things—to things themselves. Without God nothing can explain itself. Without wisdom man commits the supreme folly of seeking answers where there is no voice to reply. With wisdom man learns from the only Teacher who really knows everything.

BUT WISDOM accompanies and flows from charity. Without charity there is no gift of wisdom. Without charity there is no fellowship in the divine life. Without that fellowship man has no power to see things as God sees them. Wisdom then depends on charity.

ORDER AND PEACE DEPEND ON WISDOM, both in the individual and in society. Man needs divine wisdom to set in order the house of his own soul and the house of human society. Man therefore needs charity. He needs to preserve charity so that wisdom may grow with charity. With charity and wisdom man can remake the world according to the plan of a God Who is love. With charity and wisdom man escapes from the dark narrow prison of selfishness into the great wonderful free world of God's love. God does His part when He gives man that share in His own life which is charity. All that man needs is the generosity of spirit to use charity, to give himself in love to God and his fellowmen.

CHAPTER IV

Prudence:
Happiness in Action

CHAPTER IV

Prudence: Happiness in Action

IT IS A WONDERFUL PRIVILEGE to be able to talk to a friend over the telephone. It is even more wonderful to enjoy a friend's company face to face. But if your friend is in another city, then you can only enjoy his company face to face by making the long journey to him.

SPEAKING VERY BROADLY we might say that faith, hope and charity enable us to enjoy God's company, but over the telephone, not face to face. Through faith we hear His voice telling us wonderful news about Himself and His love for us. The sound of love in His voice and in His promises to us lifts our hearts up in hope. The love we return to Him in charity impels us to give up all things for Him and to undertake the long journey which will bring us to Him. But still, before we can see Him face to face, we must actually set out on the road that leads to Him.

AS WE HAVE SAID PREVIOUSLY, we walk to God by our human actions. But the field of human activity is broad and deep. In the course of the average human lifetime a man must do many things besides believe, hope and love. He must eat and drink, work and rest. He may marry and beget children. Then he must provide food, clothing and shelter for his family. He must provide intellectual, moral and religious training for his family. He may enter politics. Then he must govern his community well. He may become a soldier. Then he must defend his country well. But no matter what life may demand of him, he must direct all his actions to the goal of happiness. He needs therefore the moral virtues of prudence, justice, fortitude and temperance. The moral virtues will enable him to set in order the wide field of human activity and direct all his actions to God, the object of the theological virtues. We all admire the man who orders his life well. Such a man knows the goal of human life. He knows how to suit his actions to his goal. Everything that he does turns out well. The virtue which enables such a man to direct his actions to the goal of human life is the virtue of prudence. Prudence is the virtue which directs human action to the goal of happiness. In this chapter we shall consider the virtue of prudence.

PRUDENCE DIRECTS HUMAN ACTS to their proper goal. But direction is first of all a work of reason. Prudence therefore is an intellectual virtue. If a man were to set out for the North Pole we should think him imprudent if he wore only a light summer suit. We should say that he did not have enough foresight to realize that his body could not stand the intense cold of the Arctic region unless it were warmly clad. Prudence implies foresight—an ability to foresee what things must be done to attain the goal and what things must be avoided. But foresight of this kind must be based on a remembrance of past experience and a correct estimate of the present conditions of human action. Prudence then is a perfection of man's reason. It enables him to direct his actions to their goal intelligently.

BECAUSE IT DEALS with human actions it is a work of man's practical reason. It is not, like the other intellectual virtues of understanding, science and wisdom concerned with speculative truth or theories. It is concerned with the details of human actions, with the living of life itself. It adapts human actions to the attainment of the goal of life—happiness. As the good mechanic chooses the right tool for the task at hand, so the prudent man chooses the right human action for the goal of human life.

B ECAUSE PRUDENCE ACTUALLY directs human actions it is a perfect virtue. It is a perfect virtue because it directs man to what is morally good precisely as good. The prudent man not only knows what should be done, he also applies that knowledge to his action. Prudence then is not found in the dreamer who never acts on his dreams, nor in the impulsive, impatient man who is always acting, but without forethought either of the proper goal or of the proper means to the goal. Prudence presupposes that a man's will is good, that is, it presupposes that the will is actively tending toward good. Without this active tendency of the will to good, a man is at best an ineffective dreamer who refuses to apply his knowledge to action, and at worst, a crafty schemer who applies his knowledge to evil action.

T HIS ACTIVE TENDENCY of the will toward human good is the work of the other moral virtues of justice, fortitude and temperance. The function of prudence is to direct the actions of these virtues to their goal. The proper goal of each of these virtues consists in conformity with right reason. Now the conformity of an act of justice, fortitude or temperance with right reason is appointed by reason itself. It is not the role of prudence to find or appoint the goal of these virtues. But it is prudence which determines in what way man shall act in order to attain the goals appointed by reason. A man, for example, has borrowed fifty dollars from a neighbor. The end or goal of justice is to give each man what is due to him. Justice, in conformity with right reason, demands therefore that the fifty dollars be paid back. But how and when shall it be paid back? A man without prudence might never pay it back, and so he would fail to observe the rule of reason in a matter of justice. Such a man would not have the foresight and the resolution to set aside a small sum from his wages each week until he had saved the entire sum and could pay his debt. Instead he might wait for some windfall to drop the money in his lap, or he might waste his own money betting on horseraces in the vain hope of getting the fifty dollars quickly. But the prudent man will save according to his ability so that he can repay his neighbor as soon as possible. In this case prudence has determined exactly how the debt shall be paid. It determines, for instance, to open a savings account in a bank and deposit five dollars each week until the whole amount is saved.

PRUDENCE, WE SAY, decides or determines just what act or acts will attain the goal of moral virtue. This shows that the chief act of the virtue of prudence is to command. In any matter of human action reason has three tasks to perform. Reason must take counsel, judge and command. If a man owes money which he must repay, he must first take counsel, that is, consider the different ways in which it may be possible to save the money he owes. He might simply wait until times get better or until he is making more money. He might borrow from Peter to pay Paul. He might gamble in order to get the money quickly. He might save a little of his wages each week until he has the sum owed. Then reason judges the relative merit of each of these different ways of paying the debt. It finds that waiting for better times is unsatisfactory because it offers no real assurance that the debt will ever be paid. Borrowing from Peter to pay Paul just transfers the payment from one man to another. Gambling is too risky. Only a real effort to save through some sacrifice offers a likely solution to the problem. Lastly, reason commands that this last solution be put into action. Since prudence is concerned with human action, it is clear that the chief act of prudence is neither taking counsel, nor judging, but commanding. For only the command results in proper action.

THE FACT THAT SO MANY PEOPLE act imprudently shows that prudence is a virtue that implies maturity of mind. This is even clearer to us when we consider all the virtues of mind that real prudence requires. Take the case of a man in Phoenix, Arizona who is offered a better position in New York City. Shall he accept or refuse? Before deciding, he must recall that his wife has a bad case of asthma and that while the climate of Phoenix is very beneficial to asthmatics, the climate in New York is not. Then he must understand that his wife's health is more important than a larger income. But perhaps his employers will be angry at him if he refuses to move from the branch office at Phoenix to the home office in New York. He ought to be wise enough and docile enough to seek the advice of older and wiser men than himself. It will help too if he is shrewd enough to see the solution that is best among those suggested. The ability of his mind to reason will be a factor in reaching the right decision. He also needs foresight to determine the exact degree of danger to his wife if he goes or to both of them if he refuses to go, as well as the probable effect on his employers of the reasons for refusal. If he intends to refuse, he must determine circumspectly just what reasons he can give to gain his point without offending his employers. Lastly, he must be cautious not to endanger his whole future by his refusal or the way in which he refuses. Let us say that he makes a prudent decision. Quite properly for his wife's sake he refuses to go to New York. But he explains this reason so well to the home office, he appeals so successfully to the fundamental humanity of his employers that he retains their respect. In reaching this decision he has made use of memory, understanding, docility or teachableness, shrewdness, reason, foresight, circumspection and caution. All these habits of mind are required for perfect prudence.

THE GREAT NUMBER of mental talents required for prudence should not make us think that it is almost impossible to be prudent. There are two kinds of prudence possible to man, namely, natural or acquired prudence and supernatural or infused prudence. Natural prudence is acquired slowly with age, experience, education and character training. Memory, foresight, circumspection and caution require experience and therefore time before they can be acquired. Understanding, shrewdness and perhaps docility require both experience and training or education before they can function perfectly. But all these things are possible to a human being with good will. If the will remains steadfast in its pursuit of moral good, then natural prudence will mature in a man.

BUT, AS WE HAVE ALREADY SEEN, the will of man cannot remain constant in the pursuit of good without grace and the infused virtue of charity. Perfect prudence can be found then only in those who are and remain in the state of grace. More important even than this is the fact that the infusion of grace and charity in the soul by God brings with it also the infusion of the supernatural virtue of prudence. Supernatural prudence does not have to be slowly and laboriously acquired by men. It is a gift from God. It is given even to children through the sacrament of Baptism. It is possible therefore for everyone to begin his life with some prudence, with supernatural prudence. And this prudence is superior to natural prudence. Natural prudence conforms human actions to the rule of human reason. But supernatural prudence conforms them to the rule of the Eternal Law of God. In this way it prepares men for the happiness of the vision of God. Through supernatural prudence the divine light of the Eternal Law guides human acts to the eternal destiny of man safely and surely and divinely.

MOREOVER, TO INSURE the proper functioning of supernatural prudence God also gives through grace the gift of counsel. We are not speaking here of natural human counsel, but of that supernatural gift of the Holy Spirit which is called counsel. This gift of God makes the mind of a man docile under the guidance of God Himself. Through this gift it is the eternal wisdom of God which enlightens man in the choice of human actions which will lead man to happiness.

IT IS TRUE of course that supernatural prudence will not function perfectly in a human being from early childhood. Some training in natural prudence will be helpful. But as long as a human being retains the good will of charity, supernatural prudence and counsel will in turn be helpful in the attainment of natural prudence.

THE OBJECT OF PRUDENCE is the good of the moral virtues, human good. But, as we have seen elsewhere, human good may be the good of the individual or the common good of society. Hence it is possible to divide prudence into prudence for the individual—which is called simply prudence—and prudence for society—which is called domestic prudence when it deals with the good of the family, political prudence when it deals with the good of society or the state, and military prudence when it deals with the problems of defending the good of the state or nation against attack. Everyone needs prudence in the management of his own individual life. Those who have the care of families, states, or military forces will need respectively either domestic, political or military prudence to provide for the common good of society.

THE NECESSITY OF PRUDENCE for successful living makes it important to consider briefly the vices opposed to prudence. First of all there are the vices which are evidently opposed to prudence, the vices of imprudence and negligence. Imprudence is the vice of not following the rule of reason in human action. As we have seen, the prudent man takes counsel before acting. He uses his memory, understanding, docility, shrewdness, reason, foresight, circumspection and caution. But the imprudent man will not take counsel. He will not use these mental talents. He rushes headlong into action, without caution or circumspection, thoughtless of his past experience or ability to reason, inconstant because of lack of foresight. Negligence is the failure of a man to be alert in his human actions. It indicates that a man is not sufficiently interested in the proper goals of human activity to take the means to be prudent.

SECONDLY, THERE ARE THE VICES of carnal pru dence, craftiness and excessive worry, which resemble prudence. Many people even think that these vices are true prudence. Carnal prudence is the prudence of the man who looks upon the goods of the flesh as the goal of his life. He is alert and shrewd in obtaining the goal of his desires, the satisfaction of the needs of the body. But his prudence is a false prudence because it prevents him from obtaining eternal happiness, the satisfaction of the needs of his soul. Craftiness is the sin of using fictitious or evil means to gain the desired goal. Excessive worry is the sin of being so solicitous of obtaining worldly goods or of providing for the future that a man forgets to work for the true goal of eternal happiness.

THESE SINS OF IMPRUDENCE arise from the capital sins of lust or avarice. Since the goal of human life is the eternal happiness of the vision of God, anything which withdraws the mind and heart of man from God and the things of God will lead to the loss of prudence. But men turn from God to the world either through lust for the pleasures of the flesh or through an inordinate desire for the goods of this world of time and space. The prudent man, on the contrary, is always sufficiently farsighted to realize that all human activity is worthwhile only to the extent that it leads man to God. For prudence is concerned ultimately with the direction of human activity to the great goal of human life, the vision of God.

IMPRUDENCE LEADS TO UNHAPPINESS. We might even say that it is unhappiness. It condemns a man to the futility of achieving goals that do not satisfy him. The imprudent man is imprisoned in the dense jungle of base desires and ignoble satisfactions. He cannot escape from the tyranny of the flesh. The prudent man finds happiness in human action. His activity is always satisfying because he knows that it is leading him to eternal happiness. His prudence frees him from the tyranny of the flesh and the despotism of inordinate desire. It has been said that vigilance is the price of liberty. We might paraphrase the statement and say that prudence is the price of the freedom of the sons of God.

CHAPTER V

Justice:
Happiness in Society

CHAPTER V

Justice: Happiness in Society

MEN ARE BY NATURE SOCIAL BEINGS. They live together and work together for their mutual advantage. This cooperation of men with one another is necessary if men are to achieve real success in human living. If all parents abandoned all children immediately after birth, the children would not live and the human race would perish. If all the patrons of department stores took the merchandise but refused to pay the price, all department stores would be bankrupted and soon there would be no stores at all and no goods to be purchased. If, from birth to death, every man had to do everything for himself, provide his own food, his own clothing, his own home, his own medical care, his own defense against thieves and murderers, his own education, then the human race would perish. The fullness of human living is possible to mankind only through the cooperation of all in the pursuit of the common good of all. Men must live together and work together if each man is to have his chance to lead a full, rich human life. Briefly, men must live in society.

SOCIETY SUCCEEDS IN PROMOTING the common welfare of its members only to the extent that the common life of the members is ruled by order and peace. The United States of America is rich in natural resources. Millions of human beings can live richly and fully through the proper use of these natural resources. But imagine for a moment that the peace and order of the United States did not exist. On Monday farmer Jones might plant his fields in wheat. But on Tuesday farmer Smith would plough up the fields again and plant rye. And before either one of them could harvest the crop, some marauders from the next county might drive up in force and harvest the rye for themselves. This same situation would prevail in all the fields of human endeavor. The storekeeper would never know from day to day whether he had any goods to sell or whether his customers would pay their bills. The lonely traveler would never know whether or not he would complete his journey without being robbed or murdered. The householder would never know when he might be driven from his home by an invader stronger than himself. Without peace and order no society could live long. Without peace and order the life of mankind would be a will-o'-the-wisp tossed about violently by the hurricane winds of brute force.

BUT THE PEACE AND ORDER of society are attained through the practice of the virtue of justice. It is justice which leads the customer to pay the merchant the proper price for his merchandise. It is justice which leads the farmer to respect the fields and crops of his neighbors. It is justice which leads the policeman to enforce the laws without fear or favor. It is justice which prevents a man from stealing the money, the home or the wife of another man. In a word, it is justice which leads each man to give to every other man what is due to him. It is justice which leads men to respect each other's rights. In this way justice gives to society the stability and efficiency which are necessary for successful living.

THE VIRTUE OF JUSTICE is based on the recognition in each man of both rights and obligations. We are all familiar with the notion that men have rights. A man, we say, has a right to his own life.

The worker has a right to his wages. The citizen has a right to be protected by the police against thieves or murderers. A right is something that is due to a man, something that he can claim as his own.

THE RIGHTS OF A MAN may be either natural or positive, that is, they may be due to him simply because he is a man, or because of some agreement reached between men. By nature, for example, each man has a right to his own life or good name. By private agreement the man who sells an automobile has a right to be paid the purchase price. By public agreement—law—each man has a right to the inviolability of his own home. Not even a policeman may enter or search his home without a duly authorized search warrant.

THE NOTION OF RIGHT cannot be divorced from the notion of obligation. If one man has a right, then other men have the obligation to respect that right. If a man has a right to his own life, then no other man can murder him. If a storekeeper has a right to his goods, then his customers have the obligation to pay him for any goods they wish to take for themselves. If every man's home is his castle, then not even the police may enter without his permission or without a search warrant. Every right walks hand in hand with the obligation to respect that right. The action of men —in their dealings with one another—must be so regulated that the rights of all are safeguarded.

THE VIRTUE WHICH INCLINES MEN to respect the rights of others is the virtue of justice. Justice is a habit by which a man, by a perpetual and constant will, gives to each one what is due to him. It is a virtue because it makes human acts good. It is a virtue of the will of man because it is concerned not with the knowledge of man or the internal passions of man but with man's external actions in relation to other men.

As we look at other men we can see them from two points of view. We can look upon them simply as other individuals or we can look upon them as members of the community. Each man is both of these things, himself and a member of the community. And in both ways he has rights and obligations. Our actions in relation to another man considered only as a private individual are ruled by particular justice. Our actions in relation to other men considered as members of the community are ruled by what is called general or legal justice.

Particular justice regulates the relations between men considered as individuals. When one man pays another two dollars to mow his lawn, it is particular justice which directs both the making and the fulfilling of the contract. When a man buys vegetables from his grocer, it is justice which inclines the man to pay for the vegetables and the grocer to give his customer both the quantity of potatoes agreed upon by both and the exact change required.

General or legal justice regulates the relations between men considered as members of the community. Its object is the common welfare of all the members of the community. It is general justice which regulates the laws prescribing the requirements for voting. Since its object is the common good of all, and since the moral goodness or virtue of men leads to the attainment of the common good, it it within the province of general justice to direct the acts of all the virtues to the common good.

T HE PROPER ACT of the virtue of justice is to give to each man exactly what is due to him. The customer in a store must give to the merchant exactly the price agreed upon, no more and no less. The burdens of taxation should be distributed among the citizens of a state in proportion to their real ability to pay. It follows from this that the mean of justice is not simply the mean of reason. It is also the real mean. Through justice we give to other men exactly what is theirs. If we give more, the excess is due to liberality, not to justice. If we give less, the defect is due to injustice.

T HE VIRTUE OF JUSTICE is the mortar that binds together the bricks of the house of mankind. It is justice which gives to human life the stability which men need to work without fear or anxiety in the search for happiness. Where justice rules, there men need not fear that their food will be taken from their mouths or their homes burned to the ground by vandals. It is justice which gives men the inspiration to work fruitfully. Where justice rules, there men know that the fruits of their labor are their own. Justice is more excellent than the other moral virtues. It surpasses fortitude and temperance because it is a perfection of the rational will of man, which is a more excellent power than the sensitive appetite, the subject of fortitude and temperance. It is more excellent than prudence, for general justice seeks the common good—which is superior to the private good of the individual—and particular justice is directed also to the good of another.

T HE VALUE OF JUSTICE can be measured also by the evil of injustice. The unjust man despises the rights and the persons of his fellowmen. He takes what is not his without regard for the rights of others. The money, the good name, the property, even the life of his neighbor he will destroy in pursuit of his own selfish ends. In this way he becomes an evil force destroying the unity of society. Every unjust man is a threat to the peace and order of human social living. As the number of the unjust increases, the stability of social life dies. Men lose their incentive to work for themselves or for the common good. Suspicion and hatred replace trust and love in the hearts of men. The law of force and cunning replaces the law of justice.

SINCE INJUSTICE always consists in an injury inflicted on another person, it is contrary to the law of charity. By its nature then it is mortally sinful. But it may sometimes happen that the injury is so slight that it is not altogether contrary to the will of the person injured. To steal five cents from a millionaire can hardly be a mortal sin. Basically the gravity of the injustice will be measured by the will and the circumstances of the person injured. To steal even a small sum of money from a very poor person can be mortally sinful. On the other hand one cannot steal large sums even from the wealthy.

PARTICULAR JUSTICE is either distributive justice or commutative justice. Distributive justice governs the distribution of the goods or the burdens of society to the individual members of society. It is distributive justice, for example, which provides for public education and public hospitals. The burdens of taxation and military service fall under the province of distributive justice.

COMMUTATIVE JUSTICE, on the other hand, rules the relations between individual men. It governs all the actions by which things are transferred between men. If the transfer is involuntary on the part of the original owner, as in the case of theft, then the action of the thief is an injustice and commutative justice demands that the stolen object be restored to its owner. If the transfer is voluntary, as in the case of buying and selling, then commutative justice rules the action of both the buyer and the seller.

THE MEAN TO BE FOLLOWED in distributive justice is the mean of geometrical proportion. The common goods of the community are to be distributed according to the relation between the citizens and their usefulness or prominence in the community. The mayor of a city, for example, will be paid a higher salary or pension than any lesser employee of the city.

ON THE OTHER HAND, the mean of commutative justice will be the exact arithmetical mean. If a man has borrowed twenty-five dollars from someone, he must repay twenty-five dollars. If he has stolen ten dollars, he must restore ten dollars.

THE FACT that commutative justice demands the restitution of what has been taken from someone else shows the foolishness of commutative injustice. The thief who has stolen money is obliged to restore it. The liar who has ruined a man's reputation is obliged to do what he can to retract his lies and their evil effects. As long as he clings to his injustice, the unjust man is an enemy of society and of himself. As long as he refuses to restore the order of justice, he is outside the order of charity and so cannot find true happiness.

THE SINS against justice are many. One sins against distributive justice by respect of persons. Distributive justice demands that the common good be distributed to persons according to their dignity or usefulness to the community. Thus justice demands that only a qualified person should be appointed to a judgeship. But the sin of respect of persons consists in giving a man something simply because he is the person he is. Thus the mayor who would appoint as judge a relative who was not qualified for the position would be guilty of the sin of respect of persons.

SINCE COMMUTATIVE JUSTICE regulates the relations between individual men, and since the actions of men in relation to one another are by far more numerous than the actions of distributive justice, the sins against commutative justice are more numerous also. We can injure our neighbor unjustly by murder or bodily injury, by theft and robbery, by bearing false witness against him in a court of law, by accusing him unjustly, or, if you are a judge or juror, by giving an unjust judgment against him, by reviling or backbiting him so that he loses his good reputation, by cheating him in a contract of sale, by lending him money at an exorbitant rate of interest, and so on.

SINS AGAINST JUSTICE are the cause of tension and unrest in human society. Sins against distributive justice cause either anger or cynicism in the citizens. Anger can lead to sedition or revolt. Cynicism leads either to the moral corruption or the civic apathy of the members of the community. In either case the moral temper of society declines and men forsake the order of charity for the disorder of selfishness.

SINS AGAINST COMMUTATIVE JUSTICE are even more destructive of the peace and order of society. Lying and stealing and murder destroy men's trust in one another and so prevent the harmonious cooperation of men with one another for the common good of all. When men cannot trust their neighbors, then they cannot work together effectively. When no one can be sure from day to day that what he has is his and will remain his, then all incentive to fruitful work is destroyed.

INJUSTICE THEN DESTROYS both the common good and the good of individual men. It destroys the happiness of society. Justice, on the other hand, means happiness in society. When men are just, then all can feel easy and secure. Human energies can be directed without anxiety to the search for real happiness. Without the fear and anxiety born of injustice men can direct their hearts and minds to the fulfilment of the law of charity. From one point of view charity is the cause of justice. For when men love one another they will be just to one another. From another point of view, justice is indispensable for charity. For when injustice reigns in society, then men find it hard to love one another and easy to love only themselves. The happiness of society then demands both charity and justice as the motive of justice and justice as the strong bulwark of charity.

CHAPTER VI

Religion:
Happiness in the
Service of God

CHAPTER VI

Religion: Happiness in the Service of God

GOD HAS CREATED MAN. He is therefore man's beginning. He has created man for Himself. He is therefore man's final goal. The proper order of the universe demands that men recognize these two facts and act accordingly. Men must give God His due, just as they must give each other what is due. Since God is the source of man's existence, life and action, it is clear that man can never fully repay God for all that God has done for him. Man can never fully repay God because all that he gives to God already belongs to God. But man must give to God, as the source and final goal of his existence, all that he can give Him, the full service of his body and soul. Religion is the virtue by which man gives to God the service and the honor which are due to God.

MEN PAY HONOR TO GOD not for God's sake, but for their own sake. Since God is absolutely perfect and perfectly happy in Himself, the honor men pay him in religion adds nothing to the perfection or happiness of God. But it does bring happiness to men because it places them in their proper relationship to God. It gives men their proper place in the universe. A fruit tree exists to bear fruit, and it achieves its true destiny when it actually bears fruit. Man exists as the spokesman of the universe. It is his function in the world to recognize God's dominion over all creation, to adore God as the Creator and the goal of all creation. When man recognizes God's dominion and adores God's majesty, he achieves his true destiny and so he finds happiness.

THROUGH REASON man recognizes God's dominion over man and over the universe. Through free will man voluntarily submits himself to God's sovereign dominion. Religion is, then, chiefly an affair of the mind and heart of man. External actions alone are not the essence of religion. The religious man worships God in his mind and heart.

NEVERTHELESS THE EXTERNAL ACTIONS OF MAN, his gestures of reverence such as genuflections or prostrations, his vocal prayers or hymns, his external sacrifices—all these visible and audible actions are necessary and useful to the virtue of religion. Man is not simply a spirit. He is also a body. His soul and body are a unit—the unit which is the whole man. Man's body, just as well as his soul, is subject to the divine dominion. Moreover, as all reasonable men know, even man's spirit cannot rise to the contemplation of God without the assistance of his body. A man can conceive in himself an intense spiritual love for a woman, but not until he has seen her, or heard her voice, or read her letters. If he does not know her at all through his senses, he cannot love her at all. In the same way, man rises to the thought of God through his knowledge of God's power and goodness as they are manifested to him in the visible world of creation. Again, any intense action in man's soul tends to manifest itself in the gestures or attitude of his body. We can tell that a man loves a woman by the way he looks at her, or the sound of his voice when he speaks to her, or by the things he does for her. So, too, when a man loves God and wishes to serve Him, he will express his internal religious acts in the external attitude, gestures or actions of his body.

MAN'S NATURAL TENDENCY to express the acts of his soul in the actions of his body accounts for the externals of religion, for churches and statues, for paintings and stained-glass windows, for altars and crucifixes, for priestly vestments and for sacrifices. All these externals of religion are meant, not to draw men away from God, but to enable them to approach God more easily. But it is still true that these external actions of religion are secondary. They must be subordinated to those acts of reason and will by which men subject themselves to God as His rational creatures.

BECAUSE RELIGION IS ESSENTIALLY a virtue of the spirit of man, the first act of religion, the heart of all other acts of religion, is devotion. Devotion is the will to do readily whatever concerns the service of God. The religious man is always ready to do whatever is necessary or useful for the worship of God. Of course this readiness of will, like all the attitudes or acts of the will, is based on man's recognition of his obligation to surrender himself to God. In this sense we say that devotion to God is based on meditation or contemplation. By meditation man perceives that he can find his true place in the universe and his real happiness only through the surrender of himself to God. In meditation man perceives the goodness and the kindness of God to himself, and this begets love which is the cause of devotion. Through meditation man also perceives his shortcomings and unworthiness, which leads him to lean on the strength of God for his salvation, and so to submit himself to God. The knowledge of his own defects may make a man sad, but the knowledge of God's goodness gives him joy. This is the explanation of the joy of truly religious people. Their minds and hearts are firmly anchored in the goodness and strength of God, and no difficulty or disaster can shake their souls from this firm foundation on which they stand.

NATURALLY, THE DEVOUT MAN who recognizes both the goodness of God and his own need of God's strength will praise God and thank Him for His gifts. These acts of praise and thanksgiving are prayers of praise and thanksgiving. There is also a place in religion for the prayer of petition. In the prayer of petition man raises his mind to God to ask Him for the things he needs. The prayer of petition is a part of God's plan for man. When we say that God answers prayers, we do not mean that prayer can cause God to change His mind. God has made the whole world and governs it by His providence. Everything that occurs in the world takes place according to the plan of divine providence. But it is part of God's plan that certain gifts will be given to man only in answer to prayer. We pray, not to change God's plans, but in order to receive from God those things which He has planned to give us in answer to our prayers.

IN ANSWERING THE PRAYERS of men, God will follow the order of divine wisdom and love. He will put first things first—first the spiritual and then the temporal needs of man. When a man prays for what is necessary for his own salvation, God will answer his prayer by giving him what he really needs for salvation. But when a man prays for temporal things—a special job, or money, or fame, and so on— God will or will not grant such gifts in so far as He sees that they are or are not good for this particular man.

CHRIST HIMSELF has given us the perfect prayer in the Lord's Prayer, the "Our Father." In the Lord's Prayer we ask for all the things we may rightly desire, and we ask for them in the order in which we ought to desire them. As a rational creature, man should seek first the goal of his life, God Himself, and secondly the things which lead to this goal. In the first petition of the Lord's Prayer, "Hallowed be Thy name," we express our love for God in Himself. In the second petition, "Thy kingdom come," we ask to attain the goal of happiness in the kingdom of God. In the remaining petitions we ask for the things which will lead us to our goal. When we say: "Thy will be done on earth as it is in heaven," we are asking for the grace to fulfill God's will so that we may merit happiness. When we ask: "Give us this day our daily bread," we are asking for the means of meriting happiness, either the Body of Christ in the sacrament of the Eucharist or the temporal necessities of life in so far as they will lead us to God. In the next petition, "Forgive us our trespasses," we plead for the forgiveness of the sins which would prevent us from reaching happiness. When we ask God: "Lead us not into temptation," we are asking Him to protect us against the future danger of sin. Lastly we pray: "Deliver us from evil," begging God to free us completely from the evil of this present world.

PRAYER MAY BE SAID aloud or in the silence of one's own soul. Individuals can pray in either way; but when a group or community prays, it is better for the prayer to be said aloud. In this way men can achieve a unity of mind and heart in their communal prayers.

IN ONE WAY OR ANOTHER God answers all prayers. Even the prayers of the sinner, when he prays for repentance, will be answered through the mercy of God. But the prayers of God's friends, that is, of those who are in the state of grace and charity, are meritorious.

BESIDES THE INTERNAL religious acts of devotion and prayer there are also external acts of religion. Man's internal religion tends to express itself externally. The external acts of religion are adoration, sacrifice, oblation, the support of God's ministers, vows, oaths, adjuration and the reverent use of God's name.

ADORATION WAS ORIGINALLY a general term which meant to pay tribute to someone's excellence. The young man who is in love says that he adores the woman of his choice. He means that he honors the virtues which she possesses. When we use the word adoration in relation to religion, the word retains this original meaning. We adore God or His saints because of the excellence of their holiness. The adoration we give to God is called latria. Latria is the honor we pay to God as the infinitely perfect being, the Creator and Lord of the universe. The adoration we pay to the saints, their relics or images, is called dulia. Dulia is the veneration we give to the saints because, through the grace of God, they have achieved real holiness and union with God in heaven. Because the Blessed Virgin Mary is the Mother of God, and because God's grace has made her the most excellent of all the saints, we pay her the tribute of hyperdulia or superveneration. The veneration which we pay to Mary or to the saints is ultimately an adoration of God Himself, because what we honor in Mary or the saints is the share in the divine life which God has generously given them.

SACRIFICE IS AN ACT of religion that is made only to God. Sacrifice is the offering to God of something that is visible and sensible. It is offered as a sign of the subjection and honor which man owes to God. It is a sign of man's inward submission to God as his Creator and final goal. In the full sense, then, sacrifice always demands these two things: the inward submission of man to God and the external action which is a sign of this submission. We can see these two elements of sacrifice in the sacrifice which Christ offered on the Cross of Calvary for the salvation of all men. On the Cross, Christ was offering His human life to God as an acknowledgment of God's supreme dominion over all human life. In the shedding of His Blood, He symbolized externally His inward offering of Himself to God. In every sacrifice we must have these two elements: the inward act by which man offers himself to God and the external offering of something to God which symbolizes the inward offering.

A**N OBLATION OR OFFERING** is the giving of something to God. If it is offered in such wise that it is destroyed in God's honor, then the offering is a sacrifice. If it is not intended to be destroyed, but rather to be used in the worship of God or given for the use of God's ministers of religion, then it is simply an offering to God.

M**EN MAKE OFFERINGS** to God as an acknowledgment of the fact that all they possess comes to them originally from God. They may offer something to be used in the worship of God, such as a chalice, a set of priestly vestments, the first-fruits of their labors, or the money to provide for a fitting worship of God. Or they may make offerings to provide a suitable livelihood for God's minister. Men must worship God not only as individuals, but also as social beings. Hence there must be ministers of religion—priests—

who will mediate between God and men, carrying the prayers of men to God and bringing God's graces down to men. But those who devote their lives and labors to God and men in the service of religion must live as other men. They need food and clothing as other men do. It is fitting, therefore, that the rest of men—for whom they labor in the service of God—should make offerings for their support. If a man loves God, he will worship God and he will see to it that the worship of God is carried out in a fitting manner. This means that he will make offerings to God for the objects used in religious worship, and for the support of the priests who act as man's representatives in the worship of God.

MEN ALSO WORSHIP GOD by vows, oaths, adjurations and by praising God. A vow is a promise by which a man binds himself to do something for God. It is the generosity of love which impels a man to vow something to God. In an oath we call upon God to witness the truth of what we say. In an adjuration we either beseech our superiors or command our inferiors to do something in the name of God. In oaths and adjurations we are, as it were, asking God to take part in our human affairs. It should be clear that man cannot ask God to do this unless there is a serious reason for so doing. It is even more obvious that man cannot—without sin—ask God to bear witness to a lie, or to aid a man to do something that is evil. Lastly, the religious man will use the name of God reverently. He will praise God openly in word and even in song. Prayers of praise and hymns are really the natural outpouring of the great love for God found in the heart of the religious man.

O N THE REVERSE SIDE of the picture, there are many sins which men commit against the virtue of religion. Basically, they may be reduced to sins of either superstition or irreligion. The superstitious man either worships a creature instead of God, or he worships God in a way that is displeasing to Him. The irreligious man really feels contempt for God or for the things of God.

T HE SUPERSTITIOUS MAN may worship God, but in a way displeasing to God. In some of the old pagan religions, for example, men committed acts of impurity as acts of worship. Certainly God, Who is all holy, cannot wish men to commit sin as an act of worship. Or the superstitious man may worship a creature instead of God. He may do this by outright idolatry, the adoration of a creature, such as the sun, the stars, the moon, idols of stone or wood, the devil, the world, or other men. Again, the superstitious man may attribute to creatures perfections and powers which can be found only in God. A man who seeks to learn the uncertain future through the devils, through the examination of the entrails of animals, or through observing the flight of birds, is committing the sin of divination, the sin of attributing to creatures a knowledge of the future which God alone possesses. A man who attempts to shape life to his own purposes by the practice of black magic, a man who seeks to direct his life by the forecasts of fortune-tellers, or a man who seeks to procure good fortune or ward off bad luck by wearing charms or carrying a rabbit's foot is guilty of the sin of superstitious observances. He is attributing to creatures powers which belong to God alone.

T HE IRRELIGIOUS MAN despises God or the things of God. He may tempt God to do things as a test of His power. The liar who asks God to strike him dead, if he is not telling the truth, is tempting God. The man who perjures himself after asking God to bear witness to the truth of what he testifies in court is guilty of the sin of perjury. The man who treats with irreverence persons, places or things consecrated to God is guilty of the sin of sacrilege. A man who would kill a priest just because he is a priest of God, a man who creates a disturbance in a church, a man who would wantonly destroy a consecrated chalice, or trample on the linens used in the sacrifice of the Mass, such a man is sacrilegious. The man who thinks that spiritual things can be sold, the man who sells or attempts to sell spiritual things is guilty of the sin of simony. In all these ways a man shows his contempt for God and for the power of God and he is an irreligious man.

SINS AGAINST THE VIRTUE of religion destroy man's proper subjection to God. The superstitious or the irreligious man is out of order in the universe. He is like the soldier marching out of step, or like the disgruntled and discourteous suitor at a marriage feast. Religion, on the other hand, enables man to fulfil his role in the universe. Through religion man becomes the voice of the whole world, the high priest of all creation, honoring and praising God as the Creator and goal of all creation. As justice establishes peace and order among men, so religion establishes peace and order between man and God.

CHAPTER VII

Happiness in the Service of Man

CHAPTER VII

Happiness in the Service of Man

THE VIRTUE OF JUSTICE is the necessary foundation of peace and order in human society. Justice, in the strictest sense of the term, regulates the relations between persons who are equal to one another. But there are many relations between men and other men and between men and God which are not relations of equality. Man is related to God as the creature to his Creator, not as one equal to another. Religion, as we have seen, is the virtue which enables man to give to God what is His due. But one man may be related to other men by way of the subordination of one man to another, or the dependence of one man on another. There must also be parts of the virtue of justice to establish order in relationships of this kind.

MEN OWE THEIR EXISTENCE, their lives and their actions to the influence of God. But, after God, they owe their lives and their opportunities to pursue happiness to their parents and their country. Without their parents they would not exist at all. Without their parents they would lack the necessities of human life, food, clothing, shelter, intellectual and moral training. Without their country they would not have the real opportunity to develop their talents and work for their own welfare and for the good of all. Consequently, men owe to their parents and to their country a debt of honor, reverence and service. It is the virtue of piety which directs a man to the fulfilment of his obligation to honor and serve his parents and country. Even when a man is an adult and his own master, he is still under an obligation to serve his parents or country if they have real need of his services. If his parents are in need of money, medical care, or human consolation, the pious man will provide them according to his ability. If his country has need of his money, or of his services in some government agency or in the armed forces, he will provide them according to his ability and his country's need.

AGAIN, IN ANY COMMUNITY OF MEN, there must always be some who, by virtue or position, are placed over others to rule or inspire the rest. The authority they possess or the good they bring to the community merits for them the tribute of honor, respect and gratitude. Men pay them this tribute by exercising the virtue of observance.

THE VIRTUE OF OBSERVANCE includes the virtues of dulia—or veneration—and obedience. By dulia men bear witness to the dignity or power of other men. To praise the President of the United States, to bow to him as he passes in a parade, to erect a statue in his honor—all these are acts of the virtue of dulia. To venerate the saints by asking them to intercede with God for us is an act of dulia. It pays tribute to the spiritual dignity of the saints as the friends of God in heaven. Because the Virgin Mary is the greatest of all the saints and the Mother of God Himself, Christians pay to Mary the tribute of hyperdulia or superveneration.

OBEDIENCE IS THE VIRTUE by which a man submits his own will to the commands of a superior. It is natural that children should obey their parents, that citizens should obey their government, that soldiers should obey their commanders, and that all men should obey God. Without obedience to their superiors, men can never establish in society that order which is needed if they are all to obtain that share of the common good which is necessary for their own happiness. And without obedience to God, men can never attain happiness at all.

THERE ARE ONLY TWO EXCEPTIONS to the rule of obedience. If a higher authority should countermand the order of a lower authority, then a man must obey the higher authority. If a general tells a soldier to advance on the field of battle, whereas a lieutenant orders him to retreat, the soldier must obey the general. Again, if a superior gives an order, but in a matter where he has no authority, then a man need not obey the order. A salesman in a store must sell the merchandise at the price commanded by the owner of the store. But if the owner should presume to dictate to the clerk which woman he should marry, then the clerk need not obey the merchant. The merchant has no authority to interfere in the private life of his employees.

IN A LESSER WAY, benefactors are related to those who receive gifts from them, as God is related to men or parents to their children. Of their own free will they have given something to others. The whole world recognizes that a debt of gratitude is due to them. The grateful man will give to his benefactor heartfelt thanks and, in proper time, a gift in return. The virtue of thankfulness—or gratitude—makes a man recognize that someone has done him a favor; it makes him acknowledge the favor with thanks, and it makes him repay the favor at a suitable time. St. Thomas, with a fine feeling for graciousness in human affairs, remarks that the grateful man does not return the favor immediately. To do so is to make the whole affair seem like a contract of buying and selling, and it deprives the benefactor of the pleasure he found in making the original gift. St. Thomas also remarks that gratitude makes a man return a favor in abundance. If one man gives another a hundred dollars, he does so out of the goodness of his heart. To give him a hundred dollars in return is to give him the exact sum he gave you, but it does not imitate the same fullness of heart. The grateful man will try to imitate the fullness of generosity of his benefactor. This means that he will try to surpass his benefactor in the return gift. If he cannot match the original gift in value, at least he will try to surpass his benefactor in the generosity of heart with which he repays the favor.

TO BE UNGRATEFUL IS SINFUL. It is a failure to repay a moral debt. There are degrees of ungratefulness. The first degree is to neglect to return the favor. The second degree is to take no notice of the favor, to overlook thanking the one who so generously did the favor. The lowest degree of ingratitude is to fail even to admit to one's self that a favor has been given. We are all familiar with ungrateful people —people who accept favors as if they were theirs by right, people who never thank anyone for favors, and people who never return a favor. Such people are like sands in the workings of a fine watch. They grate on other people's feelings and remove the pleasure from human relationships and love.

TRUTHFULNESS IS ANOTHER VIRTUE that is necessary in the social life of man. Men cannot live and work together without communicating their thoughts to one another. This implies that men must be able to trust one another, but trust is impossible unless they tell one another the truth. We all remember the story of the boy shepherd who cried "Wolf!"

once too often. Because he had fooled his fellow shepherds so frequently, they did not believe him when he was telling the truth. As a result, the flock of sheep was lost. If society is to function smoothly, men must be able to believe one another. Truthfulness is a virtue necessary for social life.

LYING, THEN, IS SINFUL. The sinfulness of a lie may vary according to the conditions in which the lie is told, and according to the seriousness of the matter about which the lie is told. But all lies are dangerous because they tend to make men distrust one another. Hence they serve to destroy that spirit of cooperation which men need if they are to work together efficiently and live together harmoniously.

SOME TYPES OF LIARS are more harmful than others. The hypocrite—the man who pretends to be what he is not—is a great evil in society. He feigns to be a good man although he is evil. This leads him to lie about his neighbors, or to spread scandalous stories about them, in order to glorify his own virtue. The boaster is a nuisance to society. He tries to make people believe that he is better than he is. Of course this blind illusion about his own excellence makes him overlook the virtues of others or even deny the real virtues of others. In a lesser way, the man who belittles himself and makes it appear that he is less than he really is, also deceives other men. This can be harmful, too, because it prevents the community from ever using his real talents for the benefit of all.

THUS FAR WE HAVE BEEN SPEAKING of virtues that are necessary if order is to be preserved in human society. Now we must mention the virtues which make the social life of man pleasant and delightful. Strict justice can give order to human relations, but something more is demanded if human relations are to be pleasurable and inspiring to all men. There must be, as it were, a surplus of good will among men if life is to seem worth living.

THE FIRST OF THE VIRTUES to add zest and enjoyment to social life is the virtue of friendliness or affability. The cheerful "Hello" of neighbors as they pass on the street, the friendliness of one housewife to another when she lends a cup of sugar or volunteers to mind the children for a while—gestures of friendliness such as these add the glow of love or charity to human life.

OF COURSE FRIENDLINESS must be sincere, or it turns to ashes in the hearts of men. It is for this reason that the sin of flattery is so despicable. The flatterer pretends to be friendly. He praises people, but he does so only to gain some advantage for himself. When his flattery becomes apparent, people recoil from him as a traitor to the unselfish love on which real friendliness is founded.

QUARRELING is another defect that destroys friendliness. The quarrelsome man is always contradicting others, in little matters or great. If anyone says anything, he must contradict it; if anyone does anything, he must criticize it. In this way he shows his contempt for others and his colossal pride in himself. Such a man makes cooperation among men difficult, if not impossible.

LIBERALITY is another virtue which gives life a pleasant flavor. The liberal man knows how to use his money and possessions well for the benefit of others. He takes pleasure in giving things to others, in doing favors. His generosity helps both himself and others. He himself, by his liberality, protects himself against the danger of becoming too attached to the goods of this world. His neighbors benefit by receiving both the gifts he gives them and the example of generosity which he affords them.

AS LIBERALITY is a virtue which enables a man to use his external possessions well, covetousness and prodigality are vices that move a man to use external possessions poorly. The covetous man is ruled by an overwhelming desire to acquire riches. In his mad desire to acquire wealth, he will have no pity or mercy for others. His mind will be perpetually restless with schemes to enrich himself. He will be inclined to use violence to gain his ends; he will perjure himself; deceive others by fraud, or even destroy them by treachery. Covetousness is a capital sin which leads men into other sins.

PRODIGALITY is the opposite extreme. The prodigal man wastes his possessions; he gives away his money and his goods, but without prudence. He deceives himself by thinking that he is generous, even virtuous; but he wastes his possessions until he becomes a burden to the community.

THE LAST OF THE VIRTUES which St. Thomas lists under justice is the virtue of equity. For him equity is a virtue by which man seeks to preserve the equality of justice and the common good, outside the letter of the law. The mind of man is not perfect enough to make laws that will cover all the actions of men in society. If a man asks another to mind his gun, for example, the law might say that the gun must be returned to its owner on demand. But suppose that the owner demands it when he is drunk and threatening to kill someone with the gun. Surely in such a circumstance the common good demands that the gun should not be returned to him. Equity is the virtue which enables a man to act outside the letter of the law, when real justice or the common good demands it.

IN THE CASE OF JUSTICE, as in the case of the other virtues, God has also given man, through grace, a gift of the Holy Spirit to perfect human justice. This gift is called the gift of piety. It is a gift by which the Holy Spirit moves man to worship God as his Father. It subjects man to God as to his father. Justice and its related virtues put order in the social life of man. The gift of piety gives man the most perfect element of order—perfect submission of man to God.

IN THESE DAYS when tyrannous dictatorships and wars direct the course of human life, when even peaceful countries are suffering from the strife between labor unions and corporations, from the tensions due to race prejudice and religious intolerance, we can all see the need of justice and its related virtues. Justice itself will give to each man security in his own possessions. Religion will put man into his proper relationship to God. Piety will enable him to honor and serve his parents and country. Observance—dulia and obedience—will ensure the proper functioning of society. Gratitude and truthfulness, friendliness and liberality will make life gracious and enjoyable. Equity will prevent harshness and frustration.

BRIEFLY, JUSTICE AND ITS RELATED VIRTUES will ensure men's observance of the ten Commandments of God, and when these precepts of both the Natural and the Divine Positive Law are observed by men, human life will be ruled by both human and divine wisdom. Wisdom directs all things well. Where justice reigns under wisdom, there men will establish peace and order. In peace and order it is possible for men to find happiness.

CHAPTER VIII

Fortitude:
Happiness and Heroism

CHAPTER VIII

Fortitude: Happiness and Heroism

EVERYONE ADMIRES A HERO. We are all thrilled by the courage of the man who faces the danger of death without flinching. We are impressed, too, by the man who refuses to be defeated by difficulty, disease or disaster. We like the man who does not weep in the face of trouble, or run away from responsibility. We know that life is not all peaches and cream. We know that every life must weather its share of storm and stress; and so we respect those who are strong enough to oppose difficulty with strength, danger with courage, and death without fear.

IT IS THE VIRTUE of fortitude which enables men to overcome difficulty in the pursuit of good. Fortitude is the virtue which moderates the powers of the irascible appetite of man. Imagine for a moment the problem faced by a soldier in the midst of battle. He is comparatively safe in his foxhole, but his friend is lying wounded on the open ground fifteen feet in front of him; he wants to rescue him, but he is afraid he will be killed himself. In the face of these two dangers, the danger to his friend and the danger to himself, he becomes angry at the enemy and then he becomes daring. He decides to rescue his friend. But how shall he do it? Let us say that he has only two ways of trying to do it. He can run across the fifteen feet, pick up his friend and run back; or he can crawl slowly over the fifteen feet, take hold on his friend and crawl slowly back, dragging his friend with him. It is more daring to dash out and back; but it is more likely that he himself will be killed, for he will present a better target to the enemy. It is less daring to crawl out, but the slowness of this method will require greater self-control. He will die a thousand deaths as he inches his way forward; but he will be more likely to succeed this way. Summoning all the strength of his soul and body, he crawls out and drags his friend back to safety.

NOW, IN PERFORMING this act of courage, this act of heroism, the soldier needed the virtue of fortitude to direct the actions of the passions of fear, anger and daring. If fortitude had not curbed the power of his fear, he would never have attempted the rescue at all. If anger at the evils he faced had not roused him, he would never have been daring enough to make the attempt. But if his anger had been too strong, his daring would also have been excessive, and he would have thrown caution to the winds and rushed out screaming defiance at the enemy and he himself would have been killed. Fortitude curbed both his anger and his daring and directed them prudently to the best method of rescuing his friend. Briefly, we might say that without fortitude, either the passion of fear would have made him fail his friend, or the passion of excessive daring would have made his attempted rescue a failure. Without fortitude either he would not have tried at all, or he would have tried badly and so failed.

FORTITUDE IS THE VIRTUE which directs the movements of the passions of the irascible appetite—especially the passions of fear and daring—in the face of a good that is difficult to achieve. The intellectual virtues perfect human reason in the pursuit of both speculative and practical truth. Justice perfects the human will in the field of human relations. Temperance perfects the will by moderating the tendencies of the concupiscible appetite and subjecting them to the rule of reason. Fortitude perfects the will by removing the obstacles which fear and daring raise in the pursuit of good.

FORTITUDE IS CONCERNED with the pursuit of good in the face of danger, but the greatest danger to man in this world is the danger of death. Fortitude, then, is concerned especially with the fear of death. If a man is ready to die in the pursuit of moral good, then certainly he is ready to face any lesser danger in the same pursuit. The man who is ready to die for his faith in God, is certainly ready to face the loss of his money or imprisonment for the same good.

AS WE HAVE SEEN ABOVE in the story of the soldier who rescued his friend, courage—or fortitude— is not irrational. It is a virtue, a moral virtue. It must be directed by reason, by the virtue of prudence. It is right reason which tells a man that he must endure bodily evils—even death—rather than lose his soul. It is true prudence which tells a man that he must endure the martyrdom of death rather than give up his faith in God or Christ. It is reason also that tells a man when his daring is excessive and foolhardy and unlikely to succeed. It is true prudence which tells a man who cannot swim that he should not jump into a turbulent ocean to rescue a drowning man. Fortitude, like all the other virtues, follows the mean of reason. It pursues the right path between excessive fear and excessive daring; it is neither the cowardice of the timid and fearful, nor the foolhardiness of the reckless and inexperienced. It is the sure strength of the virtuous, rational man. It gives a man the strength to endure pain and even death, when they cannot be avoided; it gives him power to face danger and overcome it, when it can be overcome.

THE MOST PERFECT ACT of fortitude is martyrdom—the sustaining of bodily suffering and death for faith in God and Christ. Because of his faith in God, the martyr is not only ready to die rather than give up his belief in God, but he actually does give up his life for his faith in God. His martyrdom is the final proof of his great love for God. "Greater love than this no man hath, that a man lay down his life for his friends" (*John* XV, 13.)

THE ENEMIES OF FORTITUDE are cowardice, fearlessness and daring. Cowardice is an inordinate, an excessive fear of death. Through cowardice a man refuses to endure what right reason tells him he should endure rather than lose the moral good he should pursue. It is cowardice which makes a man deny his God rather than suffer or lose his life. It is cowardice which induces a married couple to practice illegal birth control rather than suffer the restraint of continency or the danger of suffering or death. When cowardice leads a man to shun his serious obligations, it is a mortal sin.

FEARLESSNESS is also opposed to true fortitude. The fearless man—as we are now speaking of fearlessness—is the man who rushes into danger without measuring either the danger, his own strength, or the chances of success. Such a reckless disregard of danger is due either to pride, or a lack of love or understanding. The man who does not love his life as much as he ought will rush into danger because he does not care what happens; it is carelessness, not courage, which influences him. The proud man, overestimating his own strength, cannot conceive of any danger he could not overcome; it is not courage, but vainglory, which actuates him. The dull or stupid man walks into danger without knowing where he is going; it is ignorance, not courage, which moves him. In all these cases we find, not true fortitude, but a cheap imitation of it, founded on an inability to love, an excessive love of one's own excellence, or a lack of intelligence.

EXCESSIVE DARING is also a sin against fortitude. When a man is excessively daring, he rushes into danger without taking counsel either with himself or with others. He measures neither the extent of the danger nor his own strength. His actions are not directed by right reason or prudence; hence, even if he is successful, his acts are not virtuous. They lack the direction of right reason, and therefore are not truly acts of fortitude; on the contrary, because they lack the moderation of reason, they are sinful.

LIKE THE OTHER CARDINAL VIRTUES, fortitude has other virtues which are related to it. Fortitude itself is concerned with the fear of death. But there are many other lesser fears which plague men in this life. There must, therefore, be virtues to moderate these fears also. The virtues which strengthen men in the face of evils or dangers less than the danger of death are magnanimity, magnificence, patience and perseverance.

MAGNANIMITY is the virtue which enables men to do great things. Now a human act may be great in either of two ways: it may be great in relation to some particular person, or it may be simply a great thing in itself. If a poor widow with only five dollars to her name gives it to a neighbor for medical care, she does something which is very small in itself, but which is very great in relation to herself and to her circumstances. If a man, such as George Washington,

devotes his time, his brilliant talents and his possessions to the liberation and development of his country,
what he does is great not only in relation to himself,
but it is simply and absolutely great. The virtue of
magnanimity is concerned chiefly with things that are
great, absolutely and simply. Because great deeds
usually bring great honor to a man, magnanimity is
concerned with great honors. The magnanimous man
tends to do things that are deserving of great honor.

WE MUST NOT, however, make the mistake of
confusing the magnanimous man with the vain
man. The vain man seeks honor among men simply
for the sake of honor; or he seeks honor beyond what
is due to him; or he seeks honor for what is not really
honorable. Magnanimity is a virtue, and it is concerned with the best use of the greatest things. The
magnanimous man does great things for God, or for
the benefit of his fellowmen. He seeks honor not so
much for himself and in the eyes of men as for God
and in the eyes of God. Because he loves God and
men, he dares to do great things for God and men.

THE MAGNANIMOUS MAN is a man of confidence,
assurance and, usually, wealth. He is a man of
great hope, and this gives him confidence. He is a man
of fortitude, and this frees his mind from fear and
gives him assurance. Wealth is not absolutely necessary for magnanimity, but there is no doubt that it is
a great help. The wealthy man can easily accomplish
great things by means of his riches, power and friends.

THE VICES OPPOSED to magnanimity are presumption, ambition, vainglory and pusillanimity. The
presumptuous man is one who seeks to do great things
that are beyond his powers. Presumption is a vice
because the actions prompted by it lack the prudent

direction of right reason. The ambitious man—naturally, we are speaking of the vice of ambition—is one who wants honor for its own sake alone, or looks for recognition and honor when he has done nothing to merit them. The vainglorious man wishes to be honored for something that is not honorable, or he seeks honor from men alone. Vainglory is a capital vice that leads to disobedience, boasting, hypocrisy, quarreling, obstinacy, discord and a restless search for new and novel ways of exciting admiration. Pusillanimity is a vice that leads a man to refuse to do what is really possible to him.

MAGNIFICENCE is the virtue which enables men to make something which is great. It is magnificence which enables a man to give several million dollars for the erection of a public hospital, library or university. Because it is concerned with making great things, magnificence requires great expenditure of money. It is related to fortitude because it is concerned with something difficult. It is difficult to build a large hospital, and it is difficult for a man to part with several million dollars. But magnificence is a lesser virtue than fortitude because it deals, not with the fear of death, but with the loss of one's own property.

MEANNESS is the vice opposed to magnificence. The mean man—as St. Thomas uses the term here—is the man who tries to make something great but with insufficient means. The mean man, for example, tries to build a million dollar hospital with a half million dollars. He always wants to get more for his money than it will buy. He is the type of employer who will always underpay his employees.

PATIENCE is the virtue which enables man to endure hardship in the pursuit of good. Hardship is always an evil to man. It causes sorrow, and might make a man forsake the pursuit of good in order to banish his sorrow. The husband whose wife is seriously ill for a long time may be tempted to drown his sorrow in alcohol or the affection of another woman. He needs the virtue of patience to enable him to bear his sorrow without failing in virtue.

PERSEVERANCE is the virtue which enables a man to endure delays in the attainment of good. A man wants to save money to pay for an expensive operation to restore sight to his son, but it takes him a long while to save the money, and every so often some unexpected expense delays him even more. It is perseverance which enables him to endure the delays until he accomplishes his desire.

SOFTNESS—St. Thomas calls it effeminacy—and pertinacity are opposed to perseverance. Softness is a vice that makes a man ready to forsake any good intention when difficulties arise. Pertinacity is a vice that makes a man cling to his own opinion and judgment long after facts have shown that he is wrong. The soft man has no perseverance at all. The pertinacious man perseveres in his wrong course of action even after right reason shows that he is wrong.

OF COURSE, the highest kind of perseverance is perseverance in the pursuit of God. For this reason God has given men, through grace, the gift of fortitude. This is a gift of the Holy Spirit which enables man to persevere in moral good until he attains the vision of God. The Holy Spirit infuses into man's mind a confidence that through the grace of God he will win through to Heaven.

EVERYONE with any experience of life knows the great need men have for the virtue of fortitude and its related virtues. Life is not easy; good is not accomplished without difficulty. Perseverance in good is a tremendous trial of man's strength, but only the brave deserve the prize. The kingdom of heaven is won by violence, that is, by strength. Only the heroes of this life can find the happiness of heaven. The secret of heroism is fortitude, and the secret of fortitude is love. When a man has a great love of good—the moral good—then he can find the strength to be brave in the pursuit of good.

CHAPTER IX

Temperance: Happiness and Control

CHAPTER IX

Temperance: Happiness and Control

DID YOU EVER INVITE a family to dinner? And had you cooked a large roast and an abundance of vegetables? Did you think that you had enough food for an army? And were you embarrassed when your guests and their children ate as if they had not had a meal in a month? Remember how your heart sank as the food vanished through their mouths like water poured into a glass with a hole in the bottom?

OR WERE YOU EVER embarrassed by a guest who drank too much and proceeded to make himself a nuisance to all the other guests by his vulgar language, his obscene jokes, or his too amorous attentions to the ladies present?

IN ALL HUMAN SITUATIONS of this kind, the cause of the trouble is lack of control. People are unable to control their desires. They can never have enough of what they want. They eat too much, or drink too much, or seek too much sexual excitement. The man or woman with unbridled desires is a danger to himself or herself and a nuisance or a scandal to society. In a brief phrase, the happiness of both the individual and society demands self-control. Man is full of desires, but they must be regulated by reason. Left to themselves they will bring man to disaster; hence they must be subject to the control of right reason.

IT IS THROUGH THE VIRTUE of temperance and the virtues related to it that the desires of man are brought under the control of reason. Man is not simply an animal; he is a rational being. Man does not live simply by instinct or desire; he lives by reason. Reason must direct his actions to the goal of human life—happiness in the vision of God. But man is also an animal; he has the same tendencies to eat and drink and to procreate his kind that we find in animals. The good of the individual, the life of his body, requires that man eat and drink to preserve his life. The good of the human race demands that men and women marry to preserve the human race. It is nature which impels a man to eat and drink and marry and raise children; but because man is also a rational being, all these tendencies must be brought under the control of reason. If they are not, man descends to the level of the beasts and forsakes what is highest and noblest in his human nature—the spiritual soul, with its capacities for knowledge and love, which raise him above the beast and make him capable of living forever with God in friendship and love. It is temperance and the virtues related to it which give man the control he needs to achieve true human happiness.

MAN HAS MANY TENDENCIES, and so many desires, which could draw him away from God. The strongest of these are his inclinations to eat and drink and to beget children through marriage. The virtue which moderates or controls these strong inclinations is temperance. If a man's cravings for food and drink and the pleasure of sex are not controlled by reason through the virtue of temperance, then he is in danger. His uncontrolled appetite for food or drink or sex will lead him to forsake God for creatures. He will ruin his own health and life by gluttony, drunkenness or sexual excess. He will destroy the order of society in his eagerness to gratify his own desires. He will lose his immortal soul because the intensity of his desires will lead him to abandon God for the pleasures of his own body. The needs of the body are natural and impelling, but they must be brought under the control of reason or they will destroy man. It is temperance which brings these imperious forces under control; it enables a man to master his own inclinations and direct them to the good of himself and the whole human race.

LIKE ALL THE MORAL VIRTUES, temperance follows a mean between excess and defect. It does not deny that man has natural inclinations to food and drink and the use of sex. It gives man the means to master these inclinations for his own good. It admits that man requires these things for his own preservation and that of the human race. A man would sin by defect, then, if he refused totally to satisfy these needs of nature. The man who refuses to eat at all for no good reason would be guilty of the sin and the vice of insensibility. On the other hand, the man who eats too much, or drinks too much, or who makes a sinful use of sex, sins against temperance by intemperance. Temperance enables a man to satisfy these tendencies within reason.

FORTUNATELY FOR MOST MEN, the two qualities most necessary for temperance are found in the majority of men. They are shamefacedness and honesty. Shamefacedness is a passion in man which makes him fear to do a base or ignoble action. It is shamefacedness which prevents a man from overeating or getting drunk in the presence of others. It may not be the most noble motive for avoiding evil and doing good, but there is no doubt that it is a very good means of acquiring the virtue of temperance and keeping it.

HONESTY is the quality of spiritual beauty in things, actions, or men. Man has a natural tendency to honesty in things, actions, or men. The honest is the good, and man has a natural bent toward what is good. Honesty is opposed to what is disgraceful. Honesty works hand in hand in a man with shamefacedness. Man hates what is disgraceful and loves what is honest or good. Honesty, then, is also a great help in building up the virtue of temperance and preserving it.

TEMPERANCE is concerned chiefly with the greatest pleasures which attract man in this present life— the delights of eating or drinking or sex. It is divided into the virtues which regulate man's use of these pleasures—the virtues of abstinence, chastity and virginity. Abstinence enables a man to eat and drink in moderation according to the rule of human reason. When a man eats more than he needs to preserve life, he is guilty of the sin of gluttony. It is abstinence or fasting which leads a man to use food for the good of his body and soul.

FASTING is the act of the virtue of abstinence. A man fasts when he abstains from eating all that it is possible for him to eat. Fasting is good for many reasons. In the first place, overeating often dulls a man's moral sense and leads him into temptation. It incites him to acts of lust. Fasting destroys this hazard to human action. Secondly, gluttony dulls a man's mind and prevents him from using it properly. Above all, gluttony prevents a man from devoting his mind to God and the things of God, because the glutton is always too sleepy for prayer or meditation. Lastly, fasting is good for man because it enables him to make acts of reparation to God for his sins. By denying himself the pleasures of eating, a man does two good things: he brings his body into subjection to his soul, and he can repay God by this self-inflicted punishment for the sins he has committed.

S OBRIETY is that part of the virtue of abstinence which enables a man to practise temperance in drinking. The harmful effects of alcohol on the human system and human behaviour are too well known to need any lengthy description here. The drunkard brings disgrace and disaster to himself and to his family. Sobriety is the virtue which enables a man to make use of the pleasures of drinking—or to abstain from them entirely—for the good of his human nature.

C HASTITY is the virtue which moderates man's use of sexual—or venereal—pleasure. The common good of the human race impels men to beget children so that the race will not perish. Nature has given men an added motive for begetting children by associating one of its most intense pleasures with the act by which children are conceived in the wombs of their mothers. This pleasure does not exist for itself, but is intended to lead men and women to perform their duty to propagate the human race. It should be sought and used, therefore, only for the good of the race and in accordance with the rule of right reason. But the intensity of the sexual drive in human beings will run away with man unless it is brought under the control of reason. It is the virtue of chastity which makes it possible for men to use their sexual instincts properly.

V IRGINITY is a virtue by which men or women abstain entirely from sexual pleasure. It represents the highest degree of control of the sexual appetite. As a virtue it makes men and their actions morally good. It should be clear, then, that when we speak of virginity here we are not referring to any of those unfortunate human beings who through some physical or mental defect are incapable of desiring or obtaining sexual pleasure. We are talking of the virtue that exists in those human beings—capable of sexual acts and pleasure—who voluntarily renounce such acts or pleasure for a higher good. In virtue of the basic natural tendency of human beings to perpetuate the human race by begetting children, only a higher goal makes voluntary virginity good. Men find three kinds of good in this life: the external possessions which enable them to live well, the goods of their bodies (such as health), and the goods of their souls (such as knowledge and virtue). Now it is reasonable to forego a lesser good for a higher good. The athlete gives up liquor and tobacco for the good of his body. The scholar gives up liquor, food and amusement for the good of his mind. So, too, the virgin gives up the pleasures of sex in order to have more time and mental ease to devote his or her mind to God and the contemplation of God. It is precisely the infinite character of the good that the virgin seeks—God Himself—which makes virginity more excellent than marriage. Married persons have to spend a great deal of their time, and energies and talents on one another and their children. The virgin can consecrate this time, energy and talent to the worship of God. Nor is the intention of the virgin a selfish one. In the first place, the virgin gives the world an example of the possibility of controlling the sexual drive of human nature. From this point of view alone the virgin is a boon to society. The virgin proves that self-control is attainable. Secondly, the true virgin practices virginity out of love for God, and hence out of love for men. No one can truly love

God without loving men. As the virgin grows in the love of God, so does she grow in the love of men. Her virginity then becomes a sacrifice in the eyes of God for the good of mankind. As the married woman provides for the bodily preservation of the human race, so the virgin, by the sacrifice of her flesh provides for the spiritual preservation of the human race. Through her sacrifice and intercession in prayer, the grace and the power of God descend into human life, making men better and procuring the salvation of the human race.

THE VICE OPPOSED to chastity and virginity is lust. Lust is an inordinate tendency to indulge in the pleasures of sex. As we have already said, the pleasures of sex are legitimate as long as they are sought in accord with reason. Since God and nature direct these pleasures to the preservation of the human race through the begetting of children, reason demands that these pleasures should not be sought or used unless they are directed to the procreating and raising of children. It follows, therefore, that they can be sought legitimately only in marriage, for only through the institution of marriage and the human family is it possible to beget children and raise them properly. The deliberate seeking of sexual pleasure outside marriage will always be against right reason and hence sinful. Lust is a vice or a sin by which men seek and employ sexual pleasure against the order of right reason.

IT IS A CAPITAL SIN because it leads to other sins. The lustful man becomes blind to all else as he seeks to gratify his base desires. He becomes thoughtless, refusing to take counsel even with himself about his evil way of living. Because his mind is blinded by his insane desires he is inconstant, swearing to give up his lustful cravings, but rushing back to them at the first smile or affectionate gesture from the object of his lust. Throwing caution to the winds, he becomes rash in seeking to satisfy his ignoble yearnings. By pampering his own desires, he succumbs to an inordinate self-love and begins to hate God. Hating God, he comes to love this present world in which all his temporary wishes seem to be fulfilled, and to hate the next world in which he could find true happiness. And so the lustful descends from the world of the spirit, for which he was made, to the world of the beasts, which he was meant to dominate. Refusing to be ruled by God, he finds himself ruled by the blind impulses of the beasts beneath him.

THOSE WHO HAVE FALLEN VICTIM to lust need the virtue of temperance to restrain their inordinate desires. But there are other inclinations in man which also need the moderation of reason. Because the virtues which direct these tendencies do so by regulating them, these virtues are said to be related to the virtue of temperance. They enable man to reach self-control or self-mastery.

CONTINENCE is a virtue of the will by which a man checks the strong impulses of desire for pleasures of touch—such as the pleasures of food, drink and sex. It is distinct from temperance as the imperfect is distinct from the perfect. When a man has the virtue of temperance, the passions of his concupiscible appetite are subject to his reason and will, and they cannot strongly resist the power of his will. In the continent man his passions strongly resist his will, but his will remains firm in the face of their onslaught. In the incontinent man, on the contrary, the will gives in to the vehemence of the passions and he falls into sin.

CLEMENCY AND MEEKNESS are virtues which moderate the passion of anger. Meekness restrains anger itself, whereas clemency directs its external effects. Meekness keeps a man from becoming angry at all; clemency prevents a man from taking too much revenge on those who have injured him.

MODESTY is the virtue which subjects to the rule of reason those tendencies of man which are weaker than his inclination to the pleasures of food, drink or sex. Briefly, we might say that modesty directs man's desire for his own excellence and for knowledge, and man's external behaviour and dress. As we have already seen, men have a natural tendency to avoid difficult things. They need the virtue of magnanimity to move them to the accomplishment of hard things. Men also have a natural leaning to great things, but since lofty things are often beyond their powers they need a virtue to keep them from tending immoderately to high goals. The virtue which restrains man's mind from aiming at big things against reason is the virtue of humility. Humility is a virtue of the will, but it depends on knowledge. To be humble, a man must realize the lack of proportion between his own powers and the great things toward which his will tends. Humility does not make a man think less of himself than he ought; it is based on an honest estimate of one's own capacities, and hence enables a man to see what he cannot do and to abstain from trying to do the impossible. Humility is a very important virtue in relation to the pursuit of happiness. It is humility which makes it possible for a man to see that he cannot find happiness without the assistance of God's grace and love. The humble man does not try the impossible—to save himself without

God. The humble man subjects himself to God, worships God and asks the divine assistance in his pursuit of happiness.

PRIDE is the vice opposed to humility. The sin of pride is an inordinate desire or love of one's own excellence. Through pride a man either thinks himself better than he is, or he thinks he can do things which are beyond his own power. The proud man thinks that all his talents are his own; he will not even acknowledge that he owes them to God. Or, if he acknowledges that they come from God, he still thinks that they are due to his own merit rather than to God's generosity. He boasts of gifts which he does not possess. He despises other men and imagines he is the exclusive possessor of whatever talent he has. The proud man knows everything and can do anything. He must be the leader, or else he will not work or play. Pride is a very serious sin because it leads a man to resist even God Himself. A man may fall into other kinds of sin through ignorance or weakness, and in such a case he fears the just judgment of God. But the proud man rebels against God, and will not be subject to Him. He resists all God's efforts to lead him back to virtue, and will have none of His help. He will save himself by himself or perish.

THE SIN OF ADAM AND EVE, our first parents, was a sin of pride. By the gifts of grace and integrity Adam and Eve were free from the temptations of the flesh; they could only fall into sin through the spiritual faculties of reason and will. When the devil, in the guise of a serpent, tempted them, he attacked them by appealing to pride. He told them that if they would eat of the forbidden fruit, they would become as gods, knowing good and evil. Through pride, through a disordered desire to attain some spiritual perfection without God, Eve fell and then seduced Adam. The consequences of this first sin of pride are apparent to all of us. Because of it the human race was expelled from Paradise and man became subject to inordinate concupiscence, disease and death.

AS PRIDE EXPELLED Adam and Eve from Paradise, so it can prevent men from finding happiness through the grace of God. Humility, man's recognition of his dependence on God and of his absolute need for submitting himself to God, is the only remedy for human pride. The humble man trusts not in his own strength, but in the power and love of God. Unable to do anything of himself for his own salvation, he can do all things in God.

MAN HAS ALSO AN INTENSE DESIRE to know, to learn everything; but it is neither possible nor convenient for man to know everything. This desire also must be moderated according to the rule of reason. Studiousness is the virtue which directs man in his desire to learn the truth. Curiosity is the vice which impels man to seek knowledge which is not proper to him. It is curiosity which sends men and women to fortune-tellers to learn what will happen to them in the future—a knowledge which is proper to God alone. Curiosity impels women—or men, for that matter—to seek to know all the secrets of their neighbors, so that they may slander them behind their backs.

MODESTY is also the virtue which directs a man's external behaviour and dress according to the rules of right reason. Modesty makes a man act in the fashion that befits a human being. It is modesty which prevents a man or woman from behaving lewdly in public, and enables a human being to seek legitimate recreation in a decently human way. The modest man does not insist on being the life of every party. He may tell a joke, but never a "dirty" one; he laughs at what is humorous, but not hysterically like a man out of his mind. Or again, it is modesty which makes a woman dress decently, and prevents her from making herself a temptation to lust in the men she meets. Briefly, modesty is a virtue which gives a man or woman self-control.

IT IS AN UNFORTUNATE FACT that the world today has glorified intemperance, impurity and immodesty. Through the newspapers, radio and television, men and women are led to believe that "glamor", sophistication, "sex appeal", the right silhouette, and the right liquor are the only things in life worth striving for. This is an appeal to what is lowest in man, his animal nature. That is why the virtue of temperance and its related virtues are a necessity in the modern world. Man is made for God, not for the beasts. Man's problem is to use the things of this world to lead him to God. He must be the master of his animal nature, or he will be its slave. He must subdue his body for the good of his soul. He must conquer the world so that he may go to God. Temperance is the virtue which makes man ruler of himself and of the material world in which he lives. The intemperate man is a plaything in the grip of the debasing forces of the material world. The temperate man is the master of material forces, and his self-control enables him to use the world as a stepping-stone to God. The temperate man finds happiness through rational self-control.

CHAPTER X

Intimations of Happiness

CHAPTER X

Intimations of Happiness

THE LIFE OF FAITH that leads to happiness is not an easy one. One of its darkest difficulties is the fact that it is a life based on faith. The vision of God—man's final destiny—is not on display in the windows of our large department stores. You cannot find it enthroned in the main room of our museums. A man cannot see it in this life; he must believe in it, hope for it, work for it in the darkness of this present life.

BUT GOD IS GOOD AND WISE. He knows that those who toil in the dark depths of the mine of life must glimpse an occasional pinpoint of light to strengthen their faith in the existence of the sun. In His great generosity God gives man intimations of His own existence and power and love. In this way He confirms man's faith, strengthens his hope and increases his love for Himself. God gives these intimations to man in the gifts of prophecy, speech and miracle.

THROUGH PROPHECY God reveals to man things that are knowable only to God Himself. It is by prophecy that man has come to know the deep secrets of the divine life, such as the mystery of the Trinity. More importantly, from the point of view of man himself and his need for certainty, the prophets of God have been able to foretell the future, especially the free future acts of God and men. The mysteries of the divine life are so profound that man might not accept them from a prophet; but the accurate forecasting of free future acts is a clear sign of the divinity. It is an intellectual miracle confirming the truth of the divine revelation given to men by God through the prophets.

GOD CAN SPEAK to His prophets in different ways. He may send them visible and audible sights and sounds in which His message to men is contained; He may act directly upon the imagination of the prophet; or He may illumine the intellect of the prophet immediately, making him aware of the divine judgment he must manifest to men.

THE PROPHET HIMSELF needs no previous preparation or disposition to be the recipient of a divine message. He may not even fully realize the meaning of what he himself sees or transmits to men; but in the hands of God he is a chosen vessel carrying the light of divine wisdom to men.

OCCASIONALLY the prophet is carried out of himself in rapture. His soul remains in his body; but it withdraws or is withdrawn from the turmoil of the life of the senses, and the prophet gazes for a moment on the face of Divinity Itself. Refreshed and inspired by this glimpse of God Himself, the prophet can speak with authority to men and impart to them his own conviction of the truth and love of God.

AS FAR AS PUBLIC REVELATION is concerned—that is, the revelation which God has entrusted to His Church to be proposed to all men for belief—the age of prophecy ceased at the time and with the work of Christ and His Apostles. But God still sends private revelations to men as signs of His continuing love and care for them.

IF GOD'S MESSAGE to men is to be properly appreciated by men, it must be preached to them. This means that it must be preached in all the languages of all the nations of the earth, and it must be preached forcefully and persuasively. In the long course of man's history on earth, God has not left the preaching of His message to the unaided efforts and talents of men. In order to give the infant Church of Christ a good beginning, God bestowed on the Apostles the gift of tongues. He infused into their minds a knowledge of the various languages of men, so that they could preach God's message to all men and understand their questions. In addition, down through history He has given His missioners—from time to time —the power to preach His word persuasively. Finally, throughout the history of His Church, God has continuously confirmed the preaching of His word by miracles. Through the power of God, the blind have their sight restored to them, the deaf hear again and the lame walk. The preachers of God's word heal the sick and forecast the future, to confirm the truth of God's message to men. In all these wonderful ways God gives to men an occasional glimpse of the splendor which is Himself, of the great light of happiness which awaits those who love and serve God.

MAN HIMSELF stretches his hand out to this happiness by living a life of virtue. And as he lives this life of virtue, his very life becomes to him a source of hope and happiness. The life of virtue in man may be either active or contemplative. The contemplative man devotes most of his energy to the truth, especially that sublime Truth which is God. The active man gives most of his energy to action, especially the action of the moral virtues in his life. Of course, when we speak in this way of the contemplative or the active man, we are not saying that the contemplative never acts or the active man never contemplates truth. It is a matter of proportion and intention. The contemplative dedicates himself chiefly to the contemplation of God, and the active man intends to devote himself principally to the work of the moral virtues.

THE CHIEF ACT of contemplation is a simple contemplation of the truth, especially divine truth. This is an act most natural to man. The life of plants is said to consist in nourishment and generation. The life of animals consists in sensation and movement. But the life of man consists in intellectual understanding and in moral action according to reason. In the intellectual contemplation of truth man, then, finds the fulfilment of his noblest human endowment, the power to know. But the intellect of man is moved to action by the human will. Love, therefore, is the motive cause of contemplation. A man pursues contemplation because he loves the truth, and wishes to know it and understand it.

NOR CAN IT BE SAID that the moral virtues have no relation to contemplation. The mind of man cannot raise itself easily to the contemplation of truth unless his passions are under control. The lustful man can hardly find time to consider the sublime truths of the divine life. The moral virtues, then, are a disposition of man to contemplation. When the moral virtues have given a man control of himself, then he can raise his mind and heart to God and the thought of God.

AS WE HAVE ALREADY SAID, contemplation consists in the act of gazing at truth. But before a man reaches the perfection of this simple gaze at truth, ordinarily there will be many other intellectual acts to be performed. A man must first of all accept the principles from which he will proceed to the contemplation of truth. These principles are chiefly the

truths that God has revealed to man about Himself
and His action in the world. Then man must meditate
on, or reason out, the meaning of these principles.
Finally he arrives at the simple contemplation of
truth. The truth which man contemplates will be God
as He can be known through the world He has made,
and God as He is in Himself.

TO THE CONTEMPLATIVE MAN contemplation is a
delight. The very act itself is the perfect act of
man's highest faculty, the power to know the truth.
This alone brings the highest satisfaction to man. Besides, in true contemplation God Himself is the object
of the mind's gaze, and so through contemplation man
receives a foretaste of the perfect happiness of the
vision of God.

THE ACTIVE MAN gives himself principally to external actions; he is more concerned with external
good works. Since we are speaking here of the good
human life, it is clear that these exterior works will
be works of virtue, especially of the moral virtues.

OF THE TWO TYPES of human life possible to men,
the contemplative life in itself is more perfect
and more meritorious. Man's ultimate goal is the contemplation of God face to face. The contemplative,
then, is already directly preparing himself for his chief
act in Heaven. The active man is preparing himself
for Heaven, but not so directly. However, this does
not mean that every man must seek contemplation
rather than action in this life. Some men are called by
God to contemplation, and others are destined for
action. By temperament and virtue, some are more
prepared for contemplation than others. Some need a
life of action to keep their passions in check. In any
case, since the active life depends on the moral vir-

tues, even the contemplative must prepare himself for contemplation by a life of action, that is, he must practise the moral virtues so that his passions may be brought under control and offer no hindrance to contemplation.

BASICALLY, OF COURSE, a good man chooses either the active or the contemplative life only as a means of achieving his ultimate goal, the vision of God. Naturally, too, since every man is unique— unique in the freedom of his own deliberate choices in life—he will build his life and realize his goal in his own inimitable way. But despite the uniqueness of each human life, it is possible to distinguish the states of life in which men actually work for happiness.

THE TERM "STATE OF LIFE" as St. Thomas uses it here is not the equivalent of the expression "station in life". By "station in life", people usually mean such things as whether a man is rich or poor, a professor or a postman, a banker or a politician. By the expression "state of life" St. Thomas means something more permanent and stable than a temporary station in life. It implies a certain immovableness in a man's moral position in life, and a relation to the obligations which bind his person. In the moral order, there are two basic states of life. A man is free or he is a slave; he stands on his own or depends on another.

UNDER THESE GENERAL STATES OF LIFE—freedom or servitude—there will be many more particular states of life, according to the various works to which men must devote themselves. St. Thomas, naturally enough, since he is a theologian, concerns himself here only with states of life in the Church and therefore spiritual states of life.

I N THE SPIRITUAL ORDER, different states of life are distinguished by their relation to moral or spiritual perfection. Spiritual perfection consists in charity, which unites a man to God. From this point of view, we can distinguish two freedoms and two slaveries. A man may be a slave to sin, and this is the state of the habitual sinner; or he may be a slave to justice, and this is the state of the habitually just man. A man may be free from sin, and this is the state of the good man who has mastered himself; or he may be free from justice, and this is the state of the man who is not held back from evil by the love of justice.

T HE MAN who is seeking true happiness strives to be free from sin and a slave to justice. The root of this spiritual freedom is charity, and the freedom itself grows out of charity commanding the other virtues to their acts. As in all cases of growth, we can distinguish three stages of the perfection of charity: the beginners, the proficient and the perfect. It is important to remember that in all three stages charity itself is present as the basic cause of freedom from sin.

S PIRITUAL PERFECTION consists primarily in the observance of the commandments, that is in the love of God and our neighbor. To sin against the commandments is to act contrary to charity, and therefore to lose charity, the essence of perfection. Secondarily and instrumentally, perfection is found in the observance of the counsels, poverty, chastity and obedience. Wealth and marriage, for example, are neither sinful nor contrary to charity itself, but they may hinder the act of charity. The father of a family cannot devote as much time to the service of God as the nun who is observing the vow of chastity.

THIS DOES NOT MEAN that real perfection is impossible to anyone but priests and religious. Through the grace of God, it is possible for anyone to be spiritually perfect, that is, to live well the life of charity for God and man. The housewife who lives across the street from the convent may be more perfect than some of the nuns in the convent. Yet, in technical language, the nuns are living in a state of perfection, and the housewife is not. The term "state" means something permanent and immovable, and the nuns have bound themselves by their vows of poverty, chastity and obedience to a way of life to which the housewife has not bound herself.

BISHOPS OF THE CHURCH and religious—that is, those who have freely bound themselves by the vows of poverty, chastity and obedience—are in the state of perfection. Bishops are in the state of perfection because their office binds them to work for the spiritual perfection of the flock entrusted to their care, and in order to bring others to perfection they must be perfect themselves.

RELIGIOUS are in the state of perfection because they are bound by the vows of poverty, chastity and obedience. The essence of perfection is charity or the love of God above all things. Now a man can fail to love God above all things because he loves external possessions too much, or his body too much, or his own will too much. By the vow of poverty the religious gives up external possessions. By the vow of chastity he gives up the legitimate use of the pleasures of his body. By the vow of obedience he gives up his own wilfulness and submits himself to God through his superior. In this way the religious voluntarily withdraws himself from the things which might lead him away from God. By pledging himself to a life of poverty, chastity and obedience, he binds himself to seek perfection, that is, to seek to love God perfectly. His vows give him a certain stability or immovableness in the search for spiritual perfection, and it is for this reason that he is said to be in a state of perfection; he has promised, by his vows, to seek perfection.

THE SPIRITUAL PERFECTION of bishops and religious is a sign of their success in the search for happiness. It is an example to all men. Their wholehearted pursuit of God is like a beacon on a mountaintop showing other men the way to happiness. As we said in the very beginning of this essay on man, the image of God, the final goal of every human life is happiness—the vision of God. And the meaning of every human act is found in its relation to this goal. If it turns a man away from this goal, it is evil and leads to unhappiness. If it leads man on to this goal, it is good and will bring man to happiness. If men are to fulfil the true destiny of human nature, they must use all their powers to seek God. The human body, the human soul, the passions of man, his reason and will, his habits and virtues, the grace of God and the supernatural virtues which come to man with grace— all these wonderful powers must be used in the pursuit of happiness. Through temperance man learns to control himself in the pursuit of pleasure. Through fortitude man strengthens himself in the pursuit of good in the face of difficulty and danger. Through justice man learns to establish peace and order between himself and the rest of men, between man and God. Through prudence the mind of man becomes capable of directing all his human actions well. Through faith man learns for the first time of the great goal of human life—the vision of God. Through hope his heart is raised up to this goal. Through charity man begins to love God as he ought. Through charity man already possesses God. If charity directs all his human actions, his life on earth will be filled with the beauty and the strength of God. As long as grace and charity remain in man's soul, man is the image and the likeness of God. Like God, he has the power to see and to love God. If man perseveres in the love of God, one day he will reach his goal, his ultimate happiness. He will see God face to face and he will love God as God loves Himself. Then man will be what God always meant man to be—the image and likeness of God.

✠✠✠✠✠✠✠✠✠✠✠✠✠✠✠✠✠✠✠✠✠✠

PART III

✠ ✠ ✠ The God-Man

*Refers to questions in the Summa

✠✠✠✠✠✠✠✠✠✠✠✠✠✠✠✠✠✠✠✠✠✠

CHAPTER I

The Incarnation

The Mystery of the Incarnation
Reasons for the Incarnation
The Problem of Nature and Person
The Union of Natures in Christ
The Human Nature of Christ
The Grace of Christ
Christ: The Head
The Mystical Body of Christ
The Knowledge of Christ
The Power of Christ
The Weakness of Christ
Union of Wills in Christ
Christ's Subjection to His Father
The Prayer of Christ
Christ: The Priest and Victim
The Adoration of Christ
Christ: The Mediator

CHAPTER I

The Incarnation

THE VISION OF GOD is the goal of human life. It is divine grace and the supernatural infused virtues which come to man with it that enable him to attain the vision of God. But by sin, Adam lost grace and the infused virtues for himself and for the whole human race. How, then, can man ever reach his true destiny? Must we say that real happiness is forever impossible to him? By sin he has cut himself off from God. Like a petulant child, he has run away from the home of God's love. But the love of God for man is strong and deep and wise; it has reached down from heaven to earth and rescued him from sin and death, and the manner of its coming is beyond the understanding of man. "By this hath the charity of God appeared towards us, because God hath sent his only begotten Son into the world, that we may live by him. In this is charity: not as though we had loved God, but because he hath first loved us, and sent his Son to be a propitiation for our sins" (I John, IV, 9-10).

THIS IS THE CENTRAL MYSTERY of Christianity— the mystery of the Incarnation of the Son of God. To save men from their sins, God sent His own Son into the world as a man. The Word of God, the Second Person of the Most Blessed Trinity, became man and dwelt amongst us for our salvation. The Son of God is both God and man. He is one divine Person existing in two natures, one divine and the other human. Try as we may, we shall never understand in this present life how the Son of God could become man and still remain God. But this is the mystery of God's love for us which He has revealed to us. Christ Himself, the Son of God in human flesh, proclaimed this stupendous truth. His miracles proved His claim. He was put to death by the Sanhedrin for making this claim. Christ died on the Cross rather than retract it; and He rose from the grave to prove that He, Who was really man, was also really God.

THOUGH WE CANNOT UNDERSTAND this great mystery, still, as St. Thomas and the Fathers of the Church point out to us, by it the goodness, wisdom, justice and power of God are made known to us. In the Incarnation God, Who is almighty and all-perfect, has condescended to unite to Himself a human nature which is created and limited in power. Surely this is a sign of God's goodness to man. Since Jesus Christ is both God and man, He can offer to God an infinite satisfaction for man's sins against God, and in this the wisdom of God is manifested to us. Because Jesus Christ is man, it is man who satisfied God for sin, and in this we see the justice of God. Lastly, to unite a human nature to the Son of God as His very own human nature—this is a work that demands divine power.

THE LOVE OF GOD for man shines out more clearly in the mystery of the Incarnation when we realize that God did not have to become man in order to save man from his sins. God could simply have forgiven man his sins and restored grace to him; or He could have been content with any satisfaction for sin that man himself might make. But the love of God for man was not content with half-measure or with what was simply necessary. God chose the best possible means of saving man, the best possible means of leading man to good and withdrawing him from evil.

THROUGH THE INCARNATION, God leads man to good. The Incarnation is the firm foundation of the virtues of faith, hope and charity. It is the foundation of faith because in Christ we hear the voice of God Himself. It is the foundation of hope because it is a manifestation of the strength of God's love for us. It is the foundation of charity because God's great love for us cannot but enkindle our love for Him. Moreover, in the Incarnation men find the example they must follow to reach the vision of God, for in the life and actions of Christ we see the work of the Christian virtues in their full perfection. Lastly, through the Incarnation the divine life of grace is restored to man, and it becomes possible for him to live divinely here on earth so that he may inherit the vision of God in heaven.

THE INCARNATION withdraws man from evil. First of all, it shows him that he must prefer God and himself to the devil, who brought about the ruin of human nature. Secondly, it shows man his own great dignity. God has united to Himself no other nature but the nature of man. Surely, then, man is something wonderful in God's eyes and in the universe. But the Incarnation also preserves man from presumption, for grace is restored to him through Jesus Christ and not because of his own merits. Then, too, in the Incarnation the love of God dissolves the hard ice of human pride. If God is humble enough to become man, can man be too proud to become godlike through divine grace? Most importantly, Jesus Christ, the God-Man, satisfied God for man's sins and so merited for him the forgiveness of his sins.

THE SON OF GOD became man to save man from sin. Some theologians have held that God would have become man even if man had not fallen into sin. But St. Thomas remarks that God has not told us what He would have done if man had not sinned. It is better, therefore, to say no more than God Himself has said, that the Son of God became man to redeem man from sin. He came into the world to take away all sin, both actual and original sin. Since original sin infects the whole human race, it can be said that, though Christ came to take away all sin, nevertheless He came principally to rescue man from original sin.

St. THOMAS ALSO REMARKS that Christ came into the world at just the right time. Had He come immediately after Adam sinned, man would not have appreciated the value of his redemption by Christ. To appreciate the value of the divine gifts he threw away by sin, man needed to live for some time on his own resources. Moreover, the dignity of the Person Who was coming to save man—the Second Person of the Trinity—demanded that the world be prepared for His coming by the long line of patriarchs and prophets who preceded Him. Again, if Christ had come at the beginning of the history of the human race, faith in Him might be weakened in the time to come. On the other hand, had Christ delayed His coming until the end of men's history on earth, it is very likely that by that time men would have forgotten about God and His commandments.

IN ITSELF, THE INCARNATION is a mystery that surpasses human understanding. We can do no more than state it correctly. St. Thomas begins his statement of the mystery with the infallible definition of the Council of Chalcedon: "We confess that in these latter times the only-begotten Son of God appeared in two natures, without confusion, without change, without division, without separation—the distinction of natures not having been taken away by the union." If we strip this definition down to its essentials, we might say that in the Incarnation we have one Person, the Son of God, and two natures, one divine, the other human, and these two natures are united in the one Person. To understand what we mean, we must recall what is signified by the terms "nature" and "person", and by a union in a person.

ALL OF US KNOW, at least in an elementary way, what is meant by the terms nature and person. We know that a dog has a nature, an animal nature, the nature of a dog; but we realize that a dog is not a person. We know that John Smith has a human nature and is a person, and we understand, too, that his nature is not precisely the same thing as his person. His human nature is the same as the human nature of all other men, but his person is not. We can assert that all men are rational animals, that they all have bodies and souls. But if John Smith steals ten dollars from Mary Jones, we can say that he did it, but we cannot say that anyone else did it. As a human being John Smith has a body and soul like all other men, but only the person known as John Smith, and no one else, stole Mary Jones' ten dollars. We might state all this simply by recalling that the answer to the question, "What is it?" gives us the nature of a thing; and the answer to the question, "Who is it?" gives us the person. If we ask, "What is that coming down the road?" the answer may be, "It is a human being". The answer gives us the nature of what is coming down the road. But if we want to know the person coming down the road, we must inquire, "Who is it?"

THE NATURE OF A THING tells us what it is; but the person tells us who it is. This implies, too, another important distinction between a nature and a person. The answer to the question, "What is it?" might be anything—an atom, a boat, a rose, a horse, a man, or even the divine Nature. But the reply to the query, "Who is it?", must always be—a rational being, an intellectual being. If we ask, "Who is it?", we never expect to be told, "A rose," or "A boat". We expect to hear that it is John Jones, or St. Thomas, or the Archangel Raphael, or the Son of God. A person is always a rational being, and therefore a being with free will—a being who has control of his own actions, someone who is master of himself, someone who is responsible for his own actions. A person is always, then, someone who is unique, who is himself and nothing else and no one else. A nature may be common to many individuals. There may be thousands of dogs, but they all have in common the same kind of nature. There may be thousands of men, and they all have in common the same kind of nature. But every human person is himself and no one else; his personality is not possessed in common by anyone else.

NOW IN THE INCARNATION we say that there are two natures but only one Person. In the Person of Christ, the Son of God, there are two natures, one divine, the other human. Christ is God, the Supreme Being, the Omnipotent Creator and Lord of the world. The Person, Christ, is the divine Nature. But He also has a human nature, a human body and a human soul. The one Person is both God and man. There are two "Whats" in Christ but only one "Who". If we ask, "What is Christ?", we must give two answers; we must say, "He is God", and "He is man". But if we inquire, "Who is He?" then we must have only one reply; we must declare, "He is the Son of God". It does not matter that we might also state, "He is the Second Person of the Trinity", or "He is Jesus Christ, the son of Mary of Nazareth", or "He is the Messias". All these are only other names for one and the same Person. In Christ, then, we have one divine Person Who exists in two natures, one human, the other divine.

IN CHRIST, THE DIVINE NATURE and the human nature are united. In what way are they united? Here we find ourselves in the very heart of this great mystery. Obviously, they are not simply united in the way in which two stones lying together on the ground are united. If that were the case, then there would be two persons in Christ, the divine Person and a human person. This would not be a union, but simply a juxtaposition, a placing together of the two natures. Nor can we say that the two natures are fused together, in the way, for example, that hydrogen and oxygen are mixed together to make water. This is impossible, first of all because it would mean that the divine Nature of Christ would have to be changed in some way, and the divine Nature is absolutely unchangeable. If the divine and the human natures in Christ were really fused together, either the divine Nature would become human, or the human nature would become divine, or the resulting mixture would be something that was neither human nor divine. But none of these things is possible. The divine Nature cannot be changed at all; the human nature cannot become divine; and Christ is not something that is neither divine nor human. He is both God and man. In Christ we find both natures in their full perfection.

Nor can we say that the two natures are united to one another as the soul and body are united together to form one man. In this case, soul and body are two incomplete principles which complete one another in their union. But the divine Nature is not at all incomplete or imperfect. It cannot directly unite with a human nature as one incomplete principle with another. Besides, as in the case of hydrogen and oxygen, the union of body and soul brings into being something which is different from either the body or the soul alone; it brings into being the whole man. But in the Incarnation the union of the two natures does not bring into being any third being distinct from the divine and human natures. In the Incarnation the two natures are complete, not mixed or confused with one another, not forming any third thing distinct from both.

THE UNION BETWEEN THE TWO NATURES in Christ is a personal union. It takes place in the Person of the Son of God. The two natures are not united to one another directly. They are not mixed or fused with one another to form a third thing distinct from both. Rather they are united to one another indirectly in the Second Person of the Trinity. Nor is this personal union of the two natures in Christ like the union between soul and body in a man. In an ordinary man, his person or personality is the result of the union of soul and body. There is no human person until a human soul and a body are united to one another to form the whole man. But in the Incarnation, the person pre-exists the union of the two natures, because it is the Person of the Eternal Son of God. In the Incarnation the Son of God, Who is eternal, assumes to Himself a complete human nature, a body and soul. By this union the human nature becomes the human nature of the Son of God. He is the Person existing in this human nature, the Person responsible for all its actions, the responsible Agent acting in and through this human nature in the world of men. It should be clear at once that the human nature of Christ has no human personality. If we were to look at the human nature of Christ and ask, "What is it?" the answer would have to be, "It is a human nature". But if we were to inquire, "Who is he?" then we could not give in reply the name of any human or created person, because there is no created personality present in Christ. We should have to say, "He is Christ, the Son of God".

B ECAUSE THERE IS ONLY ONE PERSON in Christ, and because that Person exists and acts in two natures, one human and one divine, it follows that all the actions of both natures can be and must be attributed to that same one Person. It is the person, not the nature, which is the responsible agent. Hence we can say of Christ that He created the world, that He performed miracles by His own power, that He is immortal and eternal; and, on the other hand, that He ate, drank, slept, suffered, died, rose again and ascended into heaven.

S URELY THIS IS A PROFOUND MYSTERY. We cannot hope to understand it until we see it clearly in the vision of God. We cannot positively understand how it is possible for God to assume to Himself a human nature. We even find difficulty in seeking to understand how the human nature of Christ can exist without a human personality. But this is a mystery revealed to us by God Himself. With the humility of faith, we submit our own minds to the infinite wisdom and truth of God. Because God has revealed this sublime truth to us, we know that it is possible for the Son of God to assume to Himself a human nature without a human personality. Because God has said so, we know that this staggering possibility is an actual fact, a consoling fact. For, if God has so loved men that He sent His only-begotten Son into the world as man, then surely God's love can raise man up to the unfathomable happiness of the vision of God.

IN MANY WAYS, as we have already seen, it was becoming that the Son of God should assume a human nature. We might add here that it was more fitting for Him to assume a human nature than any other kind of nature. From the point of view of dignity, it is fitting that the Son of God, Who is the absolute perfection of divine Knowledge, Who is the divine Intellect, should assume to Himself a nature that is also rational and intellectual. Again, even though the angels are also intellectual beings, it was more fitting that God should become man, because man needed salvation and could be saved, whereas the evil angels, the devils, could not be saved, and the good angels do not need redemption.

SINCE THE PURPOSE of the Incarnation was the salvation of the sinful race of Adam, it was also fitting that the Son of God should assume to Himself an individual nature of the race of Adam. In this way, the same human race that had offended God in Adam and had lost God's grace could satisfy God for man's sin and regain the grace of God.

FOR THIS REASON, too, the Son of God assumed to Himself a complete, a perfect human nature, a human body united to a human soul, a rational, intellectual soul. If He had not done this, then He could not have satisfied God for sin as a real human being, a true representative of the race of Adam. We cannot escape from this mystery, then, by saying either that God only appeared to us as a man, but that His body was only the appearance of a body; or that His body had no human soul, no human intellect or human free will. In all these hypotheses, Christ would not have been a real man and He would not have been able to offer God a man's reparation for sin.

THE SON OF GOD assumed to Himself a complete human nature. Now, because this human nature is the human nature of a Person Who is God, it is only natural that this human nature will have all the perfection that is possible to a human nature and that is not opposed to the purpose of the Incarnation—the redemption of mankind. We must consider briefly both the perfection of Christ's human nature and its weaknesses.

IN THE ORDER of divine grace, the human nature of Christ is the most perfect of all human natures. Since the human soul of Christ is so intimately united to the Person of the Son of God, it is only natural that His soul should be perfectly sanctified by divine grace. Divine grace made His soul holy and pleasing to God, just as it does in the souls of other men. Moreover, the soul of Christ was to be the source of the supernatural acts by which the redemption of man would be accomplished. But sanctifying grace is necessary for meritorious supernatural acts; hence the soul of Christ was given this grace. In addition, Christ was to be the source of grace for all other men. But how could He give grace to others if He did not possess it Himself?

A S IN OTHER MEN, so too in Christ, sanctifying grace brought to His soul the perfection of the supernatural virtues. But because of the perfection of Christ's grace, not all of these virtues were necessary to Christ. In the perfection of His grace Christ already possessed the vision of God. His soul already enjoyed from the beginning of its existence the happiness of seeing God face to face. Hence there was no need in Christ for the virtues of faith or hope. He did not need faith, for He saw God face to face; and He did not have to hope for what He already possessed. But Christ had the other supernatural virtues and gifts of the Holy Ghost in a pre-eminent degree.

C HRIST ALSO POSSESSED to the fullest degree the gratuitous graces of which we have already spoken—the gift of prophecy, the gift of tongues, the gift of preaching well and the power to work miracles. In God's plan, Christ was to be the perfect teacher of all men; hence God gave Him these gifts to fit Him for this task.

T O SUM IT ALL UP, we must say that Christ possessed the fullness of all grace. His soul is intimately and substantially united to God in the Person of the Son of God. Because it is more closely united to God, the source of divine grace, than any other creature, it receives the greatest outpouring of grace. Since Christ is to communicate the grace of God to others, it must possess the greatest degree of grace. It might be well to remark here that Christ possessed an absolute fullness of grace. We say of Mary, His Mother, and of some of the saints that they also were full of God's grace. In their case we are referring to a relative fullness of grace; they possessed as much grace as they needed to perform the work God gave them to do. But Christ had the most stupendous task of all: He had to redeem the whole human race; He had to restore grace to the whole human race. Hence He had to possess an absolute fullness of grace.

ALTHOUGH THE SOUL OF CHRIST possessed the fullness of grace, His grace was still a created reality; it was something finite and limited in itself. It was the greatest possible participation in the divine life, the greatest share in the divine life given to any creature; from this point of view it might be called infinite. No other degree of grace, in fact the grace of all other men and angels put together cannot surpass the grace of Christ; but in itself the grace of Christ is still a finite, created reality. However, unlike the grace of other men, it was not capable of any increase; no one can gain more than the greatest degree of anything, and Christ had from the beginning the greatest degree of grace.

THIS GREAT GRACE was given to Christ also because in the divine plan He was to be the head of the whole human race in the spiritual order. Adam is the head of the whole human race in the natural order of the body. He was also, before his sin, the spiritual head of the human race. By his sin he lost God's grace for himself and for all his descendants, and in this way he ceased to be the head of the human race in the spiritual order. However, God determined to restore grace to the human race, and He made Christ the new spiritual head of all men. It is in this sense that the Fathers of the Church called Christ the "second Adam." From Adam to the end of time, all grace comes to men from Christ. Since His own personal sanctifying grace is the source of grace for all men, His grace is sometimes called capital grace, or the grace of headship.

CHRIST IS THE HEAD of His Church. This is a truth which is profoundly significant for all men, especially the members of His Church. Christ is the head of the Church and the Church is His Mystical Body. The terms "head" and "body" are used in comparison with the head and body of a man. The head of a man is the first part of his body, beginning from the top down. The head is also his noblest part, for in it we find all the senses of man—sight, hearing, taste, smell and touch, the imagination and reason—whereas in the rest of the body we find only the sense of touch. The head is also the power which rules the rest of the body, for in it we find the brain, which moves all the parts of the body to their different actions for the good of the whole body. Now Christ plays all these roles in relation to His Church. He is the first, or the topmost, part of the Church, for He is the first-born of all the sons of God through grace. He is the noblest or most perfect part of the Church, for He possesses the absolute fullness of grace. Through His graces, He is the closest human being to God and His soul is the instrument by which the wisdom and power of God become active in the world of men. He is the Teacher, the Ruler and the Sanctifier of all men. Lastly, as the head directs the members of the body to the good of the whole, as the head gives life and movement to the body, so, too, Christ directs the members of the Church to the good of the whole Church and imparts life to all the members of His Church. Christ possesses the grace of headship because He bestows grace on all.

CHRIST IS THE HEAD of men principally in relation to their souls. However, the bodies of men are the instruments by which they act in the world; hence, Christ can be said to have an influence on the bodies of men in so far as He sanctifies and moves their souls by grace. In a man whose soul lives by the grace of Christ, the body is an instrument for the performance of works of justice, rather than for works of iniquity. In this way Christ sanctifies both the souls and bodies of men. We can say, also, that at the time of the resurrection of men at the end of the world, the souls of those who are in heaven will glorify their risen bodies. The glory of the saintly soul will flow into the risen body. In this way, too, Christ is the head of men's bodies as well as their souls.

CHRIST IS, in the divine plan, the head of all men. Now in a human body the head and all the members exist together and simultaneously. This is evidently not the case in the headship of Christ. All men do not live at the same time, nor are they all actually united to Christ, their head. Christ, then, is the head of all men, but in different ways. If we consider all the men who have existed or who will exist in the course of time, then we may express their relation to Christ as their head in the following way. Christ is the actual head of all those who are already with Him in heaven enjoying the vision of God, the final fruition of the life of grace. He is also the actual head of all the men who are not yet in heaven, but who are united to Him in grace and charity. He is actually the head of all those who are united to Him by faith, even though, through mortal sin, they have lost grace and charity. In this case, though, it is clear that such men are less perfectly His members than those who are in the state of grace. Lastly, other men, while they are still in this life, are the members of Christ's Body in potentiality. They are not actual members of His Church, but they can become members. Of these men some will, in the providence of God, become actual members of Christ, but others will not. After death, those men who did not die as members of Christ will cease even to be potential members of Christ.

CHRIST IS ALSO THE HEAD of the angels. The perfection of His grace places Him nearer to God than even the highest angel. In addition, Christ uses the ministry of angels in working out the salvation of men; and in this way He adds to their accidental glory and happiness, and directs their actions to the good of the whole Mystical Body which is His Church.

CHRIST IS THE HEAD of His Church, both because He is the source of the grace by which its members are spiritually alive, and because He governs the whole Church. Now He has given to men a share in these powers. Christ Himself has ascended into heaven. He is no longer with us in the flesh; but He has remembered that we are only human beings, that we cannot live solely in the realm of the spirit. He has, as it were, left behind Him other Christs who continue to exercise His functions as Head of the Church. It is true that only Christ, because of the close union between His soul and His divinity, can directly cause grace to flow into the souls of the members of His Church. He alone, as the Son of God, can send the Holy Spirit, the Sanctifier, into the world to cause God's grace to exist in the souls of men. But He has given His bishops and priests the power to act on the souls of men through the sacraments which He Himself has instituted. When a priest baptizes an infant, or when a bishop confirms someone, it is Christ Himself who acts through the priest or bishop and through the sacrament, to introduce God's grace into the soul of the person baptized or confirmed. In the sacrament of matrimony it is the bride and groom who make the sacrament, and the power of Christ acts through them and through the sacrament to give them the grace of the sacrament.

CHRIST HAS ALSO ENTRUSTED the external government and instruction of His Church to men. To the Pope and the bishops He has given authority to rule and to teach His Church. In a sense, then, these men may also be called heads of the Church. But they are subordinate heads, like the heads of the various departments in a giant corporation. They rule some particular section of the Church, as a bishop rules and teaches one particular diocese. The Pope of Rome, however, is the Vicar of Christ. He takes Christ's place on earth as the ruler and the teacher of the whole Church on earth. It is this participation of the Pope and the bishops in the headship of Christ which merits for them the respect, obedience and love which all the members of Christ's Church give to them. They speak to men for Christ. They speak with His voice. He speaks through them, and hence in matters of faith or morals they can speak infallibly. The Spirit of Christ, the Holy Spirit, reminds them of all that Christ has commanded them.

IF CHRIST IS THE HEAD of His Church, then the Church is His Body. As the term "Head" is used figuratively of Christ in relation to the Church, so also the term "Body" is used figuratively of the Church in relation to Christ. It is obvious that the Church is not a physical body as the body of a man. It is rather a body in the sense in which we speak of a moral body, such as the body politic. The body politic is a group of men united to work together under some authority, to achieve the common goal of all men in the temporal order. Now the Church is a group of men united to work together under the authority of Christ for the good of the whole Church, which is the attainment of the vision of God. However, the Church is even more than a moral body. In a moral body, the only means of union between the members is the free decision of their wills to work together. But in the Church the members of Christ's Body are united to Christ and to one another by the supernatural bond of God's grace and charity. All the members of Christ's Body, the Church, are united, not by a natural union of wills, but in the divine life of grace and in the supernatural bond of Christian charity. Because both grace and charity are supernatural realities which are not fully understood by men in this life, we call this union a mystical, or mysterious, union. Hence, the Church is called not simply the Body of Christ, but the Mystical Body of Christ.

A S A NATURAL BODY is alive, so the Mystical Body of Christ is alive in the supernatural order. As the soul is the source of the life of the human body, so the Holy Spirit, the Third Person of the Most Blessed Trinity, is the life of the Mystical Body of Christ. From heaven, Christ, as the Son of God, sends the Spirit into the world to give supernatural life to His Church. The Holy Spirit communicates life to the Church in the order of truth, holiness and discipline. He is the source of truth in the Church, because it is the Holy Spirit Who imparts infallibility to the Pope and bishops in the teaching of Christian doctrine. He is the source of truth for all the members of the Church, for it is He Who bestows on all the gift of divine faith whereby they lay hold on God's revealed truth. He is the source of holiness, since He is the principal agent infusing grace—a share in the divine life—into the souls of men. He is the source of discipline, as it is He Who chooses—in a mysterious, invisible way—those who will be the visible rulers of the Church in the world. He is the primary source of all vocations to the priesthood or the religious life, to the episcopacy or the papacy. It is for these reasons that the Holy Spirit is called the Soul of the Church, the Soul of the Mystical Body of Christ. He is the source of all its supernatural life. He is the source of the charity which binds together all the members of the Church.

A S THERE ARE MANY and different members in a living human body, so, too, Christ and the Holy Spirit have placed numerous and diverse members in the Church. As we have just said, some members of the Church are placed in positions of authority, and they are endowed with the graces necessary for teaching, ruling and sanctifying. To the others are given the graces required for obeying and serving the Church. But in all the members of the Church, whether they be rulers or ruled, God produces an astonishing variety of graces which gives the Church the great beauty that is to be found in any living body. In the Church there are humble missioners with the gift of tongues or of persuasive preaching. We can find, also, intellectual geniuses such as St. Thomas or St. Bonaventure. In the Church God produces the zeal of St. Paul, the charity of St. John the Evangelist, the fortitude of Pope Gregory VII or of St. Ambrose, the temperance of Matt Talbot, the humility of the Cure of Ars, the purity of St. Agnes, the crusading spirit of St. Louis of France, the martyrdom of St. Maria Goretti.

IN ALL THESE MYSTERIOUS WAYS, God works out His divine plan for men and for His Church. All the members of His Church labor together for the building up of the Body of Christ, for the salvation of men. Christ, His Blessed Mother, the angels and saints in heaven work for the release of the souls in purgatory—the Church Suffering. They work also for the salvation of the Church Militant—the Church here on earth. Seeing us in their vision of God, they know all our needs, our trials and difficulties. Through their prayers, a constant torrent of God's graces is pouring into purgatory and into the world to redeem men. The souls in purgatory—the Church Suffering—expiate their sins in the purifying fires of purgatory. Some theologians think they also can pray for the Church Militant on earth. At any rate, when their souls are fully cleansed and they are admitted to heaven, then they, also, as saints of God, intercede for us who still remain here on earth. The members of the Church here on earth—the Church Militant—in their turn toil and pray for their own salvation and for the release of the souls in purgatory. In addition, they praise God in Himself and in His saints. In all these wonderful ways, the grace of Christ circulates through the three great sections of His Church, the Church Triumphant in heaven, the Church Suffering in purgatory and the Church Militant on earth, binding them all together in the Communion of Saints.

THIS MARVELOUS SUPERNATURAL LIFE of the Church is all traceable to the grace of headship which is Christ's. From this point of view, we can say that the Church is Christ; it is from Him that supernatural life flows to all its members. Christ lives on forever in His Church; here on earth the Church is the continuance of His life. In the Church, Christ still teaches men the truths of salvation, sanctifies their souls, and rules them for the salvation of the world.

THERE ARE, UNFORTUNATELY, some men who are not under the headship of Christ. These are they who are either already in hell for their sins, or who will be condemned to hell for their sins. These men have lost their true head, and now are under the rule of the devil. They have no real head in the sense of a source of supernatural life; but they are subject to the external government of the devil.

SINCE THE HUMAN NATURE of Christ is the human nature of the Son of God, and since Christ in that nature is the head of men and angels, it is natural to expect that it will have all the excellence that is possible to a human nature. This is precisely the case: in knowledge and power, the human nature of Christ possesses all the perfection possible to a human nature.

FROM THE POINT OF VIEW OF KNOWLEDGE, it would have been absurd for God to give Christ a human mind without endowing it with all the knowledge possible to it. As God, Christ possessed the perfection of the divine knowledge. As God, Christ knew everything that could be known about God and the world, about the past, the present and the future. But, still, the perfection of the human nature of Christ demands that the soul of Christ should know everything that a human soul may know, and in the way in which it is possible for a human soul to know anything. This means that the soul of Christ must have been enriched from the beginning with the vision of God. If Christ was to make it possible for other men to see God, certainly He must have seen God with His own human intellect. Obviously, this vision of God in the human intellect of Christ cannot be equal to the infinitely perfect vision of God which is proper to God alone. But since Christ, in His human nature, is the head of all creatures, He will see in His vision of God all that can be known about creatures—that is, He will see everything that is real about creation: all that has been, that is, or that will be. He will not see everything that is possible to God; only God can fully realize the infinite power of God. In addition, the human soul of Christ possesses infused knowledge. We realize that this is possible, because the angelic intellects know by means of infused knowledge, and the souls of the dead also know by infused knowledge, since they no longer have any eyes, ears, and so forth by which they could know anything. If the angels and the souls of the dead are to know the things in the world, they must know them through knowledge which God infuses into their minds. Since knowledge of this kind is attainable by a created mind, it must exist in the human mind of Christ. Surely, God would not allow the mind of His own human nature to lack any possible perfection. Through this infused knowledge Christ would not know the essence of God; He knew the essence of God through His beatific vision of God. But through this infused knowledge He would know everything that is possible for a created intellect to know. Lastly, the human intellect of Christ could acquire knowledge just as other men obtain it. Through the senses He would come to learn the world in which men live; by the power of His mind He would come to understand the meaning of things just as other men do. It follows, then, that while the vision of God in the soul of Christ and the infused knowledge in His soul could not grow or increase, the acquired knowledge in the soul of Christ could increase. This is the meaning of the statement in sacred scripture that the Boy Christ advanced in wisdom. Neither His beatific vision of God nor His infused knowledge increased, but His natural acquired knowledge was augmented. Naturally, since the human nature of Christ was a perfect human nature, since the power of Christ's mind was never weakened or darkened by sin, even the acquired knowledge of Christ surpasses the knowledge of all other men. We do not say that Christ, in this way, knew even things of which He had not experience, such as the television or the atom bomb. But His mind grasped the essence of all things. Naturally, too, since Christ is God, it was not fitting that Christ should learn anything either from angels or men. God is the source of all knowledge; therefore, even in His human nature, He acquired all that He knew without any angelic or human teacher.

As WE HAVE ALREADY NOTED, the great perfection of the human knowledge of Christ is due to the fact that it is the knowledge of the human nature that is God's, the human nature that was assumed by the Son of God. The absolute perfection of the Son of God demands that the human nature He assumes be as perfect as it can be. The necessity of this perfect knowledge in Christ appears even more clearly when we recall the role that Christ plays in the universe. He is the head of men and ange's, and must direct them; therefore, He must know perfectly the world of men and angels. In addition, He is to lead men to the vision of God. But unless He knows the destination well, how can He lead men to it? It was necessary then, for Christ to know God and the whole universe as perfectly as possible.

WE MAY SAY THE SAME about the power of Christ. Since He is God, it is fitting that His human nature possess all the power possible to a creature. As He is the head of men and angels, it is fitting that He have all the power necessary to fulfil this role in the universe. Because the human nature of Christ is a creature, it cannot have the omnipotence of God. It cannot create anything or annihilate anything; these actions are proper to God alone. But Christ had the power to work miracles through His human nature; it was the instrument used by His divinity to produce miraculous effects in the world. Obviously, too, the human nature of Christ, in virtue of its fullness of grace and perfection of knowledge, had the power to instruct all creatures.

THE PERFECTION of the human nature of Christ is an inspiration to all men. It shows them what God wants them to be; not that all men, or any one man, could ever reach the excellence of Christ. But it is the will of God that all should approach the perfections of Christ as closely as possible. Still, God, in His wisdom, did not make the human nature of Christ so perfect that men might not recognize Christ as one of themselves, as another human being. In Christ we find those human imperfections which are not contrary to His human perfection, and which are useful in the work of redemption which Christ was to accomplish. Christ was hungry at times, and thirsty, and tired; He could feel pain. He could suffer and die, and He did suffer and die for the sins of men. By His sufferings and death He paid the penalty of the sins of men. He could feel sorrow at the prospect of death; He could weep over the death of Lazarus, His friend. But He did not have those defects of human nature which are due solely to sin. Since He had to suffer and die to redeem men from sin, He assumed in His body the defects of suffering and death; but He Himself, because He was sinless, did not contract the penalties of suffering and death as a punishment for His own sins. He assumed these defects only to pay the penalty of other men's sins. He Himself was absolutely sinless; the perfection of His holiness did not even tolerate in Him any inclination to evil, any disordered concupiscence of the flesh. But the sufferings and the death He endured for men are an example of patience and love to all.

THE SON OF GOD has become man. Christ is both God and man. Important consequences result from this tremendous fact. From the point of view of Christ Himself, it follows that since there is only one Person in Christ, whatever we can say of either of His natures can be said of that Person. Hence, we can declare that Christ is God, or that Christ is man. We can state that the Son of God is eternal, and that He died on the Cross at Calvary. Because the Person in Christ is a divine Person, the Son of God, we can call Mary the Mother of God; she has given birth to God in His human nature. However, it is important to remember that the two natures of Christ remain themselves; hence, we cannot say that the divinity of Christ is human, or that the divine Nature died on the Cross, or that the human nature of Christ is eternal or strictly omnipotent.

IN VIRTUE OF THE ONENESS of personality in Christ, we must also assert that there are not two Christs, the one human and the other divine. We must affirm that there is but one Christ, Who is both human and divine. Because there is but one Person, one responsible Agent in Christ, it follows that there must also be a unity or a conformity between the divine will of Christ and His human will. Since Christ possessed a perfect human nature, He also possessed a free human will. The human will of Christ was perfectly conformed to the divine will of Christ. It did not will anything against the divine will, nor did it refuse anything the divine will commanded. This does not mean that Christ did not suffer at all in undergoing death on the Cross. Christ allowed His sensitive appetite to function quite naturally during His Passion and death. As in other men, His soul, through the action of the sensitive appetite, feared the prospect of suffering and death. This is the meaning of Christ's statement in the garden of Gethsemani: "My soul is sorrowful unto death". His will, considered simply as a tendency to good, also shrank from suffering and death. But His will as a rational appetite, as an inclination to good under the control of reason, accepted suffering and death as the will of God. In the action of His human will, then, Christ gave us the example of a perfect will. While still subject to the movement of the passions, the will of Christ was rationally obedient to God, even unto the death of the Cross.

AS A HUMAN BEING, Christ had also the power to act in a human way. He was capable of acts of reason and will. In fact, all the actions of the human nature of Christ, even the purely vegetative functions of His body, were under the control of His rational human will. Moreover, since Christ was able to act freely, He was capable of meriting grace for Himself and for others. But here we must make an important distinction. Since Christ did not exist in His human nature until the Son of God assumed a human nature to Himself in the womb of the Virgin Mary, Christ did not merit for Himself either the personal union of His human nature with the Son of God, nor sanctifying grace, nor the perfection of His knowledge. But He merited for Himself the glory of His body after His Resurrection and His Ascension, and, in general, all the perfections which He acquired in the course of time. In addition, He merited by His free actions all the graces given to men as members of His Mystical Body, and even the graces whereby the angels assist Him in the work of building up His Mystical Body.

WE MAY ALSO CONSIDER the consequences of the Incarnation from the point of view of the relations between Christ and His Father. As God, the Son of God is equal in divinity to the Father; but in His human nature, the Son of God is subject to the Father. In the first place, all the goodness of the human nature of Christ comes from God the Father. Secondly, the human nature of Christ, as all creatures, is subject to the divine governance of the world by God the Father. Lastly, since the will of the human nature of Christ was perfect in grace, it was fully and freely subject to God the Father. Christ, then, gives us once again a perfect example of the proper subjection of men to God.

BECAUSE CHRIST was human, He prayed to His Father. In this, also, He afforded us a perfect model. He asked for those things which God wished to give Him through prayer, such as the glorification of His body after the Resurrection. But He also offered to God in prayer the desires of His sensitive appetite. Thus, at the beginning of His Passion He prayed: "Let this chalice pass from Me". By so doing He showed us that it is possible for man to desire what God does not wish. But He also taught us on the same occasion that our rational wills should be conformed to the will of God against the tendencies of the sensitive appetite, for He concluded His prayer with the words: "Nevertheless, not as I will, but as Thou wilt." Because His prayers were always in conformity with the will of God, they were always answered.

THROUGH THE INCARNATION, Christ is the high priest of God and the human race. It is the function of a priest to act as a mediator between God and men. He must bring the gifts of God to men, and he must take the offerings of men to God, and make satisfaction for their sins. Now Christ fulfilled this role perfectly. He is the perfect Mediator between God and men, because He Himself is both God and man. He brings God's gifts to men, because it is through Christ that divine grace is given to men. He offered Himself on the Cross to God as a satisfaction for the sins of men, and in this way He both brought to God the offering of mankind and made satisfaction for sin.

THE OFFERING which Christ made to God for men was the sacrifice of Himself on the Cross. In this sacrifice, Christ was both the victim and the priest. As we have already seen, every visible sacrifice is a

sign of an invisible sacrifice. The death of Christ on
the Cross was the visible sign of the internal act of
will by which Christ offered Himself to His Father for
the sins of men. Christ was thus both the priest offering the victim of sacrifice to God and the victim. His
sacrifice on the Cross accomplished the three goals of
sacrifice: the remission of sin, peace between God
and men, and holocaust. By His death, Christ redeemed men from sin and won for them the grace
which establishes peace between God and men.
Through His death, Christ offered Himself wholly to
God for men, and so was made a holocaust, that is, a
victim wholly burnt or offered to God. Because it is
God Himself, the Son of God, Who offers this sacrifice,
the sacrifice is of infinite value and it purchases an
eternal reward for men, the vision of God in eternity.
For this reason, the priesthood of Christ is eternal.
It is important to note that Christ is the natural Son of
God. Other men may become the adopted sons of
God through grace; but since Christ is the Second
Person of the Trinity, He is the natural Son of God
and not the adopted son of God.

THE INCARNATION is a work of God in the world.
It was, therefore, a part of the plan of divine providence from the beginning. From all eternity, God the
Father intended that His Son should become incarnate in Jesus Christ. We can say, then, that Christ as
man was predestined to be the Son of God.

FROM THE POINT OF VIEW of the relation of Christ
to men, it is important to remember both that He
is man and that He is God. Because He is man, all
men can be inspired by His example, attracted by His
humanity, and ennobled by a familiarity with Him in
prayer and grace. But since He is God, all men owe

Him adoration. Adoration, as we have seen, is paying tribute to someone's excellence. When it is homage to God's perfection as the Supreme Being, the Creator of the world, then the adoration is latria. When it is any lesser tribute to some lesser excellence, then it is veneration or dulia. Since Christ is God, we must pay Him the adoration of latria. We must acknowledge Him as the Supreme Being and the Creator of the world. Since there is only one Person in Christ, we must even give this adoration to Christ in His human nature, or in the images of Him which men make for use in religious actions. Naturally, we do not give the worship of latria to the human nature of Christ, or to images of Christ insofar as they are creatures. We give this worship to Christ in or through His human nature, or the images which represent Him to us. We might put it in another way by saying that we give an absolute adoration to the Person of Christ, but a relative adoration to His human nature and to images of Him.

WHEN MEN ADORE CHRIST, they truly adore God. Christ is Emmanuel, that is, God-with-us. In Christ we can, so to speak, see the face of God. It is His human face, it is true. But even this vision is a foretaste of the beatific vision of God which is the inheritance of all those who are members of Christ's Body, the Church. It is their inheritance because Christ is the perfect Mediator between God and men. He stands between God and men—He mediates between them—because He brings God's gifts to men and He takes men to God. As man, He is the perfect Mediator because He occupies a position midway between God and men. As man He is not God, and so He stands below God. But as a man possessing the fullness of grace, knowledge and power, He stands above men. He is thus in a perfect position to mediate between God and men. And this is what Christ is doing ceaselessly for men in and through His Body, the Church.

THE INCARNATION is God's answer to the misery of men without God. God stoops to man to raise him to Himself. "And I, if I be lifted up, will draw all things to Myself". Man has only to accept freely Christ as his Mediator. Not even Christ saves a man against his will. Because man is proud, God has stooped down to him. Since man is disobedient, God has given him the example of the perfect obedience of Christ. As man is ignorant and in error, God has given him Christ, the perfect Teacher. Could the love of God do more for man? "By this hath the charity of God appeared towards us, because God hath sent his only begotten Son into the world, that we may live by him".

CHAPTER II

Mary: The Virgin Mother of God

CHAPTER II

Mary: The Virgin Mother of God

THE WISDOM OF GOD reaches from end to end mightily and it arranges all things sweetly. Everything has its place in the pattern of divine providence. God fits everything and everyone to its place in His plan for the world. When God the Father resolved to send His only-begotten Son into this world to be born of a woman, He chose and fashioned a woman to be the worthy mother of so great a Son. When we meet a very good child, we are quite likely to say, "He must have a very good mother". We explain the child's goodness by the goodness of his mother. We believe that it is the mother's goodness which has made the child good. But in the mystery of the Incarnation, it is the contrary which is true. Mary of Nazareth is the perfect Mother of God because her Son, Who is God, has made her so. Because the Son of God is all holy and all perfect, Mary, His Mother in the flesh, must be as holy and perfect as she can be. God did not cast His eye over all the women in the world, seeking to discover which one was best fitted to be the mother of His Son. Mary was not chosen by God because He found her to be the most perfect of women. Rather, He made her the perfect woman because He had chosen her to be the Mother of His Son.

AS GOD, Christ is the essense of holiness. Even as man Christ is absolutely sinless. His human nature was never stained either with original sin or with actual sin. Nor did He experience that disordered concupiscence which is the result in man of original sin. Surely, then, it was fitting that the Mother of a Son so holy should also be sinless. Because she was to be the Mother of His Son, God preserved Mary from both original and actual sin.

THE BLESSED VIRGIN MARY was a human being descended from Adam by way of carnal generation. She had a human father and a human mother. If she had not, therefore, been chosen to be the Mother of God, she would, like every other descendant of Adam, have contracted original sin at the moment of her conception in the womb of her mother. But because she was to be the Mother of His Son, God preserved her soul from the stain of original sin from the very instant of her conception in the womb of her mother. God did this by infusing divine grace into the soul of Mary at the very instant He created her soul and united it to her body. He did it in virtue of the merits of Christ. No descendant of Adam receives the grace of God except through the merits of Christ. The Mother of Christ was no exception to this law of grace. Like every other human being who is descended by carnal generation from Adam, the Blessed Virgin Mary needed to be redeemed by the Blood of Christ. But whereas every other human being needs to be cleansed from the stain of original sin—which he has contracted by way of carnal generation from Adam—the Virgin Mary did not need to be cleansed from original sin. She never contracted this stain of sin. Through the grace of Christ, she was preserved from the stain of sin from the first moment of her conception in the womb of her mother. This is the doctrine of the Immaculate Conception of the Mother of God. Because of the widespread misunderstanding of the meaning of this doctrine, it might be well to mention here that the doctrine of the Immaculate Conception of the Virgin Mary is a different doctrine from the doctrine of the Virgin Birth of Christ. The doctrine of the Immaculate Conception means that Mary was preserved from the stain of original sin from the first moment of her conception in the womb of her mother. The doctrine of the Virgin Birth of Christ means that Christ was conceived in the womb of Mary by the Holy Spirit without the agency of any human father.

OBVIOUSLY, since God preserved Mary from the stain of original sin because she was to be the Mother of His Son, it follows that He will also have preserved Mary from the stain of any actual sin. As the goodness of the parents brings honor to their children, so, too, does the sinfulness of the parents bring shame to their children. But it is not fitting that the Mother of God should bring shame to her divine Son. Therefore, God preserved Mary from any personal sin, whether mortal or venial. Through the grace of God, which was infused into her soul at the moment of her conception, Mary was absolutely sinless. She was never stained with original sin, nor did she ever commit any personal sin, not even the least venial sin.

THE SINLESSNESS OF MARY is due chiefly to the fullness of grace which God gave her. Christ is the source of grace to all men. But Mary is closer to Christ than any other human being, because He took His flesh from her and dwelt in her womb, and lived intimately with her for approximately thirty years. The closer one is to Christ, the source of all grace, the greater the degree of grace one receives from Christ. Mary, therefore, received from Christ a fullness of grace not granted to any other creature. Her Immaculate Conception made her worthy to be the Mother of God. When the Son of God became incarnate in her womb, and while He dwelt with her until the time of His public ministry to men, the constant presence of the source of all grace confirmed Mary in the state of grace. Finally, after her death and Assumption into heaven, Mary enjoys in heaven the fullness of grace and glory.

ONE OF THE MOST ASTOUNDING PRIVILEGES of Mary is the fact that she is not only the Mother of God, but the Virgin Mother of God. Mary conceived Christ as a virgin. She gave birth to Christ while remaining a virgin. And she remained a virgin throughout her life. We are confronted here with two miracles of nature, and, if we use the term miracle in the wide sense, with one miracle of grace. In the first place, Mary conceived a Child in her womb without the agency of any human father. Normally, a woman conceives a child by having carnal relations with a man. Normally, in so doing, the woman loses her virginity. Normally, conception does not take place without the male seed of the human race. But in the conception of Christ, there was no human father and no male seed. Instead, God Himself, the Holy Spirit, miraculously conceived Christ in the womb of Mary. Hence she remained a virgin in the conception of Christ. Again, even if we imagine that a woman has retained her physical virginity in conceiving a child, normally she will lose this physical virginity in giving birth to the child. But Mary gave birth to Christ miraculously, that is, Christ came forth from the womb of Mary without destroying her virginity. Lastly, though Joseph and Mary were really married, through the superabundant grace of God, they kept a vow of virginity throughout their married lives. They never had conjugal relations with one another. In this way Mary remained always a virgin. The perpetual virginity of Mary is both a testimonial to God's power and holiness, and to the loving obedience of Mary to the will of God.

THE PERPETUAL VIRGINITY OF MARY is not so surprising when we reflect that Mary is the Mother of God. Christ is the true and natural Son of God. It is not fitting that He should have any other natural father. It was not fitting that God should share His parenthood with a man. Christ is also the Word of God. As the Word of God, He proceeds from His Father without corruption. It was fitting that He should proceed from His Mother without corrupting her virginity. He came to take away the sins of men. But if He had been conceived of Mary by a human father, He Himself would have been subject to original sin. It was not fitting that He should be subject to the sin which He came to destroy. He came so that men might be reborn spiritually of the Holy Spirit. It was, therefore, fitting that He Himself should be conceived by the Holy Spirit. He came to restore the integrity of human nature. It was not fitting that He should destroy the physical integrity of His Mother. Lastly, it is He Who has commanded us to honor our fathers and mothers. It was fitting that He should not lessen the honor due to His Mother by destroying her virginity in His birth.

IN ORDER that her virginity might be perfect, Mary consecrated it to God by a vow. Since the Old Law made the generation of children a matter of obligation for God's Chosen People, Mary did not make an absolute vow of virginity until, through the Angel Gabriel, she knew she was to be the Mother of Christ. Then she took this vow in conjunction with St. Joseph, her husband.

IN SPITE of her perpetual virginity, Mary was really married to St. Joseph. In justice to her Son, to herself, and to society, it was necessary that she be married. If she had not been married, men would have said that her Son was an illegitimate child, the fruit of some sinful union. Christ needed the name, the protection and the care of a human father. If Mary had not been married, the Jews might have considered her an adulteress, and so might have stoned her to death or ruined her reputation. Again, because Joseph was the husband of Mary, he is a witness to the miraculous conception and birth of Christ. He confirms Mary's story about the conception and birth of her divine Child.

THE MARRIAGE of Mary and Joseph was a real marriage. They were united to one another by the bond of mutual love, a love of the spirit. They gave to each other those conjugal rights which are of the essence of marriage, although, by their vow of virginity, they agreed never to use those rights. And their marriage was blessed with a Child to Whom they gave parental love, care and upbringing.

MARY BECAME THE MOTHER OF GOD at the moment of the Incarnation. It was a moment for which God had richly prepared her. Through the fullness of grace which He gave her, Mary had lived a life of obedience to the will of God. Her every thought and action had been formed in the burning crucible of charity or the love of God. She had even conceived the resolution to devote herself to the service of God by a vow of virginity. At the moment chosen by God, the Archangel Gabriel appeared to her in bodily form and announced to her the great purpose for which God had chosen her. "Hail, full of grace," he said, and his words signified her worthiness to fulfill the role for which she was destined. "The Lord is with thee," he continued, and in these words he announced the conception that was to take place. When Mary gave the full consent of her loving, obedient heart in the words, "Be it done unto me according to thy word," the marriage between God and human nature was complete. God had become man, and in the consent of Mary all mankind consented to its own ennoblement in the God-man, Christ. Eve had seduced Adam to the destruction of the human race. Mary conceived Christ for the salvation of the human race.

THE SON OF GOD, JESUS CHRIST, was conceived of the flesh of Mary, the Virgin of Nazareth. He was, therefore, a man like other men. He was of the race of Adam. He was also, as had been foretold by the prophets, of the family of David, a member of the royal house of Israel. But the active principle of His conception in the womb of Mary was the Holy Spirit, God Himself. Of course, it is true that it was God, all three Persons of the Trinity, Who conceived Christ in the womb of Mary. But God Himself attributes this action to the Third Person, the Holy Spirit, because it is a work of divine love, and in God the Holy Spirit is the love of the Father and the Son. This does not mean that the Holy Spirit is the father of Christ. To be a father, a person must beget a child who is similar to himself in nature. God the Father begets in God a Son Who is like to Him in the divine nature, Who is, in fact, identical with Him in the divine nature. A human father begets a child who is like to himself in human nature. But the Holy Spirit, when He conceives Christ in the womb of Mary, does not beget a child similar to Himself in the divine nature. As God, the Son of God is already divine, begotten only of God the Father. The action of the Holy Spirit forms in Mary the human nature of the Son of God. Hence, the Holy Spirit is not the father of the Son of God in Mary.

THE CHILD CONCEIVED IN MARY is the most perfect Child the world has ever known. Because the active principle in the generation of Christ was God Himself, the body of Christ was perfectly formed from the first instant of its existence. It had a rational soul. The Son of God assumed this body at the very moment of the infusion of the rational soul. In this way, Mary is the Mother of God from the first instant of the conception of Christ in her womb. In fact, if it were otherwise, Mary would not be the Mother of God, but the Mother of a human being who was later assumed by the Son of God.

IN ADDITION, Christ was, as we have already seen, spiritually perfect. He possessed, from the first moment of His existence, the absolute fullness of God's grace. His soul was united to God in the glory of the beatific vision of God. He possessed infused knowledge, and hence was capable of free acts of His will. Hence, too, He was capable of meriting grace and redemption for men from the very beginning of His existence as man.

MARY IS TRULY the Mother of God. When we consider the absolutely infinite perfection of

God, the obvious humanity of Mary and the no less obvious humanity of her Son, Christ, this might seem a startling statement. But it is none the less true. When any mother gives birth to a child, she gives birth not only to a human nature but also to the person who exists in that human nature. We do not say that Mrs. Smith is the mother of a human nature. We say that she is the mother of John Smith, or of Richard Smith, or of Helen Smith. In other words, we say that she is the mother of the persons to whom she gave human nature. So, also, in the Incarnation we do not say simply that Mary is the Mother of the human nature of Christ. We say, and rightly, that she is the Mother of the Person Who exists in that human nature, of the Person to Whom she gave that human nature. Since that Person is God, the Son of God, we say rightly that Mary is the Mother of God. This Divine Maternity is the greatest of Mary's privileges and the source of all her other divinely given privileges.

A S IS THE CASE with every mother, her life is closely interwoven with the life of her Divine Son. She bore Him in her womb. She gave birth to Him at Bethlehem, in fulfilment of the ancient prophecy. She fled with Him to Egypt to escape the murderous wrath of Herod. She lived with Him for years in the obscurity of Nazareth. She asked Him to perform His first miracle in His public ministry. She was with Him on Calvary. On Calvary, in obedience to the will of God, she renounced her maternal rights to the life of her Son, her rights to His continued filial love and care in this world. She offered her own maternal agony to God for the salvation of men. In union with Christ, she offered the life of her Son for the redemption of man. In this way, she merited the right to dispense all God's graces to men to the end of time. After her own death, her Divine Son, because of His filial love for her, raised her body from death and she was assumed body and soul into heaven. In heaven she reigns as the Queen of angels and men.

WHEN WE CONSIDER the unique position given by God to Mary, when we reflect on the great privileges God has granted Mary, then we are not surprised at the great devotion of Catholics to Mary. If God has so honored Mary, can we do less? Since all her privileges, all her great dignity are due to the perfection and dignity of her Son, then the honor which we give to Mary does not detract from the honor we give Christ. Rather, it is a fitting tribute to the Son Who could fashion for Himself so great a Mother.

CHAPTER III

Christ:
The Savior

CHAPTER III

Christ: The Savior

THE SON OF GOD came into this world to save men from sin and the consequences of sin. The whole life of Christ, therefore, is dominated by this purpose. From the very beginning of His human life, from the moment of His conception in the womb of His Mother, Christ is the Savior of mankind. Moreover, since He was capable of rational acts and therefore of free acts from the first moment of His existence in the womb of Mary, He began even at that very moment to give to God that perfect obedience which is the soul of the sacrifice of Himself whereby He has redeemed mankind. As Adam had destroyed all human nature by his disobedience, so Christ restored human nature by His obedience to God. And that perfect obedience began at the very first instant of His existence in His human nature. It is true that the principal redeeming act of Christ is the shedding of His precious blood on the Cross of Calvary. But, it is also true that from the beginning of His human life, Christ directed all the acts of His will to their final consummation on Calvary. From the very beginning, the will of Christ was perfectly conformed to the will of God.

IT IS FOR THIS REASON that Christ was content to be born of a poor woman of Nazareth, in the poverty of a stable at Bethlehem. It is for this reason that Christ was content that His Divinity and Majesty as the Son of God should be manifested only gradually to mankind. Had He made His divinity known to all men at once and unmistakably, then there would have been no room for faith in Himself; and, in the plan of God, men must be saved by faith. Hence, in the beginning, the divinity of Christ was manifested only to His Mother and to St. Joseph, to the shepherds and to the Magi from the East. In this way, too, God safeguarded men's belief in the reality of the human nature of Christ. For had Christ manifested Himself as God at once—by some stupendous manifestation of His divine power—men would have doubted that He was really a human being, and so would have missed the awe-inspiring message of the Incarnation, the magnificent love of God for man. On the contrary, God saw to it that men of good will should be able to perceive both the divinity and the humanity of Christ. The humble circumstances of His birth, the obscurity of His life at Nazareth, His familiar intercourse with men during His public ministry—all these would convince men of the reality of His human nature. On the other hand, the Star from the East which announced His birth to the Magi, the prophecy of Simeon, the angels who appeared to the shepherds—all these were divine signs of the divinity of Christ. When the time was right, the miracles and prophecies of Christ Himself would convince men of His divinity.

IN OBEDIENCE to the will of God, Christ submitted Himself to the Old Law which God had given to the Jews. Though He Himself was the founder of the New Law of grace, nevertheless He took upon Himself the burden of the Old Law. He submitted to the rite of circumcision, which was a profession of obedience to the Old Law. By shedding His blood in this way, He proved the reality of His human nature and at the same time He dedicated Himself to God for the salvation of men. In so doing, He also showed His approval of circumcision, which God had instituted for the Jews as a sign of their faith in the Savior Who was to come. The circumcision of Christ is also a manifestation of the wisdom of God, for if He were not circumcised, then the Jews, to whom He first preached the Gospel of salvation, would not have received Him at all.

AT THE TIME of His circumcision, Christ was given the name Jesus. This was the name that God Himself had chosen for Him. It was foretold to Mary and Joseph by angels. In Hebrew the name means "Savior". In this way, God announced the role which Christ was to play in the history of the world.

JESUS AS CHRIST gave men an example of humility and obedience by submitting Himself to circumcision; so too, Mary, His Mother, gave men the same example by going to the Temple to be purified after the birth of Christ. Like her Son she needed no purification. But like her Son she obeyed the will of God and showed her approval of the Old Law of God.

SO TOO, forty days after His birth, Christ was offered to God in the Temple in accordance with the Jewish rite. He Himself was consecrated to God as the first-born of Mary. And, even though He was sinless, the usual offering for the expiation of sin was made for Him. In this way, He taught men that they must offer themselves to God.

THE ENTRANCE of any great man into a position of power and authority is always marked by some important ceremony. This is true of the life of Christ. Before He began His public ministry for the salvation of men, He was baptized by John the Baptist. John the Baptist, a cousin of Christ, was the herald chosen by God to prepare men for the coming of Christ as their Savior. He had been sanctified by Christ Himself while he was still in the womb of his mother,

Elizabeth. He had led a life of extreme asceticism and prayer. Then, inspired by the Holy Spirit, he began to preach to men repentance for sin as a preparation for the coming of the Savior. Under the inspiration of the Holy Spirit he also baptized men with water. The baptism of John did not give men the grace of the Holy Spirit as the baptism of Christ does. But it prepared the way for the sacrament of baptism which Christ was to institute. John's preaching prepared men for faith in Christ. It accustomed men to the rite of baptism which Christ would institute. And the penance which John preached prepared men to receive the effect of Christ's baptism. Because John's baptism did not give men the grace of God, those baptized by John needed also the baptism of Christ for salvation.

THE BAPTISM OF CHRIST by John marked the beginning of the public ministry of Christ. Although Christ was sinless and needed no purification at all, He received the baptism of John. In the first place, since John's baptism did not really forgive sin or give grace, it was not unfitting for Christ, Who possessed the fullness of grace, to receive this baptism. In this way Christ showed His approval of John's baptism, and, therefore, of the efforts of John to lead men to Himself. By receiving baptism from John, Christ also sanctified baptism.

THE BAPTISM OF CHRIST by John sanctified baptism. This is made clear to us by the fact that when Christ was baptized in the Jordan, the heavens were opened, and the Holy Spirit descended in the form of a dove and rested over the head of Christ, and the voice of God was heard saying, "This is my beloved Son in whom I am well pleased" (*Matt. III*, 17). Through the sin of Adam the gates of heaven were closed to all men. But at the baptism of Christ the heavens were opened. This signified that through the sacrament of baptism which Christ would institute, the gates of heaven are reopened to man. In addition, the appearance of the Holy Spirit in the form of a dove and the voice of God the Father show us that the whole Trinity was present at the baptism of Christ. Since baptism sanctifies men in the name of the Father and of the Son and of the Holy Spirit, it was fitting that the Trinity should be manifested at the baptism of Christ.

ACCORDING TO ST. THOMAS, Christ was baptized in His thirtieth year. This St. Thomas regards as the perfect time for His baptism. At the age of thirty a man should be in the prime of his manhood. He should be fit for his life's work. Now Christ was about to begin to teach men the truths of God's revelation which they must believe to be saved. His baptism, then, at this age signaled the beginning of the important work of His life. Besides, by beginning His public ministry Christ was beginning the New Law of grace. It was fitting that He should have shown men that He was capable of keeping the Old Law. But by deferring the beginning of His public ministry to this age, He had given men the example of thirty years of conformity to the Old Law. No one could say that He abrogated the Old Law because He could not keep it Himself. We can also see a divine symbolism in the baptism of Christ at the age of His maturity. As Christ was baptized at the perfect age of manhood, so Christian baptism brings forth perfect men, men perfected by God's grace.

CHRIST CAME INTO THE WORLD to save men by His teaching, His example, His Passion and death on the Cross. The purpose of His life dictated the manner in which He lived. Because He had had to teach ignorant, sinful men the truths of God, He did not shun men. He did not lead a solitary life, disdaining the company of men because He was too perfect for them. Rather He went out into the world of men, seeking them in the towns and the villages, in the fields and on the roads, in the mountains and on the sea. How could He teach them, if He did not walk with them and talk with them? How could He lead them by His example, if He led a hidden life far from their eyes? Because He came to save sinners, He sought them out, like the good shepherd seeking his lost sheep. He became man so that men might find it easier to come to God. Hence, in His human nature, He made Himself accessible to all men, rich and poor, good and evil.

NOR DID HE REPEL MEN by an extreme austerity. It is true that Christ at times practiced abstinence in eating and drinking. He did this in order to give men good example. Because He was the perfect man, He had no need to discipline His appetites by fasting or abstinence. But He did so to show men that they can profit by mastering the tendencies of their sense appetite. On the other hand, for the most part, Christ ate and drank in the normal manner of men. Because He was always in perfect control of Himself, there was never anything excessive in His eating and drinking. But by acting as other men He made it possible for men to approach Him easily.

ONLY IN THE PRACTICE of poverty does Christ give the appearance of being different from most men. Most men either hate poverty and seek riches, or, if they are rich, they cling to their wealth. But

Christ was voluntarily poor. He knew that the cares of wealth prevent men from being good preachers of the word of God. So He Himself gave an example to all the Apostles He would send to men in the course of time. He renounced worldly wealth, so that He might preach God's word unhindered by cares. He deliberately kept Himself poor in the things of this world, so that He might enrich men in the things of God. He knew, too, that men are only too inclined to think that God's ministers preach God's word for their own advantage. Hence, He gave up the wealth of the world so that His message to men might be recommended to them by His own unselfishness. Lastly, He lived a life of poverty in order to show men more clearly the power of His divinity. He would save mankind without any of the things which men hold necessary for success.

H E ALSO ENDEARED HIMSELF to men by allowing Himself to be tempted by the devil. The great spiritual perfection of Christ might have led men to despair of their own salvation. Men, weary of the struggle against temptations, might too easily say, "It was easy for Christ to be good; He had no temptations". But Christ was tempted by the devil. When He was hungry, after forty days of fasting, the devil tempted Him with bread. When that temptation failed, the devil tempted Him first to vainglory and then to worldly power and wealth. Christ was thus tempted to sins of both the flesh and the spirit of man. As man He conquered these temptations and vanquished the devil. In so doing He has given all men an example. The temptations of the devil can be overcome with the grace of God and strength of will. He has even shown good people that their goodness does not mean that they are not still subject to temptation. If the goodness of Christ could be subjected to temptation, then temptation is the common lot of all men. But all men can take refuge in the mercy of Christ. He Who was tempted can understand the needs of other men. Christ, Who has overcome temptation, will mercifully aid those who are still subject to temptation.

AFTER HIS TEMPTATION by the devil, Christ began His ministry of teaching. He preached to God's Chosen People the Gospel of salvation. He preached it to the Jews because the promise of salvation had been made by God to the Jews. The message of God was to be preached first to the Jews and then, through them, to all men. The Jews, by believing in and worshipping one God, were nearer to God than the pagan nations of the world. It was fitting that God should reward their faithfulness by preaching the message of salvation first to them. Even from the natural point of view, it was proper that Christ should preach the Gospel first to His own people. Moreover, it was through His Passion and death that Christ merited power and lordship over all men. It was natural, therefore, that He should not wish His doctrine to be preached to the pagan world until after His Passion and death. It is even a sign of His great power that His Apostles should have converted the pagan world of Rome, while Christ Himself restricted His preaching to His own people.

CHRIST WAS ABSOLUTELY TRUTHFUL. It was natural, then, that He should preach His doctrine openly. He preached in the streets of the cities, in the porches of the Temple, in the plains of the countryside. He did not conceal His doctrine. It is true that He preached some of His mysteries in the form of

parables. The meaning was there for those with good
will to perceive His meaning. But, in His mercy, the
parables sometimes concealed His true meaning from
those who were not ready to receive His doctrine. On
the other hand, He never concealed or "toned down"
His teaching because of the malice or the sensibilities
of His enemies. He did not hesitate to reproach the
Scribes and Pharisees for their hypocrisy. He would
not retract His promise of the Eucharist because the
Jews refused to accept the idea that He would give
them His flesh to eat and His blood to drink. On that
occasion He even offered His chosen Apostles the
choice of believing Him or abandoning Him. He
taught openly and as one having authority.

BECAUSE HE TAUGHT as one having authority, He
never committed His doctrine to writing. The
actual work of writing would seem an imperfection in
one Who was God. It would seem that God had no
other means of transmitting His doctrine to men. To
teach is to impress a doctrine firmly in the minds and
hearts of men. Certainly Christ, the God-man, is the
perfect teacher. He could transmit His message to
men by word and example more perfectly than any
written work. Moreover, He could send other men to
bring His message to all men. He could so train and
inspire and guide them that they would preach His
message perfectly, whether by word or by writing. In
addition, it is natural for men to be taught by other
men. Hence, it was fitting that Christ should train
His Apostles to speak for Him to other men.

HIS DOCTRINE WAS A REVELATION from God to
man. He revealed to men the deep secrets of
God, the mysterious inner life of the Trinity, and the
secret of God's relations with man, the Incarnation

and all that it implies. Because it was a message from God and because its truth was beyond the grasp of the human mind, it was necessary for Christ to give guarantees of the truth of His message. This He did by the miracles He performed. A miracle is a work or an effect that can be produced only by the power of God. It is a finger of God pointing to truth—either the truth that Christ was the Son of God, or the truth of the divine message He was teaching to men. Christ worked miracles to prove that His doctrine was really a divine message. Since only God can work miracles, it follows that the claim of Christ was true. His message was a divine message or God, Who worked miracles through Him, is a liar. But God cannot lie. Therefore, the message of Christ is a divine revelation to men.

THE MIRACLES OF CHRIST proved that He Himself was God. His miracles showed that He had power over all of creation. When He expelled demons from those possessed by devils, He showed His power over the angels. When He caused the Star of Bethlehem to point out the place of His birth, when He caused the sun to be darkened for three hours at the time of His Passion and death, He showed His power over nature. When He changed water into wine at Cana, He showed His power over the inanimate things of the world. When He cured the paralytic, or the man born blind, when He raised Lazarus from the grave, He showed His power over men. He performed so many miracles, so many miracles of different kinds, and at the decision of His own will, that He manifested a divine command of the whole created world. Since He Himself claimed to be God, and since He worked so many kinds of miracles at will, we can only agree that He was God.

ONE OF THE MOST SIGNIFICANT of His miracles was His transfiguration on Mount Thabor. Christ had said to His disciples, "If any man will come after me, let him deny himself and take up his cross and follow me. For he that will save his life shall lose it: and he that shall lose his life for my sake shall find it" (*Matt.* XVI, 24-25). He was trying to teach His disciples that by imitating His own immolation on the Cross they would find happiness, the happiness of the vision of God. To convince them of this truth, and to give them some inkling of its meaning, He took Peter, James and John to Mount Thabor. There, in their sight, He was transfigured. "His face did shine as the sun: and his garments became white as snow. And behold there appeared to them Moses and Elias talking with them ... And ... behold a bright cloud overshadowed them. And lo, a voice out of the cloud, saying: This is my beloved Son in whom I am well pleased. Hear ye him" (*Matt.* XVII, 2-5). The brilliance which shone from the body of Christ on this occasion was the light of glory transmitted from His divinity to His human soul and from His soul to His body. Because He possessed the vision of God, Christ had the right to this light of glory from the beginning of His existence in His human nature. But, for the sake of men, this light of glory was deferred until after His Passion and death. On this occasion Christ worked a miracle. He allowed the light of glory to shine in His body. He did this, first to confirm His Apostles in their belief in His words. He did it, secondly to give them a glimpse of the meaning of His words. If a man denies his baser tendencies, if He believes in Christ and keeps the commandments of God out of love for God, he will gain eternal life. After death He will see God face to face, and his soul will be resplendent with the light of divine glory. At the last resurrection, when his body is reunited to his soul, the light of glory in his soul will give even his body a reflection of the light of glory. When Christ allowed Peter, James and John to see Him transfigured on Thabor, He was giving them a preview of the glory that would come to all men of good will through His Passion and death. The transfiguration of Christ is both a testimonial to the truth of Christ's message and a glimpse of the world to come for all those who love Christ.

BUT THE GLORY OF CHRIST in His body, and the glory that is to come to all men at the end of the world are purchased with a great price. Before the body of Christ could be confirmed in the glory of His sanctified soul, before men could have any chance to emulate His glory, Christ had to win redemption for mankind by His Passion and His death upon the Cross of Calvary.

CHRIST DID NOT SUFFER and then die upon the Cross because God was under any compulsion to demand so great a recompense for the sins of men. God could have simply condoned men's sins and granted them pardon when they repented of their sins. Nor was Christ Himself under any compulsion to suffer and die for the sins of men. He offered Himself freely and voluntarily as a sacrifice for men. But Christ suffered for men because this was the will of God. God willed that His only-begotten Son should become man to suffer and die for the salvation of men. This divine decision manifests both the justice and the mercy of

God. It manifests His justice, because it shows that God has actually demanded satisfaction for the sins of men against Him. It manifests His mercy, because no one but a God-man could have offered a suitable satisfaction for the sins of men. Because He was God, Christ could offer God an infinite satisfaction for the infinite malice of sin. Because He was man, Christ could offer a man's satisfaction for man's sin.

THE WISDOM OF GOD'S PLAN in the Passion and death of Christ is shown, too, by the other purposes which God accomplished in this way. Christ suffered and died to win God's pardon for the sins of men. But His suffering did more than this. In the first place, since He was both God and man, His suffering was a staggering proof of God's love for men. Could God do more for men than suffer and die for them? Secondly, in His Passion and death Christ gave to men an example of the perfect virtue which will lead men to heaven: obedience to God's will, humility, constancy in following God's will, fortitude in the face of death, a love of justice even unto death, and so on. Thirdly, by His suffering Christ merited grace and glory for men, and so made it possible for men to attain their real happiness. Fourthly, by suffering and dying for all men, Christ gave to men a strong additional motive for avoiding sin. If a father sold all his possessions in order to pay the foolish debts of his son, would not the son have a strong reason for behaving prudently in the future? If the Son of God suffered and died because of the sins of men, to pay the debt of men's sins, should not all men have a good reason for avoiding sin in the future? Lastly, the Passion and death of Christ are a divine tribute to the dignity of man. Man had destroyed himself by falling victim to the devil in the garden of paradise. Through Christ, a man conquers the devil and restores mankind to the friendship of God. Men can point to Christ with honest pride and say that their Brother Man has saved them.

IN HIS PASSION AND DEATH Christ endured extreme suffering. He suffered at the hands of both men and women. A man betrayed Him; a woman betrayed His Apostle Peter; the Sanhedrin condemned Him; His own people cried out for His blood; Herod and Pilate washed their hands of Him; Pilate delivered Him over to scourging and the crucifixion on the cross; the soldiers and servants mocked Him and spat upon Him and beat Him; He was abandoned by His Apostles and friends; His reputation was destroyed by the ignominy of His trial and death as a criminal; His soul was sad and weary at the prospect and the reality of suffering and death; His sensitive nature flinched from suffering and death; His hands and feet were pierced by nails; His brow was crowned with thorns; His whole body was torn with the lashes of the scourging. And because He had a perfect human nature He felt this suffering all the more keenly.

IT IS TRUE that the higher part of His soul continued to enjoy the vision of God. But the lower part of His soul, His power to feel sensitive joy or pain, was inundated with the anguish of His torments. Christ allowed His human nature to experience the length and the breadth and the depth of human suffering. Because He suffered to atone for the sins of all men, He allowed Himself to endure the fullness of human pain. In Him the words of the prophet Isaias were fulfilled: "There is no beauty in him, nor comeliness: and we have seen him, and there was no sightliness, that we should be desirous of him: despised and the most abject of men, a man of sorrows and acquainted with infirmity: and his look was as it were hidden and despised. Whereupon we esteemed him not. Surely he hath borne our infirmities and carried our sorrows: and we have thought him as it were a leper, and as one struck by God and afflicted. But He was wounded for our iniquities: he was bruised for our sins. The chastisement of our peace was upon him: and by his bruises we are healed" (*Isaias* LIII, 2-5).

T HE SUBLIMITY OF CHRIST'S LOVE for men is shown by the fact that He did not have to suffer and die. Because He was God, He could have prevented His enemies from doing Him any injury. Because His soul had perfect control of His body, He could have prevented the wounds from achieving their normal effect. But, in obedience to the will of His Father, He submitted Himself to the violent hands of His enemies. God and Christ Himself, out of love for men, delivered Christ to the hands of His torturers and executioners. But it was these latter who scourged Christ, crowned Him with thorns, nailed Him to the Cross and so killed Him. His own people handed Him over to the Romans to be put to death, and the Romans crucified Him. In this way Christ suffered both from the Jews and from the pagans of the world. Since He came to save not only the Jews but also the rest of men, it was natural that He should suffer at the hands of both.

T HE GUILT OF THOSE who brought about the death of Christ varies with their knowledge of what they were doing. Least guilty of all were the pagan soldiers who tortured and crucified Christ. They had no knowledge of the fact that Christ was the Savior of mankind, nor of the fact that Christ was God, the Son of God. More guilty than they was Pilate, who, though he also was ignorant of the true identity of Christ, nevertheless, out of cowardice, condemned an innocent man to death. Next in the mounting scale of guilt comes the multitude of simple people at Jerusalem who were misled by their leaders. They had seen the wonderful works of Christ and so might have believed in Him. But their leaders deceived them and made them doubt Christ. Most guilty of all were the arch conspirators among the leaders of the people. They knew that Christ had fulfilled in His Person and life the signs foretold by the prophets. But they were unwilling to accept Christ as their Savior. They deliberately blinded their eyes to the evident signs of His divinity. God was ready to give them faith in Christ, but, in the hardness of their hearts, they refused to accept it. Because their ignorance of His true identity was deliberate, it does not excuse their sin. They committed the most grievous of sins. They delivered their Savior and their God to death at the hands of pagans.

CHRIST SUFFERED AND DIED on the Cross of Calvary. As He hung there, suspended between earth and sky, with His life's blood draining away in agony, His enemies mocked Him. "If thou be the son of God," they said, "come down from the cross". As St. Paul has said, the crucified Christ is "unto the Jews indeed a stumbling-block, and unto the Gentiles foolishness" (I *Cor.* I, 23). Did God fail on the Cross? Was His life among men a magnificent but futile gesture? St. Paul gives us the answer: "But unto them that are called, both Jews and Greeks," the crucified Christ is "the power of God, and the wisdom of God. For the foolishness of God is wiser than men: and the weakness of God is stronger than men" (I *Cor.* I, 24-25). On the Cross Christ seems most helpless. But it is on the Cross that He is most powerful. For it is on the Cross that He accomplished His purpose, the salvation of men.

A<small>S CHRIST HUNG ON THE CROSS,</small> He willingly offered His human life and the sufferings and death of His body for the salvation of men. In the plan of God, Christ was the new Adam, the new Head of the human race. Because He offered His life willingly out of charity and obedience to His Father, His human will merited from God the salvation of mankind. Because He suffered and died out of love and obedience, Christ gave God more than was required to compensate for the sins of the whole human race. He satisfied or atoned for men's sins. He offered His life to God to honor God and to appease Him for the sins of men. His Passion, therefore, was a sacrifice most pleasing to God. The life which He so willingly laid down for men was the price paid to God for the sins of men and the punishment due to those sins. By paying the price of men's sins Christ redeemed men. Christ did all this—He merited salvation, He atoned for sin, He sacrificed Himself to God for sin, He redeemed men —in obedience to the will of God. His human nature was the instrument of His Godhead, the instrument which the Son of God used to save men. Because it was the instrument of His Godhead, Christ accomplished what He had come into this world to do.

B<small>ECAUSE CHRIST IS GOD</small> as well as man, His Passion delivered men from sin and from the power of the devil. It freed men from the penalty of sin, death and the loss of the vision of God. His Passion reconciled men to God and reopened the gates of heaven to all mankind. His Passion merited for Himself the exaltation of His own human nature. Because He was put to death unjustly, God raised Him from the dead. Because His body had suffered the humiliation of burial, He ascended into heaven. Because He had endured the mockery of men, He now sits at the right hand of the Father in heaven. Because He had been delivered over to the power of men, He has been made the judge of all men in the world to come. In the Passion of Christ the weakness of God is stronger than men. Through the human death of Christ the divine life is restored to men.

CHRIST REALLY DIED on the Cross. His human soul was separated from His body. But His Divine Personality remained united to both His body and His soul. For this reason the dead body of Christ was still infinitely precious. Because it was still united to the Person of the Son of God, any indignity inflicted upon it by the soldiers who lowered it from the Cross, any gesture of reverence paid to it by His Mother or the holy men and women who reverently buried it, was of infinite value for the salvation of men.

AS SOON AS HE DIED, the soul of Christ descended into hell. The hell of which we speak here is limbo, the place in which the souls of the just were awaiting deliverance. He hastened to limbo to announce to the just the reopening of the gates of heaven. Through His Passion, He had made it possible for them to find glory in the vision of God. He did not descend into the hell of the devils and the lost human souls. There was nothing He could do for them. By their own free decision, they had cut themselves off from God forever. Only those united to

Himself in faith and charity could obtain the benefits of His Passion.

O N THE THIRD DAY after His death Christ rose again. His soul was reunited with His body and He rose from the tomb glorious and immortal. He waited three days to convince everyone that He had really died. He rose from the grave to confirm our faith in His divinity. Because He has risen, we can also hope to rise again at the end of the world. Because He has risen from the grave, the new life of grace is given to our souls. Because He was God, He gave to His body and soul the power to unite with one another again. By the power of God Christ, Who had died on Calvary, rose again on the first Easter Sunday.

C HRIST ROSE again in His own human body. His body still bore the scars of His Passion. He could have removed these scars, if He had wished. But He chose to retain them. In this way He could prove to men that it was really Himself who had risen. Besides, He was to ascend into heaven to plead with His Father for the salvation of men. In heaven His scars would be a perpetual reminder to the Father of His suffering for men. In heaven, too, the marks of His wounds would be an everlasting trophy of His triumph over the world, the devil and sin. But though He still bore the marks of His wounds, His risen body was glorified. It was immortal. He could never die again. The glory of His soul, united to God in the beatific vision, flowed over into His body and made it shine with a divine light. His body was completely under the control of His soul.

A FTER HIS RESURRECTION He appeared to His Mother, His Apostles and to His disciples. He walked with them, talked with them, ate and drank with them. In this way He gave them convincing signs of the reality of His resurrection. Through their testimony the truth of His resurrection has been given to the world. Those who believe in Him and in His resurrection can hope to rise again also.

THE RESURRECTION OF CHRIST is the cause of the resurrection of all men. Only God has the power to make men rise again. But Christ is God. And God intends to make the resurrection of Christ the efficient cause of the resurrection of all men. At the end of time it will be the risen Christ who will make all men rise again. His risen human nature will be the instrument by which His divine power will reunite the souls of all men to their bodies.

THE RESURRECTION OF CHRIST is also the model or pattern according to which the souls of the just shall rise on the last day. Christ will make sinners rise, but to their condemnation. Because they have no faith in Him nor love for Him, they can have no part in His glory. But the just will rise in the likeness of Christ. His body is now glorious and immortal. The bodies of those who had faith in Him, who loved Him and kept His commandments, will be glorious and immortal, too. The resurrection of Christ is both the pledge of the future resurrection of men, and the model of the resurrection of the just who die in the grace of Christ.

FORTY DAYS after His resurrection Christ ascended into heaven. He went to heaven to receive the glory which was due to Him. There He pleads with His Father always for the souls of men. In heaven He sits at the right hand of God. As God He is equal to the Father and to the Holy Spirit. As man, as the perfect man, possessing the absolute fullness of God's grace, and as the glorious Head of the whole human race and of the angels, He sits at the right hand of His Father, that is, He has been given the power to judge all men and angels. At the General Judgment it will be Christ Who makes the final truth known—the true character and the true meaning of the actions of men and angels. At this judgment it is Christ Who will give the final decision. At His word the damned will go into hell forever to satisfy the justice of God, and the good will enter forever into the bliss of heaven to manifest the mercy of God.

THE HUMAN RACE TODAY needs a savior. Men are seeking salvation in ideas, in fascism, in nazism, in communism. Men are seeking salvation in science, in electronics, in atomic fission, in dreams of flights to the moon or Mars. Men look for the promise of strength in dictators or military geniuses or financial wizards. But there is no salvation for man except in Christ the Savior. It is Christ Who has re-established order in the world. Man introduced chaos into the world by disobedience to God. Christ has reintroduced the principle of obedience to God. By His obedience He has opened the floodgates of heaven to the world of men. Because He died on the Cross out of love and obedience, the living waters of God's grace are ready to quicken the parched souls of men. Because He was humble, even unto death, men can be raised up to the dignity of sons of God. Because He loved both God and man, it is possible for men to love God and one another.

BUT CHRIST SAVES no one against his will. He can give salvation only to those who believe in Him, hope in Him and love Him. He has merited grace for all men. But men must freely accept this grace and use it for their salvation. We are all saved in Christ, our Head and our Savior. But only on condition that we freely unite our minds and hearts with His. Christ is not a dictator. He does not bend men to His will with guns and secret police and concentration camps and slave labor. He is a loving Savior. He compels no one to march with Him or for Him. He hangs on a Cross between earth and sky, between men and God. He has nothing to recommend Him but humility and a great love. Yet His outstretched arms are big enough to hold the world. The road to happiness lies through His Cross. If any man will save his life, he must first lose it. He must deny himself and follow Christ.

CHAPTER IV

The Sacramental System

CHAPTER IV

The Sacramental System

BY HIS PASSION, Christ has merited for men the grace which leads to salvation in the vision of God. But this grace must be given to men if they are to be saved. It is Christ Who distributes God's grace to men. He does this through His Church, the Holy, Roman Catholic Church. The Church is, as it were, the continuation of Christ on earth. He has won all graces for men. He distributes all graces to men. But He Himself has ascended into heaven. Nevertheless, from heaven, He distributes grace to men through His Church. He does this through His Church, which is His Mystical Body. How does He do this? Because His love for men is infinite, He is prepared always to give grace from heaven to those who will sincerely repent of their sins and come to Him in faith and love. In fact, Christ, through the Holy Spirit, is always inviting men to repentance, to faith and to love. But Christ is too wise to think that men will seek the grace of God efficiently, if its distribution to men were something purely invisible and intangible. Men are not angels. Their minds and hearts cannot rise to the thought of spiritual things except through the medium of what is visible and tangible. Because man is man, that is, because he is a body as well as a soul, he needs some visible, some sensible means of knowing that the grace of God is accessible to him. In His wisdom and love, Christ has made it possible for men to receive His grace in a way that takes their humanity into account. He has done this through the institution of the sacraments. The sacraments are the ordinary channels through which the grace of God comes to

men. Christ has instituted them and entrusted them
to His Church. Through the sacraments men receive
the grace of God—both sanctifying grace, a share in
the life of God, and the actual graces needed to live
as a Christian.

WHAT IS A SACRAMENT? As the very word itself
suggests, it is something sacred or holy. As it
is used here, it means a sacred or a holy sign of something sacred or holy. We all know what a sign is. A
word is a sign of the idea we have in our minds. The
word "Exit" on a highway or parkway is a sign or indication that motorists may leave the highway at that
point but not enter it. A red light on a traffic signal is
an indication that traffic in that direction must stop. A
sign, then, is something that indicates something besides itself. When a man at a party raises his eyebrows, it may seem to some that he is just raising his
eyebrows. But to his wife, who knows him well, it may
be an indication that he thinks it is time to go home.
The raising of the eyebrows is a sign or indication of
something else. Now a sacrament is a sign. It indicates something besides itself. It indicates something
holy, something sacred. It indicates the grace of God.
The grace of God makes men holy. Hence St. Thomas
calls a sacrament the "sign of a holy thing so far as it
makes men holy". Other theologians have called a
sacrament a "sign that is efficacious of grace," that is,
a sign that effects grace in the souls of men. Now
grace sanctifies the souls of men; it makes them holy.
And in the sanctification of our souls there are always
three things to be considered: the Passion of Christ,
which is the cause of our sanctification; sanctification
or holiness itself, which is grace and the supernatural
virtues; and the goal of sanctification, which is eternal

life, the vision of God. Now every sacrament is a sign of these three things: a sign of the past, the Passion of Christ; a sign of the present, grace in our souls; and a forecast of the future, the eternal life, which is the consummation of grace.

A SACRAMENT IS A SIGN. Hence it must be something sensible, something men can see and hear or touch. If it were not sensible, it could not be a sign. An invisible red light will never stop traffic. A man's desire to go home will never reach his wife unless he gives her a sensible sign, a gesture, a shrug of the shoulders or a word. A sacrament, then, must be something sensible. It is a sensible thing or action which indicates or symbolizes a spiritual reality, grace.

A S A SIGN a sacrament must be something specific. It must be something that can be recognized as indicating the spiritual reality which it signifies. If men could not agree on whether a red or a green light should be the traffic signal to stop, then neither signal would be any good. So, too, with the sacraments. If they are to be good signs, they must be something specific. But the grace which they signify comes from God only. Hence, only God could determine what signs were to be used in the sacraments. Moreover, since signs, especially when they signify something difficult or mysterious, are not always easy to understand, it is also natural to add to any action or gesture or thing some words to convey the full meaning of the sign. Hence, in the sacraments instituted by Christ we find both things or actions and words. The things or actions are called the matter of the sacrament. The words are called the form of the sacrament. In baptism, for example, we find not only water and the action of pouring the water on the head of the person to be baptized, but also the words, "I baptize thee in the name of the Father, and of the Son, and of the Holy Ghost". Baptism cleanses the soul from sin. But the water alone, even the pouring of the water alone, might not convey the real meaning of the sacrament. But when the words are added, then there can be no mistake about the signification of baptism. To baptize means to cleanse, and to baptize in the name of the Trinity means to cleanse a soul in the name of and by the power of God—in other words, to expel sin by the infusion of grace. Of course, since it is God Who has instituted these sacred signs—the sacraments—it follows that both the sensible things and the words which He instituted cannot be substantially changed by men. Only God can give grace. Only He has the right to decide which signs shall convey grace to men.

GOD HAS CHOSEN to give grace to men through these sacramental signs because He knows human nature. Since the fall of Adam the mind of man has been immersed, for the most part, in material, sensible things. Before Adam's sin, his soul was in perfect control of his body and his senses. It was easy for Adam to raise his mind to the contemplation of spiritual things. Hence Adam had no need for sacraments. But since the sin of Adam, the mind of man finds it difficult to think of spiritual things. It must be led to the heights of spirituality gently, through the contemplation of material things. If the way to a man's heart is through his stomach, then the way to the higher reaches of his mind is through his senses—through his eyes, his ears, his hands, and so on. It is also a delicate touch of divine wisdom that man, who falls away from God by seeking the gratification of his senses, should be led back to God through his senses. Man has turned from God to the things of the world. God will lead him back through the things of the world.

HUMAN SIGNS DO NOT HAVE THE POWER of producing what they signify. A traffic light may turn red, but the motorist may ride through it. A husband may yawn, but his wife may still refuse to go home. A man may speak, but his words may not communicate his real thoughts. But the sacramental signs which Christ has instituted are effective. They do confer the grace which they signify. Baptism really does expel sin from the soul of the person baptized. It really does bring grace to the soul of the person baptized. Sacraments cause the grace which they signify. Since grace is a participation in the life of God, a share in the divine life, the principal cause of grace is God Himself. No one else, and nothing else, can give grace to men. But God can use instruments to produce His effects, in this case, grace. A paint brush could never paint a picture. But an artist can use a paint brush to produce the portrait of George Washington. Water alone and human words alone could never expel sin from a man's soul by infusing God's grace into that soul. But in the hands of God the pouring of the water and the words of baptism can forgive sin and introduce grace into a man's soul. The sacraments are instruments which God uses to give grace to men.

WE MAY SAY, THEN, that the sacraments of Christ contain the grace which they signify. Principally, they signify the grace which is a share in the divine life, sanctifying or habitual grace. Since the supernatural virtues accompany the infusion of grace in the soul, the sacraments also confer these virtues. But each sacrament is directed to a special effect.

Baptism, for example, is directed to the spiritual rebirth of a man and to his incorporation in the Church as a member of the Body of Christ. Baptism, therefore, will signify and confer the divine assistance necessary to achieve this spiritual effect—that a man be reborn as a member of Christ and be able to live as such. Since all grace was won for man by the Passion of Christ, it is clear that the sacraments contain grace and confer grace because of Christ's Passion. They derive their power to sanctify men from the power of Christ's Passion.

THE SACRAMENTS have a twofold purpose. They are a remedy for the disease of sin, and they make the soul of man capable of worshipping God properly according to the rites of the Christian life. But whenever a man is given some special work to do, he is usually given some external sign to signify his power. The cashier of a bank has a sign at his desk to tell the world that he is the cashier. A policeman wears a uniform to proclaim his position and authority. This principle is observed in the rites of Christian worship. Those who come to God through Christ, those who worship God according to the rites established by God Himself, are marked for that worship. They are given marks or characters to signify their right and power to worship God according to the rites of His Church. These marks are called characters. They are indelible marks imprinted on the souls of men.

THESE SACRAMENTAL CHARACTERS are spiritual powers given to men to enable them to take part in the worship of God. The worship of God consists either in receiving divine gifts or in bestowing divine gifts on others. In either case a man needs the power to receive or to give divine gifts. Now all spiritual gifts come to men from Christ. Hence the sacramental characters give men a share in the priesthood of Christ Himself. Since the sacramental character is given to men for the purposes of divine worship, it deals with action, and therefore resides in the powers of the soul, the intellectual power of the soul. Since the intellect is incorruptible, the character will be indelible. It cannot be blotted out of the soul.

SINCE THE SACRAMENTAL CHARACTER gives a man power to receive or to dispense divine gifts, not all the sacraments imprint characters on the soul. Baptism and confirmation give a man power to receive the other sacraments. Hence they confer a character. Holy orders gives a man power to confer the sacraments on others. Hence holy orders also confers a character. But the other sacraments give men no new power to receive or to confer the sacraments. Hence they confer no character.

GRACE AND THE SACRAMENTAL CHARACTERS are spiritual effects produced in the spiritual souls of men. God alone can be the principal agent producing these effects in the souls of men. But God can use both the sacramental signs and the men who administer these signs as instruments by which He produces His interior sanctification of the souls of men. The men who act as God's ministers in the conferring of the sacraments are only instrumental causes. They are like the brush in the hand of the painter. Through them God blots out the sins of men and paints in His grace.

CHRIST IS BOTH GOD AND MAN. He produces the interior spiritual effects of the sacraments both as God and as man. As God he has both the power and authority to produce grace in the souls of men.

As man He produces these effects meritoriously and efficiently, but instrumentally. He uses His human nature as an instrument in the production of grace. But His human nature is the chief instrument used by God to produce grace in the sacraments. By His Passion He won the grace which is given to men in the sacraments. Hence He had the power to institute the sacraments. Hence all other human ministers of grace derive their power from Him. They act in His name.

SINCE THE HUMAN MINISTERS of the sacraments of Christ are only His instruments, the efficacy of the sacraments does not depend on their personal virtue. They may be evil. But they are only instruments. The power of Christ can pass through them to sanctify the souls of those who receive His sacraments. Obviously, a sinful man sins grievously when he administers a sacrament while in the state of sin. But his sin does not prevent the sacrament from having its effect. He may not even have faith in Christ or in the power of the sacrament to sanctify. But as long as he acts as the instrument of Christ, the sacrament will confer grace. This is another proof of God's great love for men. He will not even allow the sinfulness of some to prevent others from receiving His grace. As long as the minister of a sacrament has the power to confer that sacrament, and as long as he intends to do what the Church of Christ wants done, then the sacrament he confers will give grace.

CHRIST INSTITUTED SEVEN SACRAMENTS: baptism, confirmation, the holy Eucharist, penance, extreme unction, holy orders and matrimony. If we examine them closely, we can see that they show a parallel between the life of grace and the natural life of man. Before a man can live at all, he must be born.

Before he can begin to live spiritually in Christ, he must be reborn into the life of grace. Baptism is this spiritual birth. Secondly, man must grow to maturity so that he can do a man's work. This growth is necessary also in the spiritual order, and the sacrament of confirmation confers the strength of spiritual manhood on men. Thirdly, men need nourishment to preserve life and strength. In the spiritual order, the sacrament of the holy Eucharist gives spiritual nourishment to men. In the natural order men become ill. They need to be cured and restored to their former vigor. Men can become ill in the spiritual order through personal sins. The sacrament of penance removes sin and restores spiritual health. The sacrament of extreme unction restores a man to spiritual vigor by removing the remains of sin from his soul and preparing him for eternal glory. Man is also a social being. Some men must be given the power to rule the community and perform public acts. The sacrament of Orders does this in the spiritual life of the Church. Priests offer sacrifices for themselves and for the people. Men must propagate the race. The sacrament of matrimony sanctifies them for the accomplishment of this obligation.

THE GREATEST of all the sacraments is the holy Eucharist. In the Eucharist Christ Himself, the High Priest, the Savior, the source of all grace, is present substantially. The other sacraments are all directed to this great sacrament. Holy orders gives a man power to consecrate the Eucharist. Baptism gives men the power to receive the Eucharist. Confirmation strengthens a man so that he will not fear to receive the Eucharist. Penance and extreme unction prepare a man to receive the Eucharist worthily. Matrimony signifies the union of Christ with His Church, and the Eucharist is also a figure of this same union.

ALL THE SACRAMENTS are necessary for men, but not in the same way, or to the same degree. Baptism is necessary for all if they are to be saved. Penance is necessary for those who have fallen into mortal sin after baptism. Holy orders is necessary for the Church. Confirmation perfects baptism. Extreme unction perfects penance. Matrimony preserves the membership of the Church.

THE SACRAMENTS are a wonderful gift of God to men. Through them, the power of Christ's Passion is applied to the souls of men for their salvation. Through the sacraments men are reborn and remade into the likeness of Christ. Through the sacraments men become the children of God and the heirs of heaven. Because they are effective signs of the grace which they signify, they give men an easy way to obtain the grace of God. They are another tender sign of God's mercy. He has not left men to wonder whether or not they have obtained the grace of God or can obtain the grace of God. In the sacraments, God has given men a sure way of obtaining His grace. No one need roam restlessly through life seeking in out-of-the-way places for some uncertain sign of God's mercy. The sacraments are the visible signs of God's love for men.

CHAPTER V

Baptism and Confirmation

CHAPTER V

Baptism and Confirmation

CHRIST INSTITUTED the seven sacraments in order to give men a share in the divine life—that share in the divine life which is called grace. Now every life must have a beginning, and the beginning of life we call birth. The supernatural life of grace has a beginning, and we call that beginning baptism. Through the sacrament of baptism a man is born spiritually of water and the Holy Spirit.

AS WE HAVE ALREADY SEEN, this sacrament was instituted at the moment Christ was baptized by John. The baptism of John did not give Christ the life of grace. He already possessed the fullness of grace. But when the waters of John's baptism touched Christ, at that moment water itself was sanctified and received, through Christ, the power to sanctify the souls of men. The power of water to give grace to men comes from the power of Christ's Passion. Hence, even though the sacrament of baptism was instituted at the baptism of Christ by John, nevertheless the sacrament was not to be administered to men until after Christ's Passion, death and resurrection. For this reason Christ did not order His Apostles to baptize men in the name of the Father, and of the Son, and of the Holy Ghost, until after He had risen from the tomb. But from that time on baptism is a necessary means to salvation. Unless a man be born again of water and the Holy Spirit, he cannot enter the kingdom of heaven.

IN BAPTISM, as in all the sacraments, we can distinguish three things: the sacrament only, the reality and the sacrament, and the reality only. These terms may seem mysterious, but when we apply them to the things for which they stand, they lose their mysteriousness. In baptism, the sacrament only is the external rite, the sensible sign, that is, the cleansing with water and the pronouncing of the words of the sacrament. The reality and the sacrament is the baptismal character which is imprinted on the soul. The reality only is the grace which the sacrament confers on the person baptized. To put the point in another way, in baptism, the pouring of the water and the words pronounced while the water is poured are called the sacrament only, because this sensible rite is only a sign, a sign of the baptismal character and of the grace of God which is being conferred. The character is called both a reality and a sacrament because it is something in itself, the spiritual reality imprinted on the soul, and it is also a sign of something else, a sign of the grace to be given by the sacrament. The grace given by the baptism is called a reality only, because it is the reality in which the sacrament terminates. It is called reality only because it is something real in itself, the grace of God, and it is not a sign of anything besides itself.

I F THE BAPTISMAL CHARACTER and the grace of baptism are to be given to the person seeking baptism, the sacrament must be administered properly. This means that the external rite of baptism must be performed in the manner determined by Christ, Who instituted the sacrament. Now baptism consists essentially of two parts: the cleansing with water of the body of the one to be baptized, and the pronunciation of the words, "I baptize thee in the name of the Father, and of the Son, and of the Holy

Ghost." These two parts of the sacrament are called, respectively, the matter and form of the sacrament. Each of the seven sacraments has its own matter and form. In each case it is the form which gives the proper meaning to the matter. In baptism, for example, the words pronounced give the true meaning of the cleansing of the body with water. A man might be washed simply to cleanse his body, or to cool it off, or to refresh it. But when the words of baptism are added, then we know that this particular cleansing is a cleansing of his soul. His sins are being washed away by the grace of God. In baptism, as in every other sacrament, both the matter and the form are necessary. To wash a man without pronouncing the words of baptism is simply to clean his body. To pronounce the words of baptism without washing a man with water is to beat the air with meaningless words.

THE MATTER OF BAPTISM is the action of cleansing a man with water. To baptize, then, we need water, and we need to cleanse a man with the water. Christ chose water because it is the element most frequently used in cleansing things, and especially because it is most easily accessible to men. Men cannot live without water. Hence they usually live where water can be found easily. Because it is the will of Christ that everyone be baptized, He chose as the matter of baptism an element which all men—rich and poor alike—could obtain easily. In baptism the water must be used to cleanse the person who is being baptized. This means that the water must flow over the body of the person. To achieve this effect the Church has, in the course of time, baptized men by immersing them in water, by sprinkling them with water, and by pouring water over them. At the present time, baptism is administered by pouring water on the head of the one being baptized.

THE SACRAMENT OF BAPTISM can be administered only once to any one person. As a man can be born in the body only once, so also he can be born in the order of grace only once. Again, Christ died but once, and those who are baptized are baptized in the death of Christ. Baptism also imprints on the soul an indelible character which can only be given once. Baptism, too, is chiefly a remedy for original sin, but once original sin is wiped out of the soul, it cannot return. Hence, baptism is not necessary as a remedy against original sin after a man has been baptized once.

BAPTISM ACHIEVES ITS EFFECTS through the power of Christ's Passion. But the power of Christ's Passion is more extensive than baptism of water. The president of a business concern may give a man the power to admit men to the concern on condition that they fill out satisfactorily a prescribed application blank. But the president himself still has the power to admit someone himself, and even without the filling out of the application blank. So too, Christ has the power to give grace to men even outside the sacraments which He has instituted as the normal means of obtaining grace. Normally, men cannot even begin the life of grace unless they receive the sacrament of baptism. But Christ knows that it may be impossible for some men, through no fault of their own, to receive baptism of water. In His mercy, He has made it possible for men to receive grace through what we call baptism of blood or baptism of desire. In baptism of blood a man gives his life for his belief in God and in Christ. He is martyred for his faith in God. Because he gives his life for God as Christ did, Christ will give him the grace needed for salvation. In baptism of desire a man repents of his sins and desires to do whatever God wants him to do, even to be baptized, if he knew that God willed it. If, in such a case, it is impossible for the man to receive baptism because, for example, there is no one to baptize him, then Christ will give him the grace he needs. Of course, neither baptism of blood nor baptism of desire is the sacrament of baptism. Hence, they do not imprint on the soul the baptismal character which enables a man to participate in the priesthood of Christ.

BECAUSE OF THE NECESSITY of baptism of water, Christ has made it easy for men to receive the sacrament. Ordinarily, the minister of baptism is a priest of Christ's Church. But in cases of necessity, that is, when a person is in danger of death and a priest cannot be found quickly enough, then anyone may baptize—a man or a woman, a good man or a sinner, a Christian or an unbeliever. All that is necessary is that the person should administer the sacrament properly, according to the mind of the Church. Of course, if there are several persons present, then it is preferable that a believer in Christ should baptize rather than an unbeliever, a man than a woman, a cleric rather than a layman.

THE SPONSORS OR GODPARENTS in baptism are intended to be teachers of the faith to those who are baptized. Just as a child needs the loving care and instruction of its parents if it is to develop properly as a human being, so too, it needs the care and instruction of godparents, that is, instructors in the spiritual order of faith. Godparents assume, then, a serious responsibility. They are responsible for the Christian training of the person to whom they are godparents.

Β Y THE WILL OF GOD, baptism of water is the normal, necessary means of salvation. Everyone, then, must be baptized. Children should be baptized as soon as possible and convenient, that is, within a few weeks after birth. Normally adults, who must make the decision to be baptized of their own free will, have to be instructed in the truths of the faith before they are to be baptized. Through baptism they embark on the Christian life. They ought to understand the nature of the Christian life and the obligations it imposes upon them. In danger of death both children and adults should be baptized at once.

O F COURSE, the children of unbelievers are not to be baptized against the will of their parents. If this were done, the children might lose their faith through the unbelief of their parents. Obviously, too, adults should never be baptized against their will. Sinners can be baptized, but on condition that they are willing to give up their sin.

S INCE THE SACRAMENT of baptism takes away sin and the punishment due to sin, no satisfaction for sin can be demanded from those who have just received the sacrament of baptism. Nor can those who are about to be baptized be asked to make any confession of their sins. All that is required is that they wish, either by their own will, if they are adults, or through the will and faith of their parents or the Church, if they are children, to be baptized.

T HE FIRST EFFECT of baptism is the expulsion of all sin and the debt of punishment for sin from the soul. Both original sin and personal actual sins are removed from the soul by the waters of baptism. The debt of punishment for sin is also removed by baptism. Through baptism man escapes the punishment of hell in the next life. The temporal punishment of sin in this life—disordered concupiscence, sickness, pain and death—is not removed in this present life. But, through baptism, it will be removed after the resurrection of man. Baptism destroys sin by giving man sanctifying grace and the supernatural virtues and gifts of the Holy Spirit. It also incorporates a man in Christ, that is, it makes him a member of the Mystical Body of Christ, which is the Church. Because man is incorporated in Christ through baptism, he is enlightened by Christ through the gift of faith. Hence baptism is sometimes called the sacrament of faith. Because man is made one with Christ and the grace of Christ through baptism, he becomes capable of performing the works of grace, those good, meritorious acts which lead to the vision of God. Hence it is through baptism that the gates of heaven are opened to a man. When he is baptized he begins that supernatural life which will be perfected in heaven. He sets out on the road which leads to heaven.

W HEN INFANTS ARE BAPTIZED, the grace given to them is equal in all. But when adults are baptized, the degree of grace will vary with their voluntary dispositions. Those who approach the sacrament with greater sincerity, with greater repentance for sin and with greater love for God will receive greater grace. If a man should receive the sacrament with absolute insincerity, that is, if he is a sinner and intends to remain a sinner, he will receive the sacrament and the sacramental character, but he will not receive the grace which expels his sins. Sin is a matter of will. If a man wills to remain a sinner, not even God, much less a sacrament of God, will do violence to his free will. But the sinner who receives baptism receives the baptismal character. If he later repents of his sins, this baptismal character will bring God's grace to his soul for the forgiveness of his sins. This is another indication of the great mercy of God. Baptism can be received but once. But even those unfortunate men who receive the sacrament unworthily and sinfully can receive the grace of the sacrament if they will repent of their sins.

I N THE NATURAL ORDER a man is not only born, but he grows to manhood or maturity. When a man is mature he is, so to speak, perfect. It is in his maturity that a man is really capable of acting perfectly as a man. In the order of grace a man is born through the sacrament of baptism. He comes to spiritual maturity or manhood through the sacrament of confirmation. In the natural order of life it is the child who is protected and nourished. The man must go out into the world to struggle for himself and for others. In the spiritual order of grace this growth is repeated. Baptism sanctifies a man in and for himself. Confirmation makes him a spiritual adult. It sanctifies him for himself and others. The spiritual man must defend his faith against the attacks of the world, the flesh and the devil. He must give others the example of courage and steadfastness in the profession of the faith. The grace to live his faith amid the dangers of the world comes to him in the sacrament of confirmation.

T HE GRACE OF CONFIRMATION is aptly symbolized in the matter and form of the sacrament. The person to be confirmed is anointed on the forehead with chrism. Chrism is a mixture of olive oil and balm. Oil is a familiar symbol of strength and fullness. It signifies the spiritual fullness of grace that comes in confirmation. Balsam is a fragrant substance. Its fragrance is intended to show that the interior grace of the man confirmed must make itself known in the world by the odor of good works and constancy in the faith. While the man being confirmed is anointed with chrism, the bishop says, "I sign thee with the sign of the cross, I confirm thee with the chrism of salvation, in the name of the Father, and of the Son, and of the Holy Ghost. Amen". In this formula the Church expresses the cause of the grace of confirmation, the Trinity; the strength given by the sacrament is expressed in the word "confirm". And, as the soldier is given a helmet to wear in battle, so the confirmed man is signed with the sign of the cross on his forehead to show that he must do battle for the faith and for Christ. Since the confirmed man must do battle for the faith, confirmation gives him an indelible character which marks him as a soldier of Christ, appointed to bear witness to the faith in the world.

NATURAL MATURITY comes slowly to men. But the spiritual maturity of confirmation comes in an instant. God, Who is the cause of the grace of confirmation, is not limited by the restrictions of space and time. In an instant He gives to the confirmed soul the fullness of spiritual maturity. In the spiritual order, as in the natural order, everyone is intended to grow to maturity. Hence this sacrament should be administered to all who have been baptized. For, even though some may never live to be adults physically, nevertheless their souls are immortal and will live forever. God wants their souls to be mature in the spiritual order.

SINCE CONFIRMATION gives a man the fullness of grace, it is usually administered only by the bishop, who possesses the fullness of the priesthood.

As in baptism, the one to be confirmed is assisted by sponsors. The sponsors show that he is passing from spiritual infancy to spiritual manhood and needs mature assistance to make the change easily. The sponsors also act as seasoned officers in the battle of the Christian life, leading and advising the new soldier in the field.

WHAT WE HAVE JUST SAID of the sacraments of baptism and confirmation should emphasize the fact that Christianity is a way of life, a divine way of life. Baptism opens the soul of man to the life of God. It breaks the bonds of sin which chain man to the earth. It sets man free in the limitless world of divine knowledge and love. Through faith, hope and charity, man must grow in this world of God. The sacrament of confirmation gives him in an instant the perfection of spiritual manhood. In the changing tides and floods of human doubt and uncertainty, his soul is held by the unmoving anchor of faith. Other men may sink in the quicksands of fear and despair. But his soul soars aloft on the strong wings of divine hope. In a world that has grown cold because it cannot love, his soul is warmed by the flame of charity. Strengthened by the grace of confirmation, he is ready to bear witness to the power of the Passion of Christ.

CHAPTER VI

The Holy Eucharist

CHAPTER VI

The Holy Eucharist

FOOD SUSTAINS LIFE. Without food, no living being can remain alive and active. Grace gives to man a share in the divine life. Baptism gives man birth in the divine life. Confirmation gives man maturity in the divine life. But this life cannot continue to grow without food, spiritual food. Like every other life, the divine life of grace must be nourished. It must be fed. The food of the life of grace is the sacrament of the holy Eucharist. In this sacrament, the life of grace feeds on the very Body and Blood of Christ Himself. If, in the natural order, bread were the only substance that men could eat, then all men would eat bread always. For a man needs food to live. In the supernatural order of grace, the Eucharist is the necessary food of the supernatural life of grace.

OF COURSE, the Eucharist is not necessary in the same way that baptism is necessary. Baptism is necessary as the beginning of the supernatural life of grace. But the Eucharist is necessary as the consummation of the life of grace. Baptism is necessary because it makes a man like Christ, and so fits him for the reception of Christ in his soul. In the Eucharist, man is united to Christ Himself. In the Eucharist, the very Body and Blood of Christ come to dwell in the body and soul of man. In the Eucharist, the Body and Blood of Christ become the spiritual food of man's soul, increasing grace in the soul and so increasing man's likeness to Christ.

THE EUCHARIST is called by many names in Christian tradition. It is called "the Sacrifice," because it is a remembrance of Christ's Passion. It is called "Communion," because it is the cause of unity or union between Christ and the members of His Church. It is called "Viaticum," because it gives man the way to win the vision of God. To put it in another way, in the Eucharist we have a renewal of Christ's Passion, which saved men by meriting grace for men; in the Eucharist we have Christ Himself, Who gives grace to men; and in the Eucharist we have Christ Himself, Who enables the souls of men to pass through death to eternal life.

CHRIST HIMSELF instituted this great sacrament at the Last Supper. He knew that He was shortly to leave this earth. He knew that He would not remain in this world much longer in His bodily presence. But He did not wish to leave His faithful disciples entirely. He wished to remain with His followers in some way. And so He gave us His presence in the sacrament of the Eucharist to take the place of His historical bodily presence. Besides, He wished to leave men a remembrance of His Passion. Faith in His Passion is necessary for salvation. But in the course of time men might forget His Passion and death on the Cross. In the Eucharist He has given men a perpetual remembrance of His Passion. He instituted this sacrament at the Last Supper, because He knew that the last words and actions of men who are about to leave this world are more likely to be remembered with love and devotion than any other words or actions. The Eucharist was, as it were, His last will and testament to the human race. Shortly before His death, resurrection and ascension into heaven, He left men His Body and Blood as the food of their souls. It was the most precious gift

He had to leave us, because the Eucharist is Christ Himself, the Author and Dispenser of God's grace.

IN THE MIND OF CHRIST, the Eucharist is to be the food of souls. "I am the living bread which came down from heaven. If any man eat of this bread, he shall live forever: and the bread that I will give is my flesh, for the life of the world . . . Except you eat the flesh of the Son of man and drink his blood, you shall not have life in you. He that eateth my flesh and drinketh my blood hath everlasting life: and I will raise him up in the last day. For my flesh is meat indeed: and my blood is drink indeed. He that eateth my flesh and drinketh my blood abideth in me: and I in him" (*John VI, 51-55*).

BECAUSE THE EUCHARIST is the food of souls, Christ chose bread and wine for the matter of this sacrament. Bread is the staple food of all mankind, and wheaten bread is the bread most commonly used among men. For this reason, Christ chose bread to be the sacramental sign of His Body. But man not only needs solid food, he also needs liquid refreshment. Wine is a liquid nourishment universal to mankind. Wine made from grapes is the only true wine. Hence Christ chose wine to be the sacramental sign of His Blood. When He instituted this sacrament at the Last Supper, Christ, according to the custom of His country, mixed a little bit of water with the wine. In the Mass, a little water is mixed with the wine which is to be changed into Christ's Blood. This water represents the Christian people, the members of the Church. This represents the union of the faithful with Christ. Christ wanted to give men His own Body and Blood as the food of their souls. Hence, as the sacramental sign of His Body and Blood, He chose elements that would be recognized as food by men.

IN THE SACRAMENT of the Eucharist, bread and wine are changed into the Body and Blood of Christ. Christ Himself is truly present in the Eucharist under the appearances of bread and wine. The Eucharist is, then, the perfect sacrament of the New Law. In the other sacraments, the sensible rite signifies and causes the grace of Christ to come to the souls of men. In the Eucharist, we have Christ Himself and the grace which He brings to the souls of men. This is a testimonial to the depth of Christ's love for men. His delights are to be with the children of men. In the Eucharist Christ, Who has ascended into heaven, still remains with men on earth. Because He cannot be seen by human eyes in the Eucharist, because His presence in the Eucharist is sacramental and mysterious, the Eucharist is a challenge to the faith of men. By believing in the truth of this great mystery, by believing that He Who could feed five thousand men with a few loaves of bread, can feed millions of men with His Body and Blood in the Eucharist, men prove the strength, the splendor and the perfection of their faith.

IN THE EUCHARIST, at the words of consecration uttered by Christ at the Last Supper, or now by the priest at Mass, bread and wine are changed into the Body and Blood of Christ. Bread and wine are no longer present. Instead the Body and Blood of Christ are present sacramentally. We can never hope to understand in this life how this change takes place. This is a mystery beyond our comprehension. But we can so state the mystery that it is no longer absurd or ridiculous or contradictory.

LET US EXAMINE the mystery more closely. Before the Consecration of the Mass, bread and wine are present on the altar. When the priest says, speaking in the name of Christ, "This is My Body," and "This is the chalice of My Blood of the New and Eternal Testament, the Mystery of Faith, which shall be shed for you and for many unto the forgiveness of sins," the bread and wine cease to be present, and the Body and Blood of Christ become present. How does this take place? Christ, in His Body and Blood, is present in heaven. He does not leave heaven and come to the altar to displace the bread and wine. Rather, the bread and the wine are changed into His Body and Blood. The bread and the wine cannot remain. If this happened, then the words of Christ, pronounced in the Mass by His priests, would not be true. Instead of saying, "This is My Body," the priest should say "This is bread and the Body of Christ." But Christ cannot lie, and He said, "This is My Body." At the moment of Consecration, then, the bread must become the Body of Christ and the wine must become His Blood. The change must be instantaneous, for Christ did not say, "This bread is about to become My Body;" He said, "This is My Body." Naturally, the whole of the bread must be changed into the Body of Christ, and the whole of the wine must be changed into His Blood. If this did not happen, then once again the words of Christ would not be true. He should have said something like this: "This is partly bread and partly My Body." But He did not say anything like this. He said simply, "This"—all this that you see— "is my Body."

THIS IS A VERY SPECIAL KIND OF CHANGE, in fact the only change of its kind that we know. We are accustomed to many changes in the world of matter. Water and wheaten flour can be mixed together and baked. In the baking they are changed into bread. In the course of time, through the processes of nature, wine can change into vinegar. But there are three things of which we are sure in all changes of this kind. First, the new substance—bread or wine in the examples given—did not previously exist. It came into being with the change. Secondly, something of the first substance—of the wheat or of the wine—went into the making of the last substance, the bread or the vinegar. And thirdly, the sensible qualities of the first and the last substances were not the same. Wheat looks differently and tastes differently from bread. Wine tastes differently from vinegar.

NOW IN THE EUCHARIST, the substance of the Body and the substance of the Blood of Christ are in existence before the substance of the bread and the substance of the wine are changed into them. Secondly, and consequently, nothing of the bread and nothing of the wine are used in making the Body or the Blood of Christ. Instead, the bread and the wine are changed into the already existing Body and Blood of Christ. Thirdly, although the sensible qualities of the Body and Blood of Christ are different from the sensible qualities of bread and wine, nevertheless, the sensible qualities of the bread and wine still exist in the Eucharist. The consecrated Host still looks like bread, feels like bread, and tastes like bread. The wine that has been consecrated into the Blood of Christ still looks like wine, tastes like wine. On the other hand, neither the Host nor the Precious Blood looks like the Body and the Blood of Christ. We can only say that the whole substance of the bread has been changed into the substance of the Body of Christ, and the whole substance of the wine has been changed into the Blood of Christ, but that the appearances of bread and wine still remain. What was bread has been changed, though the appearances of bread remain. What was wine has been changed, though the appearances of wine remain. Theologians call a change of this kind "transubstantiation." The word means that one whole substance is changed into another whole substance, even though the appearances— philosophers would say "accidents"—of the first substance still remain. In the Eucharist neither the bread nor the wine is annihilated. They are changed into the Body and Blood of Christ.

THE BODY AND BLOOD OF CHRIST are present in the Eucharist. By the very power of the sacrament, the Body of Christ becomes present under the appearances of bread, and the Blood of Christ becomes present under the appearances of wine. But Christ is not separated into His Body and Blood. This would destroy Christ. Hence, the whole Christ must be present wherever His Body or His Blood is present. This means that wherever the Body of Christ is present, there His Blood, His Soul and His Divinity must also be present. The same may be said of His Blood. Hence, Christ is wholly present under the appearances of bread and under the appearances of wine. He is wholly present under every particle of the consecrated Host and in every drop of the consecrated wine. Moreover, all the sensible qualities of the Body and Blood of Christ are present under the appearances of bread and wine—His size, His weight, His color, the texture of His skin, and so on. But they are not present in this sacrament as they are in heaven, or as they are in human bodies still here on earth. They are present only because the substance of Christ's Body and the substance of His Blood are present. They are present through the substance of the Body and Blood of Christ, in the manner in which a substance is present. If the quantity of Christ's Body were present in the Eucharist in the way in which the quantity of our own bodies are now present in place, then at the Consecration the host would have to become as tall as the Body of Christ, as broad as the Body of Christ and as heavy as the Body of Christ. Or else the Body of Christ would have to become as small and as light as the host. But neither of these things takes place, because the quantity of Christ's Body does not become present in this way. It becomes present through the presence of the substance of Christ's Body. As a consequence, the eyes of men cannot see Christ in the Eucharist. Not even the natural intelligence of angels can see Christ as He is present in the Eucharist. Only God, and those who enjoy the vision of God, can see Christ present in the Eucharist. Here on earth, we can only know through faith that Christ is present in the Eucharist under the appearances of bread and wine.

EVEN AFTER THE SUBSTANCE of the bread and the substance of the wine have become the substance of the Body and the substance of the Blood of Christ, the appearances of bread and wine remain. The Host tastes like bread, feels like bread. The appearances of wine taste like wine. They can nourish man physically, just as ordinary bread and wine do. They can be corrupted, just as ordinary bread and wine. This is truly a miracle of divine power. Ordinarily, the feel, the taste, the shape and the weight of bread cannot exist except in bread. But here they exist by the divine power. The same must be said of the appearances of wine. These appearances of bread and wine do not exist in the Body and Blood of Christ. They exist only because the power of God sustains them in existence as the sign of the presence of the Body and Blood of His Son. When they are corrupted, for example, by the digestive processes in the body of the man who receives them, it is these appearances of bread and wine that corrupt, not the Body and Blood of Christ. Christ remains present under these appearances just as long as they are the appearances of bread and wine. As soon as they cease to be such, then the Body and Blood of Christ are no longer present.

THIS WONDERFUL CHANGE of bread and wine into the Body and Blood of Christ is accomplished through the words of Christ—words which He pronounced for the first time at the Last Supper, words which are pronounced in His name daily in the sacrifice of the Mass. These words are the form of the sacrament of the Eucharist. Bread and wine are the matter, and the words of Christ are the form of the sacrament. It should be noted here that the other sacraments are accomplished in the use of the consecrated matter. Baptism is accomplished when the blessed water is poured on the head of the man being baptized and the baptismal formula is pronounced. But in the case of the Eucharist the sacrament is accomplished when the words of Christ are pronounced over the bread and wine. Again, whereas in the other sacraments the priest either speaks in his own name or prays that God will accomplish the effect of the sacrament, in the Eucharist the priest merely pronounces the words of Christ. It is Christ Himself Who changes bread and wine into His own Body and Blood. The priest acts as the instrument of Christ, pronouncing the words in His name.

THE WORDS OF CONSECRATION—"This is My Body," and "This is the chalice of My Blood, etc.,"—effect the change of bread and wine into the Body and Blood of Christ immediately. It is God Who performs this wonderful work, and He works in an instant. In both cases the word, "This," refers, not to the bread or the wine, but to the Body and to the Blood of Christ. These words not only signify the change which takes place, they cause the change to take place. They are instruments which God uses to change bread and wine into the Body and Blood of Christ. Hence both the statements are true, even though the one be pronounced without the other. If a duly ordained priest of Christ were to pronounce over bread the words, "This is My Body," the bread would be changed into the Body of Christ, even though the priest did not go on to consecrate wine into the Blood of Christ. Each formula effects exactly what it says. "This is My Body" changes bread into the Body of Christ; and "This is the chalice of My Blood, etc." changes wine into the Blood of Christ.

LIKE ALL THE SACRAMENTS, the Eucharist gives divine grace to man. In the first place, through the reception of the sacrament of the Eucharist, Christ Himself, the cause of grace, becomes present in man. Secondly, the Eucharist represents the Passion of Christ. But the Passion of Christ is the cause of grace. Thirdly, the Eucharist does for the spiritual life of man all that material food does for his body. But it is grace which sustains, restores and increases the life of the soul of man. Lastly, the Eucharist is a symbol and cause of the unity between Christ and the members of

His Mystical Body, the Church. Just as many grains of wheat are united to form one bread, and the juice of many grapes to form one wine, so in the Eucharist and through the Eucharist the many members of Christ's Church are united to Him and to one another in charity to form the one Church, the Mystical Body of Christ. But charity only comes to men with grace. Therefore the Eucharist gives grace to men.

THE EUCHARIST is also the means by which men attain to the eternal glory of the vision of God. "He that eateth my flesh and drinketh my blood hath everlasting life: and I will raise him up on the last day" (*John* VI, 55). This sacrament does not give glory to a man immediately. But it gives him Christ, through Whom he can attain to glory. It brings him the power of Christ's Passion, by which he can attain to glory. The appearances of bread and wine also signify the spiritual food and the unity of Christ's followers with Himself and with one another, through which men attain to glory.

BECAUSE THIS SACRAMENT contains Christ Himself and the Passion of Christ, it has in itself the power to forgive sins. But the sinner himself must be considered. If a sinner, in the state of mortal sin, should receive this sacrament while intending to remain attached to his sin, then he will not be forgiven. On the contrary, he will commit a sacrilege in profaning in this way the Body and Blood of Christ. But if he is ready to give up his attachment to sin, and if he approaches the sacrament in forgetfulness of his sin, then his sin will be forgiven. The sacrament will give him charity, which will perfect his contrition and bring forgiveness of sin. Of course, if he remembers his sin, he ought first to obtain the forgiveness of his sin in the sacrament of penance. No one should approach the sacrament of Christ's Body and Blood while still consciously in the state of mortal sin. Since the effects of this sacrament are grace and charity, it will forgive venial sins and restore the fervor of charity.

THE EUCHARIST can also release man from the punishment due to sin. It is both a sacrament and a sacrifice. As a sacrament, it unites a man to Christ through charity. But it is by the fervor of charity that a man obtains the forgiveness of the punishment due to his sins. The degree of fervor will determine the amount of punishment which is forgiven. As a sacrifice, the Eucharist can also forgive the penalty of sin. In itself, the Eucharist is powerful enough to forgive all the penalty for all the sins of all men. But, in matters of satisfaction, the disposition of men must be taken into account. The Eucharistic sacrifice will remit their punishment according to the measure of their devotion.

THE EUCHARIST is the spiritual food of the soul. As food it strengthens the soul. Hence it will protect a man against future temptations and sin. It is also a sign of the Passion of Christ which conquered the devils. Hence it will protect men against the attacks of the devils.

THE EUCHARIST produces these wonderful effects when it is properly received. Because the Body and Blood of Christ are present under the appearances of bread and wine as soon as the bread and wine are consecrated, anyone who receives Communion will receive the Body and Blood of Christ. But not everyone will receive the effect of the sacrament, grace. The unbeliever and the Catholic in mortal sin will receive the Body and Blood of Christ. But they will not receive the grace of the sacrament. They are said to receive the Eucharist sacramentally, but not spiritually. On the other hand, it is possible to receive the grace of the sacrament spiritually by desiring it. Lastly, the man in the state of grace who receives Christ in Communion also receives grace, the spiritual effect of the sacrament. In this case he receives the Eucharist both sacramentally and spiritually.

THE SINNER who receives the Eucharist while conscious of his sin is guilty of sacrilege. The reception of this sacrament is an expression of a man's union with Christ and with the members of His Church in faith and charity. But the sinner is not united in charity to Christ. In receiving this sacrament he is guilty of lying. He uses the sacrament to lie. This is a grave abuse of a sacred thing, the sacrament of the Body and Blood of Christ.

ALTHOUGH THE SINNER HIMSELF is under a grave obligation not to receive Christ in the Eucharist until he has repented of his sin, the Church is most just and wise in distributing this sacrament. If a man's sins are not public and well-known, she will give him Communion when he approaches the altar rail. In this way she protects the reputation of the sinner. Even Christ Himself gave the Eucharist to Judas. On the other hand, if a man is an open sinner, and his sinfulness is surely known to the world, then the Church will refuse this sacrament to him. This prevents both the profanation of the sacrament and scandal to the people. But, generally, it is so difficult to know that a man is still in the state of sin, that this drastic action is taken only rarely and with great caution.

THOSE WHO ARE TO RECEIVE the Eucharist in Communion are obliged to fast from food and drink (except water) from midnight of the night before they receive. This is commanded out of respect for the sacrament. It does not seem fitting that a man should eat or drink other substances just before receiving the very Body and Blood of the Lord Himself. But, like a good Mother, the Church grants special exceptions to the sick, the dying and those who might otherwise be unable to receive Communion.

WHEN WE CONSIDER the wonderful benefits which come to men through the reception of Christ in Communion, we can understand the great desire of the Church that all her members should receive Communion as frequently as possible. The Church urges her members to receive daily. The sacrament itself can be received daily. But, of course, the dispositions of those who are to receive must be considered also. Because of the great dignity of this sacrament, a man should not approach It unless he is prepared to receive It worthily. By a law of the Church, all those who have reached the use of reason are obliged to receive Christ in Communion at least once a year.

WHEN CHRIST instituted this sacrament, He commanded His Apostles to administer It as He did. This means that both the Apostles and their successors, the priests of the Church, must consecrate both bread and wine and receive Christ under both species. The priests of the Church must, when they celebrate Mass, receive Christ under the appearances of bread and under the appearances of wine. But, since Christ is wholly present under both species, a man can receive the whole Christ under either species. Since the Church has grown so greatly, and since so many of the faithful receive Communion, the Church gives this sacrament to the faithful only under one species, the species of bread. The chief reason for this is the great respect due to the Blood of Christ in this sacrament. When so many people receive Communion and many of them are children, there is a serious danger that the Precious Blood of Christ might be spilled on clothing, on the altar rail, or on the ground, if It were administered to all.

A S WE HAVE ALREADY SAID, in this sacrament, bread and wine are changed into the Body and Blood of Christ by the words of Christ Himself. The man who performs this rite acts in the name and the person of Christ Himself. Now no one can act in the name and person of someone else, unless the power to do so is given to him. Christ has given this power only to His priests. Only the ordained priest can change bread and wine into the Body and Blood of Christ in the name of Christ. Ordinarily, too, only the ordained priest can dispense this sacrament to the people in Communion. The priest does what Christ did at the Last Supper. Christ consecrated bread and wine and He distributed His Body and Blood to His Apostles. The priest consecrates bread and wine and distributes Communion to the people. By office a priest is an intermediary between God and the people. He offers the people's gifts to God and God's gifts to the people. The Eucharist is God's gift to the people. Again, the Eucharist is a sacred thing. It can be touched only by consecrated or sacred things. The linen cloth—the corporal—on which the Body of Christ rests on the altar, the chalice in which the Blood of Christ rests are consecrated for this purpose. So too, the hands of the priest are blessed and consecrated so that they may handle the sacrament worthily.

THE PRIEST CONSECRATES bread and wine in the sacrifice of the Mass. But whoever offers sacrifice must share in the sacrifice. The outward sacrifice is a sign of the inner sacrifice by which he offers himself to God. By sharing in the external sacrifice he shows that he is making the internal sacrifice. For this reason, the priest who celebrates Mass must receive the Eucharist in Communion at that Mass. Moreover, he dispenses this sacrament to others in Communion. He himself ought to receive first. In this way, he proves to the people that he is the dispenser of divine gifts.

THE PRIEST who approaches the altar to offer the sacrifice of the Mass, to change bread and wine into the Body and Blood of Christ, ought to be a spiritual man, a holy man. He ought to be united to Christ in faith and charity. But Christ remembers the weakness of men. In His great desire to give Himself to the faithful, He has not linked either the reality or the power of this sacrament to the changeable dispositions of men. As long as a man is a validly ordained priest, he can validly perform and administer this sacrament. He may be a sinner. He may even be a heretic, or a schismatic, or excommunicated by the Church. Still, if he consecrates bread and wine, they become the Body and Blood of Christ. Of course, such a man is guilty of grave sacrilege in celebrating Mass. But his Mass is a Mass, and he does change bread and wine into the Body and Blood of Christ. Since Christ Himself is the chief Priest in every Mass, and the Victim of every Mass, then even the Mass celebrated by a wicked priest is fruitful for the Church. Obviously, the great devotion of a good priest will make the Mass he celebrates more fruitful than the Mass of a sinful priest. But the essential fruitfulness of the Mass can never be lost, for even the sinful priest offers Mass in the name and by the power of Christ.

THE POWER OF A PRIEST to offer Mass is not so much an obligation as a privilege. Theologians teach that a priest is obliged to offer Mass at least several times each year. This is a reasonable obligation. Surely a man must use the graces and powers which God gives him. Hence, the priest ought to use his power to celebrate Mass. Sometimes a priest is obliged in justice to say Mass. Thus, pastors are obliged to offer Mass for the people of their parish every Sunday, and on other specified feast days during the year. But the priests of Christ appreciate the great gift that has been given them. Normally, every priest says Mass as often as he can. Usually, the priest offers Mass every day of the year.

THE MASS IS A SACRIFICE. The Eucharist is both a sacrament and a sacrifice. When the priest says Mass, he not only changes bread and wine into the Body and Blood of Christ, he also offers to God the sacrifice of the Body and Blood of Christ. Earlier in this book we said that sacrifice is an act of religion made to God alone. It is the offering of something sensible to God, in recognition of God's supreme dominion over man. Normally, in a sacrifice, the thing which is offered to God is immolated or destroyed. In this way men signify God's absolute dominion over man. The sensible thing is destroyed in God's honor to show that both it and man belong absolutely to God and to no one else. The offering is made by a legitimate minister, that is, by a man duly chosen to represent the whole community.

AS WE HAVE ALREADY SEEN, Christ offered the perfect sacrifice to God in His Passion. He was a legitimate minister, that is, He was the Priest appointed by God to offer this sacrifice. He offered His own sufferings and life to God. He was Himself the Victim of the sacrifice, because He was immolated on the Cross. By giving His life to God, He paid tribute to God's supreme dominion over life and death.

NOW IN THE MASS we have the renewal of the sacrifice of the Cross. The Mass is a representation and a renewal of the sacrifice of the Cross. In the Mass, Christ is offered to God and mystically immolated in an unbloody sacrifice under the appearances of bread and wine. On the Cross, Christ offered Himself to God in a bloody manner. In the Mass, Christ is offered to God in an unbloody manner. But in both sacrifices the principal Priest and the Victim are identical. In both, Christ is the principal Priest offering the sacrifice. In both, Christ is the Victim Who is offered to God. On the Cross, Christ merited grace for men. Through the Mass, His merits are applied to men for their salvation. On the Cross, Christ offered His Passion immediately to God for the salvation of men. In the Mass, through the mediation of the priests of Christ, the Passion of Christ is offered to God for the salvation of men. In the Mass it is Christ, the Eternal Victim, Who is offered to God in recognition of God's supreme dominion, and in expiation of the sins of men. The sacrifice of the Cross is a true sacrifice. The Mass, which is a re-presentation, a renewal of the sacrifice of the Cross, is also a true sacrifice.

BECAUSE THE MASS is the sacrifice of Christ's Body and Blood, it is offered with great solemnity. The essential element of the sacrifice—according to theologians—is found in the consecration of the bread and the wine. But this essential rite is surrounded with other fitting ceremonies. The ceremonies of the Mass are intended to emphasize and enhance the dignity of the sacrifice of the Body and Blood of Christ. They also serve to instruct the members of Christ's Church in the truths of faith and in the meaning of Christ's sacrifice. When the faithful participate in them intelligently and devoutly, they help the faithful to offer themselves with Christ to God.

THE SACRIFICE of the Mass is the sacrifice of the Body and Blood of Christ. Because of its great dignity, it is offered usually in churches and chapels consecrated or blessed for this purpose. The altars, the cloths and the sacred vessels used in the Mass are blessed or consecrated for their sublime function. This is a fitting tribute to the Body and Blood of Christ, the Head of men and angels.

THE MASS ITSELF is divided into two parts, the Mass of the Catechumens and the Mass of the Faithful. The Mass of the Catechumens is a period of preparatory prayer and instruction. It begins with the praise of God in the prayers at the foot of the altar and the Introit. In the Kyrie, eleison and the Christe, eleison—Lord, have mercy on us and Christ, have mercy on us—we pray to the Trinity for God's mercy. In the Gloria, we give glory to God and meditate on the glory which awaits us in heaven. In the Collect, the priest prays for the people that they may be worthy of the great mystery of the Mass. In the Epistle, Gradual and Alleluia, the people are instructed by the Church. In the Gospel, they are instructed by Christ Himself. After the Gospel, the people profess their faith in the Creed. This closes the Mass of the Catechumens.

THE MASS OF THE FAITHFUL is the actual celebration of the mystery of the Eucharist. It consists of three principal parts: the offering or Offertory which the people make to God; the Consecration, in which the sacrifice and the sacrament of the Eucharist are perfected; and the Communion, in which the priest and the people receive the sacrament.

THE INCIDENTAL CEREMONIES of the Mass are intended either to symbolize Christ's Passion or to incite the people to devotion and reverence. The many signs of the cross, for example, signify the Passion of Christ. The outstretched arms of the priest recall Christ stretched out on the Cross. The washing of the priest's hands, the inclinations of the head of the priest and the faithful, the genuflections, and so on, signify the devotion and reverence of the priest and the people for the dignity of this great mystery.

THE PRIEST who offers Mass, and the people who participate with him in this offering are only human. They can make mistakes, or forget some ceremony of the Mass. Or the material elements may be defective: the wine may be imperfect, may have turned to vinegar, and so on. As far as is humanly possible, the Church has made regulations to cover any possible defect in the Mass. The Mass is the principal prayer and action of the Church. She is extremely careful to see that the Mass is offered properly.

THE EUCHARIST, both as a sacrifice and as a sacrament, is a great gift to man. In the Eucharist, man achieves that perfect union with God for which he was made. Man was made to live in union with God both in this life and in the next. By sin, man voluntarily destroys his union with God in this world. If he dies in his sins, he remains separated from God for all eternity. By sin, man refuses to recognize the supreme dominion of God. The Passion of Christ made it possible for man to be released from the bondage of sin and restored to union with God in divine grace. In His Passion, Christ, acting for the whole human race, gave God that obedience and submission which every man ought to give to God. In this way, He satisfied God for the offense of man's disobedience. In this way, He restored to the human race grace and charity, which are the source of order in man's world, the source of man's union with God. Through the sacrifice of the Mass, the power of Christ's Passion is applied to men. In the Mass, men give to God that perfect sacrifice which is pleasing to God. In the Mass, men offer to God the perfect obedience of Christ and the obedience of their own wills. In union with Christ they also become pleasing to God. Their sacrifice is acceptable to God. Because it is acceptable, God generously returns to them the sacrament of the Eucharist for the nourishment of their souls. When they receive the Eucharist, they receive Christ Himself, the Author of grace. Receiving Christ they receive grace and charity. They are united in love and obedience to God. The disorder of sin is destroyed. Man is once again on the royal road, the divine road to happiness.

CHAPTER VII

Penance

The Sacrament of Penance

The Virtue of Penance

The Effects of Penance

Contrition

Confession

Satisfaction

Indulgences

The Minister of Penance

CHAPTER VII

Penance

BY HIS PASSION AND DEATH, Christ has made it possible for every man to reach the vision of God. The power of Christ's Passion comes to men through the sacraments. In baptism men die to sin and are spiritually reborn in the grace of God. In confirmation those who have been baptized attain spiritual maturity. In the holy Eucharist men receive the spiritual food which nourishes their souls with grace and protects them against sin. If God's grace destroyed the free will of men, we could say that these three sacraments would infallibly save all those who received them. But grace does not destroy free will. As long as men remain in this life, they are free. They can fall from grace by sin. Christ knew that many men would lose grace by personal mortal sins committed after baptism. In His mercy, He has given men a remedy for the sins committed after baptism. This remedy is the sacrament of penance.

PENANCE IS A SACRAMENT, a sacred sign, through which God's grace is given to men for the forgiveness of their sins. The sacred sign consists of the words and acts of the penitent, and the acts of the priest who pronounces God's pardon to the sinner. The matter of this sacrament is found in the words and acts of the sinner seeking pardon. They are the sinner's contrition, or sorrow for sin, his confession of his sins to a priest, and the satisfaction which he performs for his sin. The remote matter of penance is the sins of the penitent. These sins are to be destroyed by the sacrament. The proximate matter is the acts of the penitent, his contrition, confession and satisfaction for sin. The form of the sacrament is the formula of absolution which the priest pronounces: "I absolve you from your sins, in the name of the Father, and of the Son, and of the Holy Ghost. Amen." Through this sensible sign, the grace of God is restored to the sinner; his sins are forgiven and the gates of heaven are reopened to him.

IT MUST NOT BE THOUGHT that penance—or, as it is popularly known, confession—gives men license to commit sin at will. The sacrament of penance demands acts of the virtue of penance. By the virtue of penance, a man detests his past sins as offenses against God. He is determined to destroy these sins as far as it is possible to do so. This does not mean that he can undo his past sinful acts. What is done cannot be undone. But he can remake his will. He can withdraw it from his sins, by renouncing them, by determining never to forsake God again through sin, and by resolving to make satisfaction to God for his sins. By his sins he sought creatures to the exclusion of God. In penance he renounces creatures for God. In this way he restores the order of justice which was destroyed by his sins. By his sins he refused God the obedience which was due to Him. In penance he turns once again to God in obedience. The penitence of the sinner may begin with servile fear. The sinner is in terror of the pains of hell which await him, or he fears the loss of heaven. But then he begins to hope for pardon. This leads him to love God, Who is merciful, and so to fear God as a child fears a loving father. This true repentance gives the sinner a habitual displeasure at his past sins. It leads him to resolve never to do anything contrary to the love of God. The sacrament of penance demands true repentance in the sinner. Hence, it can never be a license to sin in the future. The thief who seeks absolution on Saturday, while intending to rob a bank on Monday, is wasting his time. The sacrament produces grace only in those who are truly sorry for their sins.

IF A SINNER IS SINCERELY REPENTANT, the sacrament of penance is an instrument of divine mercy forgiving his sins and restoring to him the grace of God. Because it is an instrument of God, it is all powerful. There is no sin which cannot be forgiven in this sacrament. Man's will is free. He can always repent of his sin in this life. The Passion of Christ has won for men the forgiveness of all sins. Through the sacrament of penance, the power of Christ's Passion is applied to the soul of the contrite sinner for the pardon of his sins. The sinner must be repentant. This implies that he must be sorry for all his mortal sins—those he remembers, and those he may have forgotten. The man who is sorry that he murdered his neighbor, but not sorry that he stole five thousand dollars from him, cannot obtain pardon through penance. Such a man is trying to say simultaneously, "I love God more than anything else," and "I love five thousand dollars more than God." True repentance demands that a man love God more than anything else. This means that he will be sorry for any and all mortal sins. When he has this kind of sorrow, the sacrament of penance will release him from sin and the eternal penalty of his sins. If his contrition is very intense, it may even release him from the temporal punishment due to his sins.

THE SACRAMENT OF PENANCE can also forgive venial sins. Since venial sins do not expel grace and charity from the soul, the sacrament of penance is not necessary for their forgiveness. They can be forgiven through any new infusion of grace in the reception of any of the sacraments. They can be blotted out of the soul by any movement of charity in the will. The use of the sacramentals of the Church— holy water, blessings, and so on—will also remove venial sin from the soul. But the sacrament of penance can also bring about the remission of venial sin. As in the case of mortal sin, the sinner must be repentant. If a man receives the sacrament while clinging to a venial sin, that venial sin will not be forgiven in the sacrament.

PENANCE REMITS SIN by infusing grace into the soul of the sinner. It restores to the sinner his dignity as a son of God. Naturally, with the infusion of grace, the supernatural virtues are also reinfused into the soul. Moreover, with this reintroduction of grace and the virtues, the merit of the sinner's past meritorious works is also restored to him. Every good act that he performed while previously in the state of grace was meritorious of eternal life. By his sin he lost the right to the reward of these supernatural acts. But through penance this right is given back to him. It is worth remembering, also, that the good acts of the sinner, while he was in the state of mortal sin, were dead in the supernatural order. Obviously, penance cannot give life to something that was always dead. Hence, not even penance can make such acts meritorious.

THREE THINGS ARE REQUIRED on the part of the penitent, if his sins are to be forgiven in the sacrament of penance: contrition, confession and satisfaction. Contrition is sorrow for sin. Now there are two kinds of sorrow. There is the passion, or feeling of sorrow, and there is that rational detestation of sin as an offence against God which is a deliberate choice of the will. It is this second type of sorrow which is necessary in penance. The glutton may be very sad because his overeating has given him indigestion, but this sorrow will not bring forgiveness. He is sorry for his indigestion, not for his offence against God. The contrition which brings forgiveness of sin in penance is a rational sorrow for sin because it is an offence against God. It extends to all the actual personal sins which the sinner has committed. It includes a resolve to avoid all mortal sins in the future. Contrition is based on the love of God. The sinner renounces his sins because they are offences against God, Who is all good and supremely lovable in Himself.

CONTRITION, as an act of virtue, can bring about the remission of sins. It is important to note, however, that true contrition always includes the desire and the intention to go to confession and receive the sacrament of penance. By the will of God, the sacrament of penance is the ordinary means by which the sins committed after baptism are to be forgiven. Now a man cannot be truly contrite unless he intends to fulfil the will of God. Hence the contrite man will desire to receive the sacrament of penance.

AS ONE OF THE ACTS of the sacrament of penance, contrition brings about the remission of sins. In this case it is an instrument in the hands of God. It is a part of the sacramental sign which God uses to blot out sin by the infusion of grace. In the sacrament, however, perfect contrition is not necessary. Attrition—imperfect contrition—is sufficient. When a man has perfect contrition, he is sorry because God is good and lovable in Himself. When a man has only attrition, he is sorry because he fears to lose heaven or be condemned to hell. In the mercy of God, either contrition or attrition suffices in the sacrament of penance. But both must be real, that is, the sinner must be prepared to give up anything rather than remain in the state of sin.

THE SINNER MUST CONFESS his sins to a priest. In confession, he must reveal to the priest all the mortal sins committed since baptism which he has never submitted to a priest for absolution. He must declare these sins in so far as it is possible for him to do so. He must confess them accurately, giving their number and kind, the external acts which flowed from them, and any aggravating circumstances which might increase their guilt. If the penitent cannot remember any particular sin, obviously he is not obliged to confess it. If he cannot remember any mortal sins at all, then he should confess a venial sin of which he is conscious, or at least some past sin previously confessed. The sacrament of penance is given for the forgiveness of sins, and therefore some sin must be confessed. If the penitent does not confess his sins properly, the priest will safeguard the integrity of the confession by asking questions designed to obtain the necessary information. Penitents should not resent the questions asked by the priest. If the confession is not made properly according to the ability of the penitent, the sacrament will not produce the desired grace. The priest asks questions, not out of idle curiosity or excessive severity, but for the sake of the penitent and the sacrament he desires to receive. A person should confess his sins to a priest as often as it is necessary. The person in mortal sin is in danger of losing his soul. When such a person is in danger of death, he must confess his sins and seek absolution. Or if a person wishes to receive Communion, and he is in mortal sin, he must first go to confession to receive absolution. By the law of the Church, every adult must go to Communion at least once a year; he must make his Easter duty. If he is in mortal sin, he must go to confession before he makes his Easter duty. When we consider the danger of sudden death, it is apparent that a wise man will seek pardon in the sacrament of penance as soon as possible after he has fallen into sin. The confession of sins in this sacrament is not an easy thing. The pride of men rebels at the thought of revealing their sins to another man. But it is a good thing for men. In the first place, a sincere, contrite confession will bring pardon and restore the friendship of God. Secondly, the shame which men endure voluntarily in confessing their sins will help to lessen the punishment due to their sins. It should also help them to avoid sin in the future.

MOREOVER, PEOPLE SHOULD NOT BE KEPT from this sacrament by the fear that their sins may be made known to the world. In the confessional the priest acts as the representative of God, hearing secrets known to God alone. The knowledge which the priest learns in the confessional belongs to God alone. The priest is under a serious obligation never to reveal it directly or indirectly to anyone. Unless the penitent gives the confessor permission to reveal his sins to someone, the seal of the confession is absolute.

WHEN A MAN HAS CONFESSED his sins properly and with contrition, the priest gives him absolution and imposes a penance which the sinner must accept and perform as a satisfaction to God for his sins. To make satisfaction for sin is a work of justice.

By his sins the penitent has offended God. When he performs the penance imposed on him by the priest, he repays God for the injury inflicted on God by his sins. This work of satisfaction is necessary if the sacrament is to achieve its effect—the forgiveness of sin and the restoration of grace. The penitent must accept the penance given by the priest and intend to perform it. If he does not, then the absolution will not bring pardon for sin nor restore grace.

THE PRINCIPAL MEANS of satisfaction for sin are fasting, prayer and almsgiving. By fasting the sinner chastises his body for the sins of the body. In prayer he turns to God his soul which had deserted God in sin. When he gives alms, the sinner freely deprives himself of those external possessions through whose pursuit or abuse he had forsaken God.

THE WORKS OF SATISFACTION are effective only when they are acceptable to God. The sinner must be in the state of grace, and his acts of penance must be informed by charity. When a man in the state of grace performs acts of penance for sin, he pays the debt of his sins and strengthens himself against future sin.

BECAUSE ALL THE MEMBERS of the Church are one in Christ, it is even possible for men to make satisfaction for the sins of others. They cannot, of course, furnish a remedy to others against future sin. One man's fast does not tame another man's body. But a man can pay the debt of punishment for another man's sin. This possibility is based on the bond of charity which makes all the members of the Church members of one family. As members of one spiritual family, they can help one another to pay the debt of sin. It is this same principle which is the foundation of the Church's practice of granting indulgences. An indulgence is the remission, in whole or in part, of the temporal punishment due to sin. It is not a forgiveness of sins, but a remission of the temporal penalty for sin. In fact, no one can gain an indulgence unless he is in the state of grace, united with Christ in charity. Indulgences are granted from the great treasury of merits gained and satisfactions made by Christ, His Blessed Mother and the saints. They are granted by the Church to those who are living members of the Church through charity.

IN THE SACRAMENT OF PENANCE the penitent must confess his sins to a priest. This requirement has been established by God Himself. When Christ gave His Apostles the power to forgive sins, He said to them: "Receive ye the Holy Ghost. Whose sins you shall forgive, they are forgiven them: and whose sins you shall retain, they are retained" (*John* XX, 22-23). Obviously, Christ did not mean that the Apostles were to forgive or refuse to forgive sins by an arbitrary decision based on their own whims, fancies or idiosyncrasies. They were to exercise this tremendous power and authority with discretion, with judgment. But the Apostles and the priests who inherit this power from them must know the state of the penitent —his sinfulness and his repentance—if they are to make a prudent judgment. This is possible only when the penitent makes known the state of his soul by a contrite confession of his sins. Moreover, the decision which the priest makes to grant or to refuse absolution is an act of authority. Because it is such, the priest needs not only the power of holy orders but also a share in the governing power of the Church. As the theologians say, he must have "jurisdiction." This jurisdiction must be given him by one who possesses it by reason of his office, the bishop of the diocese.

CHRIST HAS GIVEN THIS GREAT POWER to His priests for the salvation of the faithful. It is a proof of God's infinite mercy to men. In the sacrament of penance, the voice of Christ Himself is heard down through the centuries repeating over and over, "Thy sins are forgiven thee." St. Peter asked Christ: "Lord, how often shall my brother offend against me, and I forgive him? Till seven times?" Jesus replied: "I say not to thee, till seven times, but till seventy times seven times" (*Matt.* XVIII, 21-22). By the sacrament of penance Christ forgives man, His brother, "seventy times seven times." He came into this world to save men from sin. His mercy will not be denied. In the face of so great a love, who will be ungrateful?

CHAPTER VIII

Extreme Unction

CHAPTER VIII

Extreme Unction

THE SOUL OF A MAN in the state of mortal sin is spiritually dead. By the reception of the sacrament of penance, that soul comes to life again. Penance is a spiritual resurrection. But the recovery of spiritual life through penance may not be absolutely perfect. The use of penicillin may rescue a man from death by pneumonia, but the disease may leave the man weak and inclined to ill health or subsequent disease. Sin acts in the same way. Even after original sin or actual sin is forgiven in the sacraments of baptism or penance, sin may leave its traces in man. Even after a sinner has been justified by God's grace, his mind may still be lacking the perfect vigor needed to perform well the supernatural acts of grace or glory. This weakness in man is called the remnant of sin. Just as any physical or mental weakness will prevent a man from entering fully into the joys of living, so also the spiritual weakness of the remnants of sin will prevent a man from entering into the joys of glory, the joys of the vision of God. The soul must be cured of these remnants of sin before it is ready for the vision of God. Christ instituted the sacrament of extreme unction to remove the remnants of sin from the souls of men, and prepare them for the vision of God.

IN EXTREME UNCTION those who are in danger of death are anointed with oil, while the priest says: "Through this holy unction, and His most tender mercy, may the Lord pardon thee whatever sins thou hast committed, by sight, hearing, smell, taste, word, touch or step." As the priest says the appropriate words he anoints in turn the eyes, ears, nostrils, lips, hands and feet. The symbolism of the sacrament is simple and clear. Men anoint their bodies to give them health and strength. In this sacrament, the priest anoints the body of the sick person to signify the healing of the soul. Oil is used because it is both gentle and penetrating. Violent remedies for bodily sickness often cause a sick man to lose hope. In extreme unction the use of oil shows that the sick man must not lose the hope of salvation. Again, oil is a penetrating liquid. It seeks to cover and penetrate any surface on which it is poured. It is used in extreme unction to signify the completeness, the perfection of the effect of the sacrament, the total removal of the remnants of sin.

T HE DIRECT EFFECT of this sacrament is the destruction of the remnants of sin in the soul. Extreme unction will remove the weakness of mind that prevents a man from living fully the life of grace and glory. It will even remove the debt of punishment due to his sins. In a word, if worthily received, this wonderful sacrament will prepare a man for immediate admission to heaven.

S HOULD THE DYING MAN be in the state of sin, extreme unction will also remit the guilt of his sins, if he has the proper dispositions. The sacrament infuses sanctifying grace into the soul of the sick man. But sanctifying grace expels mortal sin. Hence the sacrament expels sin from the soul. Normally, however, this sacrament should be received by a man when he is in the state of grace and there is no need to remove mortal sin from the soul.

S OMETIMES THIS SACRAMENT not only heals the soul of the sick man, but it restores his bodily health as well. This effect is not due to the medicinal properties of the oil or the anointing. It is due to the power of God. If God sees that the spiritual health of the sick man depends on, or can be advanced by the recovery of bodily health, He will achieve this effect through this sacrament.

THE PRIEST is the minister of extreme unction. He can administer it only to those who are ill, and whose illness places them in danger of death. This condition for the reception of the sacrament is inherent in the very sacramental sign itself. In extreme unction, the sign signifies the curing of the soul which is sick with the remnants of sin. But if the man anointed were not ill, then the anointing of his body could not signify the healing of his soul. To anoint a man who is well is to make a lying gesture, at best a futile gesture. Then too, this sacrament is intended to prepare a man for the glory of heaven. But man reaches this glory only after death. Hence this sacrament should be conferred only on those who are in danger of death. Since men sometimes recover their health, even though they have been mortally ill, this sacrament can be repeated as often as a man finds himself in a new danger of death through illness.

THE ANOINTING OF THE BODY in extreme unction signifies that the soul is being cured of the remnants of sin. Every sin, as a free, voluntary act, involves knowledge and action. The senses of man—sight, hearing, and so on—are anointed, because they are the ordinary and original source of knowledge to men. The feet are anointed because they symbolize the motive power by which man moves himself to sin.

EXTREME UNCTION is not given to infants, even when they are in danger of death. In their case, baptism removes both original sin and the penalty of sin. Hence they have no need of extreme unction to prepare them for heaven. Of course, the same truth applies to all those human beings who are equivalent to infants: idiots, imbeciles and madmen who have never had the use of reason. Since they could commit no personal mortal sins, they need no sacrament but baptism. Besides, the fruitful reception of this sacrament depends on the dispositions of the person receiving the sacrament. But only those who have the use of reason are capable of disposing themselves for this sacrament.

EXTREME UNCTION will achieve its effect in proportion to the good dispositions of those who receive it. When we consider the objective of this sacrament— to prepare a man for the vision of God—the importance of proper dispositions is apparent. The better a man prepares himself to receive this sacrament by acts of faith, hope and charity, or contrition for sin, the readier he will be to receive the vision of God at his death. It is, then, no kindness to a dying man to defer this sacrament until he is so ill—perhaps even unconscious—that he cannot dispose himself properly to receive it.

EXTREME UNCTION is another proof of the love and thoughtfulness of God. He knows that impending death is a fearful trial to men. Then, if ever, the weakness of men's minds and hearts may lead them to sin and despair. This sacrament gives them strength and hope in the face of death. God knows, also, that many men are so imperfect that the moment of death will not find them fully prepared for the vision of Himself. By this sacrament He wishes to prepare them perfectly for eternity. Extreme unction is the hand of God reaching down to lift man up to ultimate happiness.

CHAPTER IX

Holy Orders

The Matter and Form of
Holy Orders

The Effects of Holy Orders

Preparation for Holy Orders

Other Christs

CHAPTER IX

Holy Orders

To the good Catholic, the most beloved member of his community is the priest. It is the priest who is the proximate source of the spiritual life of the community. The priest baptizes the new members of the community, giving them that spiritual birth which makes them children of God and heirs of heaven. He acts as a mediator between God and men, offering to God the holy sacrifice of the Mass, and bringing to men the divine graces which lead them to the vision of God. At the altar rail he gives men the Body and Blood of Christ to nourish their souls with grace. In the confessional he forgives the sins of men and restores them to the friendship of God. When they are dying, he comes to absolve them from their sins, to give them Viaticum and to anoint them for their journey to heaven. Like Christ—and the priest is truly "another Christ"—he is the center of the spiritual life of the members of Christ's Body, the Church.

The priest is a man of power and authority. By his preaching, example and counsel, he directs the lives of his parishioners in accordance with the revealed wisdom of God and the laws of the Church. In his administration of the sacraments and blessings of the Church, he is the human channel through which the power of the Passion of Christ is transmitted to men for their salvation. No man could give himself such power or arrogate to himself such authority. No mere man could even dare to choose himself for so stupendous a role in the life of men. Only God can make a man a priest, and He does so in the sacrament of holy orders.

HOLY ORDERS IS A SACRAMENT, a sacred sign of a holy thing. The sacred sign consists of the imposition of the bishop's hands on the head of the man to be ordained, and the words which the bishop pronounces in conjunction with the imposition of hands. The imposition of hands is the matter of this sacrament, and the words pronounced by the bishop are its form.

HOLY ORDERS gives the priest an increase of sanctifying grace. He is to communicate grace to others. He must be filled with grace himself. The sacrament also gives the priest the sacramental character of orders, an indelible spiritual power in his soul which gives him a share in the priesthood of Christ. This character gives the priest the power to offer the sacrifice of the Mass and to administer the sacraments to the people. The reception of the sacrament of holy orders also gives the priest a title to all the graces he will need to carry out his priestly functions worthily. If we recall the many priestly tasks which the priest must perform in his lifetime, it will be seen that this sacrament brings to the priest a veritable torrent of graces for his own sanctification and the sanctification of the world.

THE POWER AND DIGNITY which this sacrament gives to a man explain the solicitude with which the Church prepares its candidates for the priesthood. They must be recommended by the pastor of their parishes. They must be trained in all the ordinary intellectual disciplines which constitute the splendor of a well educated man. When they have completed their training in the arts, the sciences and in philosophy, they must study the science of theology for at least four years. They must also be trained in the exercise of all the virtues until they are men dedicated wholly to God and to God's people. Because they are to be leaders of the people, they cannot be ordained until they have reached maturity. The Church requires that candidates for the priesthood be twenty-four years of age before ordination. Before ordination, they must give proofs of the stability of their characters and the reality of their virtues. They must also pass an examination to prove their fitness for preaching the word of God, for offering the sacrifice of the Mass, and for administering the sacraments of the Church. Because of the extent of the powers given to them by this sacrament, they must be ordained by a bishop, that is, by someone who possesses the fullness of the priesthood of Christ.

WHEN A MAN BECOMES A PRIEST, he becomes another Christ. Before his ordination he received grace from others. But after ordination he can communicate grace to others. He is the active, human instrument through which the grace of Christ passes to men. This makes it apparent that holy orders is a social sacrament. Baptism, confirmation, Communion, penance and extreme unction sanctify the individual for his own advantage. But holy orders sanctifies a man for the benefit of others. It makes him holy so that he can communicate holiness to others. Holy orders has a social aim—the spiritual care and rule of the Christian community. It is through the priesthood that Christ provides for the continuance of the spiritual life of the Church. In priests Christ still walks the earth, seeking the salvation of men, preaching the Gospel, administering the sacraments of His grace. By the agency of His priests, Christ still offers Himself to His Father as the eternal Victim of the sacrifice of the Mass, acknowledging God's dominion over the universe, thanking Him for His gifts, praying to Him for the needs of men, and expiating men's sins. With His priests Christ visits the sick, comforts the afflicted, gives alms to the poor, shelters the homeless, instructs the ignorant, feeds the hungry, and forgives the sinner.

THE IMPORTANCE of the priest's role as mediator between God and men makes it necessary for the Church to see that no unworthy or unsuitable candidate is raised to the priesthood. She has drawn up a long list of the impediments which render a man unfit for the reception of holy orders. It is the duty of the bishop to see that no unfit candidate receives this sacrament.

THE DIGNITY AND POWER of the priesthood are derived from the dignity and power of Christ Himself. The priest receives them, not for his own vainglory, but for the salvation of men. They are a sacred trust, a holy responsibility given him by God. He stands before God and men, a mediator between both. The magnitude of his task appalls him, but the grace of holy orders sustains him. He is another Christ, not by his own merit, but by the love and the power of Christ. Through the sacrament of holy orders, Christ lives in him and acts through him for the salvation of men, for the building up of the Church, the Mystical Body of Christ.

CHAPTER X

Matrimony

CHAPTER X

Matrimony

IN THE LONG HISTORY of man on earth, no institution has been more admired, nor more sought after than the institution of marriage. Married life is the state of life which the majority of human beings choose for themselves. In so choosing they are following one of the deepest instincts of human nature. In the first place, it is through marriage that the human race propagates and so preserves itself. Without marriage and the children that are born, educated and developed in marriage, the human race would perish from the face of the earth. Secondly, nature itself shows men that the two sexes exist to be of mutual help to one another. Neither sex is complete without the other. The man, for example, may be quite capable of working for a living for himself and his family, but not so capable of making a home, rearing and forming the character of his children. The woman, on the other hand, may not be so capable of earning a livelihood for herself and her family. But she is very versatile in the making of a home, in the care and training of children. In the building and the maintenance of a human family the man and the woman complement each other. They pool their talents, as it were, and make up for each other's deficiencies. In this way they round out each other's personalities, for their own advantage and for the preservation of the human race.

MATRIMONY, then, is an institution of nature. It is nature's way of preserving the human race. The natural law imposes on the human race the obligation of preserving itself through marriage. This precept of the natural law is binding on the race, but not on particular men or women. Nature's only concern is that the race of man be preserved. This means that the human race must beget children, but it does not mean that every man and woman must be involved in the begetting of children. Only on the supposition that the human race was in imminent danger of perishing through a lack of children, could any argument be advanced that all men and women should marry and produce offspring.

CHILDREN ARE BEGOTTEN by the sexual union between a man and a woman. But marriage is much more than a casual union of the sexes. In the lower orders of the animal kingdom, a casual encounter between the sexes may be all that is necessary to preserve in existence a particular type of animal. In such cases, either the female of the species is able to care for her offspring until it can fend for itself, or the newborn animal is already perfectly equipped to take care of itself. But human beings are different. The newborn infant cannot care for itself. It must be protected and nourished by its parents for a long period of time. It must be educated intellectually and spiritually. This demands a stable union between the man and woman who beget children to one another. They must give themselves to one another; they must help one another; they must live a common life. Only in this way can nature's primary purpose in marriage be achieved. Nature preserves the human race, not by casual unions between the two sexes, but in the permanent union of matrimony.

IN THE ANIMAL KINGDOM below man, the union of the sexes for the preservation of the species is a matter of blind instinct. Given the appropriate circumstances, they cannot but unite to propagate their own kind. But among men, marriage is a matter of free choice. As we have just said, the human race must preserve itself, but no particular man or woman is obliged to fulfil this obligation. This is due primarily to the fact that the good of the community may also be advanced by the practice of virginity or of religious vows on the part of some. There is no doubt that the good example and the prayerful lives of those who dedicate themselves to God are of immense benefit to human society. We might mention here in passing that the attitude of the Western world toward celibacy and virginity is not quite honest. On the one hand, men will reproach the Catholic clergy, brothers and sisters for not marrying and begetting children. On the other hand, they will often, though married and with the obligations of marriage, do all they can, by artificial birth control, to prevent the birth of children. But perhaps this mistaken attitude will only help to emphasize the point we are making here. Marriage is a human institution, a state of life of human beings. It involves the granting of rights to one's own person and body, and the assumption of permanent and serious obligations. To grant rights over one's self, to assume obligations—these are human actions. They are, therefore, free actions.

SINCE MARRIAGE involves rights and obligations, it involves the virtue of justice. Marriage, as an institution of nature, is essentially a contract—a contract between a man and a woman, whereby they give to one another the right to use one another's bodies for the procreation of children. But contracts are subject to the virtue of justice. Matrimony, then, is founded on the bedrock of justice. Without justice, no marriage can be a marriage; without justice, no marriage can be successful.

L ET US HASTEN TO ADD that justice does not destroy the romance or the love of marriage. On the contrary, justice is the indispensable basis of real love. Can a man really love a woman, if he will not respect her rights? A man may remember his wife's birthday and their wedding anniversary. On such occasions he may send her flowers, give her expensive presents, take her to dinner and the theatre. But if, all the while, he is unfaithful to her, he does not really love her. If she should discover his treason to their marriage, what seemed to be love will turn to ashes in her mouth. Without justice, there is no true love. The great love which should flourish between husband and wife must be founded on justice, on respect for the marriage contract.

I N MATRIMONY, two people surrender themselves to one another to beget children and to lead a common life. The mutual self-surrender of matrimony demands a life of self-sacrifice from husband and wife. The common marital life they are to lead can be successful only if it is based on love and justice. They must face joy and pain together, triumph and defeat. The dangers and difficulties of married life can be surmounted only by great virtue. That is why it is important to remember that matrimony is not only a contract; it is also a sacrament. Christ has raised the contract of marriage to the dignity of a sacrament. He made it a symbol of the union between Himself and His Church.

L IKE ALL THE SACRAMENTS, matrimony is a sensible sign of an inward grace. The remote matter of the sacrament is the very persons of those contracting marriage. The proximate matter is the signs or words by which each gives to the other the rights over his own body for the ends of marriage. The form is the mutual external acceptance of these rights. The ministers of this sacrament are the contracting parties themselves. This is the only sacrament which lay Catholics can ordinarily give themselves. The priest who officiates at a wedding only assists at and blesses the marriage; he is not the minister of the sacrament. The sacrament, like all the sacraments, gives sanctifying grace to the couple who receive it. It also gives them a title to all the graces necessary to make their marriage happy and successful. This means that God will give them all the supernatural help they may need through all the years of their married life. In all the trials and difficulties, dangers and disappointments they may have to face, they can call upon God for the help they need. Because they have received this sacrament, they have a right to the divine assistance to preserve the happiness and the holiness of their marriage.

THE SACRAMENTAL SIGN is perfected in the making of the marriage contract. In the contract of marriage, we can distinguish its cause, its essence and its effect. The cause of the marriage is the mutual consent of the people who marry one another. The essence of marriage is the union which results from this consent. The effect is the common life to which the bride and groom dedicate themselves.

THE CONSENT, which is the cause of the marriage, has as its object the persons of the contracting parties; the consent is a deliberate surrender of rights over their own bodies for the purpose of marriage, the procreation of children. We must remember here that marriage, both as an institution of nature and as a sacrament, is good. Its primary end—or purpose—is good. Hence, the sexual act by which married persons procreate children is neither shameful nor evil. Marriage is in accord with the natural law. It is even a divine command, for God told Adam and Eve to "increase and multiply." Once the contract of marriage is made, it is a matter of justice for the husband and wife to give each other the use of their bodies for the purposes of marriage. In marriage, then, the sexual act can be a matter of virtue. When married people perform this act with one another as a payment of their marital debt to each other, it is an act of justice. When they perform it in order to procreate children to worship God, it is an act of religion. Because this act can be virtuous, it can also be meritorious of grace and glory. It is not Christian to consider marriage or the marital act as something evil. On the other hand, it is also worth remembering that the marriage contract is concerned with the transfer of the right to the use of the body. It does not demand the actual use of the body. The rights must be transferred, but they need not be used. The Blessed Virgin Mary was really married to St. Joseph, even though neither one ever used the rights which they had given one another.

TO RECEIVE THE SACRAMENT of matrimony validly, a person must be baptized and free to marry. He must manifest his consent in some sensible way. He must give his consent in the presence of a priest and two witnesses. If he would receive the sacrament lawfully, he must also be free from any of the impediments which would make the marriage illicit. To receive the grace which the sacrament confers, he must be in the state of grace when he receives the sacrament of matrimony.

MATRIMONY IS AN INSTITUTION of nature and a sacrament. It is good and holy. It will, therefore, bring blessings or good things to those who enter the married state. The blessings of matrimony are the child, the good of faith and the good of the sacrament. The child is the first blessing of marriage. The child is the expression and the fruit of the mutual love of husband and wife. Children are both the primary end of marriage and the first good or blessing of marriage. In the child, the parents fulfil their duty to the human race, to society. In the child, the parents find their own happiness, for the child is something of both of them. By caring for him, educating him for life in the world, they perfect themselves in the virtues of love and self-sacrifice. By impressing upon him the outlines of their own personalities, they have, in a wide sense of the word, made themselves immortal in the history of man on earth.

THE SECOND BLESSING of marriage is the good of faith. Basically, the good of faith means the fidelity which husband and wife owe to one another. By the marriage contract they have, as it were, deeded themselves to one another and to no one else. The good of faith, then, demands that they should render the marital debt—the marital act—to one another whenever it may be legitimately sought. It also demands that they should never surrender the use of this right to any other person. Over and above this fundamental obligation, the good of faith signifies the mutual trust and confidence that husband and wife give to one another. Fidelity to the marriage bond makes a man and a woman two in one flesh. Mutual trust and confidence make them two in one spirit.

THE THIRD BLESSING of matrimony is the good of the sacrament. As a sacrament, matrimony is a special good in itself. As a sacrament, it gives the married couple the sacramental grace to make their marriage happy and holy. As a sacrament, it is a sign of the indissoluble union between Christ and His Church. To be a sign of this indissoluble union, matrimony must itself be indissoluble. The union between Christ and His Church can never be broken. The union between a husband and his wife in the sacrament of matrimony can never be broken as long as they both shall live.

IN ITSELF, MATRIMONY is a noble institution. As a sacrament, it is a holy institution, a symbol of the union between Christ and the Church. But in the world in which we live today, many men seek to degrade it, to make it a plaything of human desire, a toy for lust and selfishness. The destruction of the institution of matrimony involves the destruction of the goods or blessings of marriage. Those who advocate or practice artificial birth control or abortion, those who abandon children or neglect to raise them properly, sin against the blessing of children. Those who practice or condone adultery attack the fidelity of the marriage bond. Those who refuse the legitimate use of the marriage act also sin against the fidelity of marriage. Those who allow or seek divorce and remarriage attack the indissolubility of the marital union.

IN A WORLD THAT CONDONES and even exalts these attacks on the sanctity of matrimony, it is no wonder that the Church insists that persons contemplating marriage should think long and seriously before they enter the marriage contract. The obligations of marriage are serious and long lasting. They should not be assumed without careful consideration of all the factors involved. Since the primary purpose of marriage is the procreation of children for the preservation of the race, matrimony is a social institution. The family is the fundamental unit of society. Hence society as such is interested in every marriage. It has a stake in every marriage. The Church, too, exists and functions not just for individuals, but for society. She also has an interest in every Christian marriage. The man and woman who contemplate entering the married state must recognize their obligations to society, and the right of society and the Church to make regulations for the proper celebration of matrimony. The regulations of the Church are made for the protection of the marriage and of the persons involved. The publication of the banns of marriage is intended to forestall the ruin of the marriage, that would ensue if one or both of the parties were not really free to marry. The form of the marriage ceremony, that is, the making of the marriage contract in the presence of a priest and two witnesses, is a protection of the marriage bond. No one can deny a contract made in the presence of witnesses.

THE CHURCH ALSO LISTS many impediments which make an attempted marriage either illicit or invalid. These impediments are obstacles to the perfection of a marriage. Some of these obstacles make it unlawful for the parties concerned to enter the marriage contract, but if the contract is made the marriage is valid, it is a real marriage. Others make the marriage invalid, that is, it is not a marriage at all. The existence of these impediments and their danger to the perfection of a marriage make it imperative for

Catholics to follow the regulations of the Church when they plan to be married.

WHEN, HOWEVER, CATHOLICS are properly married in the Church, the dignity and power of the sacrament should be uppermost in their minds. They have entered a sacred union, a union that symbolizes to the world the sacred union between Christ and His Church. It is a union which God blesses with His grace. The common life that flows from this union may be difficult, even, at times, disappointing and exasperating. But the grace of God accompanies those who have received the sacrament of matrimony. With His grace, no problem is too big to be solved, no danger too fearful to be faced and overcome. The man and the woman who have received the sacrament of matrimony worthily, who have married one another in God and in Christ, will find the love, the peace and the happiness of Christ in their married life.

CHAPTER XI

The End and the Beginning

Death

The Particular Judgment

The Souls of the Departed

Purgatory

The Resurrection

The General Judgment

Heaven

Hell

The Choice

CHAPTER XI

The End and The Beginning

WHEN WE ARE YOUNG, we dream dreams of the future. But the future then is always a future in this present world. Because we are young and because anything is possible to the dreams of the young, the future is always bright and gay and happy. When we are older, we are perhaps content to take the triumphs and the defeats, the hopes and the disappointments of life as they come to us. But in odd moments, in times of rest and even in times of stress, the farseeing eye of youth returns to us. But then we wonder not so much about the future that may await us in this world as about the future that may await us in the world to come. Is there really a life after death? What will it be like? What part shall we play in it? Of course, we are only asking again the old question, "What is the meaning of life?" If you have come thus far with us in this book, you really know the answer to these questions. You will not ask them as if you were seeking information. You will ask them as one who yearns for the reality that awaits you in the future. You will ask them like the man who, in the midst of a trying day, will groan, "Will this day never end?" He knows the day will end. But he yearns for the rest and peace which the end of the day will bring.

WHAT WILL THE END OF LIFE bring to men? We all know that death will come to us. We must all die. But after death, what? You know that the soul of man survives his body. You know that man's final goal is the vision of God. But you also know that it is possible for man to fail to achieve this goal. What happens to the human being who is unworthy of the vision of God? In this chapter we shall try to answer such questions as these. Naturally, what we say will be based chiefly on what God Himself has told us. No one of us has gone beyond this world and returned to tell us what awaits us. We must rely on the wisdom of God as it is revealed to us. Only God knows for certain what lies as yet in the dim future for all mankind.

AS WE HAVE ALREADY SEEN, this present life is a time of trial. We are being tested. If we live well, if we live according to the will of God, our human acts will merit for us the reward of the vision of God. But the fact is that we face the possibilities of success or failure, of triumph or defeat. In either case, the outcome of the trial is determined by our own free choice. We can choose God and happiness, or we can reject God and choose unhappiness. The point to remember is that we can make the choice only in this present life. After death we cannot change our minds. As we die, so shall we live after death. If we die seeking God, we shall find God. If we die rejecting God, then we shall lose God for all eternity. After death each man faces his own particular judgment. As St. Paul has said, "It is appointed unto man once to die, and after this the judgment." (*Heb.* IX, 27.)

IMMEDIATELY AFTER DEATH, each man must undergo his own particular judgment. The moment of judgment will indeed be an awe-inspiring experience for each human being. When a matador stands alone in the bull ring, with nothing but a cape, a sword and his courage between himself and death, men say that he stands in the "Hour of truth." Either he will kill the bull cleanly with one expert thrust of the sword, or he will be killed himself, or he will miss his chance and have to return again to the "Hour of truth." In the bull ring, the "Hour of truth" is the moment in which the bullfighter proves himself, the instant in which he passes the test of his training, skill and courage. There is an "Hour of truth" for every human being, a moment in which he proves his virtue, his love and his readiness to see God. This is the moment of his particular judgment. In that moment, he will either be judged worthy of heaven and so enter it in triumph; or he will be judged unworthy and so be condemned to the defeat of hell; or he will be judged worthy of heaven, but as yet not fully prepared, and he will be sent to purgatory to be purified for his entrance into heaven.

IN ONE SENSE, it is God Who judges the souls of men after death. It is God Who knows their lives and their human actions even better than they themselves. He knows to the last little detail the state of each soul at death. As the Lord and Master of all men, it is His right to reward, or punish, or purify the souls of men. It is God, then, Who will pronounce judgment on the souls of men at the moment of death. But, in another sense, it is men who will pass judgment on themselves. At the moment of judgment, the soul which has left its body in death will see clearly its own merits and demerits, its own love or lack of love for God. In a moment of blinding clarity, God will infuse this perfect self-knowledge into the soul which has left the world of time and space. The soul will see the absolute justice of the judgment of God. In that very instant, the soul will ascend to the heights of heaven, fall to the fires of purgatory for a time, or descend forever into hell. In that "Hour of truth" each soul will know itself perfectly and see the truth of its own judgment.

WHEN A HUMAN SOUL IS SEPARATED from its body by death, the body dies, but the soul lives on forever. Without the body, without the five senses and the imagination, the soul would be incapable of knowing anything but itself and God. But God will infuse into such a soul all the knowledge which is suitable to it. The intellectual power of the soul remains, and God will not see it idle. Such a soul must go either to heaven, hell, purgatory or limbo. A spiritual substance, such as an angel or the separated soul of a man, is not by nature in any place, except in so far as it either acts in that place or is acted upon in that place. A demon, for example, is not in New York, except in so far as he acts in New York. Since he has no body, since he is purely spiritual, no place can be said to contain him except in so far as he is active in that place. If a demon tempts a public official in New York to take a bribe, at the moment of the temptation that demon can be said to be in New York. We must say the same of the separated souls of men after death. As spiritual substances, they are not naturally in any particular place. But sacred scripture seems to insinuate that both the demons and the souls of men are assigned by God to particular places: to heaven, hell, purgatory or limbo. Since the fate of angels and men differs according to their merits or demerits, it seems fitting that God should assign different places in which angels and men will be rewarded or punished. The souls of the just go to heaven to be rewarded; the souls of the damned go to hell to be punished; the souls of those who die in grace but are not yet ready for heaven go to an intermediate place called purgatory, where they will be purified or cleansed for heaven; and the souls of infants who died without baptism—or those who are equivalent to infants without baptism, idiots, imbeciles, and so on—will be sent to a place of purely natural happiness called limbo.

THE SOULS OF THE DEAD are not separated from all contact with this world in which we live. In the ordinary providence of God, they cannot come to us, nor can we speak to them with the ease promised by spiritualists and mediums. Neither the ouija board, nor spirit writing, nor table tapping is a means of communicating with the souls of the dead. It is possible that God has, on rare occasions, allowed an angel to appear to men in the guise of one of their relatives or friends. God may allow this in order that the living may be incited to pray for the dead or to mend their own sinful ways of life. God might even, by a miracle, allow a departed soul to assume the appearance of its own body for the same purposes. But such events are rare. Normally, the souls of the dead remain in their own places. They are in contact with us not in the sense that they can come to us or speak to us, but in the sense that they can know, through infused knowledge or through their vision of God, what we are doing and what is happening to us. Thus the saints can know that we are praying to them, asking them to intercede with God for us. Knowing this, they can intercede for us and so help us to attain their own salvation. Some theologians think that even the souls in purgatory can know us, and so can hear our prayers to them and intercede with God for us. Whether this be true or not, one thing is certain: the souls in purgatory need help, and we can give it to them.

THE SOULS IN PURGATORY have not lost God forever. They are the souls of men who died in grace. But they have not as yet fully paid the debt of punishment for their sins. Their souls are not yet fully cleansed of the remnants of sin. Hence, they are not fully prepared to enter the absolute purity and holiness of heaven. They must be cleansed and purified of the remnants of sin and the debt of sin. They know that they have merited the vision of God in heaven, and their souls are in agony until they achieve that happiness. Moreover, because of their attachment to sin and their unpaid debt of sin, they suffer from the fires of purgatory. As the name purgatory suggests, the fire purges them of the last stains of sin. Since these souls are purely spiritual, it seems clear that fire, simply as fire, cannot pain them. But, through the power of God, the fire of purgatory detains them from entering heaven, and this is punishment enough for a soul that burns with an ardent desire to see God.

THE SOULS IN PURGATORY are in the state of grace. They are united with the saints in heaven and with us here on earth by the bond of charity. They belong to the communion of saints. Hence, the saints in heaven and we ourselves can help them. That is why the Church offers Mass for them, urges us to pray for them, and to give alms to the poor for the release of the souls in purgatory. Whether or not the souls in purgatory can pray for us while they are still in purgatory, we can be sure that when they reach heaven through our assistance, they will remember us at the throne of God.

IF, AFTER DEATH, men were to remain disembodied souls for all eternity, we could conclude our long study of God and man with a few words about the pains of hell and the glories of heaven. But, as we said so long ago, God means man to be perfectly happy, and man cannot be perfectly happy unless he finds happiness both for his body and his soul. We might say that this is due fundamentally to the fact that man is not completely man unless he is a body and a soul. At any rate, it is God's intention to raise all men to life again in the body at the end of this present world. When the last man has been born and died, this present world will pass away, and God will remake the world. By His divine power, He will reunite the souls of men to their bodies. All men will rise again in their own bodies.

WE DO NOT KNOW the day nor the hour when this will take place. God has not revealed this to us. We know only that it will happen at the end of this present world. Sacred scripture tells us that it will come to pass when Christ comes into the world for the second time to judge all men. At His coming, He will bring to pass the resurrection of all men. He will do this by the power of His Godhead, but He will use His own humanity as the instrument through which His divine power will restore the souls of men to their bodies.

ST. THOMAS TELLS US that the risen bodies of men will have identity, integrity and quality. By identity he means that the souls of men will be reunited to their own bodies, the bodies which they had in this life. In other words, each man will be truly himself. The risen bodies will have integrity in the sense that they will be complete bodies. If a man in this present life is deformed, through an accident, or by amputation, or congenitally, at the resurrection his body will be complete, as it was meant to be. The resurrected bodies of men will have quality. This means that men will rise with perfect bodies, at the age of perfection—St. Thomas thinks this is at the age of thirty. Quality also implies that, since the bodies of men will be immortal for all eternity, there will be no need for men to eat or drink to sustain their lives.

THE BODIES OF THE SAINTS will also have the qualities of impassibility, subtlety, agility and clarity. After the resurrection, the glorified souls of the saints will have complete mastery over their bodies. This mastery will manifest itself in impassibility: by the power of the soul, the body will not be subject to any injury or suffering. By the power of the soul, the body will also be subtle: the body will be spiritual, that is, completely subject to the spirit of man. The risen body will also be agile: by the power of the soul, the body will be able to move from place to place almost with the speed of thought. The glorified bodies of the saints will also be gifted with clarity: the splendor of the soul enjoying the vision of God will flow over, as it were, into the body and give it the beauty of the divine light.

THE BODIES OF THE DAMNED will not, of course, possess these wonderful gifts. Their bodies will be complete and immortal. But they will have risen, not to glory, but to punishment. Since they made no real and constant effort to bring their bodies under the domination of their souls in this present life, they will not be given the glorious gifts which flow from the complete mastery of the body by the glorified soul.

IMMEDIATELY after the general resurrection of all men, the general judgment will take place. At that time, each man will recall the story of his whole life.

His conscience will remind him of his merits and de-merits, his good deeds and his sins. He will also see the lives of all other men, their virtue and their sinfulness. Those who died in the state of grace will see themselves and everyone else in their vision of God. In an instant, then, they will see the merits and the demerits of all men. The damned, who died in sin, will not be able to see the good or the evil of all men in this way; but God will strengthen their minds so that they also will see the merits and demerits of all men in a few moments.

THE GENERAL JUDGMENT evokes different reactions from different men. The proud, whether they be weak or strong, have no wish that their sins be revealed to others at the general judgment. They cannot tolerate the thought that their hidden weaknesses might ever be made known to anyone. They will defend their own attitude by saying that they have no interest either now or later in the faults of others. The self-righteous and the vindictive sometimes profess a great interest in the last judgment. Forgetting that vengeance belongs only to God, they derive malicious pleasure from the thought of the final revelation of the sinfulness of others. Those who are sinful through weakness of will, fear not so much the manifestation of their crimes as the sentence of condemnation that may be passed upon them. Hardened sinners—those who sin through sheer malice—deliberately refuse to consider the possibility of the last judgment. Others have imagined that the revelation of the sins of the saints may prove embarrassing to them. In all cases, however, it seems probable that the thought of this ultimate trial of all men should be tinged with terror for every human heart.

A REASONABLE FEAR of the general judgment is good for all men. It is important, however, that the fear be reasonable—that is, that it be the right fear at the right time. To be afraid when there is no danger is cowardly; to be terrified by shadows is foolish. While a man is still living in this present world, he has two things to fear in the general judgment: the disclosure of his sins, and the sentence of eternal damnation which will be passed on him if he dies in sin. Both the fear of final exposure and the dread of eternal condemnation should deter a man from sin. If they do so, then they are beneficial. Neither shame nor the desire to escape eternal punishment is the best motive for avoiding sin. But, when we consider the issue at stake—the salvation of men— no motive is to be despised. On the other hand, it is a mistake to think that all men will carry these fears with them to the general judgment itself. At that time, only the damned will fear either the revelation of their sins or the sentence of condemnation that will follow their exposure. Because they are hardened in sin, the damned will resent bitterly the manifestation of their wickedness to the world. In that "Hour of Truth" they will have no complaint against the divine justice. God will show to all men the great love He had for the wicked, while they were still in this present life, and their obstinate refusal to accept that love. Their bitter envy of the saints who are blessed in God, their implacable hatred for all that is good, will make them fear the exposure of their own evil, their own lack of love, their own abysmal failure. They will dread even more the sentence of eternal damnation which will be meted out to them. It is true that they will have been suffering in their souls the chief pain of hell—the loss of God—since the time of their death. But, from this moment on, they will also suffer in their risen bodies. At the general judgment, God will condemn them, body and soul, to the fires of hell.

BUT THE JUST—those who died in the state of grace—will fear nothing at the last judgment. Because they died in God's grace, they will know that the happiness of heaven is theirs for all eternity. They need not, therefore, dread the outcome of the judgment. Nor will they be afraid of the disclosure of the sins they may have committed in this present life. The manifestation of their sinfulness will be counterbalanced by the revelation of their repentance. The shamefulness of their defeats will be overshadowed by the greatness of their final victory. Shame is fear of disgrace; but the saints, who have won through to the glory of heaven, cannot be disgraced. Rather than feel shame, they will rejoice that the mercy of God is shown in their own salvation.

THE GENERAL JUDGMENT will show to all men both the justice and the mercy of God. In this way it will both pay tribute to the holiness of God and reveal His wisdom to men. The revelation of the sins of the wicked will also emphasize the greatness of the mercy which God extended to them and which they refused. The condemnation of the wicked will manifest the justice of God. The exaltation of the just will show clearly the great love and mercy of God.

WHEN MEN SEE CLEARLY the justice and the mercy of God, the wisdom of God will also be apparent to them. All the seeming inequalities and injustices of human life—the prosperity of the wicked and the oppression of the just, the sudden and early death of the saintly and the long life of the tyrant—all these mysteries of life will be opened to the minds of men. The plan of God in the creation of human life, in all its vastness and complexity, will be seen by men.

THE JUDGE OF ALL MEN will be Christ Himself. A judge must have authority over those whom he judges. A judge without authority may give his own personal opinion, but he cannot enforce his judgment. As God, Christ is the Lord and Master of all creation. As God, then, He has the right and the power to judge all men. But Christ is also the Redeemer of all mankind. In His human nature He offered His Passion and death for the salvation of men. By His Passion and death, it is possible for men to enter the kingdom of heaven. For this reason God has given Him, even in His human nature, the power to judge all men. The judgment is concerned with the admission of some men to the joy of the kingdom of heaven through the Passion of Christ and the exclusion of others. It is right, therefore, that Christ should have the power to distinguish the good from the evil, those who have been saved by the power of His Passion and those who have rejected salvation by His Passion.

WHEN CHRIST FIRST CAME into this world to make satisfaction for the sins of men, He came in poverty and weakness. He allowed men to put Him to death. But at the general judgment He will come in glory and power. "When the Son of man shall come in his majesty, and all the angels with him, then shall he sit upon the seat of his majesty. And all nations shall be gathered together before him: and he shall separate them one from another, as the shepherd separateth the sheep from the goats: And he shall set the sheep on his right hand, but the goats on his left" (Matt. XXV, 31-33).

WHEN THE ANGELS have separated the good from the evil and put the good on His right hand and the evil on His left, then Christ will judge all men. We do not know for certain just how the judgment will take place. In the opinion of St. Thomas, it is unlikely that either Christ or an angel will read aloud the deeds of all men. Such a procedure would last interminably. St. Thomas is inclined to the view that the judgment will take place mentally. By the power of God, all men will see at once their own lives and the lives of all the others. The just, of course, will see this in an instant in their vision of the essence of God. The damned cannot see God; but God will enable them to see this in a very short time, so short that it would be to us the equivalent of an instant.

THE SENTENCE OF THE JUDGE will follow this view of the lives of all men. Christ Himself has foretold the judgment He will make and the reasons for it: "Then shall the king say to them that shall be on his right hand: Come, ye blessed of my Father, possess you the kingdom prepared for you from the foundation of the world. For I was hungry, and you gave me to eat: I was thirsty, and you gave me to drink: I was a stranger, and you took me in. Naked, and you covered me; sick, and you visited me: I was in prison, and you came to me. Then shall the just answer him, saying: Lord, when did we see thee hungry and fed thee: thirsty and gave thee drink? And when did we see thee a stranger and took thee in? Or naked and covered thee? Or when did we see thee sick or in prison and came to thee? And the king answering shall say to them: Amen I say to you, as long as you did it to one of these my least brethren, you did it to me. Then he shall say to them also that shall be on his

left hand: Depart from me, you cursed, into everlasting fire, which was prepared for the devil and his
angels. For I was hungry, and you gave me not to eat:
I was thirsty and you gave me not to drink. I was a
stranger and you took me not in: naked and you
covered me not: sick and in prison and you did not
visit me. Then they also shall answer him, saying:
Lord, when did we see thee hungry or thirsty or a
stranger or naked or sick or in prison and did not
minister to thee? Then he shall answer them, saying:
Amen I say to you, as long as you did it not to one of
these least, neither did you do it to me. And these
shall go into everlasting punishment: but the just,
into life everlasting" (*Matt.* XXV, 34-46).

W HEN THE JUDGMENT is accomplished, when the
sentence of exaltation or of condemnation is
passed, then this present world will be truly ended
and the next world will begin. The life to come begins
in its fullness with the judgment. When Christ has
passed judgment on men and nations, then the damned
will go to hell, body and soul, to begin their eternal
punishment, and the just will enter, body and soul,
into the joys of eternity.

W HAT SHALL THE NEW WORLD be like after the
judgment? With the limited vision of our present
minds, we cannot say. God has told us a little, just
enough to whet our appetites and to sustain our hopes.
As St. John tells us in his Apocalypse: "I saw a new
heaven and a new earth. For the first heaven and the
first earth was gone: and the sea is now no more. And
I, John, saw the holy city, the new Jerusalem, coming
down out of heaven from God, prepared as a bride
adorned for her husband. And I heard a great voice
from the throne, saying: Behold the tabernacle of God

with men: and he will dwell with them. And they shall be his people: and God himself with them shall be their God. And God shall wipe away all tears from their eyes: and death shall be no more. Nor mourning, nor crying, nor sorrow shall be any more: for the former things are passed away. And he that sat on the throne, said: Behold, I make all things new. And he said to me: Write. For these words are most faithful and true. And he said to me: It is done. I am Alpha and Omega: the Beginning and the End. To him that thirsteth, I will give of the fountain of the water of life, freely. He that shall overcome shall possess these things. And I will be his God: and he shall be my son. But the fearful and unbelieving and the abominable and murderers and whoremongers and sorcerers and idolaters and all liars, they shall have their portion in the pool burning with fire and brimstone, which is the second death" (*Apoc.* XXI, 1-8).

AFTER THE JUDGMENT, there will be a new heaven and a new earth. The just will live in this new heaven and earth, and God will dwell with them. The damned will depart to a place of fire and brimstone, where they will be punished for their sins. God will dwell forever with the blessed who died in His grace. How will God dwell with the saints? In the first place, through the gift of glory the saints—and everyone who gets to heaven will then be a saint—will see God. They will enjoy the vision of God. They will see God as God sees Himself, face to face. They will not comprehend God—that is, they will not see all that God is; they will not see all that God can do. But they will see Him face to face, just as now we can see a man face to face. Of course, they will not see God with their bodily eyes. They will see Him with their minds.

It will be an intellectual vision of God as He is in Himself. They will see God as He is in Himself, that is, they will see God the Father, and God the Son, and God the Holy Ghost; and they will see that these three Persons are the one God. In God they will find the satisfaction of all their desires. As human beings they have sought, and needed always, the absolute perfection of all truth and all goodness. In God they will find the fulfilment of all their desires, the full perfection of all the tendencies of their humanity. The vision of God will give them the happiness they have always sought.

THE VISION OF GOD will also give the saints a mastery of the whole world. The glory which men achieve in the vision of God is also a power which sets men free in the world God has made for them. In the new world which God gives to men after the general judgment, men will be truly free. They will suffer no more from those unruly desires of the flesh, from sinful tendencies to gluttony in food or drink, from sinful desires of the flesh, which now trouble them. "They shall no more hunger nor thirst: neither shall the sun fall on them, nor any heat. For the Lamb (Christ), which is in the midst of the throne, shall rule them and lead them to the fountains of the waters of life: and God shall wipe away all tears from their eyes" (*Apoc.* VII, 16-17). The vision of God will glorify their souls, and the glory of their souls will give them complete domination of their bodies and of all the material world. They will live in the world of the earth and the sky, the planets and the skies, as masters and no longer servants. The glory of their souls will redound to the glory of their bodies. They will live in the company of their loved ones, their relatives and friends who have also died in Christ and in the grace of God. All the wonderful things that men dream of, all the good things that will make men happy, will be the lot of the saints who have lived the life of grace and died in the friendship of God.

THE HAPPINESS OF THE SAINTS will be greater after the general judgment than before. It is true that the saints will have achieved the essential element of their happiness—the vision of God—before the judgment. But after the general resurrection and the last judgment, their bodies also will find the essence of human happiness. Or perhaps we should say, that after the resurrection, man—body and soul—will find his complete happiness. For then he will be happy as man, as a composite of both body and soul. His soul will be eternally happy in the vision of God, and his body will be happy in its immortality and in its union with a glorified soul.

ALL THIS, OF COURSE, is still in the future for us. We cannot really estimate the happiness which will be ours if we live in faith and hope and the love of God. "Eye hath not seen, nor ear heard: neither hath it entered into the heart of man, what things God hath prepared for them that love him" (*I Cor.* II, 9). But one thing is clear: the goal lies before us; the gate of heaven is open to us; if we will, we can find the fulfilment of all our desires.

ON THE OTHER HAND, we can fail, we can make the wrong choice. If we choose, we can stand at the left hand of Christ at the general judgment. If we do, we shall hear the sentence of eternal condemnation. This will mean that we have lost forever the only chance for happiness which was ours. We cannot be happy unless and until we see God face to face. But if we go to hell, then we shall never see God. Because we will not have loved Him, because we will, of our own free will, have rejected Him, He will reject us forever. While we may deceive ourselves in this life, while we may choose to think that we can find happiness in something else than God, after death we shall know the truth: we are made for God, and our hearts are restless until they rest in God. Without God there is no happiness for us. If we die in sin, we die without love, and we shall spend eternity without love.

LET THERE BE no mistake about this. In hell there is no love. The demons will not love us because we have cast our lot with theirs. They will hate us because we are less perfect naturally than they are, and because God has chosen to become one of us in Christ. Nor will the human beings in hell love one another. When the grace of God is gone, there is no sure basis for love. The human beings in hell will hate one another for many reasons: for the evil which each one has done to the human race by bad example, by persuasion to sin, by injustice; because one is worse than another; or because one is better than another. This is the great tragedy of hell: the total absence of love. In hell there is no community—no mutual respect or helpfulness. In hell each one is alone, isolated in his own unhappiness, hating God, men and angels.

NOR WILL THE ULTIMATE UNHAPPINESS of hell be only an unhappiness of soul at the loss of God and the love of God. The loss of the vision of God is the most terrible punishment of hell. But, in addition, after the general resurrection, the damned will suffer not only in soul, but also in body. The fires of hell will not only restrain the souls of the damned; they will also torment the bodies of those who are lost for all eternity. The intensity of the pains of soul and body of those in hell is beyond our powers either of imagination or of description. But one thing we know: there is no cessation of torment for those in hell; they suffer, and they suffer forever.

THERE IS AN OLD LATIN SAYING: "Respice ad finem." It means "Look to the end." If our long journey through Christian doctrine under the leadership of St. Thomas means anything, that meaning can be summed up in this saying: "Look to the end!" The end for all adults, rational human beings, is either heaven or hell. Which goal men reach is within the power of their own free wills. Heaven or hell? The choice is within the power of each human being. Christ has shown us the way to heaven: we have but to follow Him. A life of virtue leads to heaven; a life of vice, to hell. The life of virtue is possible to all of us through the Church of Christ and through the means of grace which are found in His Church: the Mass, the sacraments and prayer. With the grace of Christ, virtue becomes possible to men; with virtue, holiness becomes a fact in men; and with holiness, men achieve the vision of God.

THINK BACK FOR A MOMENT on the long story St. Thomas has been telling us; not his own story, but a story originally told by the tender lips of God Himself. In the beginning there was God, all holy, all perfect, all happy in Himself, needing nothing else to make Him happy. But, in the overflowing goodness of His perfection, He created the world of angels and men. The angels were given their chance for happiness: some seized that chance and they attained their eternal happiness; others failed and they were condemned to eternal punishment. God created man and gave him the same chance for happiness. Adam fell from God's grace, and lost that chance for himself and his descendants. But the love of God for men was not to be so easily foiled. God sent His own Son into the world to suffer and die for the salvation of men. Through the Redemption worked by Christ, all men, from Adam down to the end of time, can achieve salvation. By membership in the Church of Christ—His own Mystical Body—by the reception of the sacraments of the Church, by participation in the sacrifice of the Cross through the sacrifice of the Mass, by the public and private prayer of the Church, the grace of God is restored to men and the practise of virtue is possible to men. God could not do any more for men. By the love of God, men have come into existence. By His love and by their own love for Him, men can attain happiness. God has done His part: He has restored His grace to men. Man has only to do his part: choose God and live by that choice.

Outline

PART I

God and His Creatures

PART II

Man: The Image of God

PART IIA

Happiness

PART IIB

The Divine Life in Man

PART III

Che God-Man

Accidents (Appearances): 537, 538, 539, 542.

Adam: 101, 102, 275, 276, 277, 278, 279, 281, 284, 300, 307, 318, 443, 446, 489, 512, 604. Christ the Second A.: 307, 455, 502.

Adam & Eve: 100, 103, 104, 105, 131, 426, 427, 481, 579.

Agent: 117, 451. God the Perfect A.: 31. Man the imperfect A.: 31.

Almsgiving: 181, 351, 354, 355, 356, 358, 560.

Angel(s): 13, 32, 61, 63, 65, 69, 73, 76, 79, 82, 88, 123, 128, 129, 130, 132, 141, 142, 143, 495, 589, 603. Choirs of: 65, 121. Fallen: 24, 81, 82, 124. Guardian: 71, 130, 131, 132, 134, 135, 136. Hierarchies (Orders) of: 121. Knowledge of: 70, 71, 72, 74. Love of: 74, 75, 76, 77, 80, 123. Motion of: 67. Nature of: 63, 66, 67, 68, 70, 80. Not supernatural: 63, 124. Power of: 71, 73, 115, 125, 126, 133, 215, 216.

Anger: 27, 74, 190, 191, 192, 193, 211, 220, 260, 272, 273, 280, 408, 425.

Animals: 27, 38, 97.

Anointing (Last): *See* **Extreme Unction.**

Antichrist: 131, 132.

Appearances: *See* **Accidents.**

Appetite: 101, 170, 171, 188, 190, 191, 193, 196, 197, 198, 199, 200, 201, 202, 203, 207, 210, 215, 216, 218, 224, 225, 226, 231, 232, 233, 235, 236, 237, 238, 242, 244, 246, 248, 250, 257, 258, 263, 266, 267, 270, 272, 273, 275, 277, 278, 279, 281, 283, 301, 343, 408.

Apostasy (Infidelity): 327, 328.

Aristotle: 125. "The Philosopher": 137.

Art: 225, 226, 229, 230, 231, 232, 246.

Ascension: 469, 552.

Astrology: 138.

Atheists: 112, 338.

Attrition: 557, 558.

Baptism: 371, 489, 490, 511, 512, 513, 514, 515, 516, 517, 520, 521, 522, 523, 526, 527, 529, 531, 539, 553, 557, 558, 564, 566, 567, 571, 589. Formula of: 521. B. of Blood: 523, 524. B. of Desire: 523, 524. B. of Water: 523, 524, 525. "Sacrament of Faith": 526.

Beatitudes: 256, 259, 260, 261, 336.

Beauty: 11, 25, 157. Divine: 4, 12, 22, 60. Infinite of God: 18, 65. of goodness: 2. of truth: 2, 24.

Being: Divine: 12, 317, 318. Human: 13.

Beneficence: 351, 354, 358.

Capital Sins: 279, 280, 359, 360, 373, 403, 423. *See* Sins, *also* **Anger, Covetousness, Envy, Gluttony, Lust, Pride, Sloth.**

Cause: 110, 112, 113, 114, 115, 578. First: 115, 116. Formal: 145. Instrumental: 515. Particular: 138. Universal: 138.

Character (Sacramental): 514, 515, 523, 524, 527, 528, 570.

Charity: 36, 52, 79, 80, 104, 111, 221, 227, 236, 243, 247, 248, 249, 250, 252, 253, 254, 257, 258, 264, 307, 315, 321, 322, 323, 325, 333, 334, 335, 337, 341, 342, 343, 344, 345, 346, 347, 348, 349, 350, 351, 352, 353, 354, 355, 356, 357, 358, 359, 362, 363, 365, 370, 371, 381, 383, 436, 437, 445, 457, 480, 502, 504, 529, 541, 542, 543, 546, 551, 555, 556, 560, 561, 590. *See* **Love.**

Chastity: 258, 420, 421, 436.

Choice: 95, 139, 156, 165, 170, 172, 328, 557, 576, 586, 604.

Choirs of Angels: 65, 121.

Christ: 118, 259, 260, 261, 281, 295, 296, 300, 303, 309, 318, 319, 328, 356, 389, 392, 431, 444, 445, 446, 453, 454, 455, 457, 459, 460, 461, 477, 478, 481, 484, 488, 490, 491, 492, 493, 495, 500, 501, 513, 520, 521, 522, 523, 528, 531, 533, 534, 535, 537, 539, 540, 545, 561, 562, 564, 572, 577, 581, 583, 591, 597, 601, 603, 604. Divinity of: 487, 504. Emmanuel: 472. God and Man: 101, 444, 467, 481, 494, 498, 502, 515. God Incarnate: 25, 296. Head of Angels: 458, 549. Head of Church: 456. Head of human race: 455, 502, 505, 549. High Priest: 470, 517. Humanity of: 38, 42, 463, 466, 469, 475, 487, 515, 516, 591, 596. Mediator: 470, 472, 473. Nature of: 482, 483, 487, 499, 502, 505, 516. Passion of: 470, 490, 493, 495, 496, 497, 498, 499, 502, 503, 504, 509, 510, 511, 514, 515, 516, 520, 523, 529, 532, 540, 541, 542, 546, 548, 550, 551, 553, 555, 569, 596. Perfect Teacher: 473, 494. Person of: 447, 448, 449, 451, 467, 483. Present in Eucharist: 73. Resurrection of: 469, 470, 504, 505, 520, 532. Sacrifice of: 471, 486. Second Adam: 307, 455, 502. Son of Mary: 73, 114. Victim & Priest: 470, 471, 548. Way, Truth & Life: 25. Will of: 468, 469. "The Word": 25, 51, 138, 148, 443, 479.